THE WORK OF THE HEART

JEFFERSONIAN AMERICA

Jan Ellen Lewis, Peter S. Onuf, and
Andrew O'Shaughnessy, Editors

The
WORK
of the
HEART

*Young Women
and Emotion
1780–1830*

Martha Tomhave Blauvelt

University of Virginia Press
Charlottesville and London

University of Virginia Press
© 2007 by the Rector and Visitors of the University of Virginia
All rights reserved
Printed in the United States of America on acid-free paper

First published 2007

1 3 5 7 9 8 6 4 2

LIBRARY OF CONGRESS CATALOGING-IN-PUBLICATION DATA

Blauvelt, Martha Tomhave, 1948–
 The work of the heart : young women and emotion, 1780–1830 / Martha Tomhave Blauvelt.
  p. cm. — (Jeffersonian America)
 Includes bibliographical references and index.
 ISBN-13: 978-0-8139-2597-4 (cloth : alk. paper)
 1. Women—United States—Psychology—History. 2. Young women—United States—Psychology—History. 3. Young women—United States—Diaries. 4. Emotions. I. Title.
HQ759.B614 2007
305.242′2097309033—dc22

2006022268

To

Anne Rukavina Tomhave

John F. Tomhave

The memory of Andrew H. Blauvelt (1947–2004)

CONTENTS

Acknowledgments ix

Introduction:
The Theory and Practice of Emotion 1

1. The Work of the Heart:
Emotion, Class, and Performance 15

2. Schooling the Heart:
Education and Emotional Expression at
Litchfield Female Academy 50

3. Discerning the Heart:
Fear and Fancy in Courtship 82

4. Losing It:
Anger and the Boundaries
of Female Behavior 116

5. Reconstructing the Heart:
Religion, Marriage, and Motherhood 146

Conclusion 184

Notes 203
Bibliography 241
Index 263

ACKNOWLEDGMENTS

Through scholarship I sought to discover the innovative, but found instead an old truth, that no one works alone. Many years of sampling diaries and musing about their meaning have increased my indebtedness to family, friends, colleagues, the scholarly community, archivists, and, often, total strangers who were unexpectedly generous in their help.

Having written a book about emotion, I feel obliged to begin with the heart, rather than employ the conventional academic ordering. My deepest gratitude goes to my mother, Anne Rukavina Tomhave, who provided the gift of a lifetime by teaching me to love learning; and to my brother, John F. Tomhave, whose eclectic interests, acute mind, and story-telling skills first showed me what a scholar could be. Loving thanks to my husband, Andrew H. Blauvelt, who died while this book was still in progress, but whose good heart, comradeship, and faith in me I will never forget; and to our children, Katie and Will, whose company has been a continuous delight. To all, loving you has never been work.

If family constructed the feelings that committed me to history, James M. Banner, Jr., taught me the historical discipline. As my Princeton University mentor and, in the years since then, good friend, he astutely criticized rough drafts, helped me navigate publishing, and persistently demanded my best. Warm thanks to him for his generosity and acumen. Thanks also to College of St. Benedict and St. John's University colleagues, with primacy of place to Norma Koetter, History Department secretary, whose kindness, patience, and expertise eased many a crisis; S. Mary Reuter, OSB, who reminded me of the curve in the road; S. Mara Faulkner, OSB, who kept me out of the ditches; Beth Wengler, Ken Jones, and especially Jean Keller, who read early drafts; Cynthia Curran, whose London hospitality led me to Kenwood, which inspired this work; librarians Nicole Reuter and Tom Nichol, who calmly and capably fielded obscure questions; the late Linda Mealey for her psychology of emotion books; and the Information Technology staff who solved numerous computer problems without losing their good humor. Colleagues from the broader scholarly community were equally helpful, especially Michael Kay for reminding me of the importance of class, Peter Stearns for his encouragement and comments, Lynne Templeton Brickley for her expertise on the Litchfield Female Academy, and the anonymous readers of the book manuscript and previous articles. Thanks as well to Beverly Korstad Tomhave, whose genealogical skills were indispensable, and to Aaron Slater of Rutgers University, who helped me complete my New York City research. As I visited archives, friends provided hospitality, for which I thank Hilde and Jim Lindeman Nelson, Betty and Winston Perry, Jr., George and Aurelia Pouder, and Pamela Rask; while at home, Florence Amamoto, Jeanne Anderson, and Sue Weaver provided tea and sympathy. Warm thanks to Christopher Beal, New York City, for his gracious help in providing information on his family history.

My gratitude goes also to the College of St. Benedict Faculty Research and Development Committee, which provided generous support for the sabbaticals, research trips, and expenses necessary for this project; to Studium at St. Benedict's Monastery, St. Joseph, Minnesota, which provided an ideal place for study and community; and to the University of Virginia Press's staff, which patiently and expertly guided me through the many details of publishing. Warm thanks to Richard K. Holway, history and social sciences editor; Jan Ellen Lewis, coeditor, Jeffersonian America Series; Ellen G. Satrom, managing editor; the ever-steady Angie Hogan, acquisitions assistant, and the very able Kathryn Krug, copyeditor.

Thanks to those who provided permission to quote from the materials in their possession: Litchfield Historical Society, especially the immensely helpful Linda Hocking, curator of the library and archives, as well as Catherine Fields, director, and Julie Frey, curator of collections, who handled illustrations; Schlesinger Library, Radcliffe Institute for Advanced Study, Harvard University; Marilyn J. Easton, Ph.D.; New York State Historical Association Library, Cooperstown; University of Pennsylvania Press; The Connecticut Historical Society Museum, Hartford; The New-York Historical Society; Connecticut State Library/State Archives; Manuscripts and Archives Division, The New York Public Library, Astor, Lenox, and Tilden Foundations; Phillips Library, Peabody Essex Museum, especially Irene Axelrod; and the Massachusetts Historical Society, with special thanks to the New

Hampshire Historical Society, especially David Smolen. Thank you also to the Bristol (Connecticut) Public Library; Office of the Town Historian, Bedford Hills, New York, especially Rosemary Mahoney; the late Richard Lander, Town Historian of Armonk, New York; New York State Archives, Albany; LDS Family History Center, St. Cloud, Minnesota; Westchester County (New York) Historical Society; St. Matthew's Church, Bedford, New York; Maine Historical Society; G. W. Blunt White Library, Mystic Seaport Museum; the American Antiquarian Society; and Phillips Exeter Academy, especially Edouard Desrochers, archivist.

I have incorporated several articles published elsewhere, which are reprinted by permission as follows: "The Work of the Heart: Emotion in the 1805–35 Diary of Sarah Connell Ayer," *Journal of Social History* 35 (Spring 2002): 577–92, which forms part of chapter 1; and "Making a Match in Nineteenth-Century New York: The Courtship Diary of Mary Guion," *New York History* 76 (April 1995): 153–72, which I drew on in chapter 3. I also incorporated into chapters 3 and 5 "'this altogather precious tho wholly worthless book': The Diary of Mary Guion," 125–41, reprinted by permission from *Anxious Power: Reading, Writing, and Ambivalence in Narrative by Women,* edited by Carol J. Singley and Susan Elizabeth Sweeney, SUNY Series in Feminist Criticism and Theory, the State University of New York Press © 1993 State University of New York, All Rights Reserved.

INTRODUCTION
The Theory and Practice of Emotion

> Tuesday the 20 I tok a ride to the Weavers to carry some filin & from there to Bedford after some notions. . . . I was left entirely to my own meditations for Indeed thinking of the last Ball but not of it's pleasure but of the dificulties that Occurd to my Going with Mr —the one that came after me & to se to the man that treated me with so much Neglect not so much as offer one Apology but appeared to be offended wich I thot I had the most reason for Engrost all my thots thro the ride.
> —Mary Guion, Diary, 20 May 1800

In this journal entry, Mary Guion of Westchester County, New York, described several types of work: productive work, which she carried to the weaver, and consumption, when she rode to Bedford to buy some "notions." Scholars have studied household labor and consumption patterns extensively, but the main subject of Mary Guion's entry, and indeed of her entire diary, is a third kind of work, which centered on her emotions: she struggled to discern and shape what she did and should feel, in this case about a suitor who invited her to a ball but failed to appear, yet who was then angry when she attended with another man. Her ruminations on that spring day might seem insignificant, but they were at the heart of her life, her society, and women's emotion history.

To study emotion's history is to study one thing and everything; the field, like emotion itself, both suggests and defies clear boundaries. As Andrew Burstein said in his *Sentimental Democracy*, "All history is, in essence, emotional history. Terming this book an emotional history merely calls attention to its particular emphasis."[1] Over the last twenty years, emotion history has become a distinct field with a specific subject and vocabulary. A substantial part of that subject is what Peter N.

Stearns and Carol Z. Stearns have called "emotionology," society's conventions and expectations of emotional expression, a top-down understanding of feelings.[2] Adopting a social constructionist stance and exploring popular culture, Peter Stearns has studied society's rules for specific emotions such as anger and jealousy, as well as contemporary efforts to "cool" feelings generally.[3] It has proven more difficult to determine how people responded to those standards. Historians are still struggling to implement the Stearns's 1985 admonition that "thinking about emotion" should not be mistaken for "the experience of emotion."[4]

While increasing numbers of scholars have made emotion history their focus, others have addressed it obliquely, often in the process of pursuing other interests. As social history has gained prominence as an essential lens through which we understand change, and as therapeutic culture has pervaded contemporary life, many historians have found elucidating their subjects' emotional implications irresistible. Family history, men's studies, gay history, and women's history have been especially attentive to emotional dynamics. In the case of women's history, issues of emotion underlie patriarchy: men have held the power to decide that women are emotional and men rational, to define the meaning and worth of those characteristics, and to control women through controlling their emotions.[5] Historians have also studied emotion to understand the quality of women's personal lives: Carroll Smith-Rosenberg, Ellen K. Rothman, Karen Lystra, Catherine E. Kelly, and Jane H. Hunter, for example, have shed light on women's friendships, romantic love, village relationships, and school experiences.[6] Such studies have made major contributions to emotion history, but their vocabulary and conceptualization of historical change are largely situated within the historiography on women's status or sphere. Burstein is right that "all history is, in essence, emotional history," and the name "merely calls attention to its particular emphasis," but without that particularity it is difficult to gain a systematic understanding of how emotions develop and what they mean for not only women but American culture. While I began this book as a historian of women, as I worked, I realized that I could not understand women's lives unless I focused on their construction and experience of emotion and employed a conceptual framework specific to that purpose. In that sense, if this book must be categorized, it falls into the slot of emotion history that has implications for women's history, rather than the other way around.

My basic question is this: how did young American women construct and express their emotions between 1780 and 1830? Historians have long since chronicled the familiar story of the new American nation's halting and incomplete steps toward a more commercial, democratic, and evangelical future. They have been less attentive to the fact that young women stood at the center of many of this era's transitions, and that these changes included shifts in emotionology which conveyed often contradictory messages, especially for females.[7] Multiple developments implicated women and their feelings: by the late eighteenth century, a steady rise in literacy and a "reading revolution" created a new influence on emotions by connecting women to print culture, especially to sentimental fiction, with young women comprising its most eager readers; an aspiring society valorized a sincere and feeling heart as a class and gender marker, especially for young women, but sought to control those feelings; a revolutionary republic politicized womanhood and expanded young women's educational opportunities without questioning their domestic location; a romanticizing culture expected marriage to unite hearts, but maintained inequality between husbands and wives; and an evangelical nation demanded regeneration of sinful hearts, even as it assumed women were naturally moral.[8] How did young women enact, shape, or deny the confusing emotional directives implicit in these developments? How did they experience them? How much agency did individuals have in shaping and expressing feelings, regardless of emotional expectations? What influence did factors other than these rules have on emotional expression? In short, what happened in between emotionology and the lived experience of individuals such as Mary Guion?

Mine is a historical question, but I make extensive use of other disciplines in conceptualizing the answer. I place feeling within the social constructionist framework that emphasizes context rather than biology: how society shapes people's feelings by providing language, ideals, rewards, and punishments. Social construction has served historians well in directing them to the advice manuals, sermons, and popular literature that convey an era's emotionology. But unless we assume that individuals played no role in emotion management or historical change, we cannot rely on these alone. As anthropologist Michelle Z. Rosaldo put it, "emotions are about the ways in which the social world is one in which *we* are involved."[9] How, then, do historians discover how individuals are involved in their culture's emotionology? Clearly, studying a society's emotional directives is not enough, lest we fall into what Jonathan Rose has called the "receptive fallacy": "try[ing] to discern the messages a text transmits to an audience by examining the text rather than the audience."[10] To get beyond the text to the readers and from emotionology to emotion itself, I have drawn on the insights and language of sociologists Erving Goffman and Arlie Russell Hochschild.

In his brilliant *The Presentation of Self in Everyday Life*, Goffman theorized that social status was not an object, but an often polished performance, "coherent, embellished, and well articulated . . . something that must be enacted and portrayed, something that must be realized."[11] In his conceptualization, the self is simultaneously "a social product, with no underlying personal core," and the creator of social performances, including emotion. Individuals move between a front region, where they perform for society, and a back region or backstage, where they may both act contrary to socially recognized rules and prepare for their expected social performance. Society's "framing" rules assess and give meaning to that performance.[12] Applied to women's emotional expression during the early republic, Goffman's theories raise intriguing questions: In what sense did women perform emotions for their society? What areas functioned as front and back regions? Exactly how did they prepare an emotional performance, how often did they indulge in rule-breaking behavior, and where did this entire process leave their sense of self? Goffman's insights are particularly useful for the early republic, when classes were re-conceptualized, theater and novels gripped the popular imagination, and both philosophers and poets placed the senses at the center of human motivation. However, Goffman resisted the idea that an independent self existed behind social masks, and his approach concentrated more on the exterior than the interior. Given his focus, historians such as Karen Halttunen have used Goffman's concepts to understand social performance in etiquette and parlor theatricals.[13] I employ Goffman's ideas along similar lines, but use his concept of the backstage to understand how people write about and produce not just manners, but feelings themselves.

Like Goffman, Arlie Russell Hochschild uses theatrical metaphors, but she is more interested in inner feelings than outer display, and she theorizes emotions as not just performance, but work. Although her concepts are based on twentieth-century service workers, they are extraordinarily insightful (and disturbing) in explaining women's emotions two hundred years ago. Hochschild posits that in back of framing rules are "feeling rules," which provide "guidelines for the assessment of fits and misfits between feeling and situation."[14] Most importantly, through paid "emotional labor" and unpaid "emotion work," individuals incorporate, modify, or subvert those rules by shaping their own feelings. Such work entails two types of acting: "surface acting," purposeful body language such as smiling on cue, and "deep acting," the construction of internal feelings that produce other feelings, such as inducing the conviction that customers deserve good cheer and then displaying that emotion.[15] In that the airline attendants Hochschild studied produced certain emotions for their jobs, their employers compelled, and in a sense owned, their employees' feelings. However, emotion workers retain some degree of agency and remain the subjects rather than the mere objects of their culture; at the very least, they function as co-workers in constructing feeling. As she discovered, when people no longer support a feeling rule, they subvert it by doing less or different emotion work and not producing the emotion required for that rule. Conversely, their efforts to produce socially demanded feelings "can be a form of obeisance to a given ideological stance."[16] Thus, emotion work becomes a vehicle for historical change and continuity, and since everyone performs emotion work, all serve as historical actors on this most intimate level.

In making visible the often invisible tasks which comprise a significant proportion of women's paid and unpaid labor, Arlie Russell Hochschild contributes to a well-established theme in women's history: the discovery of female labor that had been previously dismissed or unnoticed, whether that be women's employment in a society supposedly of housewives, money-making chores by farm wives, childcare by "nonworking" mothers, use of the time and judgment necessary for consumption, or volunteer endeavors that comprise full-time occupations.[17] Inherent in this reconsideration has been a conviction that labor need not be paid or public to comprise work; if understood as time-consuming and compelled effort, work extends into the supposedly private world of the family. To regard emotions as labor is to question the nineteenth-century removal of women's toil from the realm of work, move labor fully into the "private" sphere, incorporate the efforts of all family members, consider forms of wages where none seems to exist, and explore the costs to workers whose labors remain invisible.[18] For the new republic, the concept of emotion work suggests that women's production meant not just making candles and textiles, but producing feeling, and that even when physically productive work declined, emotional production remained. For today, the concept recognizes what most women acknowledge to each other if not to scholars: that suppressing anger, working up enthusiasm, and charming relatives requires self-aware and often strenuous labor.

Arlie Russell Hochschild's concept of emotion work also suggests a new approach to a difficult and elusive subject: the construction of the self. Unlike Goffman, who was more interested in masks than the people behind them, she recognized a self which chooses the kind and degree of emotion expressed. As she put it, "every emotion does signal the 'me' I put into seeing 'you.'"[19] Historians have suggested that some time between 1600 and 1800 a "modern" self-concept appeared, but they do not agree on what that was, when and how it evolved, or who experienced that transforming change. Scholars such as Cecile M. Jagodzinski have maintained that during the early modern period, the English shifted from locating the true self in one's "public" performance to perceiving "authenticity" in more private arenas. Especially through reading, people developed a "private self," by which she means "the right to personal autonomy, as opposed to the requirement that one submit to authority; a consciousness (and potential manipulation) of the split between the internal self and the public face presented to the rest of the world; and the right to conceal or keep secret the workings of this inner self."[20] Similarly, Colin Campbell found that "words prefixed with 'self' in a hyphenated fashion" emerged in the 1500s and 1600s, to become common in the succeeding century, with Coleridge first using the word "self-consciousness."[21] In her study of eighteenth-century English literature, Patricia Meyer Spacks concurs, but she finds a persistent emphasis on social claims and fear of private wrong-doing throughout that era.[22] For Americans, Mechal Sobel has suggested that a communal "we-self" prevailed during the colonial period, to be succeeded by a "far more individuated 'I,'" fashioned and enlarged through dreams.[23] In all these histories of self-development, reading and writing were crucial, a finding my own research echoes, but I differ in singling out feelings as their essential subject. If we apply Arlie Russell Hochschild's insights, we see that between the I and the we, the "internal self" and "public face," lies another process: emotion work. To link emotion work to the self is to contribute two essential elements to the study of that self: work, in that we can glimpse people actively shaping the self through constructing feeling, and in that sense becoming agents of their own selves; and emotion, the element that both creates distinctiveness and signals social belonging. In the particular case of young women during the early republic, I chart their self-evolution as they move through the life cycle from daughters to students to young women in search of a husband to matrons. In each of these cases, emotion work reveals them working between the poles of individuated self-expression and social regulation of feeling, as they shape and reshape what may be termed a negotiated self.

In constructing a self, these young women also constructed femininity: in Candace West and Don H. Zimmerman's words, they were "doing gender." Much as Arlie Russell Hochschild saw emotion as the intersection between individual work and social demands, West and Zimmerman argue that gender "is not a set of traits, nor a variable, nor a role, but the product of social doings of some sort," and in that sense is "constituted through interaction." In other words, gender is not a given, but a mutual creation that requires work.[24] Building on West and Zimmerman's 1987 essay, psychologist Stephanie A. Shields theorizes that our sense of self is created largely through gender, which is in turn performed and evaluated through emotion. As she writes, "doing emotion the 'right' way, which is often a gendered way, serves as verification of the authenticity of the self. Not 'I feel, therefore I am,' but 'I feel as I believe I ought to, therefore I am the person I believe I am.'"[25] In that regard, the degree to which early republican women felt as they believed they "ought to" reveals whether they accepted or challenged their society's gender ideals, how gender translated into emotion, and who they felt they as women were. Gender was not, however, the only component of these young women's selves. They were not only women, but women of the rising classes, "doing" class as well as gender, and the relationship between socioeconomic standing and gender identity provides a major theme of this narrative.

Historians are traditionally leery of social scientific theories, and I am no exception. I try to bring them down to earth by using women's diaries as my main source and placing women's individual stories at the center of my analysis. Journals' mundane, intimate, and highly specific entries remind us that the theoretical must submit to the particular, while they provide an extended narrative of individual women's development over years and often decades. During the early republic, journals (a term I use interchangeably with diaries) took a shape especially revealing of emotion. Their authors often sewed together blank sheets for their diaries or purchased blank books; unlimited by the one-page-an-entry journal books that developed in the nineteenth century, these diarists could inscribe their emotions in detail. Susan M. Stabile has vividly described the eighteenth century's fascination with the physical process of putting pen to paper as ink traced the feelings of the heart.[26] At the same time, young women of the early republic showed few signs of the parental control over journals which was common in the later Victorian period. Influenced by novels, which were often epistolary or in journal form, diaries moved beyond traditional religious and book-keeping models by the late eighteenth century and became much more attentive to feelings, which were the subject of much sentimental literature. Increasingly, young women found self-writing irresistible; as twenty-year-old Jemima Condict wrote in 1774, "Sometimes after our people is gone to Bed I get my Pen for I Dont know how to Content myself without writing Something."[27] These women were readers as much as writers, and their reflections on political, religious, and sentimental texts enable us to glimpse how they maneuvered between the feeling rules they read and the emotions they inscribed. As William M. Reddy has argued, through articulating their feelings, people came to identify and shape those feelings. In that sense, diaries functioned as "emotives" or tools of emotion management.[28]

If privacy is essential to the modern self, the journal, as the most private form of writing, should be a key resource for the self's creation. Diarists might well say of their journals, as Nancy Thompson Hunt did of her "closet," "Here I can converse with my own heart read my own errors and find out what I am and what I ought to be—."[29] "I find a real pleasure in it when my mind is animated, and a sympathising friend when dejected—," Mary Guion concurred.[30] The eagerness with which they wrote, efforts to preserve their words, lengthening entries, and faithful chronicles over many years suggest the salience of diaries in these women's lives. Moreover, modern psychologists have found that the more quickly people report on their emotions, the less likely they are to fall back on gender stereotypes. In that sense, diaries kept daily are especially revealing of women's individual and actual experience of feeling.[31] Where possible, I have supplemented women's diaries with additional primary sources such as letters, but I focus on journals as a form particularly revealing of the self. In all these regards, journals are an ideal means for understanding young women's emotion work. For many young women, they are also our only means of understanding their feelings, since their diaries comprise our sole surviving source for their lives. In short, diaries enable us to not just make theory concrete, but to discover "the 'theory' of the actual practice" of emotional expression.[32]

To understand exactly how women engaged in emotion work and negotiated the boundaries between their broader culture and their individual needs, I have studied diaries of fifty young women who kept journals between 1780 and 1830. Of these, I have chosen eight for close analysis on the basis of their length, detail, and attention to self and society, and employed an additional eighteen for an intensive study of emotions within female academies; the remainder I draw on for additional comparisons.[33] These diarists were young, white, single women who resided in the middle and upper classes of the northeastern United States during the late eighteenth and early nineteenth centuries. Many were only in their teens, and I have felt free to use their first names in those instances. Since youth, time, money, and education all encouraged first-person narratives, this was the group most likely to faithfully record their lives in journals. All the authors were Protestant, and I make denominational distinctions where appropriate, but none were members of the Society of Friends.

Diaries are not without disadvantages as sources. While often the only source we have on an individual's emotions, diaries do not represent all the feelings that individuals experienced. Narrative conventions circumscribed description of the emotions reported, and we should not mistake written representations for feeling itself. However, as is the case with religious conversion narratives, even if the narrative is not the conversion *per se*, there is always some relationship between the two.[34] That society's conventions influence how people express emotion does not render those forms of expression inauthentic, but, rather, contextual.[35] Similarly, while diaries do not convey the totality of authors' feelings, they do reveal how people constructed feeling, and that construction is the central concern of this book. In any case, historians can make reasonable accommodations for diaries' limitations. Journals may rarely describe the physical dimensions of emotion, such as blushing, but they often record embarrassment. Diarists may have expressed feelings differently orally, but they quoted a surprising number of conversations, so that we have some sense of the role oral culture played in emotional expression. I also do not argue that these diaries are representative of anyone but their authors and, more generally, well-off, well-educated, young, white, single Protestant women in the Northeast. Since my main concern is the process by which emotions are constructed and expressed, I have focused on the journals that best addressed that question, and I have employed the early republic's extensive secondary literature for verification and context. Within this seemingly small sample, I found both considerable diversity in language, purpose, and feeling, and several common themes. In fact, this book is as much a study of the diary form as of emotion. Each diarist had a different relationship to her journal, and that relationship reflected, shaped, and served her particular emotional task.

Scholars conventionally begin books by delineating the economic, geographic, social, or ethnic community in which their subjects lived. But as medievalist Barbara H. Rosenwein has suggested, historians of emotion might better understand locality in terms of "emotional communities." She understands these as "precisely the same as social communities," whether families, towns, or churches, but entities in which to study "systems of feeling," or what emotions are valued, how they are understood, and "the modes of emotional expression that they expect, encourage, tolerate, and deplore." Rosenwein speculates that it is possible to move from one emotional community to another, and that the same social organizations might tolerate conflicting emotional communities.[36] To apply Arlie Russell Hochschild's terms, each emotional community is a different workplace whose wages and conditions of labor vary. If emotion work is the site where we create self and do gender, Rosenwein's conceptualization suggests that our sense of that gendered self shifts with our emotional community.

With the exception of chapter 4, I have organized chapters around not different emotions, but the emotional communities which women entered and left, depending on what they read, where they lived, and which life stage they faced; in this regard, women negotiated not only their relationship between self and society, but the emotional community in which they resided. In each of these emotional communities, women performed on a different social stage, experienced different conditions and pay, and encountered different emotional tasks. I have arranged the chapters to proceed chronologically, from women's younger years through adulthood in their twenties; they also chart change in place, from the family through school and the town and back again to the family. In each chapter, young women faced a contradiction that dominated their emotional community, shaped their emotion work, and pulled them between two poles: self-expression and society's regulation of feeling.

Chapter 1 considers the development of an aspiring class community shaped not just by money, but by what its members read and felt. That emotional community originated in the imagination, as mediated by books, and the diarists who most fully engaged that dream world were Sarah Connell, Mary B. Howell, and Elizabeth Cranch. These women performed mainly on a family stage, and their diaries served as the means to both produce and display their sensibility. They struggled to balance the contradictory demands of sentimentality, which expected that women feel spontaneously but confine themselves to certain emotions. Since gentility was supposed to be "easy," and they were expected to influence others largely through example, within this community women's emotion work was often invisible to others, and their pay was largely in self-admiration.

In chapter 2, I analyze a highly specific and institutional emotional community: the Litchfield, Connecticut, Female Academy, which used not sentimental texts but school rules, pedagogy, and a watching public to shape women's emotional expression on the academy stage. This school demanded that students achieve academically without forfeiting the fine feeling expected of genteel ladies. Here I examine eighteen short diaries of schoolgirls who struggled with this contradiction, not always to their teachers' satisfaction. Since their diaries were a class assignment, they comprise an official story of what they were supposed to feel, but their subversive comments and friendship albums suggest that these young women were multilingual in emotional discourse.

Chapter 3 compares the courtship diaries of Martha (Patty) Rogers and Mary Guion. While hoping to follow their hearts, they knew that courtship and marriage placed them in a highly unequal position over against men. In this chapter we move beyond Arlie Russell Hochschild's concept of emotion work to a new area: emotional judgment. In courtship, women's emotion work required not just producing or suppressing certain feelings, but discerning which men they could trust and the inclinations of their own hearts. The prime emotions they struggled with were fear and "fancy," or irrational affection. Guion and Rogers resided partly in the imagined world of sensibility, but also in the geographically bounded world of oral village culture, and they played out their parts on that larger stage, an emotional community that they ignored at their peril. They also provide examples of successful and unsuccessful deployment of diaries in emotional problem solving.

Chapter 4 differs from the other chapters in exploring a single emotion, anger, which cuts through all these emotional communities. Here I compare all the forgoing diaries, plus the diaries of Rachel Van Dyke, Abigail May, and Susan Heath, to understand how women expressed or suppressed this supposedly dangerous and unfeminine feeling. To express anger was to refuse to do socially expected emotion work; nevertheless, women voiced anger surprisingly often and almost invariably about issues of misrepresentation and identity. Such concerns reflected their frustrations with their status and with emotion work itself, since the very process of emotion work raised questions about authentic feeling and the self. Even then, these diarists were cautious, and they used their journals to explore the boundaries of allowed feeling.

Although this book primarily focuses on single women, in chapter 5 I suggest how these diarists faced the transition from girlhood to young womanhood, moved to the emotional community of matrons, and often reordered their feelings through religious conversion, marriage, and motherhood. As they negotiated this transition, they faced almost overwhelming demands that they sacrifice self-expression for social control of their feelings and embrace resigned gratitude. Marriage and motherhood returned them to the familial stage of their youth, but with very different emotions. Although women might enter the emotional community of matrons through religious commitment or encounters with death, single women were more likely to experience emotional continuity than their married sisters.

Just as women's history has contributed to emotion history, this book places emotion within the context of female lives, and hopes to shift how we understand women's history during the early republic. By seeing women's emotions as work, I reconfigure our approach to women's labor—who controls it, who profits, and who pays for it—and suggest that class is about displaying not only money, but feelings. But incorporating emotion into women's lives and perceiving it as work does not stop there. It raises questions about the most prominent themes of women's history, from our conceptualization of public and private to our understanding of female friendship, heterosexual love, domestic ideology, women's education, religious conversion, and status. As Catherine Lutz has reminded us, "talk about emotional control in and by women, in other words, is talk about power and its exercise."[37] By examining the everyday lives of women from the perspective of their feelings, Sandra Lee Bartky has further argued, we begin to see "the 'micropolitics' of our most ordinary transactions, the ways in which we inscribe and reinscribe our subjection in the fabric of the ordinary."[38] As helpful as sociological theory may be, it is women's history that most forcefully reminds us to respect these diarists on their own terms. Their tears, sarcasm, wit, and sadness, expressed in their best hand in their private journals, remind us of their individuality. They also remind us of the simple but essential point that emotion is work.

Note on Definitions

This book is about emotion work, not just emotions, but what are emotions? Psychologists, sociologists, anthropologists, and historians provide such a range of definitions that, after surveying many texts, I was relieved to see Ronald de Sousa throw up his hands and declare, "I concede that I am unable to give a definition of emotion." Undeterred, he suggested that emotion takes up the "negative space" not occupied by "*perception, belief,* and *want*," while, in turn, these three can be understood as "analogies" for emotion, or, alternatively, emotion can be conceptualized as "complexes" of this trio.[39] While admitting such definitional difficulties, other psychologists have pursued alternative understandings. In their *Psychology of Emotion*, John G. Carlson and Elaine Hatfield write that "psychologists tend to define emotion in a way that emphasizes those aspects of emotions that interest them." Their own definition is broad enough to please both psychologists and historians: "a genetic and acquired motivational predisposition to respond experientially, physiologically, and behaviorally to certain internal and external variables."[40] That definition is not too different from the one Peter N. Stearns and Carol Z. Stearns employ, although as scholars interested in "emotionology," they are more attentive to the cognitive dimension.[41] Arlie Russell Hochschild also defines emotion to include inner and outer experience: her definition is highly cognitive in that it stresses that emotion "is a way of knowing about the world" and communicating to that world; in turn, she pictures a culturally aware self experiencing but also managing the emotion's physical dimension. With her characteristic attention to context, she finds emotion is not a thing but a process: "something we *do* by attending to inner sensation in a given way, by defining situations in a given way, by managing in given ways." Since understanding emotion as a process rather than an external object renders it more visible to historians, reveals its construction, and connects the individual to society, I have found this "social theory of emotion" most helpful in discovering what women do with their culture, and how they "do" culture itself.[42]

Throughout this text, I use the words feelings and emotions interchangeably. Some psychologists distinguish the two, with the former being one dimension of the latter; when we ask the general question, "how do you feel?" people often respond with a specific named emotion: depressed, delighted, and so on.[43] For variety, I have used the words interchangeably; for clarity, I distinguish emotional subcategories where necessary.

Note on Transcription

Devising a common transcription policy for so many diaries, each with its own peculiarities, was difficult. My goals have been to convey the author's idiosyncrasies and relationship to print culture without sacrificing clarity and ease of reading. I have preserved the original punctuation, especially the dashes and exclamation points which characterized the era's sentimental emoting, but have silently added terminal punctuation where that was needed. In a few instances, I have silently corrected minor errors and slips of the pen, but generally have preserved original spelling, and used brackets to indicate those spelling corrections necessary for clarity.

1

THE WORK OF THE HEART
Emotion, Class, and Performance

> We have had a delightful walk. The scenery around was romantic and calculated to excite the most agreeable sensations. Hills towering above every other object, the soft verdure of the fields, and gentle rivulets winding along the grassy vales. These all met my view, and together with the soft murmur of the brooks, and the sweet music of the little warblers, soothed my mind into the most perfect tranquility. . . . I was so happy that I thought not of returning, till the "Sun's last rays slept upon the plain."
> —*Sarah Connell, Diary, 12 August 1808*

Between 1780 and 1830, the journal of sensibility emerged and flourished as a distinctive category of first-person narrative for young American women. Defined by one diarist as "that acuteness of feeling which is natural to those persons who possess the finer perceptions of seeing, hearing & feeling," sensibility periodically marked the verse and letters of some elite women between the 1720s and 1760s, but did not significantly influence their journals until the late eighteenth century.[1] By 1785, Elizabeth Cranch (1763–1811) of Braintree, Massachusetts, had begun incorporating sentimental passages in her entries, while other young women found sensibility so irresistible that it pervaded virtually every line of their journals. The 1800 diary of Bostonian Abigail May (1775–1800), sporadically kept 1799–1805 entries of Rhode Islander Mary B. Howell (1779–1811), and 1805–10 journals of Newburyport's Sarah Connell (1791–1835) reveal residence in an intensely sentimental world, one in which Connell's references to "agreeable sensations," "romantic" scenery, and "little warblers" formed a common language.[2] Although such rhetoric had become commonplace by the early nineteenth century, even during its height sentimental self-writing never entirely displaced other modes of journalizing. Some diarists echoed the rhythms of Calvinist sermons, Biblical verses, or everyday chat rather than sentimental literature, while still others combined these in their own multilingual discourses. By the 1820s, first-person narratives couched in the language of eighteenth-century sentimentality had begun to fade, as more distinctively Victorian words and images succeeded them. But for a brief period during the late eighteenth and early nineteenth centuries, the diary of sensibility expressed and shaped the emotional universe of many young women, especially those of the middle and upper classes.

Ethereal and overblown, sentimental language seemed to transcend the material world, but was anchored in consumption culture and circumscribed by class. Mary Howell captured the relationship between sensibility and the economy when she admired a "delightfull" "prospect" which combined "retiring waters" and "green banks" on one side of a cove and "busy commerce, houses, spires and trees" on the other.[3] The authors of this chapter's diaries of sensibility were all positioned in the rising middle to upper-middle classes and lived within easy reach of the Atlantic coast; as such, they increasingly enjoyed the luxury goods which provided the comforts associated with fine feeling.[4] Elizabeth Cranch's journal illustrates the close fit between sensibility and the upper reaches of society: daughter of an impecunious watchmaker and farmer but niece of John and Abigail Adams, Cranch revealed only occasional sensibility in her journal until she visited her prosperous Haverhill, Massachusetts, kin during 1785–86. In their circle, her diary adopted a more consistently literary and sentimental tone. Scholars of colonial, Revolutionary, and early republican America have copiously chronicled the commercial transformation that brought Cranch's relatives prosperity and formed the context for Howell's casual entry, "walk'd out shopping."[5] During the early eighteenth century, at first mainly the colonial elite had purchased British luxuries, but even before the Revolution, and with increasing speed thereafter, easy credit and improved transportation made everything from teapots to card tables more widely available. By the late eighteenth century, Americans avidly read advertisements, clamored for goods from peddlers and merchants, and spent a significant portion of their income on English manufactures. Even modest farmers remodeled domestic exteriors with fanlights and symmetrical windows, although house interiors were constructed around traditional economic needs.[6] Republican ideology warned of consumption's dangers and suggested that spending encouraged profligacy, but had little success in stemming the tide. By 1815, "fully half the number of families in the country, 400,000, owned luxury goods worth two hundred to six hundred dollars."[7] Compared to the material indulgences of England's upper classes, these were modest trimmings, but for Americans they marked a new interest in refinement and comfort that reached well beyond the elite. As T. H. Breen has expressed it, for a middle class eager to prove its claim to a better social position, "consumer goods became the props in a new public theatre of self-fashioning."[8]

Women played major roles in performing this class identity by purchasing and displaying luxury goods: by 1781, "Dear bought and far fetched is fit for Ladies" had become a truism that Betsey Heath copied in her penmanship book.[9] Even before the Revolution, wives had exhibited their husbands' wealth: unconstrained by her husband's pennypinching aphorisms, Benjamin Franklin's wife had determined that "*her* husband deserv'd a silver spoon and China bowl as well as any of his neighbors."[10] Matrons and daughters employed these goods in the social rituals over which they presided, such as afternoon tea and formal dinners; the words "drank tea" form a regular rhythm in Elizabeth Cranch's 1785–86 journal.[11] Textiles were a major British import, and their choice was also women's province; commissioned portraits of leading families dwelt on the sheen of fine fabrics, and the middle classes purchased mirrors so they could admire their new appearance.[12] In 1771 Anna Green Winslow of Boston was only twelve, but she already sensed her society's preoccupations and complained to her mother: "you don't know the fation here—I beg to look like other folk," even though this "cost an amasing sight of money."[13] Harriet and Maria Trumbull agreed; during their six-month stay in New York City, they studied the dancing, drawing, and music making designed to "finish" young ladies, but knew that their purchases were equally important. "You are very good my dear Papa, to be so indulgent to us in letting us have new dresses and encouraging us to appear in a style suited to your station in life," Harriet wrote her father, Connecticut governor Jonathan Trumbull.[14] In 1800 Abigail May recorded the era's sartorial extravagances in a Mrs. Fell, who flaunted her status through both the scale of her wardrobe—seven trunks and a half dozen hats—and its richness: "a spotted muslin trim'd round with green velvet and lace—a band of the same round her head—and a chip Chapeau with a painted handkerchief and wreath of roses upon it a pearl comb &cc—."[15] Clothes, china, and tea parties emanated from the home, rendering that presumably private and feminine sphere the site of conscious public display.

As they fashioned these new selves, women displayed not only material objects associated with refinement, but new manners. These, too, were British imports, conveyed in conduct books which ambitious middle-class Americans studied carefully. Although a number of these books drew on court culture, an estimated "two-thirds of revolutionary-era conduct books clearly addressed the middling sort," a trend that continued into the early national period.[16] Once prudish publishers deleted the immoral parts, Lord Chesterfield's letters to his son were especially popular, providing a detailed guide to graceful advancement. Echoing the new interest in appearance, Mary Howell called his advice a "mirror" by which readers could be "taught the *Philosophy* of life." "Manners, some one says is of more importance to a state than Laws," she observed, "and if so, should we disdain to take lessons in *that science* from the greatest master in the world?"[17]

External manners taught the bows, bodily restraint, and polite phrases which signaled rising class status, but were insufficient without gentility, a quality distinctly different from the "appearance of whalebone and buckram" which had characterized the more formal early eighteenth century.[18] According to Richard Bushman's *The Refinement of America*, gentility can be summed up in three popular and interlocking eighteenth-century words: delicacy, sensibility, and taste. "Delicacy in the larger sense meant the capacity for fine discriminations and an appreciation for all that was refined and gentle," while sensibility was the emotional expression of delicacy, and taste comprised the indefinable but crucial ability to convey delicacy and sensibility in beautiful forms.[19] All three were to be conveyed with an easy, graceful manner. As Nancy Shippen's mother advised her in 1777, "you may be sure you improve in proportion to the degree of ease with which you do any thing as you have been taught to do it . . . (for you must not only feel easy but appear so)."[20] Similarly, the period's portrait painters insisted that female figures "should be drawn like *Fancy*, light and airy, in a loose flowing robe," in order to embody "ease and elegance."[21]

As the emotional face of gentility, sensibility provided an index of internal delicacy, which could be judged by public expression of taste, then understood to convey character as well as aesthetics. When Abigail May visited Ballston Springs, New York, in 1800, she observed the rising classes in search of health and entertainment, and scrutinized not only their wardrobe and manners but their internal qualities, including their emotions. In a striking passage, May contrasted two women's behavior at a ball and revealed the subtle distinctions that marked sensibility. "I confess I felt my doubts as to her real character," she wrote about a Miss Kissam,

> —last evening she was dressed with great taste—and moved like a fairy, but there was a voluptuousness and *expression* in her every look—not exactly characteristic of delicacy or even decency— . . . Mr. Morgan would look at her, and then at me as if reading my opinion of her appearance—but all the Gentlemen appear'd in raptures with her *exhibition*—how great a contrast was the modest but elegant Mrs. Galla[g]her, she moved with such ease and delicacy one could almost describe her virtue personified—from her steps and gestures—tis strange that the same exercise in two beautiful women should excite such contrary sensations. both keep good time, both go the same figure almost the same steps, yet one charms us by her softness and delicacy—the other disgusts by forwardness and impudence— —.[22]

Miss Kissam failed May's test for sensibility in her lack of ease: her *"exhibition,"* "forwardness and impudence" were too overt and rendered her feelings crude and possibly sexual. Abigail May did not confine these criticisms to women, but also castigated a suitably named Oliver Pain, who "pretends to any quantity of sentiment" and thought he epitomized "'the sublime and beautiful.'"[23] His narcissism and pretense contrasted with the modest Misses Clarke, who "converse upon every subject with such fluency and propriety" yet were "only sufficiently conscious of their advantages to give them an easy dignified manner."[24] Sensibility established an elite world of feeling and virtue, and May was well aware that although her wardrobe was not fashionable, her friendship with the most delicate and genteel woman at Ballston Springs gave her "considerable consequence in the eyes of all—."[25]

In assessing Miss Kissam's sensibility, Abigail May participated in a more general construction of not only class, but race and the republican state. The consumer goods Americans clamored for were obtained from a multicultural empire which had propelled consideration of racial identity since the seventeenth century. During the early republic, the northern states progressively dismantled the African slavery which had prevailed in all parts of colonial America, but racial associations continued and influenced emotional standards. These diarists rarely spoke of race, but Mary Guion's ambivalent comments and behavior are telling. In 1805 her uncle presented her with a little boy, Harry, as a birthday present, and she matter-of-factly accepted him as her slave until New York law freed him, even though she had earlier cried during a play when a slave begged to be freed and returned to Africa. She both questioned and reflected her culture's expectation that whiteness, refined feeling, and humanity were synonymous when she wrote of Harry, "his skin I know is black but his heart is human."[26]

In characterizing Mrs. Gallagher's "ease and delicacy" as "virtue personified," Abigail May associated sensibility not only with class and race, but with republican ideology; like her contemporaries, she found political meaning in the feeling heart. Sensibility, in fact, offered a solution to Americans' fears of both tyranny and luxury. British Real Whig thought and American Revolutionary rhetoric had associated tyrants with extravagant luxury and self-interest, while the liberty-loving republican was to embrace material simplicity and the common good. Virtue, upon which the republic rested, was understood as self-sacrifice for the good of others.[27] Applied to consumption, these ideas led some Patriots to criticize the new enthusiasm for imported goods as selfish and dangerous to the new republic, and American newspapers frequently deprecated women's alleged purchasing proclivities and the "effeminacy" of luxury. In terms of gender, republican ideology initially cast virtue as male and vice as female. But these same political ideas contained an emotional subtext: the aristocrat was not only corrupt but unfeeling, while the republican's heart warmed with affection for others. As Lori Merish has argued, during the course of the eighteenth century, the Scottish Enlightenment philosophers so popular in America linked gender, feeling, and consumption in new ways: by reinterpreting luxury goods as signs of feminine refinement, they recast women into the role of "republican consumer." Material and emotional gentility fused, and refinement in manners and possessions began to suggest feminine sympathy, not selfishness, while warmhearted gentility succeeded coldhearted aristocracy as characteristics of the elite. In this context, it is appropriate that Adam Smith, author of *An Inquiry into the Nature and Causes of the Wealth of Nations*, also wrote *The Theory of Moral Sentiments*, with women figuring into emotional as well as mercantile exchanges.[28] This emotional dimension of women's gentility enabled Revolutionary Americans to retain republican identity while emulating British etiquette and eased anxiety over their eager consumption of material goods. As long as Americans' feelings were heartfelt and tender, virtue might be maintained and the republic saved.

Sentimental novels, verse, and essays were even more significant than etiquette manuals in conveying the sensibility republicans prized; possession of such books was itself a sign of gentility. Living within easy reach of maritime traffic, these diarists enjoyed access to the latest publications through bookstores and circulating libraries, whose numbers had increased significantly during the 1790s.[29] Young women often obtained books through their fathers, who subscribed to lending libraries and in that sense influenced what their daughters read, while mothers occasionally deprecated and redirected their daughters' fondness for fiction. Nonetheless, these diarists seem to have enjoyed more freedom from parental supervision of their reading than their Victorian descendants.[30] Peers also provided reading material. Within Sarah Connell's prosperous circle, sentimental books were the currency of friendship: she borrowed volumes such as Mrs. Elizabeth Rowe's letters from her friend Lydia and took turns reading out loud with her classmate Harriot.[31] In addition, young men sought favor by giving her books. A Mr. Gleason plied Connell with Shakespeare and the *Boston Mirror* with little effect, but finally won her approval when he presented her "with a large Volume, entitled *'Elegant Extracts.'* I am much pleased with it, the pieces are well selected," she observed. "I received it with pleasure as the gift of a friend whom I esteem. It will oft, remind me of the *Donar*," Connell concluded, recognizing how books formed an extension of the self.[32] In his choice of literature, Mr. Gleason confirmed his own elegance and gentility. Similarly, when Abigail May asked the residents at Ballston Springs for books to read, they offered her Tobias Smollett's *Peregrine Pickle*, Laurence Sterne's *Tristram Shandy*, and Oliver Goldsmith's *Vicar of Wakefield*, the latter being the period's most famous sentimental text.[33]

Middle- and upper-class status also provided many young women with the time to read sentimental literature and emulate its values. In her study of Victorian girlhood, Jane Hunter has argued that "the elevation of reading to a central and defining aspect of bourgeois girls' lives helped to define a specifically Victorian adolescence," a situation made possible by a decline in their housework sometime during the nineteenth century. These early national period diaries suggest that limited physical labor and the prominence of reading were already well established in many young women's lives by the late eighteenth century, at least in the middle and upper classes.[34] A much-indulged only child, Connell was expected to spend her days not on household tasks but in developing the "complaisance" and delicacy of feeling appropriate to her rank. "I rose early, and employ'd the Morning in reading," she wrote; afternoons were typically spent visiting.[35] Mary Howell reported an equally leisurely life, writing, "In the morning, wrote to Louisa, then drew a flower, read the mirror, *made* anecdotes, and *eked* out a rainy Sunday." Occasionally, she mentioned gardening or sewing, but often linked these tasks to beauty or "to oblige *Master* Fashion," rather than to necessity.[36] Some well-off young women toiled at more tasks than Connell and Howell, but, especially if they were sentimentalists, brushed them aside in their journals. Patty Rogers, the daughter of a small-town New Hampshire minister, was comfortable rather than wealthy and obliged to care for her ailing father, but in her diary she dwelt almost exclusively on her emotional state and dismissed her household efforts with the perfunctory comment, "Set down to work as usual—." Susan Heath's Brookline, Massachusetts, father was wealthier than Patty Rogers's, but too cheap to spend freely on servants. She recognized that her resulting housework kept her from the sentimental literary world she longed to join: "I wished the Ironing to the Deuce—it was a tedious interruption to reading—," Heath wrote angrily. Elizabeth Cranch's housework and language shifted with her social circle: when home with her marginally middle-class family, she assisted in considerable household production and her diary showed few signs of sensibility, but as a guest of her wealthy relatives, she did no housework and instead described her feelings in newly sentimental entries.[37]

Of course, diaries may not be reliable indicators of actual household labor, and undoubtedly obscured many tasks, especially the daily household maintenance required of all but the wealthiest women. As Laurel Thatcher Ulrich has shown, the spread of spinning did not precede but accompanied the consumer revolution, so that "'store-bought' and 'homemade' fabrics developed together."[38] But for the purposes of emotion history, sentimental diaries' omission of such work is revealing. Jeanne Boydston has argued that, beginning during the early republic and culminating in Victorianism, the more cash transactions pervaded the economy, the less women's unpaid domestic work received recognition as work at all. Changing perceptions of pregnancy suggest that this erasure of women's labor was already under way during the 1700s. As Susan E. Klepp has convincingly demonstrated, during the seventeenth and early eighteenth centuries, references to "breeding" and "big-bellied" women positioned childbirth within a productive, agricultural context that they shared with men. By the eighteenth century's end, however, sensibility provided a new, euphemistic language that devalued maternal physicality and re-imagined pregnancy as a dimension of feeling separate from men's economic enterprises.[39] Upper-class diarists of the early national period reflected these cultural shifts; for them, refined emotions had become indicators of both femininity and class status, and as such succeeded housework as a noteworthy subject. Inversely, journals of women less influenced by sentimentality often teemed with chores.[40]

Whether Sarah Connell's books were purchased, borrowed, or given, a substantial number may be classified as works of sensibility, and these influenced her prose the most. Beginning her diary in November 1805, at age fourteen, she wrote entries during the last two months of that year that were cut-and-dried. Connell skipped 1806, a year during which she must have been extensively exposed to sensibility, for in her first entries for 1807, she showed familiarity with James Thomson, a leading neoclassical poet who imbued nature with emotion; and by February she and her friends were taking turns reading Goldsmith's *Vicar of Wakefield*, a premier novel of sensibility. Over that year, her prose increasingly adopted the language of sensibility as she read Frances Burney's *Camilla* and perused Elizabeth Rowe's sentimental letters, one of the eighteenth century's most popular works of spirituality, in addition to reading a variety of other Gothic and sentimental works.[41] All in all, between 1805 and her marriage at age nineteen in late 1810, Connell quoted or mentioned reading forty-nine distinct works. Of these, twenty-one were novels or romances, seven verse, six books on religion, five dramatic works, four miscellaneous essay/letter collections, three magazines, one geography, one biography, and one allegory.[42] In the range and number of these works and her continuous search for something new to peruse, she represents the turn-of-the-century extensive reader, who, especially among the well-off, was beginning to replace earlier practices of intensively reading a few texts.[43] Much as luxury goods and conduct manuals were imports, most of Connell's reading originated in Great Britain.[44]

Although young women imbibed sensibility from multiple literary forms—verse, essays, plays, philosophical speculation, and magazines—they responded to novels with an attention and enthusiasm different in kind from their other reading. Diarist after diarist described herself as unable to put down novels, an effect that verse and essays rarely had on them. Even readers who abjured sentimental language found their plots and heroines irresistible: Susan Heath of Brookline, Massachusetts, found she "could not leave" *The Romance of the Pyrenees* for several days, was so absorbed in books she forgot to dress, and shrewdly noted that authors made many true-life tales into novels, figuring that they "would get perused sooner," a maneuver that lured Heath herself.[45] As an urban, upper-middle-class woman from a mercantile family, Sarah Connell fell into the group most likely to read novels, which in fact comprised almost 43 percent of her reading. She also kept her journal just at the time circulating libraries increased their fictional offerings.[46] Unlike Connell, Elizabeth Cranch did not read more novels than other types of books, but she nonetheless gave fiction much greater attention: in her 1785–89 diaries she favored only two texts with lengthy descriptions, both of them novels, while she dismissed her other reading with at best perfunctory comments.[47] Enthusiasm did not prevent criticism: many diarists commented astutely on fictional character development and plot, but such analysis again testified to novels' singular authority, for few journal writers bothered to critique essays or verse.

Women's enthusiasm for novels was especially significant in shaping a new, more emotionally expressive diary, and in that sense was key in initiating the articulation of feeling necessary to emotion work. Readers varied in the degree to which they adopted fiction's messages and language, but in novels they found an unmistakable new focus that was much more difficult to resist: such books put a typically young female protagonist at their center, just as did young women's journals. We can see this in the prominence of women's names in novel titles: Sarah Connell read *Camilla, Caroline of Lichtfield, Emma Courtney, Julia and the Illuminated Baron, Corinna, Julia de Roubigne, Cecelia, Leonora,* and *Amelia*.[48] Even if the heroine made tragic choices, novels invited sympathy for her rather than condemnation, and in that sense taught the importance of appreciating complex and individual rather than ideal womanhood.[49] The form of eighteenth-century novels reinforced this feminine centrality; often epistolary, they pictured heroines writing about themselves, whether keeping diaries or composing letters.[50] This focus on the heroine's feelings and experiences encouraged their readers to contemplate their own lives and to inscribe them in their own book, the diary. As John Mullan has argued, "it was in novels that the individual self—the experience of the self as individual—was most affectingly represented." As a result, novels provided "the best tuition" in learning the feelings that defined the self, a lesson easily extended to the diary.[51] Much as the process of assessing their reading helped Victorian diarists develop self-consciousness, young women of the early republic authoritatively dismissed weakly plotted works or admired an author's skill.[52] In their critical comments, young women suggest how novels taught them to articulate and judge appropriate feeling. After reading Frances Burney's *Evelina*, Susan Heath reported, "I am perfectly in love with *Lord Orville*. In spite of the *malicious* endeavours of the author of *Evelina* to prejudice the world against him, I don't believe a word of his becoming *gloomy* & *morose*."[53] Heath then turned to determining a more pressing issue: her own feelings. On a more practical level, the novel taught writing conventions which young women freely borrowed. Even the most dedicated diarists bogged down in lists of who came to tea, struggled to make narrative sense of their lives, and threatened to abandon their journals; through providing language and plots, novels suggested how to shape the often unwieldy daily life which diarists chronicled. Fiction also offered a new construct: journals began to quote conversations, a deployment of "he saids" and "she saids" that provides a window into both literary influence and everyday oral transactions.

Many diarists concentrated their novel reading in adolescence, and in that sense fiction played an especially formative role in self-development and emotional construction. Catharine Sedgwick, Abigail May's friend at Ballston Springs, reported she "read constantly, but chiefly novels," at age eleven, and even though Anna Green Winslow's family monitored her activities carefully, they did not object to her beginning Samuel Richardson's *Charles Grandison* and an abridged version of Henry Fielding's *History of Joseph Andrews* at twelve.[54] By age fifteen, Laura Maria Wolcott was such an experienced reader, that she parodied fiction's often trite plots and characters: "the heroines + heros are all perfect, all are shepherds + shepherdesses. all recline 'upon the green hill side.' all 'grow up under the dews + light of heaven among the solitary hills' until they attain to perfect womanhood, never know what it is to love, consider all as brothers &c. &c."[55] Sarah Connell seems to have enjoyed fiction most in late adolescence: she read only one novel in the last two months of 1805, when she was fourteen, but read six in 1807 and one in 1808, and then jumped to ten in 1809 at ages seventeen and eighteen, petering out to three in 1810, after which she married and gave up novel reading. Novels appear to have been less prominent in the reading of diarists past their teens. Abigail May was twenty-four when she kept her diary, and she says little about novel reading, although her summer's residence at a resort provided ample free time.[56] Novels also occupied a smaller place in Mary B. Howell's reading at ages twenty to twenty-six than they did in Sarah Connell's; they comprised only about a quarter of her reading.[57] But that they read fewer novels in their twenties does not mean that sentimental fiction was not part of May's and Howells's imaginative world. Such novels dwelt on the young, imperiled girl, and these diarists may have perused novels when they were younger and more clearly the heroine's age, as Connell did. The fact that women often gave up reading sentimental novels when they married suggests that plots spoke to a highly specific and youthful audience. Given how frequently young women read novels out loud to each other, familiarity with fiction was almost unavoidable, and references to fictional figures were a staple of young women's conversation and writing.[58] While their readers were still young, novels individualized and reinforced the sentimental ideas these diarists encountered in verse and essays in addition to providing a form, a plot, and a protagonist easily transferred to the diary. Together, such reading left an unmistakable residue: the diaries of these women show that the emotive world of sentimental literature infused their imaginations.

Sensibility, in sum, established two overlapping communities in which women were prime residents. First, in Barbara H. Rosenwein's terms, it provided a distinct and real "emotional community" with values, mores, and recognizable hallmarks.[59] Its residents experienced this community through everyday activities, such as reading out loud to each other, sharing reactions, borrowing books, acting out sentimental tableaux, and speaking the language of sensibility. Emotional circles of this kind predominated in the middle and upper classes and among women, although the required manners allowed entry to less affluent whites and to men, and failures in deportment and feeling might exclude even well-off women. When Abigail May exchanged glances with Mr. Morgan in common criticism of Miss Kissam's indelicacy, they recognized each other as fellow citizens of their emotional community, but rejected that vulgar young woman. The residents of this world were also disproportionately young. While their mothers' generation had had some experience in perusing sentimental literature, the more limited availability of books before the Revolution meant that such reading had not been as common for them as for their daughters. By contrast, exchanging works of sensibility was a hallmark of the new republic's peer culture, especially in its elite circles, and the fact that fiction was about youth and that novel reading was concentrated in adolescence tended to exclude older generations.[60]

At the same time, to borrow Benedict Anderson's phrase, sensibility connected young women to a second and *"imagined"* community of readers affiliated through print media, who experienced class status through a common literature. In Anderson's formulation, such imagined communities created political nationalism through simultaneous experiences, such as newspaper reading, but his concept also explains how sensibility functioned in Anglo-American society. As he put it, residents of the imagined community "will never know most of their fellow-members, meet them, or even hear of them, yet in the minds of each lives the image of their communion."[61] In their critique of Anderson, Nancy Armstrong and Leonard Tennenhouse suggest that fiction also enabled disparate readers to experience the same event simultaneously.[62] If we apply their insight to these diarists, we can see how reading provided a sense of a larger sentimental world and an emotional elite, international in scope (although confined to whites), yet intimate in tone. This imagined community endowed women's feelings and their immediate emotional community with heightened significance.

Should these emotional communities be understood as public or private? In his groundbreaking theoretical work, *The Structural Transformation of the Public Sphere*, Jürgen Habermas conceptualized the public sphere as having two dimensions, the state and the reading public or "bourgeois public sphere." The eighteenth-century readers he pictured were typically men in coffeehouses examining newspapers and tracts, an essentially political activity that determined whether they consented to and legitimized the state, although they brought experiences from the private familial sphere to such reading.[63] Habermas had little to say about women, and subsequent scholars have puzzled over whether eighteenth-century female novel readers became more solitary and private as they perused books, or whether books pulled them into the public sphere of print culture, if not into the world of politics. But reading's effects need not be dichotomized for either men or women; as Gillian Brown reasonably observes, "reading is never exclusively public or private; it indeed epitomizes the continual flow between these realms." Moreover, she argues, eighteenth-century novels were preeminently "stories of compelled consent," in which rude men forced refined women against their wishes, and in that sense they dealt with the same issues of legitimacy as did the public sphere.[64] These diaries show that, like reading, writing created a loop that entwined the public and private. As novels spread, young women used public print to read about the private lives of fictional females; they then imitated the language and plots of public prints in their private journals as they wrote about themselves. To complete the circle, they went on to enter into sentimental exchanges with other women, their friends of everyday life, and incorporated them into the imagined community of sensibility. Sensibility's real and fictive emotional communities, then, straddled the public/private spheres, just as did the reading and writing that created them. To understand feeling's place in these overlapping developments, we need to see connections that unite rather than spheres that divide. During the eighteenth century, the private sphere, as the area outside the state, included not only the family, but also work and property, elements that modern culture has since reinterpreted as public.[65] By detaching economic functions from their conceptualization of the private, later centuries separated emotion from work, work from the family, and men from women. I suggest that if we rejoin emotion and work, we may not only better understand the relationship between the public and private, but discover how feelings themselves were created. They, in turn, will suggest the degree to which young women consented, not to the state, but to their culture's rules for emotional expression.

Young women of the rising classes possessed and read sentimental literature, but precisely how did sensibility influence their emotional expression? T. H. Breen's "theatre of self-fashioning," with its tea parties, etiquette books, and novels, framed the performances Erving Goffman found essential to the social self, but to say people behaved in a certain way does not settle how they felt or the relationship between emotions and performance. How did they incorporate literature so that sensibility was not just an object consumed, but a feeling experienced, a part of their interior? To understand how this happened, I will examine three diaries of sensibility: those of Sarah Connell, Mary B. Howell, and Elizabeth Cranch. Connell's diary is especially useful in understanding how women incorporated sensibility into their lives. "Formed by the God of Nature with a heart of Sensibility," Connell was more interested in what she felt than what she did.[66] Once she began keeping her journal regularly in 1807 at age fifteen, she transcribed her experiences almost daily, providing a detailed four-year record of her development as a sentimentalist before her late-1810 marriage. Mary B. Howell was a much less faithful writer; she penned entries for two to three months for each year from 1799 to 1803, before she concluded in 1805 that she had "no journalizing stile" and quit.[67] Nevertheless, her entries are substantial, provide a check on Connell's diary, and convey the experiences of a slightly older woman, from the age of twenty to twenty-six. While Connell's and Howell's diaries are journals of high sensibility, Elizabeth Cranch's 1785–86 journal represents a world of more moderate sensibility, a temperament she expressed during a winter visit to her relatives. Aged twenty-two in 1785 and suffering from depression induced by a long-absent fiancé, Cranch pondered how to feel deeply but without pain. All three of these women were single New Englanders living in well-off families in or near port cities.

At first glance, their focus on feelings makes these diaries seem different from journals which depict the external reality of women's work: bread baked, socks mended, floors scrubbed. But they are in fact records of another form of labor central to women's lives: in Arlie Russell Hochschild's term, "emotion work." In these journals we can observe the two types of acting which make up emotion work and through which individuals respond to society's "feeling rules": "surface acting," or purposeful body language, and "deep acting," the construction of feeling itself.[68] Sarah Connell's, Mary Howell's, and Elizabeth Cranch's diaries powerfully convey how women learned to act appropriate emotional parts, how they shaped their feelings to fit family and gender roles, and how they attempted to integrate their own needs for self-expression with cultural expectations. Although ease was supposed to characterize sensibility, it required extensive effort, and the increase in emotion work more than made up for any decline in women's housework.

Both Sarah Connell and Mary Howell turned to sentimental literature as their prime instructor in surface and deep acting. In doing so, they encountered sensibility's major paradox: it not only exalted spontaneous and expressive emotion springing directly from the heart, but defined and therefore limited what that emotion should be.[69] As a sentimentalist, Connell repeatedly decried insincerity and hated formal occasions, "where every one 'acts a part foreign to his nature.'"[70] Her favorite books illustrated the value of spontaneity and stimulated an immediate and effusive response. On completing *St. Clair, or The Heiress of Desmond,* for example, she "threw aside the book" and "wept at the fictitious sufferings of St. Clair and Olivia. The World might call it weakness," she allowed, "perhaps it is so, yet I feel that it is a weakness I have no wish to part with; for that person who can read Mrs. Owenson's works without emotion, has indeed a heart of Apathy. Hers, is the language of the heart, it speaks to the feelings, it almost steals us from ourselves, from every thing around us."[71] Mary B. Howell reacted to *The Farmer's Boy* in much the same way. "What simplicity! what pathos, in the Farmer's Boy! every description is a mirror. we involuntarily sigh when we behold—'The piteous mourner by the pathway ride.' And we seem also to 'waft the pang' when we repeat her sad, 'oh dear!' *Beautiful* in its fullest sense,—will comprise every thing I think of the Farmer's Boy."[72]

While praising spontaneity, sentimental literature instructed Connell and Howell in specific and correct emotions. "May I ever view my heart cloth'd in sincerity," Sarah prayed on her sixteenth birthday, and this literature taught the appropriate emotional clothing—or surface acting—for every occasion.[73] In their comments on novel reading, Connell and Howell deprecated those who failed to feel as sensibility suggested they should. "That person who can read Mrs. Owenson's works without emotion, has indeed a heart of Apathy," Sarah had written about *St. Clair*. Mary Howell made a similar judgment about Henry Fielding's *Joseph Andrews:* "True, 'the plot is simple and the scene is low.' but no Lover of sentiment, or son of glee, can throw it by with disgust," she declared. "If they do, they deserve to be discarded by the first, and *illegitimatized* by the latter."[74] Her strong choice of words—"discarded" and *"illegitimatized"*—suggests that the wrong emotional response was a serious social transgression.

The cult of sensibility also provided a distinctive language that both elicited and limited emotional expression. When Elizabeth Cranch was ten, her mother sent her Elizabeth Rowe's sentimental and religious letters, along with conflicting instructions which mirrored women's difficulty in finding their own words: "try to write like her; but endeavour to be as good," her mother requested. "When you have read some of it, send me what you think of it—of every Letter write your thoughts, & send them to me. ask your aunt what you ought to think, but let me have them in your own dress—."[75] This sartorial metaphor, which echoed Connell's desire for a "heart cloth'd in sincerity," suggests how sentimental language simultaneously revealed and obscured individual feeling. Such metaphors were especially significant at a time when fashion, as well as feeling, established class status.⁷⁶ As sentimentalists, Sarah Connell and Mary Howell often expressed themselves in others' "dress," rather than their own. Their diaries repeatedly employed stock terms such as "tender," "honest," "sympathetic," and "sincere." Frequently they quoted other writers to express their own feelings, often without attribution, and it can be difficult to separate their own words from those they had read. Quoting James Thomson's and William Cowper's verses not only captured what they struggled to say, but illustrated their familiarity with sentimental favorites.⁷⁷ This overlay of borrowed language often distanced Connell and Howell from the warm emotions they sought to portray. Occasionally, Connell and Cranch referred to themselves in the third person, as if they were characters in sentimental dramas and were describing someone else's feelings.⁷⁸

Just as sentimental literature offered a language for people's feelings, it devised names which provided emotional identity. Works of sensibility popularized new first names for girls, such as Clarissa, Harriot, and Charlotte, which implicitly linked young American women with sentimental novels and the feelings they cultivated. At Litchfield Female Academy in Connecticut, about one-quarter of the students had first names which echoed fictional or classical heroines rather than the English or Biblical names common during the colonial period.⁷⁹ Sentimental literature also popularized the use of cognomens, which Mary Howell regularly employed for her friends; they promised privacy, if someone should read her diary, but also heightened the importance of transactions with these figures.⁸⁰ Howell's siblings' names were the old-fashioned Jeremiah, Roger, Sarah, and Waitstill, but the likes of Orlando, Theodocia, Alcandor, and Aldrigena peopled her diary.⁸¹ These lofty names established her journal's tone and declared her residence in the imagined community of sensibility.

Sensibility also offered a mode of punctuation that influenced readers' emotions. In particular, it popularized the exclamation point, which called attention to the text's drama. In an era when readers often recited out loud, an exclamation point suggested a raised and emotionally charged voice, which in turn elicited a heightened response from listeners. Mary Howell's repeated use of the exclamation point when she described *The Farmer's Boy* comprised the written equivalent of emoting at the top of her voice. Patty Rogers, the most sentimental and emotionally uninhibited of these diarists, employed the exclamation point in almost every entry. Sentimental texts also freely employed the dash, suggesting the continuous and free flow of emotion, a punctuation Abigail May and Elizabeth Cranch used throughout their journals.[82]

Sentimental literature modeled the physical as well as the verbal expression of sensibility. Like her favorite fictional heroines, Sarah Connell threw herself on beds, into carriages, and into her loved ones' arms. Above all, she cried: tears welled up, spilled over, poured forth, and sometimes overwhelmed her.[83] Sometimes novels moved her to tears: as John Mullan has pointed out, "people were supposed to cry over books as well as in them," because "finding your feelings through novels was supposed to be a *moral* activity."[84] At other times, both the happiness and sadness of her own life made her cry. Sarah often described weeping as collective rather than individual. On visiting her Aunt Newman, her "heart palpitated with joy," "tears of affection rolled down her [aunt's] aged cheeks," and Sarah "flew to her arms and gave vent to [her] feelings."[85] Mary Howell was less lachrymose, but also saw crying as the epitome of sensibility: on viewing a set of engravings, she found herself at a loss for words, but decided, "the involuntary tear I trust will always be the reward of the Artist and the poet."[86] While cultivating tears, these diarists expunged any physical realities that disturbed their sentimental idyll, much as their broader culture hid the messy reality of pregnancy. When Connell sailed to Portland in 1807, for example, she dwelt on "the pale radiance of Cynthia dancing on the waves" and "the sailor's pensive song," but obscured her indelicate vomiting by writing, "sickness oblidged me to go below."[87]

The physical and verbal emoting characteristic of sentimental diaries may seem artificial and indeed performed the external function of demonstrating class-based gentility, but sensibility pervaded young women's emotional interiors as well. Sarah Connell's diary is especially detailed in demonstrating how sentimentalists engaged in deep acting. As Arlie Russell Hochschild explains, in deep acting, "the actor does not try to *seem* happy or sad but rather expresses spontaneously, as the Russian director Constantin Stanislavski urged, a real feeling that has been self-induced."[88] The subtle inducement of these emotions enabled young women to more fully possess feelings of sensibility and potentially eased the conflict between spontaneity and performance. Sarah Connell's chief means of inducing sentimental emotions was through making others' experiences her own. When reading, she shared in the lives of fictitious characters; similarly, she tried to enter into her friends' feelings. Sarah frequently described her heart as one that "palpitated" or "vibrated" in response to others. In a favorite word, her heart "participated" in emotion. "Alass, my Lydia!" she wrote when her friend's mother died. "Often have you been call'd to follow to the grave, friends, from whose love you derived happiness. Sarah drops a tear in sympathy with her friend. She participates your sorrows."[89]

Connell also loved to visit poor country folk in order to imbibe the contentment she believed they possessed. Like many sentimentalists, she associated delicate feeling with the genteel, but rejected the artificiality of aristocratic life and ascribed peace and simplicity to the poor, especially those living close to nature.[90] Gentility might signify the American upper classes, but these Yankees positioned their culture in between the British aristocracy and their own lower classes, a maneuver that helped them imagine themselves as virtuously middle class, even when they were wealthy.[91] "How much superior is the sweet cheerfulness of the honest rustics, and their friendly repast, to all the parade of ceremony, and the insincerity of the Great," Connell mused after one such visit, distinguishing between the financial and the emotional elite, much as Abigail May had; "retire'd from the busy World," such rustics seemed to possess a "native simplicity" without the cultivation Connell found necessary. Much as she purchased books and teapots to demonstrate her gentility, she consumed the feelings "cottagers" and nature offered. As she returned to her home on a fashionable Newburyport street, she luxuriated in the feelings these visits inspired: "After rambling round the environs of this little cot, we bade adieu to the cottagers, and set off on our way home," Connell wrote, imitating scenes common to sentimental fiction. "It was growing late, the scene tranquil, my spirits placid. The Sun's last rays tinged the summit of the lofty Mountain, and cast a mild radiance on the objects below. The little warblers were singing their evening song."[92]

As literary critic Janet Todd points out, sensibility taught its devotees not so much "what it felt like to be another person or object, but what it felt like to be looking at a person or object and how such looking affirmed their own sensibility."[93] In each of these visits, Sarah Connell moved from admiring others to admiring herself: she pictured herself seated "beneath a venerable Oak" tossing pebbles into a stream, a temporary child of nature.[94] Although she saw herself as benevolent, she brought to the poor her feelings rather than goods, exchanging refinement for contentment. Similarly, when her friend Abigail visited a poor woman with ten children, Sarah focused not on what Abigail did to help them, but on her friend's "engaging" appearance and "smile of complacency and self-approbation."[95] Melancholy was as pleasurable as contentment and produced as purposefully. Sentimentalists were particularly responsive to the moon, or "the silver crested Luna," as Mary Howell called it. Howell loved to imbibe the delicate sadness nightfall induced; she found that "pale moon beams . . . inspired the soul, with (what the world terms) a most romantic sadness. . . . I almost gazed my soul away," she confessed.[96] Sarah Connell also often stationed herself at the window during the evening, just before penning a diary entry. "A sweet melancholy diffused itself over my heart," she rhapsodized, "Memory recalled a thousand tender scenes; the silent tear fell, from an emotion, which it was impossible to controll."[97]

Yet controlling emotions was exactly what the cult of sensibility expected of its practitioners: they were to feel, but not to feel too much. In this regard, emotion work involved suppressing feeling as much as producing it. The recurrence of the words "tranquility" and "contentment" suggests sensibility's modulated tone: it demanded tears, not sobs, and tenderness rather than emotional storms. Nature embodied the tractable characteristics sensibility idealized. "We have had a delightful walk," Connell mused. "The scenery around was romantic and calculated to excite the most agreeable sensations. . . . the soft murmur of the brooks, and the sweet music of the little warblers, soothed my mind into the most perfect tranquility."[98] This concern for control was not peculiar to sensibility, although we may be surprised to find it there. As Philip Greven pointed out in *The Protestant Temperament*, early American subcultures may have differed on the particulars, but shared a concern for self-control: evangelicals sought not just to control but to eradicate the self, moderates to love the self within moral bounds, and the genteel to indulge the self, including its passions, within the bounds of etiquette.[99] Of these three, Connell's emotional world seems closest to the genteel, but studies of the eighteenth-century Virginia gentry suggest how variously gentility could express itself. The English Augustans rather than sentimentalists influenced such Southern families, and their tone seems correspondingly colder, their relationships more contractual, and their deportment less intimate.[100] Perhaps because sensibility was associated with femininity, even when advocating moderation, it echoed the warmer affective characteristics assigned to women. Even then, sensibility had rules for proper emotional expression. Although eighteenth-century Virginia gentry would have regarded Sarah Connell as emotionally unbalanced, sensibility conveyed subtle but insistent expectations of self-control.

As much as it was desired, tranquility proved an elusive goal for many sentimentalists. Sarah Connell often found it difficult to hit the emotional pitch which sensibility demanded; her deep acting occasionally left her overreacting and questioning sensibility's effects on her. "Though from it has proceeded some of my most exquisite enjoyments, yet still I am convinced that a large share of sensibility is often a cause of much sorrow to its possessor. Yet at times I share much *gaite de coeur*," she observed. "In short I always go upon the extremes. One moment I laugh, sing, and dance, thoughtless of all future evils; the smile of Youth and health sets upon my countenance, and I am the life of our domestic circle, at another I am depressed, I fly to the retirement of my chamber, & give way to the most unpleasant sensations."[101] Mary Howell also experienced her emotions swinging from one extreme to another and wondered how to incorporate reason into sentimentality's cult of the heart: "I had been passionate, had consulted nothing but the impulse of the moment, and had overtaxed her intentions," she reported after an outburst, "my *feelings* had far outstripped my *reason*—when *that* assumed her reign, I was convinced of my folly—tho sensible I shou'd do the same again, did I still follow no other guide than my heart."[102] While deep acting relieved the artificiality of surface acting, it presented its own challenges to women of sensibility.

As a more moderate sentimentalist, Elizabeth Cranch found sensibility's emotional swings especially problematic. Like Mary Howell, she used cognomens for her special friends, and like Abigail May, she strung together her observations with breathless dashes. Cranch also employed sentimental verse to shape her feelings: during an evening with her "lovely Friend" Peggy, Cranch "read to her [James] Thompsons [verse] Spring—I set this day down as one of those which I love to recollect—a calm serenity of mind, I have upon me & I felt a peculiar disengagedness from the World & its cares—," she mused. Although she admired the social affections, enjoyed "a sentimental con[versation]" and primed her feelings beneath the moon, Elizabeth Cranch was unusually critical of sensibility's effects.[103] She reminds us that readers played a role in determining the degree to which they incorporated sentimentalism in their lives. Above all, Cranch feared that sensibility would make her vulnerable and unhappy: her wealthy relatives were warm and welcoming, but, she observed, "how doth love so extend & expand our affections but in proportion, we encrease our cares & pains every object of our Love sometimes causes our Grief—the avenues to pleasure are equally open to pain—the heart which is susceptible to all the finer sensations is ever subject to the deepest wounds." Her social awkwardness seems to have heightened such concerns: "When the heart is deeply engaged in any thing I am more apt to commit inadvertencies, than when I feel an indifference—," she noted.[104] As a young woman worried about a long-absent fiancé on the frontier and plagued by depression, Cranch feared that sensibility destroyed rather than fostered contentment.

How then to protect the heart without suppressing it? Like Mary B. Howell, Cranch used reason as a counterweight, and repeatedly reported she had "reasoned upon happiness till I felt her pleasing influence diffused over my whole soul—." But her emotional frailty led her to broach an even less sentimental solution: indifference, meaning not caring, a disconnected impartiality. "[T]is then that the head reasons & the heart assents—is it not best then—always—to cherish indifference. Then, '*half pleas'd* contented will I be—Content, but *half* to please.'" To an unusual degree, Cranch's emotion work centered on producing "perfect composure & serenity." Unlike Connell, for whom contentment was a pleasing sensation borrowed from farmers, for Cranch it required purposeful inducement and suppression of unhappiness: "some *circumstances may* take place to make me more happy—*if not*, I am determined to be so independent of any other source excepting the approbation of my own heart," she vowed.[105] But Cranch could not bring herself to completely jettison sensibility, and how to feel without pain remained her central emotional task years later.

While sensibility demanded a balancing act of one kind, gender prescriptions governing emotional expression required another, as both men and women tried to express feelings appropriate to masculinity or femininity. During the early republic "doing gender" was a confusing task, especially for the upper classes. Historians of manners have argued that before 1820, American conduct manuals emphasized class over gender, and in that sense created some common ground for men and women of the same economic standing.[106] But other scholars have maintained that during the eighteenth century, gender became increasingly essentialized, as public print moved from the long-standing Western tradition of seeing women as a defective form of men, to regarding them as opposites distinguished by biology.[107] That society had begun to associate childbirth with feeling rather than physicality, while simultaneously imagining female nature to be biologically fixed, suggests this era's uneven transitions.

Within the early republic's elite, sensibility was significant for men as well as women and played a newly important role in public life. As a number of historians have insisted, for both genders, the eighteenth century was more an "age of sympathy" than of reason, with novels providing the sympathy essential to democracy; Julie Ellison has turned cultural expectations upside down by arguing that sensibility was men's province before it was women's.[108] That period's major philosophers gave "affections" a central place in human behavior, regardless of biology, a view especially prominent among Scottish Enlightenment thinkers who were, in turn, particularly influential in the United States. The male political world was also attentive to feeling: scholars have shown that during the late eighteenth century, American virtue "was experienced and seen as patriotic *feeling*," the Freemasons exalted fraternal friendship, political orations sought to convince men through "sympathetic identification rather than judgmental detachment," and Revolutionary officers sought to distinguish themselves through displaying sensibility.[109] Republican tendencies to view British aristocrats as unfeeling reveal how emotional standards had infused political discourse, and Jefferson's first draft of the Declaration of Independence posited "agonizing affection" as the basis for American nationhood.[110] At the same time, eighteenth-century portraits began to depict men as attentive to their families, and genteel males in particular felt free to express their "feminine" side.[111] In addition, Henry Mackenzie's 1771 novel *The Man of Feeling* provided a new model of the teary-eyed, sensitive male, which some men imitated.[112] The late-eighteenth-century friendship between John Mifflin and James Gibson, who employed the sentimental cognomens Leander and Lorenzo, shows the possibility of male parallels to women of sensibility, as does Philip Vickers Fithian's use of classical names and enthusiasm for sentimental letters and novels.[113] The world of sensibility even invaded rural Vermont: farmer Hiram Harwood's early-nineteenth-century diary recounts his fascination with *The Wild Irish Girl* as well as his admiration for his (appropriately named) friend Clarissa's sentimental effusions.[114]

In their diaries, sentimental women often praised such men of feeling. Abigail May repeatedly lauded a Mr. French for possessing "the most exquisite sensibility," a quality he conveyed in his "most delicate attention" to May and through "making love according to [the novelist] Sterne's definition." She was even more taken with Mr. Morgan, the gentleman who shared her low opinion of Miss Kissam. A soft-voiced widower, Morgan displayed his sensibility by pointing out "a very beautiful cloud in the west," which they admired together while he "made some delightful observations upon the 'Heavens above, and the earth beneath—.'"[115] French's sensitivity to May's needs and Morgan's responsiveness to nature and literary allusions suggested a refined feeling which she found compelling in both men and women. Inversely, she criticized not only the vulgar Miss Kissam, but also Oliver Pain, for pretending to a sensibility neither possessed. Even diarists who eschewed May's high sensibility found Mackenzie's *Man of Feeling* enthralling, suggesting new standards for male emotion: as we will see, Rachel Van Dyke, a seventeen-year-old New Jersey student, could not put the novel down, and Mary Guion of small-town New York admired the hero's tender heart and approved when her male friends wept. In their friendship albums and commonplace books, young female academy students quoted poetry that praised tears flowing "down virtue's manly cheeks."[116] For all these diarists, sensibility conveyed a delicacy of feeling that denoted social superiority and encouraged common patterns of emotional expression among men and women of the same class.

But diaries make equally clear that however much men joined women in sensibility's emotional community, they occupied subtly different terrain within that world. Sentimental effusion remained women's language more than men's, and throughout this period, male equivalents of Sarah Connell's persistent emoting were scarce. John Mifflin's 1786–87 diary shows strong sentimental influence, but remains a fainter version of the full-blown sentimentality which dominated female journals of high sensibility. As Caleb Crain notes, Mifflin had acquired "many of his sentimental habits ... by snooping on women," for whom sensibility was presumably more appropriate.[117] Even when men and women wrote the same words, they expected male penmanship to differ from women's, especially in the upper classes, with men employing the uninhibited scrawl common to business, while women wrote in a careful script that suggested not only their greater leisure but that their presumably more emotional hearts needed to be contained.[118] Abigail May's diary suggests that men's purpose in speaking the language of sensibility was also different from women's: for them, sentimental phrases were cynical tools to seduce gullible women rather than indicators of the heart. In fact, novels teemed with rakes who embodied heartless indifference to tender feeling of any kind.[119] Even sincere men established limitations on their sensibility: Philip Vickers Fithian may have indulged in surface markers of sensibility, but he also criticized himself for indulging such sentiment and regarded passion as justified on behalf of his country rather than in personal relationships. As a Vermont farmer, Hiram Harwood knew that his friend Clarissa's world did not belong to his practical realm, and he ultimately married an everyday Sally instead.[120] These distinctions aside, even if some men increased their use of sentimental expressions, so did many women, so that the distance between male and female emotional display remained substantially the same.

Even women who were themselves immersed in sensibility expected men to feel differently than women. Elizabeth Cranch may have admired many of the same traits in men and women, such as being "amiable," "unaffected," "worthy," and polite, but she expected them to be combined with gendered traits: men were to join them to "all the manly Virtues which should inspire the soldier," while women required "the sweetest disposition" and a home "perfectly elegant & neat." Even in her most sentimental journal, Cranch expected men's feelings to respect male/female boundaries: "The tear of quick sensibility filled his eye & for a moment overc[a]me manly Fortitude—," she wrote of a friend, simultaneously admiring his feeling and suggesting he should not overdo it. When her fiancé left her for the frontier, she approved the single tear he shed. Male inroads on female emotional territory bothered her more than female incursions into masculinity: in a frank dispute with a "Mr. D—" over "which was the most despicable character—'a masculine['] Woman, or an effeminate Man," Cranch unhesitatingly opted for the latter.[121] Most significantly, even women who admired "men of feeling" associated rationality with males and in that sense supported a centuries-old Western philosophical tradition. Abigail May may have praised the "exquisite sensibility" of Mr. French when he showed her "the most delicate attention," but she understood "sense" (meaning common sense) as "manly" and "tenderness" as female.[122] Similarly, while Sarah Connell admired occasional rationality in women and tenderness in men, she pointedly avoided what she regarded as assertive masculine emotions.[123] Both men and women might show tender hearts, but what Susan Juster has called the fear of "social hermaphroditism" continued to characterize public and private writings of the early national period, while the rise of biological essentialism suggested that the "man of feeling's" popularity would be brief.[124]

Sarah Connell's diary typifies upper-class women's care to observe the feeling rules which distinguished femininity. Fearing that feminine sensibility would become sexual and move from sentimental modulation to emotional storms, American culture relegated not only rationality but erotic passion to the male sphere. Connell's journal reflects this prevailing contradiction. The sentimental novels Sarah Connell read conveyed fear of unwomanly feeling in sexual terms: they commonly featured a virgin whose passion led to her seduction and betrayal, and they cautioned their readers to distrust men and contain sexual impulses. This same theme appeared repeatedly in newspapers, magazines, and almanacs of late-eighteenth-century America.[125] Connell knew just such a case of seduction in her own household. A young woman living with her family, "possessed of much beauty, and a lively disposition," met a handsome young man with "the worst of principles. He professed to love her, 'she believed and was undone.'" He seduced her, and to avoid supporting the resulting daughter, deserted the mother, who named her baby after her friend Sarah Connell, reminding the diarist of emotion's high price and specifically warning her away from passion, an emotion which belonged to men. Connell's reaction captured how little sensibility had changed gender roles: her friend's mistreatment outraged her, but she felt women brought such tragedies upon themselves.[126] Similarly, Abigail May's criticism of the unladylike Miss Kissam centered on that woman's physicality and her indelicacy, a code word for sexual passion inappropriate in females.[127]

Sarah Connell's observance of her society's feeling rules for women was most apparent in her relationship with her father, to whom she was especially close. Unlike Victorians, few of these diarists reported mothers who played prominent roles in overseeing their emotions. Connell's small, indulgent, and religiously eclectic family was similar to the "genteel" model Philip Greven has described and which both class standards and sentimental literature idealized.[128] Within such genteel groups, amiability was prized above all else. But in Sarah's late adolescence, economic circumstances tested her family's equanimity. In 1808, when she was seventeen, her father suffered major financial reversals from the Embargo; in 1809 they were forced to move from Newburyport to more modest homes in Concord and then Bow, New Hampshire.[129] Sarah Connell's response illustrates the importance of both class and gender to sensibility. On the one hand, she demonstrated that despite the loss of family money, she retained the feelings of the genteel. On the other, Connell showed her absorption of women's roles into sensibility through her desire to modify her feelings to suit her father and her care to influence him only indirectly, as a good woman should. To perform these class and gendered tasks, Sarah frankly manipulated her feelings. "We should cultivate a good disposition," she wrote. "This is a duty incumbent on all—for it will make ourselves cheerful and contented—and enable us to contribute to the happiness of those around us."[130] In other words, by displaying the right feelings herself, Connell would produce the right feelings in others. Her family's move from Newburyport to Concord represented financial failure for her father, and although Sarah was leaving behind her childhood home, she did everything she could to conceal her feelings from him. On seeing their goods boxed for moving, she "was obliged to leave the room, to prevent discovering the emotion of [her] heart." Especially difficult was the farewell to her Aunt Newman, her closest female relative. On departing, Connell at first threw herself weeping into the chaise, but remembered to hide her emotions from her parent: "Papa was low-spirited, and I endeavoured to suppress my own feelings, in order to enliven my good Father," she wrote. "My heart became tranquilized; the serenity I at first assumed, at length became real."[131]

Most striking in this account is Connell's awareness as she manipulated her feelings and performed for her audience. In this regard, despite her greater use of sentimental language, Connell shared common ground with the more cautious Elizabeth Cranch, who spoke frankly of her "duty" to be cheerful: "I will not suffer the painful sensations of my heart to overcome its native chearfulness—that, is a debt I owe to all my friends; & that I hope to preserve—."[132] Sensibility might valorize sadness, but femininity suggested melancholy should not interfere with others' happiness. Once again, sensibility idolized the spontaneous heart but could not avoid the paradox of performance: of behavior required for admission to the genteel classes; of emotions deemed appropriate to the feeling female; of gestures, words, and attitudes taught by sentimental literature; of the emotions which deep acting induced but which required control. T. H. Breen's comment that imported luxury goods were "props in a new public theatre of self-fashioning" seems even more appropriate for sensibility. Sensibility was theater in that it offered a script for performing feeling; it was public in that even within the seemingly private confines of diary, home, and family, sentimental women acted parts influenced by public print; and it was self-fashioning in that this drama created new types of women expressing emotions in new ways.[133]

Such self-aware manipulation of emotions suggests that sentimental women conceptualized a self distinct from their social performance, a self that their audience may have glimpsed. Elizabeth Cranch and Sarah Connell experienced that self and their audience in quite different terms. For Elizabeth Cranch, meeting sensibility's requirements was a difficult task which entailed numerous interior conversations, as she puzzled over how to shape her feelings. She recognized this separate self when she noted that the only source of "peace of mind" and happiness was self-knowledge. "'Know then thyself,'" she cautioned.[134] Perhaps because sensibility was so obviously trying for her, she also won recognition for her efforts. In his own diary, her cousin John Quincy Adams recorded his approval of Elizabeth Cranch, whose company he enjoyed during her 1785–86 visit. While Elizabeth Cranch was not beautiful, he wrote, "Her eye expresses the exquisite Sensibility of her heart. Perhaps this is too great for her own happiness, but although I think that feeling so keenly for the distress of others, may be productive of pains without which a person would be happier, yet I believe that this quality, (especially in a Lady) is the most amiable of all those in the human heart." Adams's recognition of what sensibility cost her, combined with the fact that her efforts "endear her to those who are acquainted with her," served as the wages for Cranch's emotion work.[135]

Ironically, Sarah Connell was more successful than Elizabeth Cranch in sustaining sensibility, but that very fact obscures her self from us and her emotional efforts from her contemporaries. Erving Goffman has suggested that every social performance has a back region, in which actors both relax from the rigors of public display by behaving out of character and prepare themselves for a convincing performance out front. Sarah's diary functioned as a backstage in that she used it to construct certain emotions, so that when she appeared before others, her words, tears, and gestures were in place. But in Goffman's terms, it was not a site of transgression: so complete was Connell's sentimentality, that although her journal had no apparent readers, she rarely stepped out of character, either in her entries or in what we know of her behavior. To Elizabeth Cranch's caution, "'know then thyself,'" Sarah might reply that her sentimental self was the only self she knew. Her diary, then, functioned as a backstage only in terms of performance preparation. How much work that took seems associated with class. Goffman has theorized that higher status means less backstage work but more time out front performing.[136] Inversely, when Sarah's family status fell, she worked harder to produce the emotions that would please her father.

While John Quincy Adams appreciated the costs of his cousin's sentimental labors, Sarah Connell's father was apparently ignorant of her efforts. Goffman believed both actors and audience sensed their common theater, but Connell's diary provides no evidence that anyone applauded her efforts or even responded to them.[137] Of course, that we have no evidence for others' approval does not mean that they did not acknowledge or appreciate her emotion work, but several factors made this unlikely. Even if her feelings "endear[ed] her" to others, that does not mean that others were aware of the work that produced those feelings; she may have received payment for the product, but no wages for the effort. Since sensibility was supposed to be natural to the elite and to women, was often subtly induced, and expressed itself in "ease," much of Sarah Connell's effort remained invisible. Women's "finishing charm," as a contemporary observed, was to appear "entirely unconscious of possessing any extraordinary gifts or graces."[138] Gender prescriptions not only increased the likelihood that Sarah Connell's emotion work went unrecognized, but limited its effectiveness: her main means of influencing her father was modeling what she hoped he would feel. The flip side of her own emotional control was her limited control over others' emotions. The fact that Connell had to change herself to change others further obscured her labors. Little wonder that her father seems not to have applauded her work in this theater of cloaked efforts. But if he was oblivious to her emotion work, her efforts were not totally without rewards. Within sensibility, Sarah Connell found at least some room for both free expression and individual affirmation.

One circle remained in which Sarah felt she could give emotions free reign: among her female friends. Much as she cried with her Aunt Newman but suppressed her tears for her father, with her female friends, feelings promised more freedom than work. In a diary striking for its emotional hyperbole, Connell saved her warmest praise for female friendship. "'Friendship! Mysterious cement of the soul, I owe thee much,'" she apostrophized, quoting Robert Blair; and again, "Friendship, sweet soother of my cares! Attend me as I journey through

Sarah Connell was only one of many young women who quoted "Friendship! mysterious cement of the soul!" in their diaries and in the albums popular among academy students. Mary Wallace Peck attended Litchfield Female Academy from 1811 to 1816 and returned as a drawing teacher in 1825. On this page of her 1825 Friendship Album, the artist amplified the words on friendship with watercolors that depicted the books and musical instruments associated with gentility. (Collection of the Litchfield Historical Society, Litchfield, Connecticut)

life." The benefits of friendship, "so dear to sensibility," were many. In Connell's favorite phrase, friendship "banished ceremony," allowing friends to put aside all social disguises. As women and members of her own class, her friends fully entered into each other's feelings, sharing their sorrows and joys. "Among all the advantages which attend *friendship*," Connell wrote, "there is none I more highly value than the liberty it allows of opening one's heart without disguise."[139] Friendship was, in short, the epitome of sensibility.

Sarah's dearest friends dated from her years at Franklin Academy in Andover, Massachusetts, which she attended for fourteen months during her mid-teens.[140] She boarded with the widow Hannah Osgood and became fast friends with her daughter Harriot and niece Maria. Her "beloved Harriot" became her closest friend, and Sarah regarded their time together as "the summit of my happiness." Years later, she lovingly described "Harriot, Maria and Sarah, seated as they often used to be at the door of Aunt Osgood's cottage, looking at the Moon shining through the foliage of the tall buttonwoods that shaded the dwelling where I was once so happy." After Connell left Andover, she and Harriot visited and wrote each other for years and enjoyed a mutuality of interests from youthful sentiment through their later turn to Calvinism.[141] Her relationship with Harriot provided a model of female friendship, so that on leaving Andover, Sarah sought out other young women with whom she could share her feelings.

Female friendship promised a sphere seemingly free from the dictates of convention and of class, not so much a backstage, which required preparatory work, as an offstage where Connell could stop performing.[142] But although Sarah maintained a life-long friendship with Harriot, class intruded on her other same-sex relationships, which could not escape broader societal demands. The Connell family's removal from Newburyport to New Hampshire in spring 1809 marked a breakdown not only in her family's wealth, but in the emotional relationships which had sustained Sarah Connell's vision of sensibility. Sentimental literature idealized harmony and contentment, but by the summer of 1810 her mother had apparently turned to drink, resulting in frequent arguments, Sarah's pleading for reform, and embarrassment for the entire family.[143] At the same time, she was cut off from her oldest Newburyport friends, in whom she had traditionally confided. Connell sought new friends, but as her class position declined, she feared to share her feelings; apparently, emotional openness depended on shared status as well as gender. Just as Elizabeth Cranch expressed greater sentimentality as she moved up in class (if only for a winter's visit), Sarah Connell retreated from sensibility as her class declined. Connell's sense that the feeling rules had somehow shifted created new emotional tasks.[144] "Old dame prudence, ever checking my visionary enthusiasm, gently wispered in my ear. . . . 'You are too much governed by impulse, learn to be more systematic,'" Connell wrote, and resolved that "my actions should be more governed by reason and that my feeling should no longer run away with my judgment."[145] Connell had by no means entirely rejected sensibility—she still read and wept over sentimental literature and corresponded with her oldest friends—but displayed a caution and a resistance to sensibility entirely new to her diary. For the first time, she monitored her emotions with her friends as well as her family. Initially, her family's economic slide had compelled her to work harder to model the sensibility that pleased her father, but with her friends, she began to question sentimentality itself. Since Sarah Connell felt greater freedom with her friends than with her father, this latter reaction may suggest how she actually felt, as opposed to how she should feel, and we finally glimpse a critical self. Her emotion work, however, continued: in this case, to dampen rather than incite fine feeling. This shift also suggests a theme that will appear in Sarah Connell's later journals as well as in the diaries of other sentimentalists: the difficulty of maintaining sensibility in the face of loss. As a result, women's residence in the imagined world of sensibility was often brief, a pleasant but intense visit at times of youth and prosperity.

All in all, how did young women experience sensibility, and what role did it play in the construction of class and gender? To varying degrees, outside forces shaped young women's feelings. Society's upper reaches provided the time, the freedom, and the obligation to display markers of sensibility. Sentimental literature also modeled the tone and language with which they expressed themselves. In Sarah Connell's case, individuals such as her father and her female friends elicited certain feelings, usually indirectly, as did Elizabeth Cranch's genteel relatives. Sarah recognized that in these regards, her feelings were at the service of others. "To love, is necessary to my very existence," she wrote. "My happiness consists in feeling that I deserve the love of my friends, in studying to make their life pass pleasantly, and in cherishing their esteem," she asserted on another occasion. "I could not exist in a state of indifference. Nature never formed me for it."[146] In that sense, her relationships to others framed her emotional self and established her womanliness.

But such conclusions can be misleading. They suggest that in their pursuit of sensibility and femininity, young women were entirely other-oriented in their emotions. This was partly true: sensibility left its practitioners open to others' feelings, just as gender roles expected women to serve others and anticipated Victorian culture's demands for self-suppression. But in practice, sensibility's effects were far more ambiguous.[147] The emotion work upon which sensibility depended required an initial recognition of self, even if that self went on to shape emotions in keeping with social demands. Moreover, the core of sensibility was not in fact empathy, but the use of others' experiences in order to stimulate and admire one's own feelings and, in that sense, it required its devotees to be attentive to themselves, not just to others. Here, Sarah Connell's case is particularly instructive, especially in terms of how she performed class. Her rural visits evoked a contentment that sprang as much from the experienced rightness of the social order and of her own feelings as from nature's beauty. In prizing her friends for the opportunity to "relieve" herself, calling a female friend an "interesting object," and visiting the poor to admire herself, Connell captured sensibility's patronizing and self-enhancing tendencies, class characteristics which challenged traditional feminine submission.[148] Simply keeping a diary suggests an assertive element; while modeling some gendered virtues, her journal's verbal facility and sentimental language also proclaimed her class and education. But above all, Sarah's diary asserted the importance of her self as a subject: her emotions were unabashedly her main interest, and she luxuriated in their expression. In this upper-class theater of self-fashioning, Sarah Connell was the unquestioned star.

Sensibility also endowed Connell with confidence in the goodness of her own heart. Rarely self-critical, she concluded an entry at age seventeen with the words, "I now retire to woo repose, of which, a guilty conscience has never yet deprived me." Her description as "pleased with myself and the World, anticipating future happiness," captures the self-satisfaction she gained from the cult of sensibility. Sarah was not alone in expressing these feelings. Mary B. Howell similarly wrote: "why shou'd I wish ought which passes in *my bosom* concealed?" "I *repent* of *nothing* I have done," she asserted on another occasion, "yet there are some things I wou'd not do again, what name shall I give to them? I am at a loss. well then we will e'en dash them to oblivion without one, they deserve no better fate."[149] The language in which that self was expressed may have been trite, and convention may have guided the emotions these young women expressed, but sensibility affirmed their being. In that sense, women were paid for their work in self-satisfaction, if not in others' recognition.

Such self-admiration suggests another metaphor for sensibility: it acted not just as a theater, but as a mirror. In the theater, others watch the performers, but those holding a mirror watch themselves. At a time when Americans purchased mirrors to admire their new appearance, labeled books of poetry and the Boston newspaper "mirrors," and called Lord Chesterfield's advice a "mirror" to learn by, the looking-glass clearly resonated with early republican culture. In her diary, Sarah Connell shows us the part she played on the social stage, but we also see her admiring herself in the mirror of sensibility; her use of the third person at moments of acute sentimentality reveals this double positioning. Here theater and looking-glass merge, for the figure reflected back was the same one that appeared on the stage: the sentimental heroine of books, rather than Sarah herself. As much as Sarah gained a sense of self-esteem from sensibility, it threatened to obscure her individuality. Both her writing voice and her performance were derivative rather than distinctive. If novels taught the feelings that defined the self, they also limited what that self could be.

Nevertheless, for young women such as Sarah Connell and Mary Howell, their pleasure in sensibility came from satisfaction in work well done; even the highly equivocal Elizabeth Cranch was pleased when she paid her social "debts" in appropriate feeling. They crafted their emotions, sometimes to order and sometimes to suit themselves, enjoyed the result, and admired their effort. To some degree, this was work they chose. Other people of their class read sentimental literature and resided in the upper classes, but their diaries were not so completely immersed in sensibility. It was also work that changed with the setting. The imagined world of sensibility was not the only emotional community available to young women; the same aspiring classes that embraced consumption and sentiment as paths to gentility sent their daughters to academies. Much as greater access to print culture distinguished young women from their mothers, academies offered an intellectual training largely unknown to pre-Revolutionary females, and in that sense separated generations, even as they re-enforced common class standing. At the Litchfield, Connecticut, Female Academy, most students "were the daughters of either the wealthy, elite upper class or of the emerging upper-middle class of prosperous merchants, businessmen and professionals."[150] Students were drawn from both the school's immediate vicinity and elite families across the republic, as aspiring parents hoped to introduce their daughters to other "genteel company" and solidify their class position.[151] Providing a wider and more public stage than the family, academies not only offered young women intellectual training, but schooled them in additional emotional tasks essential to class and gender.

2

SCHOOLING THE HEART

*Education and Emotional Expression
at Litchfield Female Academy*

> Friday I did not miss but half a Quarter in both examinations. (O, what a smart girl was I). Friday evening Miss Rowe went down to her uncle's and I had to sleep with Nancy, which I was not very much pleased with. I thought I ought to sleep with Emily; not give up my bed for Miss Waldo. Saturday the whole school read round in the Bible the first chapter of Proverbs. Miss Pierce asked what was the beginning of knowledge? The fear of the Lord. But fools despise wisdom and instruction.
> —*Eliza Ogden, Diary, February, 1817*

While sensibility gave primacy to feeling, it was not without room for rationality. Expectations that sentimentalists would modulate their feelings assumed the mind might influence the heart. Unless she consulted reason, Sarah Connell would "always go upon the extremes," and sensibility's tranquil tones would elude her. Mary B. Howell also worried that "my *feelings* had far outstripped my *reason*," and concluded that only through "reasons pure ray" could "Man throw of[f] the shackles" of folly.[1] According to a verse Elizabeth Cranch copied into her commonplace book, reason underlay emotion: "Sweet intercourse of looks & smiles: / for smiles from reason flow, / To brute deny'd."[2] Cranch reflected this belief in her persistent effort to "reason" herself into happiness. Not only did sensibility provide room for reason, it established reading as both a prime source of individual learning and the center of social gatherings. Novels of this period repeatedly described women reading and discussing books; the archetypal sentimental heroine had tears in her eyes but a book in her hand.[3] Young women who gathered to read *The Vicar of Wakefield* out loud anticipated academies in which they assembled to study nonfiction texts. As a result, although sentimentalists tended to associate rationality with men, they admired it in women as well, as long as feminine sensibility predominated. Typically, Mary B. Howell felt free to praise her friend Mrs. Vinton's mind as "masculine & capacious" and "penetrating and intelligent," but then added the necessary caveat: Mrs. Vinton "squares even her minutest actions by the line of delicate propriety . . . yet modesty and even diffidence are her characteristics."[4]

If sensibility did not prevent rationality in women, the ideological currents accompanying the American Revolution unexpectedly encouraged it. In classical theory, the republic rested on virtue; for men this signified "self-sacrificing service to the state on behalf of the common good," such as wartime heroism, with few prospects for female contributions. In fact, Whigs traditionally regarded women's sphere, the family, as the opposite of the greater good, and derided self-interest and luxury as feminine. Scottish Enlightenment philosophers were crucial in countering this association by suggesting that through refinement, both commerce and women improved society, the former through comforts and the latter through feelings. Moreover, thinkers such as Hume and Hutcheson maintained that not just law and politics but the family and manners shaped society. As wives, women might be "'faithful friends and agreeable companions,'" and not only gain "social equality" for themselves but improve civil life.[5] During the War for Independence, American women such as Mercy Otis Warren and Abigail Adams, Elizabeth Cranch's aunt, had adopted classical names to signify their new role as "female worthies" serving the republic.[6] In post-Revolutionary America, anxiety over the self-interest displayed in commerce and the first party system initially renewed attacks on female extravagance and superficiality, but such analysis moved quickly from demanding that women stop purchasing luxuries—a solution disadvantageous to mercantile men—to remaking women's character. The early republic's emphasis on women's sensibility, the belief that "their feelings are naturally more exquisite than those of men; and their sentiments greater and more refined," was part of this attempt to establish virtue in women's hearts.[7] But that era of philosophical and political flux was unwilling to rely on the heart alone and sought to secure virtue through reason as well. Although never rejecting essentialism, republican ideologues viewed the environment as a potent factor in constructing women's behavior. New forms of female education promised a milieu that taught both the rationality and social graces necessary to feminine virtue; in turn, daughters, wives, and mothers would re-enforce republicanism in their families and society.[8]

For Sarah Pierce of Litchfield, Connecticut, the ideology of "republican womanhood" provided an opportunity to found her own school, the Litchfield Female Academy, which flourished from 1792 to 1833 and taught, in all, an estimated minimum of 1,700 students, most between the ages of fourteen and sixteen and drawn from the middle and upper classes. If sensibility entailed an imagined community, Litchfield Academy provided a real and institutional emotional community with clear boundaries: membership was controlled, residence was typically for one or two semesters, and feeling rules were codified.[9] Although she was willing to tolerate selected moralistic novels, Pierce had little patience with the dream world of fiction; she forbade "light reading" on Sundays, regarded it as a waste of God's "Holy time" and required students to request permission to read fiction.[10] Instead, she was a determined advocate of "improvement," that favorite eighteenth-century word for making "good use" of an experience.[11] "Imagination is a dangerous faculty where no control exists over its exercise and if accompanied in its unshackled efforts as it too often is by warm feelings it often hurries the possessor to the very brink of imprudence," she maintained. To improve, it was "equally important to both sexes that memory should be stored with facts[,] that the imagination should be chastened and confined within its due and regular limits[, and] that habits of false judgment the result of prejudice, ignorance or error, should be destroyed or counteracted." In short, she declaimed in 1818, "the reasoning faculties should be trained to nice discriminations and powerful and regular research." In this sense, the purpose of her emotional community was, in Pierce's words, to "vindicate the equality of female intellect."[12] Upon the achievements and failures of her students rested women's advancement.

At the same time that Pierce strove to overcome limits on women's intellect, she accepted gendered social distinctions: "the employments of man and women are so dissimilar," she maintained, "that no one will pretend to say that an education for these employments must be conducted upon the same plan."[13] These reassurances were both heartfelt and practical: Pierce hoped to persuade the upper classes to enroll their daughters, but an academy labeled "female" and purporting to vindicate women's intellect (the word "vindicate" dangerously recalling Mary

Wollstonecraft's *Vindication of the Rights of Woman*) demanded that she directly address gender implications. While also concerned with women's roles as daughters and future wives, Sarah Pierce paid particular attention to what historian Linda Kerber calls "republican motherhood": as mothers, women had "the power of performing that magnificent undertaking of making our common race wiser and happier. And how is this to be done—by training up children in the fear of God—by teaching them to deny themselves to both luxury and pride, by inspiring them with true patriotism to prize the good of their country above their own private interest, to fulfill the scripture rule, of loving their neighbor as themselves. Selfishness is the great destroyer of human happiness."[14] Her curriculum combined rigorous study of "Grammar, Geography, History, Arithmatic, Rhetoric, Natural and Moral Philosophy, Chemistry & Logic" with conservative expectations of indirect maternal influence.[15] Historians have debated whether female academies such as Sarah Pierce's provided a merely ornamental education or one equivalent to men's.[16] I am interested in a different but related question: what did their education teach them about emotional expression? As we

This miniature portrait of Sarah Pierce by George Catlin, ca. 1830, conveys the directness, authority, and kindness which made her an effective leader of Litchfield Female Academy. (Collection of the Litchfield Historical Society, Litchfield, Connecticut)

will see, Litchfield Female Academy's structure and pedagogy created an intense and contradictory emotional world which mirrored women's transitional place in the early republic.

Diaries provide a major source for understanding the emotional lives of female academy students, just as they help illuminate women's experience of sensibility. But while Sarah Connell, Mary B. Howell, and Elizabeth Cranch wrote their diaries essentially for themselves, Litchfield Female Academy students wrote for others. Journal writing was to entail self-suppression rather than self-expression: "Do not let great *I* occupy too great a share of your Journals," Sarah Pierce cautioned.[17] Keeping a journal was an assignment which began and ended with the school term, rather than in response to individual needs. Students often penned entries in class; when Caroline Chester was given "permission to return home and write my Journal," she "esteem[ed] it a great privilege to compose in *silence*—."[18] Sarah Pierce also influenced diary content, as did her nephew John Brace, who became her assistant in the 1810s. "Miss Pierce has lately established rules that our journals must contain sixty lines of good writing every week," nineteen-year-old Mary G. Camp wrote in 1818, "but I fear mine will be rather deficient this week for it is required of us to attend meeting every sabbath recollect and write all we can of the sermons in our journals."[19] Noting that "Miss Pierce requested us yesterday to write an idea which we acquired during the day in our Journal," Caroline Chester dutifully recorded the invention of glass and common pins, just as Julia Cowles filled page after page with her English history lessons.[20] Students copied their journals in their best handwriting, brought them to their instructor at appointed times, and sometimes read them out loud to their teacher; Brace occasionally returned them with his comments in the margins.[21] "Persuer of these pages, know that I, the author of them, am not very well versed in polite literature," Charlotte Sheldon wrote nervously; "thou must expect to find, a dry, uninteresting, inaccurate parcel of sentences, jumbled together in a hand hardly intelligible—this is no news perchance thou wilt say—."[22]

Diary entries make clear just how public these journals were: not only Sarah Pierce but other students knew their contents. Classmates helped each other with journal writing, making even their composition a public endeavor. Mary G. Camp reported that she was "to assist Miss Bloom in writing hers but alas assistance is what I greatly stand in need of myself." Once written, diaries might be read out loud to the entire class. "What an arduous task it must be for one who is obliged to sit and hear all these dry journals read over where there is so much sameness to them," Camp complained.[23] In 1809 Henrietta Cornelia Bevier wrote that many of the girls were "heartily sick" of writing journals, but consoled herself that this "hardship" would be overcome with practice.[24] At term's end, top students reinforced the public character and importance of diaries when they submitted their journals for final awards.[25]

How can we decipher young women's emotional lives from diaries that were assigned, controlled, and scrutinized? What seems problematic in these sources actually indicates a prime characteristic of this emotional community: its public nature, in the sense of including an audience. Litchfield Female Academy students lived in a society in which people constantly watched, listened to, and compared each other. Even in their diaries, they could not retreat to a private sphere. In this sense, they were constantly on stage. Not only did this public stage influence academy students' diaries, but it marked virtually every aspect of their curriculum. Unlike the "feeling rules" of sensibility, which women absorbed through literature and observation, academy rules and pedagogical structure overtly shaped the emotional expression of female students.

Print culture may have created the world of sensibility, but oral culture dominated education in the early republic, from dame schools through academies. As William Gilmore has pointed out, "oral and print culture were, from the earliest years of an individual's life, indissolubly linked." Boys and girls first learned reading through the "pronouncing-form method," by which they articulated the alphabet, words, and sentences and finally recited set pieces.[26] In the process, they created a "soundscape" of chanting voices which characterized schoolrooms.[27] "Under speaking I comprehend reading," declared the popular elocutionist Vicesimus Knox (author of Sarah Connell's favorite *Elegant Extracts*), and anthologies of 'reading' selections emphasized the correct way to speak out loud.[28] "The teacher sought to enhance an accurate recreation of the original oration by training the student to guide the listener to the proper emotional response through display of accurate physical gestures for each emotion conveyed," Gilmore explains. "In both reading aloud and elocution, the 'passions' were to be repressed; only acceptable 'emotions' were encouraged." In many ways, elocution recapitulated the paradoxes of sensibility: as Jay Fliegelman has pointed out, "eloquence was an art of magnifying feelings actually experienced and not of deceptively fabricating feelings," yet speakers were to use specific tones and gestures, and the natural slid into the formal and theatrical. Such early elocution lessons prepared the way for further contradictory instruction in emotion management at female academies.[29]

At Litchfield Female Academy, students perused books on their own, but such private reading remained a small part of schooling.[30] The entries "studied & recited a grammar Lesson" or "studied a geography lesson & recited it" form a rhythm in Litchfield student diaries, just as they did in the classroom: individual reading regularly resulted in oral recital.[31] To "recite" was to learn to the point of memorization. Eliza Ogden suggested the scale of memory work when she noted that "Mr. Brace gave our class 15 pages of Sacred History to recite in the afternoon."[32] Recital was the chief means of examination; when Ogden recorded that she "recited a lesson in Elements without missing," she meant that she repeated the major points of the text in the original words without error.[33] Litchfield Academy students not only recited before their classmates, but also publicly did sums, ciphered, and parsed. According to Lynne Templeton Brickley, parsing "consisted of having the students analyze and break down long, elaborate sentences into their proper grammatical components, as a means of mastering the complexities of the English language." Parsing was in effect an early and oral version of diagramming sentences, an activity that would later become visual. Students took turns parsing individually and orally in class—Eliza Ogden wrote that "we were called to take our places for parsing"—or worked in small groups that competed with each other. So intense was this endeavor that students might devote an entire afternoon to analyzing less than a page of text.[34] Instructors further reinforced the oral component of Academy education by inviting select students to join them in a "philosophic conversation." After one such session, Henrietta Cornelia Bevier reflected that the "real and rational satisfaction" offered was far greater than the "trifling conversation" which wasted time better used for "improvement."[35]

Besides keeping daily journals, students composed four- to ten-page essays called "dissertations," in which they engaged in more extended reflection. The subjects Sarah Pierce chose were common to female advice literature: vanity, virtue, gratitude, children's duties to their parents, charity, and pride.[36] When her nephew John Brace became an instructor in 1814, he assigned essays on more controversial subjects, such as the soul's immortality and "the advantages and disadvantages of war," and allowed greater latitude in opinion. As the former Litchfield student Harriet Beecher Stowe recalled, these were subjects that were "not trashy or sentimental, such as are often supposed to be the style for female school." At the tender age of nine, she took great pride in her composition on "The Difference between the Natural and Moral Sublime."[37] But again the private experience of writing, like reading, transmuted into speaking as their teacher read student essays out loud to the class.

In this oral context, the consequences of "missing" during recitations or examinations were public and embarrassing. In a school whose total population varied from about 70 in 1802 to a peak of 169 in 1816, and steeply declined after 1830, everyone knew everyone else's business.[38] Students who did not know the answer were expected to admit it: Caroline Chester spoke from extensive experience when she complained that "nothing to me is more unpleasant than to be obliged frequently to say 'I do not know sir' an answer which I so often give that I fear it will never by me be forgotten."[39] Students changed places as they succeeded or failed, providing a physical illustration of their school standing. When Charlotte Sheldon was "inattentive," she moved to "the foot in spelling," while Eliza Ogden's unusually poor performance in Elements class sent her to her seat.[40] Most importantly, Sarah Pierce systematized success and failure with a credit system "founded on the principle of an emulation to excel," in which each perfect recital gained credit marks, while each miss lost them. To this she added credit or debit marks for general deportment. Individual scores were public knowledge, since students took turns adding up totals. Moreover, Pierce announced the current totals each Saturday and at a concluding public exhibition; in fact, everyone in Litchfield might know the students' scores, since these meetings were open to the town.[41] In such exposed circumstances, students naturally relished recognition of success. "The credit marks were read last week for the summer. I had 721 for what time I had been here," Eliza Ogden wrote in relief. "Miss Pierce said I had done very well indeed."[42]

Other rewards singled out students who excelled. Mary Chester reported home "the unspeakable joy of hearing my composition read in school this morning." She crowed, "It being among the first that had been read since I have been here you will doubtless think I was all tiptoe about it."[43] If students did not miss during a class, the teacher might let them have a brief holiday or go home.[44] When students did good work, such as in "writing figures," Brace announced the best ones last, so that Mary L. Wilbor "had the pleasure to perceive that mine was among the 'priveleged few.'"[45] Those who regularly excelled received official recognition by being made "lieutenants" of their division in arithmetic, parsing, or spelling; in this capacity, they acted as teaching assistants and reviewed the work of their fellow students.[46] Rewards and punishments extended into students' personal lives. Litchfield Female Academy girls typically boarded with town families, who governed their everyday behavior. Boardinghouse keepers produced weekly certificates testifying to each girl's deportment and gave them to Sarah Pierce to distribute in school. Caroline Chester took great pride in receiving good certificates from her landlady since getting up early, making her bed, and sweeping her room added credits that she regularly lost with poor class work.[47] Alternatively, students might be debarred from the social pleasure of a ball if they "missed" three or more times in a week.[48] More intrusive was the Academy's custom of publicly reviewing students' personal faults and virtues each week, an occasion Pierce used to remind students to reflect on their behavior and record their faults in their diaries. "As to my faults it would almost be impossible to enumerate all of them I have so many," Caroline Chester predictably despaired.[49] Before the assembled class, either Pierce or Brace systematically criticized the students, name by name. Sarah Pierce's assessment of her students extended from their intellectual and social characteristics to their bodies: she subtracted credit marks for slouching or, as Lucy Sheldon found, for "holding my arms stiff which made me appear awkward and which I shall certainly endeavour to correct—."[50]

In their diaries, most Litchfield Academy students professed great regard for their teachers' good opinion. "I am happy to think that my conduct this winter has been such that Mr. Brace had no fault to find with me, for I am sure it has been my endeavor and always shall be to obtain the approbation of my instructors and parents, for I think there is nothing that can afford parents more happiness than to know that their children endeavor to improve and our tutors also," Eliza Ogden preened. When Miss Pierce told her she should get a larger, "more becoming" bonnet, Sarah Beekman complied, writing, "How thankful ought we to be that we have so good a friend to tell us our faults."[51] After one Saturday morning fault session, Mary Ann Bacon reported retreating to her room "with many disagreeable feelings," as did Betsey Reynolds, but such entries were rare.[52] Diary keeping taught students to model Pierce's ideals, at least on the surface, while Academy strictures promoted internalization of its values.⁵³ Genuine fondness for Sarah Pierce encouraged compliance: Eliza Ogden reported that when students heard Pierce had returned from a trip, they were so glad, that Brace felt compelled to end classes early.⁵⁴ Student affection and attention to Sarah Pierce are especially striking at a time when mothers usually made only occasional appearances in their daughters' diaries.

In short, Litchfield Female Academy students lived on a very public stage, whether in the classroom, the boardinghouse, or their diaries; both actors and audience, they performed for and observed each other, with Sarah Pierce as their director.⁵⁵ That stage shaped their emotional world and sense of self. Sarah Pierce hoped her system would inspire emulation, the desire to imitate the best, but it also invited competition, a more assertive effort to win, with its attendant emotions of resentment, humiliation, or triumph. With emulation, selves merged in common improvement, while competition's greater individuality set selves against each other. In practice, however, the line between the two easily blurred. The academy's young ladies arrived already familiar with the "emulative consumption" which characterized fashion and the ambitious household.⁵⁶ Whether their students were male or female, academies represented the rising, consumption-oriented classes and, as J. M.

Mary Ann Bacon's miniature portrait (artist unknown, ca. 1800–25) conveys the equanimity expected of young women, rather than the pique her diary expressed at Litchfield Academy's correction sessions. (Collection of the Litchfield Historical Society, Litchfield, Connecticut)

Opal has argued, "tapped emotional currents that rural life had long restrained: pride in self, desire for praise, the urge to stand out and assert one's individuality."[57] Such traits simultaneously mirrored sensibility's preoccupation with self and challenged women's traditional place.

Surprisingly, historians have had little to say about women's competition with each other during the early republic. Carroll Smith-Rosenberg's influential 1975 depiction of a "female world of love and ritual" theorized that women lived in a separate and private sphere characterized by intimacy, warmth, and support. "Hostility and criticism of other women were discouraged" and rarely expressed in this environment of "inner security and self-esteem." Women's homosocial relations developed naturally, beginning with the mothers on whom they modeled themselves, and extended to supportive sisters and other kin. In adolescence, especially in boarding schools, girls developed friendships outside their immediate families and often maintained these for the rest of their lives, even after marriage. Such friendships were physically expressive, emotionally intense, and socially acceptable.[58]

Since Smith-Rosenberg's essay appeared, historians have offered two modifications, but have been notably reluctant to question women's sisterly bonds. First, although Smith-Rosenberg showed that eighteenth- and nineteenth-century Americans did not sexualize intense same-sex relations, her essay inspired a new lesbian history which celebrated not only female friendships but lesbian sexuality. As gay history became a distinct field, scholars such as Anthony Rotundo found that nineteenth-century men enjoyed equally intense homosocial relations, at least in youth. These historians have not so much questioned Smith-Rosenberg's depiction of warm and noncompetitive female relations as they have incorporated a sexual dimension.[59] Secondly, by the late 1980s, scholars began to question her assumption that men and women lived in separate worlds. Historians of nineteenth-century courtship and then of rural and small-town life discovered that women enjoyed close and rewarding friendships and love with men, from their single days through marriage.[60] These heterosocial relations seem to have existed alongside women's loving feelings for each other, almost in a parallel universe. Neither of these historical schools has questioned the warm and supportive emotional tone that Smith-Rosenberg originally associated with women's homosocial relations, and in that sense competition has not yet been fully incorporated into our picture of women's emotional lives during the early republic.[61]

At Litchfield Academy, where they continually and publicly vied with each other for honors, young women found comparisons often painful and experienced failure as a rejection of the self: "while the young ladies are reading their journals, I feel so anxious to know, who excels that my attention is quite fixed upon them, and it is with difficulty I can withdraw it," Mary G. Camp complained in 1818, "however in that I find little satisfaction. They so far exceed mine that it is nothing but an aggrivation, therefore I think I shall listen no more but endeavour to improve my own."[62] When they did not do well, students might feel intense shame: "recited my lesson and had the mortification to miss twise," Betsey Reynolds reported.[63] Extremely conscientious and usually at the top of her class, Eliza Ogden "felt very much ashamed" when she was sent to her seat. On another occasion, she described an incident which took place after she had stepped down as lieutenant, and therefore "was not called any more to parse the hard questions." To her mortification, she committed "a very great blunder" with an easy question by "putting a verb in the infinitive mood in the imperfect tense which I knew to be wrong and corrected myself as soon as possible, but it was too late. I could not have but five credit marks," she mourned, "but it was not for the credit marks that I cared."[64] What she cared about was the public contrast between her previous classroom status and her failure with an easy question. She had fallen from what Mary L. Wilbor had called "the priveleged few."[65] A mediocre student like Caroline Chester also felt shame in this competitive environment. She usually blamed herself for her failures: that her "unruly" tongue got her in trouble for talking in class, that she just "cannot *think*" well enough, that she wasted time and was not attentive, did not get up early enough, and allowed her thoughts to ramble. Listening to the teacher read her essay to the class, Caroline "regretted it was no better & felt that My time which I employed in writing it was wasted—."[66]

Competition at Litchfield Female Academy peaked at term's end with the "public exhibition," an appropriately named event in which the school publicly exhibited the skills of its best students. It pitted students against each other for high stakes during an intense and concentrated period. John Brace conducted examinations before the exhibition itself, and prided himself on holding them "in real college style" with the girls "all arranged in alphabetical order," as he quizzed them on eight different subjects for five days.[67] He reported the 1814 school contest in breathless tones reminiscent of a horse race: "Great struggle at present to obtain credit marks Cornelia Abbey Bradley and Ann will be the three first candidates it is very certain and for the others there is much striving—it lies between Goodrich and Pledger—at present it seems most probably that Pledger will have it—*Mary Peck* and Ruth Benedict are striving for the second—." Competition intensified as the exhibition loomed and enticed girls to attain the 9,000 credit marks required for a top student. "*Cornelia Leonard* deserves high credit for her great exertions for the last three months indeed her industry has been unparalleled in the annals of the school—," Brace wrote approvingly. "The first three months she studied *Tom Perkins* more than any thing else and permitted Miss Bradley to get above but she and Ann had studied very hard for examination and Cornelia has passed a very good one—she had upwards of 300 more than Miss Bradley [and] she received the prize for her uncommon industry and for mending her temper so much as she had—." The wide variety of prizes heightened and spread the desire to win: students could win awards in specific subject areas, as well as in composition (including of journals), improvement, politeness, industry, and, of course, most credit marks; could compete in age categories; and could try for first through fourth place. During the exhibition, residents from Litchfield and the surrounding countryside attended to examine artwork "exhibited around the school room," with the girls "all arranged in their best apparel," applaud the winners at the awards presentation, and listen to Brace's "pathetic" oration.[68]

From John Brace's perspective, the young women of Litchfield Academy were highly competitive, a situation he applauded. He described one student who "strained every nerve to reach [first prize] and accomplished it," while his repeated use of the words "exerted" and "exertions" suggests the purposeful determination of these young competitors. Carefully distinguishing each girl's abilities, he had clearly spent the term assessing who would win which prize. Brace's concluding comments on the 1814 summer session suggested that open competition was normative at Litchfield Academy: "ambition has been raised to an uncommon degree and our exertions have been wonderfully answered—."[69] Such competition was by no means peculiar to Litchfield Female Academy. Exhibitions were staples at every educational level, and many diarists reported attending them, even when they did not know the students, and often traveled to neighboring towns for the occasion. Catharine Sedgwick, Abigail May's friend at Ballston Springs, captured their popularity in her 1822 novel, *A New-England Tale, or, Sketches of New-England Character and Manners*. It described the intense academic rivalry between virtuous Jane and wicked Elvira, who tried to steal the composition prize from "our deserving young heroine" by plagiarizing her essay from a Boston newspaper. Ultimately triumphant, Jane read her winning essay demurely, but spoke from a throne before the entire community.[70]

Litchfield Academy's structure and pedagogy may have encouraged competition and rendered success and failure public, but its rules mandated suppression of any negative feelings that might result. At the beginning of every school term, students learned the Academy's rules, and each Saturday Pierce reviewed them before announcing individual student faults, reminding everyone of their importance. These rules defined the surface acting expected of Academy students, encouraged the unaffected ease associated with sensibility, and echoed the precepts taught in conduct books.[71] Most importantly, they taught that in a world of distinctions, students should feel and act as if those distinctions did not exist; the individual self might expand through academic excellence, but socially it should merge with the whole. "Persons truly polite will treat superiors with respect and deference; their equals with affability and complaisance," an 1820 definition of politeness proclaimed. "They will never smile at the mistakes of those who may be more ignorant than themselves; will never make sport of the faults or follies of their companions, much more at their misfortunes, but will on all occasions treat others as they would be themselves."[72] Neither were students to "flatter your companions by any remarks on their beauty, dress or any accomplishment, in order to increase their vanity," for "such compliments are an insult offered to the understanding," the 1825 rules stated.[73] The Academy's young women experienced embarrassment and even humiliation in public performance, but they were not to be angry. The 1814 rules copied by Eliza Ann Mulford listed as number four, "Avoid anger, Wrath and evil speaking," and the 1820 self-examination question asked if students had ever "been angry."[74] "I will endeavour to preserve a cheerful temper at all times, never giving away to fretfulness anger or discontent though my lessons are hard my companions provoke me and the weather unpleasant," the 1818 rules declared, covering intellectual, social, and climatic irritants.[75]

Aware that her own credit system threatened to foster "rivalship," Sarah Pierce reinforced school rules with official statements, speeches, and plays, all of which attempted to control assertive emotions, especially unrestrained ambition, and encouraged students to see themselves as relational rather than individual. As a woman and the female face of the school, Miss Pierce may have felt compelled to limit the effects of the competition John Brace so clearly enjoyed. In a "Moralistic Essay and anecdote," Pierce imagined a series of young women, clearly modeled on Litchfield Academy students, each of whom expressed a different form of ambition. One was ambitious to be pretty, and another to be the "worst scholar in school," but Pierce's main concern was intellectual ambition that exalted the self. She described a young woman who appeared to study for "the approbation of her teachers, the love of her companions & hope of becoming a useful member of society," and in that sense modeled feminine virtues, but in fact, "while her rival sleeps she toils & every moment which her rival devotes to pleasure is occupied by her in gaining a credit mark which she found by a shy peep at the paper [which] was wanting to complete her triumph." Pierce suggested the dangers of unrestrained ambition by comparing such women to Alexander the Great, who "trampled in his neighbours rights." "This school is a world . . . vast enough to contain many Alexanders & credit marks are weapons where with to show their dexterity— —," Pierce warned.[76] This extraordinary comparison emphasized that ambition was not only a gender transgression, but tyrannical; unlike educators later in the nineteenth century, she was concerned with Revolutionary ideals as well as femininity.[77]

No evidence indicates whether Pierce shared this "Moralistic Essay" with her students, but Litchfield student diaries reflected her cautionary views rather than John Brace's celebration of competition. Assigned many of Addison and Steele's essays, Laura Maria Wolcott summarized their criticisms of temper and complaining and their praise of cheerfulness, *"Good Nature"* and self-control.[78] Sarah Beekman's journal included essays on such "baneful passion[s]" as envy and pride, which left people in "a continual storm" of feeling. Beekman's suddenly lofty language, clearly borrowed from Miss Pierce, expressed her teacher's belief that education should teach people to "bend their tempers and to accommodate their wills to those of others," so that they became "complaisant."[79] Other students reiterated Pierce's belief that "as soon as a child begins to desire the playthings of its older brothers or sisters [you should] teach it to be content."[80] "I cannot but think that a contented mind is one of the greatest blessings which we can possess,"

Schooling the Heart 65

Caroline Chester dutifully echoed in her diary.[81] Lest students miss Sarah Pierce's determined advocacy of emotional restraint, they copied appropriate aphorisms into their penmanship books. "Let your conduct be at all times governed by reason not fancy," Maria Buel wrote fifteen times in 1830. "Malignant passions destroy all the softer impressions of humanity." "Contentment without wealth is better than wealth without contentment."[82]

Effort to control overwrought emotion is also apparent in student Betsey Clark's 1800 "Mechanical View of the Faculties of the Soul," a drawing which reflected the scientific Enlightenment's effort to organize information and balance relationships. Betsey divided the soul into "Mind or Understanding" and "Heart or Will" and listed under each its chief characteristics and effects. "Mind or Understanding" produced "Prudence," "Fortitude," "Justice," and "Temperance," all of which demanded forms of control. Justice, for example, required "Discernment"

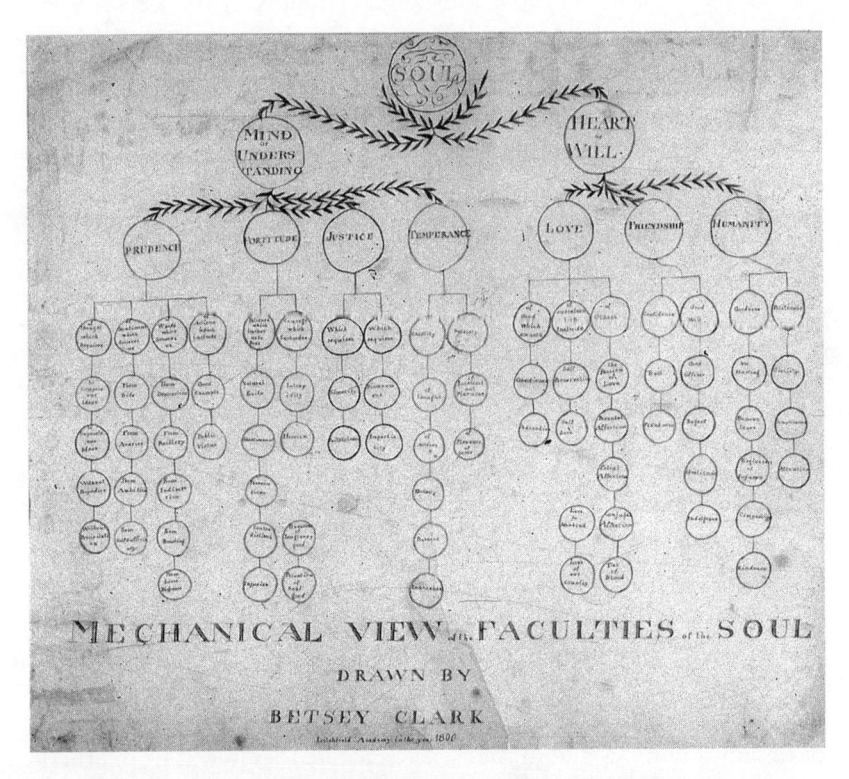

Betsey Clark, "Mechanical View of the Faculties of the Soul," drawing, 1800. (Collection of the Litchfield Historical Society, Litchfield, Connecticut)

and "Impartiality," while Prudence should appear in thought (by distinguishing ideas "Without Prejudice" or "Precipitation") as well as in words which avoided "Destraction", "Raillery," "Indiscretion," "Boasting," and "Loose Discourse." "Heart or Will" recognized that love included "Self Preservation" and "Self Love," but all the other examples advocated consideration for others. At age eleven, Betsey Clark knew that whether mind or heart dominated, she should regulate her feelings.[83]

Sarah Pierce also shaped student emotions through the plays that her pupils performed. In "The Two Cousins," the wise older woman Mrs. Leyster was clearly Sarah Pierce herself. Mrs. Leyster criticized three young women, each of whom put herself above others: Alicia, who elevated herself by class through spending more than she had, ordering "twenty volumes of new novels," and lying in bed for half the day; Harriot, who let her pet bird be mutilated so that it sang better; and Constantia, who ridiculed people who should be pitied. Mrs. Leyster's interrogation compelled Alicia to admit that her behavior, like the other girls', had shown "contempt of all that is rational." But an intellectual commitment to better behavior was clearly not enough; Mrs. Leyster instructed these malefactors not to conceal those emotions which did them "credit," especially tearful acceptance of reproof. Academy students who played the parts of Alicia, Harriot, and Constantia modeled Sarah Pierce's ideal: a kind heart, controlled by the head and subservient to authority. "Yes, my dear girl, you have an excellent heart, and that is the greatest security for all," Mrs. Leyster instructed Alicia at the play's conclusion.[84]

In sum, Litchfield Female Academy's feeling rules immersed students in a series of contradictions. These contradictions mirrored the academy's basic conflict: Sarah Pierce's simultaneous desire to "vindicate the equality of female intellect" through rigorous intellectual training, but keep women within the bounds of "republican womanhood." Just as rationality had tempered Sarah Connell's sensibility, at Litchfield Academy sensibility tempered rationality, so that women's feelings remained safely feminine, even if their minds did not. Women might study rhetoric and mathematics, but they were not to neglect relational skills, and although they competed for honors, they were not to be unduly ambitious and in that sense separate themselves from others. Above all, they were to embody the sentimental virtues of contentment, harmony, ease, and refined feeling, for these republican daughters were also to be ladies. In her essay "On Politeness," student Catherine Van Schaack emphasized that it was "particularly necessary for young ladies to acquire a polite behaviour while at school," so that their manner would be "easy and natural" rather than affected.[85] Concerns for gentility and femininity, equal parts class and gender, ran through the school rules: "Have you spoken any indecent word or by any action discovered a want of true feminine delicacy?" the 1814 and 1815 rules asked, which Eliza Ann Mulford and Caroline Boardman copied in their journals.[86] "You must come in or go out of the school in a quiet genteel manner—you must not talk or laugh loud in the street," they cautioned in 1825.[87] Academy rules made clear that students should operate from within the established social system: "Every real Lady will treat her superior with due reverence, her companions with politeness, good humor she will always show, a sweet temper, a modest deportment on all occasions, never forgetting what is due to all persons in every situation."[88] Despite his greater comfort with competition, John Brace supported these rules as well. In 1833 Miss Pierce praised his "skill in forming the female character," especially in his daughter Mary, who showed her "genteel education" by never being "out of temper" when corrected.[89]

The same contradictions appeared in parents' letters. Caroline Chester's "dear Mama," who had lacked her daughter's educational opportunities, hoped that Caroline "would appreciate [her] advantages aright" and especially improve in arithmetic. "You know not how anxiously my affection follows you & how much it depends on your improvement, in temper, industry & self-denying exertion," she wrote, seemingly encouraging her daughter's often flagging academic efforts, but then added, "to gain the love of your companions you must yourself be obliging[,] disposed rather to veil their errors than too readily mark them & to pass by observing or showing that you do their hourly actions—."[90] Caroline clearly understood her parents' priorities; "how happy it would make them to hear that none surpassed me in, amiability, kindness, and learning," she wrote, placing learning in last place, after proper feminine virtues.[91]

How did these contradictions play out in Litchfield Academy students' emotional lives? Subject to their instructors' and peers' purview, diaries reveal what Academy students believed they should say, and provide the official story of their feelings. Nevertheless, we catch glimmers of individual and unauthorized opinion. Even more clearly, we can see how the contrast between the desire to excel and to be a proper woman created emotion work for Litchfield Academy students as they sought to balance these demands. This is apparent in both their experience of competition and their female friendships.

Public, oral performance of academic ability encouraged competition and made it visible, but the Academy's restraining rules made it difficult for these young women to acknowledge feelings of academic rivalry with specific individuals. The open crowing over winning which was common in late Victorian coeducational high school girls' diaries was muted and infrequent at earlier same-sex schools such as Litchfield Academy.[92] Its diarists were much more likely to express shame from academic failure and blame themselves, than to voice resentment and blame others. Here they responded to Academy rules and their audience, but they also reflected how they were placed in society. Women were keenly aware that they rose and fell as a group: having shamed all women as well as themselves with a poor performance, they felt deep embarrassment. At the same time, all women might gain from other women's success, since any woman's achievements "vindicate[d] the equality of female intellect," which, in turn, muted individual resentment. Litchfield students might win credit marks as individuals, but their intellectual performance inevitably connected them to other women. In contrast, men's achievement in such venues bolstered male pretensions both generally and individually, while failure was experienced individually but did not call into question their power as a group. That men persistently gained as a group, win or fail, freed them to compete, while women's common situation made competition far more problematic for them.

As a result, none of the surviving student diaries expressed the fevered academic competition that John Brace observed among students during public exhibitions, and only three admitted to any feelings of personal scholastic rivalry during the school year. Of those three, Caroline Chester in 1816 named specific students not so much as rivals for intellectual honors, but as girls who had broken the school's social rules by treating her with unladylike disdain, albeit in an academic context. "Mr Brace asked me what were the four grand divisions of the globe. I misunderstanding the question answered the Eastern and Western. *Miss Staples* & *Miss Stanley* were so much gratified that they burst into a fit of laughing which was to me very embarrassing and when Mr. Brace repeated the question I could scarcely tell him though I knew it perfectly—." That she "did not miss" despite this seemed small comfort to Caroline.⁹³ The second case dates from Laura Wolcott's 1825 diary. Unlike most students, Wolcott broke Academy rules with regularity and relish, although she, too, did not name her own academic rivals. However, she leveled charges against *"S.L.B."* for having "been over" four examinations that term, and doing the same "for the prize" the last year; this seems to have denoted cheating. When she noted that this meant that S.L.B. got 160 credit marks a week, which Laura would otherwise have bested by forty, Wolcott revealed both a degree of competition and her awareness of everyone's scores. "[W]e cannot tell Mr B[race] for that would be as mean as she is," Laura wrote piously, and then proceeded to name her classmate and lambaste her as that *"artful mean* deceitful *lyeing* girl without one principle of *honour* about her, hated and despised by all her classmates. detested by her whom she thinks her best friend. this is her character & my opinion, and if I live six years until I am twenty I never shall think of her otherwise—."⁹⁴ Her language was unusually strong, but by picturing that *"lyeing* girl" as cheating and being hated by others, Laura deflected criticism that she was unduly competitive herself. In fact, throughout two years of journal keeping, Wolcott showed little interest in making top marks in her academic efforts (as John Brace well knew, since he was the instructor who read her 1826–27 diary); clearly, had S.L.B. won fairly, Laura would not have cared. Only in the third case did an ambitious student clearly name a specific intellectual and personal competitor. In that instance, Lucy Sheldon, a prize-winning student, noted: "Studied a geography lesson and recited it. had the mortification to have Miss Mary Glen get above me."⁹⁵ The infrequency and brevity of this entry is striking. Students were also reluctant to express scholastic rivalry with individuals in their letters home, although they had more control over epistolary content. Instructors sometimes read student letters, but not, apparently, out loud before class.⁹⁶ Together, academy rules, cautions to be content, and students' difficulty in separating themselves from women as a group, discouraged Litchfield's pupils from expressing personal rivalry in either letters or journals.

Caught between expectations of intellectual brilliance and femininity, some students expressed ambivalence over their academic achievements. Eliza Ogden could not help briefly bragging "O what a smart girl was I" when she "did not miss but half a Quarter in both examinations," but she also expressed hesitation when she won the office of lieutenant. "Miss Fowler informed me that I was appointed Lieutenant in her division, for which I was very sorry, as I do not think I am able to perform the office as well as it ought to be performed," she wrote; later she resigned the commission.[97] Even in announcing victory, students tried to show modesty. In 1801 Lucy Sheldon wrote that she "heard Miss Pierce tell our faults, had the pleasure to hear her say she had seen no fault in me for the week past, and hope she will ever have reason to approve of my conduct." Similarly, Frances Ann Brace was proud enough to send her essays home, but included a note that dismissed their worth.[98] Caroline Chester caught both the academy's desire to mute competitive feeling and her own modest level of achievement when she received a "good certificate" from her boardinghouse and wrote, "I was happy to find that almost all the scholars had the same."[99]

The nature of Litchfield Academy emotion work seems also to have varied individually and seasonally. A poor student like Caroline Chester recorded almost continual academic struggle, failure, and embarrassment. Moreover, she felt that if she did not do better, she would lose her parents' love. As we will see, she turned to female friends for solace, but she also scolded herself for feeling discontented.[100] Her main emotional task was to express tranquility in the face of humiliation. More intellectually gifted students faced different challenges. On an everyday basis, these young women could balance their school's conflicting demands, and experienced enough easy academic victories that they could show equanimity toward the competition. Since Sarah Pierce subtracted credit marks for poor deportment, even the most brilliant students had to be attentive to manners and attitude. But when public exhibitions loomed, the top scholars seem to have dropped gentility for open rivalry. At that point, the school itself modified its value system; it stopped restraining open competition, increased the rewards for top performance, and freed students to engage in fierce and single-minded combat. The emotion work required to balance the school's conflicting priorities declined, and school work increased. John Brace repeatedly commented on a perceptible shift in school tone as final exams and the exhibition neared. Significantly, he reported that Cornelia Leonard stopped studying Tom Perkins, the young man she had pursued, and started studying her books, a switch from women's traditional priority to an intellectual focus. Once awards were presented, either Brace or Pierce orated on the purposes of female education, elucidated the splendors of republican motherhood, and in the process returned school values to their customary balance.

The public stage of Litchfield Academy life and its contradictory rules also shaped students' same-sex friendships. In some ways, Litchfield Academy fits Carroll Smith-Rosenberg's depiction of boarding school friendships as extensions of sisterly love and the basis for lifelong liaisons among women. Sarah Pierce assigned younger girls to older students, who eased their homesickness, helped them study, and shared a bed. Academy students spent most of their days with other young women, and often expressed deep affection for their female friends.[101] Pierce herself advocated women's relations in terms very similar to Smith-Rosenberg's "female world of love and ritual," which students then copied in their journals: "Now is the time when the heart is warm to form lasting friendships—it has frequently been observed that the most lasting & sincere friendships are formed when at school. Then there is a free intercourse:—no reserve, no disguise—we get perfectly acquainted with each others' dispositions—how necessary that we make a proper choice of friends, since such friendships are so permanent."[102]

These friendships provided a world where students might enjoy freedoms denied to them in the classroom. Struggling with school rules, fifteen-year-old Laura Wolcott repeatedly conceptualized female friendship as the place where she could freely speak her heart. As she wrote in 1827, "There is no pleasure equal to that of having some 'fond, faithful friend' in whose heart you can repose every little secret. I am sure I feel the need of such a friend; Oh! With what pleasure do I look forward to next summer with dear Elisabeth, my imagination will have full range." Friendship entailed sharing feelings as well as secrets: "'I've none to weep when I am free / And when I sigh to sigh with me,'" Laura versified during a lonely moment.[103] In contrast to Sarah Pierce's continuous correcting of emotional expression, Laura declared that her friend Amelia "will never find a friend who loves her better or was more willing to pardon the inequalities of her temper."[104]

Caroline Chester also sought escape from classroom demands in the safety of friendship. Her 1815 and 1816 diaries provide more stories of both academic failure and intense relationships than any other Litchfield student journal. Caroline lavishly praised women she liked: Margaret Hopkins, who was "not only beautiful, but amiable, kind, generous and sweet tempered," and Miss F. Catlin, who "united to a lovely face all those pleasing qualities which delight and attach and make us love and admire," exemplified the femininity and gentility Academy rules praised. Caroline also delighted in the Academy's adoption system: "Miss Pierce put *Mary Elizabeth Cobb* a sweet little girl from Albany under my care—," she wrote. "She is one of the most lovely children, I have ever seen. I hope she will be very industrious and improve in all her studies, that she may gratify her friends and Miss Pierce." Caroline became fast friends with *"dear Eliza,"* and when Eliza left school, Caroline's most fervent wishes for her focused on friendship: "that she might long live & be useful to society & a comfort to her friends another that she might find all her friends well on her return & have a pleasant Journey."[105]

In contrast to the often regimented diaries they wrote for their teachers, students felt free to employ an alternative language with their peers. Throughout the term, but especially at its end, pupils asked each other to write in their friendship albums, a tremendously popular format throughout the nineteenth century, employed by young African American as well as white women.[106] Rather than use their own words, they usually quoted poems, invariably sentimental verses that Sarah Connell would have recognized. Like her, they quoted Robert Blair's "Friendship! Mysterious cement of the soul!"[107] In their best hand, they copied odes to the moon, friendship, and sensibility. While Sarah Pierce subtracted thirty credit marks for homesickness, students praised "sweet melancholy," and tears flowed in the pages of their albums, if not of their diaries.[108] In this sense, women spoke two different emotional languages and resided in two different subcultures within the larger emotional community of Litchfield Academy. For Sarah Pierce and John Brace, they modeled rationality tempered by sentiment, while for their friends, they expressed heightened sensibility. Since feelings among friends were not as publicly and systematically rewarded or punished as other behavior, students gained potential emotional freedom among their friends, just as Sarah Connell had.

But the reality of Academy life complicated this sisterly idyll. The school itself was not a totally female space, but included some male pupils and a coeducational social life stimulated by the elite male students at Tapping Reeve's nearby law school.[109] Moreover, for some female students, Academy life meant the loss of friendship rather than its creation: their diaries recorded their yearning for hometown friendships, rather than delight in creating new ones.[110] Most importantly, despite Sarah Pierce's expectation of a "free intercourse" in women's friendships, school rules shaped and constrained those relationships. Just as in the classroom, balance and emotional control were to be more important than personal expression. By curbing anger, flattery, and making fun of others, school regulations tried to find common ground among students otherwise separated by academic and class distinctions. Academy rules also attempted to control talk that might set young women against each other. An 1814 rule advised against "evil speaking," with the caution, "a tale bearer separates chief Friends."[111] "Talebearing and scandal are odious vices, and must be avoided: neither must you flatter your companions by remarks on their beauty, dress or any slight accomplishment in order to increase their vanity," the 1821 "Definition of Politeness" elaborated. But the school valued honesty as much as it did friendship, and expected Academy girls to enforce school expectations. "While you are forbidden to report things to the disadvantage of your companions," it advised, "you are at the same time requested to inform one of your teachers if you know of any conduct deserving of reproof not from malice but a true friend lest the fault should become a habit too strong to eradicate in future." Given a choice between friendship and accuracy, "The truth must be spoken at all times, on all occasions though it might appear advantageous to tell a falsehood."[112] If students did not obey these rules, Sarah Pierce herself directed their relationships; she forbade Laura Wolcott to walk with certain girls, leading Laura to complain, "I believe I am one of the most unhappy beings on the face of the earth."[113] Henrietta Cornelia Bevier seems to have echoed Pierce when she wrote that she should be careful in making friends, "for by contracting a friendship with them we shall be in danger of acquiring their faults."[114]

Student effort to direct their personal feelings into acceptable channels is apparent in their alternately insulting and demure comments about boardinghouse companions. "I should like to fathom the character of my bedfellow Miss Buell for I think her a singular girl, she has a singular peevishness of temper which is very unpleasant," Mary L. Wilbor complained in her 1822 diary, but immediately retreated: "I do not know but that is her only fault, for she is a very pleasant companion, and that excepted she is a very agreeable girl." Upset that a Miss P. would not visit Canaan with her, Mary recorded and then silenced her criticism: "I do not think it quite polite in her to refuse to go when she knows that the pleasure of the party depends in a great measure on her accompanying us, but mum! I fear I am often, too often guilty of more impolite conduct." Again, Mary briskly dismissed "D. B." as "the most unpleasant creature I ever knew," but could not bring herself to provide

D. B.'s full name. In these passages, Wilbor showed her awareness of just how far she could go in criticizing others, without crossing the line separating ladies from the vulgar. While Mary Wilbor's journal illustrates student reluctance to criticize their companions, she confidently named a Miss Austin whose talented compositions reflected school values and whom she obligingly admired.[115]

While Caroline Chester hoped to escape the classroom by cultivating friendships, she discovered competition and humiliation extended to social relationships as well. After her friend Eliza left school, Caroline devoted herself to Nancy. As a sign of her love, she gave up the rare holiday she had won in school to keep Nancy company. But Caroline soon recorded that she "had my feelings very much hurt indeed by Nancy. I think she is sometimes neglectful of the feelings of others & often very often she wounds mine most deeply, and yet I cannot but pardon her as I know it proceeds from inadvertence." She pined for the more dependable Eliza, and resolved to be content. But despite resolutions to "improve my temper, oblige all my companions & by my sweet and amiable deportment . . . endeavor to gain their esteem & love," she was again disappointed. An unnamed classmate "spoke in a very disrespectable manner," not only "of my very dear Uncle Chester who was a most excellent Christian & universally beloved by all who knew him" but of her "dear Parents." "Although what she affirmed to be true was false yet it could not but have the effect which she desired that of hurting my feelings—but the next day she told me she was in *fun*," Caroline reported in confusion. By speaking "in a very disrespectable manner," Caroline's opponent had attacked her family's gentility, even as Caroline asserted her class and femininity by not naming the other girl, although she could not resist describing the insult. Caroline was finally reconciled with Nancy, if not with this anonymous student, but consoled herself with "the happy the delightful reflection that in eight weeks I shall be at HOME [which] causes my heart to throb with JOY and though I shall leave those friends I love yet I shall go to those who are much dearer."[116]

Students' same-sex friendships not only mirrored the Academy's competition, but recapitulated sensibility's tendency to render feeling performative. Sarah Connell's experience reminds us that the emotional freedom associated with sentimentality often proved illusory: as she found, sensibility had its own feeling rules, however subtle. Because sentiment was more emotional did not mean that it was without conventions. Rather, as Litchfield Academy students found, emotion management was necessary not only to control assertive feeling to please their teachers, but to stimulate and shape refined feeling with their friends. Among friends in their boarding houses, as well as in the classroom, Litchfield Academy students needed awareness in emotional performance similar to Sarah Connell's manipulation of feeling to please her father, and in that sense, they were never offstage. Female friendship provided some relief from Academy strictures, but in many regards reflected limitations of the larger institutional culture.

By the 1820s and '30s, students seem to have found meeting Litchfield Academy's contradictory emotional demands increasingly difficult. A desire to express the individuated self appeared in consumption patterns, intellectual competition, and even a renegade diary, as Sarah Pierce aged and her influence waned, and John Brace's role increased. Much as Sarah Connell had discovered that class difference intruded upon her friendships, the Academy found that competition in dress invited divisive passions and distracted students from serious work. As daughters of the elite, students arrived well trained in fashion as a marker of class status. As early as 1796, Charlotte Sheldon regularly reported she "went a shopping with the girls" and bragged that she "began to alter my muslin into a robe which is the most fashionable dress in Hartford."[117] In 1803, Lucy Sheldon reported that she "went a shopping" in New York City, felt she had become "a city Lady," and concluded her letter home, "I fear I shall want some more money." Academy students need not have traveled so far to view "the *fashionables*," for Mary Wilbor discovered them at a nearby boardwalk, and Litchfield's shops advertised the latest hats, ribbons, and fripperies.[118] Concern for consumption appeared in student journals which, in turn, reflected Sarah Pierce's view that souls were "brands plucked out of the fire—the fire of fashionable life—." In 1806 Betsey Reynolds copied into her journal warnings that "trifling articles of dress" left women "continually tortured with the fear of being outvied" and destroyed contentment. "How often do we see young people especially of our sex who prefer company dress and amusements to study and the acquirement of useful knowledge?" Sarah Beekman dutifully declaimed. Such inessentials would "please for the [mom]ent" but leave women "comfortless."[119] School rules reflected these concerns: in 1815 Caroline Boardman copied an Academy rule that listed "Profusion in expences, [and] a want of neatness and economy" among "indications of a bad heart most to be avoided."[120] By the 1820s, more elaborate dress succeeded the simpler classical forms that had prevailed since the 1790s and focused attention on surface finery, and by 1825, Litchfield Academy felt compelled to address the issue directly: "You must not wear your party dresses, or any handsome lace, neither your best hats or shawls to school."[121]

The unpleasant emotions attendant upon academic competition also became more problematic. In the 1832 Academy by-laws and constitution, Sarah Pierce reminded students and parents that "the formation of character; the acquisition of correct habits; the control of temper, and the restraint of appetite; the discipline of mind . . . are of more importance than the principles of science, than the refinement of manners, or the elegancies of literature."[122] By 1833, the Academy's last year under her leadership, Pierce complained that the "ambitious" older students openly expressed jealousy of their competition and accused their teachers of partiality. She imputed this to "the indulgence & overweening fondness of parents" who raised children unwilling "that others should be wiser, more genteel, or handsomer than themselves." She complained, "I am afraid that the next generation instead of showing the hardy Roman virtues, will be mere Italians, without energy, patriotism or humility—." Fortunately, Pierce reported, for most of the school's history, she had "lived in an age of parental discipline, Or I would never have discharged the duties of my office as many years as I have done."[123]

Laura Maria Wolcott's fall 1825 and winter 1826–27 diaries exemplify Sarah Pierce's difficulty in controlling Academy students during its later years. While other student diaries were similar in their tone, subject, and structure, Wolcott's spoke with a fresh, distinctive voice. It is difficult to say whether she articulated what others felt but did not write, or whether her views were exceptional. As the granddaughter of a signer of the Declaration of Independence, daughter of a prominent Litchfield family, local girl familiar with Sarah Pierce and John Brace outside classes, and a student who attended the Academy for five years rather than one term, Laura may have felt unusual freedom to break the rules.[124] But she also seems to have been responding to overall changes in the Academy peculiar to the 1820s. In the school's declining years, John Brace moved from assistant instructor to vice-principal, and his ease with competition, encouragement of intellectual debate through writing assignments, and participation in social events with students may have invited rebellion. Laura submitted her journals to him rather than to Sarah Pierce, and although Brace occasionally penned comments, none of them corrected her feelings. During the last years of Litchfield Female Academy, Laura seems not to have been the only one to kick over the traces; Mary Wilbor's half-insulting comments on her boardinghouse companions also date from the 1820s.

Laura Wolcott's outbursts suggest an overwhelming need to express the self forthrightly rather than engage in multiple balancing acts. "Do not let great *I* occupy too great a share of your Journals," fifteen-year-old Laura quoted Pierce in the first entry of her 1826–27 journal, but retorted, "I suspect I shall be [a] little of an egotist + use 'I' pretty often."[125] "I am not in the habit of saying what I do not feel," Wolcott wrote, and did not hesitate to announce those feelings: she made fun of her classmates' singing, rejoiced at Miss Beecher's departure, declared her school assignment "not very interesting," repeatedly expressed anger, despised a woman who broke into her trunk, and professed admiration for the notorious and impassioned Lord Byron. Rejecting the emotion work required to balance head and heart, she indulged in "*sneers + smirks*" not found in any other surviving Academy diary.[126] Laura was not completely oblivious of Academy norms. Like her classmates, she rarely expressed feelings of competition with individual students but admired girls who excelled, knew that her "spirits frequently pass the bounds of moderation," and periodically vowed improvement.[127] As the public exhibition approached, she, too, found her "ambition is very much excited" and voiced the views Sarah Pierce demanded in her girls. "I suppose it is useless for me to wish so," she admitted, "but I can assure myself that *self denial* + pains will not be wanting. I shall not be so wicked as to be envious if others succeed + and enabled to control my feelings if I am unfortunate."[128] But denying her self was the one thing Laura could not bring herself to do; if she was going to excel, she wanted to do it for herself, not for others. On submitting an essay, she declared, "I suspect Mr Brace will think it a *spruce* one, but it is for my own advantage not the *opinion* of any one that I intend trying."[129]

At fifteen years old, Laura had a sophisticated understanding of her refusal to do the emotion work expected of her. She mused that if the grandfather who raised her had taught her "to correct the extravagance of her temper," she might have been able to resist her "evil genei" which said, "'sit a little longer a few more jokes, and a little more nonsense, the time will soon come when you will not enjoy such pleasure.'"[130] On reading the *Spectator*'s essay on imagination "unguided by the restraints of reason + judgment," she explained her position more analytically: "I am one of that sort of persons commonly called castle builders; I do not confine my mind to earth, but erect my structures in the most unstable of *elements* the air . . . magnificent palaces, stately porticos, blooming gardens shady groves have bounded into being thro the powerful feat of a warm fancy; I should be the most contented + happy being existing were the chimerical happiness springing from the vividness of my fancy less fleeting + visionary." However, Wolcott ended the entry with the flip remark, "I appeal to you for a relief from this fantastical evil + wish you to accommodate me with some method how to settle my head + cool my brain pan."[131] In what seems to have been her motto, Laura repeatedly inserted "ANYTHING BUT INDIFFERENCE" in code, rejecting the emotional detachment that Elizabeth Cranch had advocated to protect her too sensitive heart.[132] Laura's flip comments, references to her "evil genei" and "unstable" and "chimerical" visions, and use of code suggest awareness of her rule-breaking, but throughout her diary she expressed her right to criticize her teachers, assignments, and texts and asserted a self at odds with academy rules.[133] For Sarah Pierce, Laura Wolcott clearly represented the triumph of the Italians over the Romans.

Framed by public demands, rules, and constant oversight by instructors and peers, Litchfield Female Academy was an institutional community that seems a far cry from the world of sentiment, but the two worlds were not without similarities. While the imagined community of sensibility favored the heart, Sarah Pierce's academy inclined toward the head, but in either case moderation was essential. Both sentimentalists and academy students showed "emulative zeal," the former in trying to imitate fictional heroines and the latter in attempting to match the best students, and both emotional communities obscured the line between public and private.[134] The imagined community of sensibility and the institutional community of Litchfield Academy were most alike in demanding emotion work from their residents. Sarah Connell, Mary Howell, and Elizabeth Cranch were to manufacture the refined feeling and tears expected of sentimental women without falling into passion, and Academy students were to produce intellectual brilliance in competitive situations without forfeiting fine feeling, which they could then model to their friends.

Although it shared these similarities, Litchfield Female Academy entailed far deeper contradictions than the imagined world of sensibility. Sensibility promised a feeling heart, but shaped the emotions expressed; in expecting modulation, it elicited a difference in degree, not kind. In contrast, Sarah Pierce's Academy demanded not only far more—for young women to be rational beings, indeed "to vindicate the equality of the female intellect"—but contradictory qualities: that its students also behave and feel like conventional ladies. The much more public character of Litchfield Academy life also made its efforts to restrain the individuated self more difficult to attain. If "public" life

"Minerva Leading the Neophyte to the Temple of Learning," a work of silk embroidery and paint attributed to Lucretia Champion, ca. 1800, combines classical references, love of learning, and women's traditional skills with needle and brush. In that regard, it represents Litchfield Female Academy's uneasy balance of intellectuality and gentility. (Collection of the Litchfield Historical Society, Litchfield, Connecticut)

is understood as process rather than place, in particular the process of being observed, life at Litchfield Female Academy was thoroughly public, and that fact alone discouraged individuals from merging into the whole. In theory, students represented collective womanhood, but they experienced both praise and humiliation standing alone before their peers. The Academy's emotional community was also more complex than the world of sensibility. It included subcultures of friends, who expected different emotions than did their teachers, while Sarah Pierce and John Brace conveyed conflicting attitudes toward competition. To balance these contradictions, Litchfield Female Academy had multiple rules, but those same rules heightened and made visible its contradictory expectations.

Litchfield Female Academy also distinguished itself in the wages it granted for emotion work. Unlike sensibility's subtle wages of self-admiration, the Academy granted overt recognition through a carefully calibrated credit system. These publicly celebrated rewards reflected the difficulty of what the Academy demanded: not just emotional production, but a balancing act: "'to feel but to feel in subordination to reason,'" as John Brace put it.[135] Historians remember Litchfield Female Academy for the intellectual rigor of its curriculum, but the emotional tasks it set its students were equally significant: their emotion work required awareness, sophistication, and self-control as they calculated the appropriate feelings for different occasions. Its central lesson in "doing gender" seems to have been that femininity was a demanding and contradictory performance required for the privilege of education.

Litchfield Female Academy's emotional lessons stand in striking contrast to young women's education in late-nineteenth-century high schools. Much like well-off females of the early republic, affluent late Victorian girls did little housework, read novels, and kept diaries, but their education often culminated in extended periods at coeducational and competitive schools rather than one or two terms at a single-sex institution. The length of that later education resulted in the creation of a new stage in female development: girlhood, which extended from early teens through graduation. That much longer, more competitive, and more egalitarian education with boys flew in the face of larger cultural norms and challenged their future role as submissive wives, so that they scarcely knew what to do with themselves after graduation.[136] Litchfield Female Academy, by contrast, was a brief stop on a continuum rather than a major diversion. Its students experienced a short but intense education which incorporated the contradictions of female life into the curriculum rather than overtly challenging gendered prescriptions. The recurring references to "young ladies" in Litchfield Female Academy's documents reflected its orientation to an immediate future rather than an extended past. That future was marriage, and the Academy quickly launched its students into the prime task before them: choosing a husband well. In taking up that task, they rejoined the vast majority of young women during the early republic who never attended academies at all, and students traded the Academy's watching and critical schoolroom for a gossiping village culture. In courtship, young women would find not passivity and malaise, but a challenge which exercised all their emotional skills, demanded heightened awareness of self, and promised women more agency than in any other period of their lives.

3

DISCERNING THE HEART
Fear and Fancy in Courtship

[Captain Jasup] wished to have a Corespondance with me in writing. to that I would not consent for I am very sensible it is an easy matter for the pen to write expresions that the heart never experienced or at least not more at that time than any other and as I detest flattery so much I would not with my own consent indulge him with so fair an oportunity of that kind . . . then one of my companions, reason, Tells me I ought not to thinck of such a thing as an union with one so far above my years but I have another companion that I call Fancy wich is apt to intrude itself unless I keep a wachful eye—.

—*Mary Guion, Diary, January 1805*

During the early republic, courtship comprised the key emotional passage in most young women's lives, and the one that was most dangerous. Between their late teens and early twenties, men and women found themselves "continually marching to the land of matrimony," with twenty-two as the average age of marriage for New England women in the late eighteenth century.[1] In Mary Guion's words, either "happiness or misery" awaited them in wedlock: common law gave husbands control of family property, divorce was socially unacceptable and legally extremely difficult, and husbands determined their family's class, residence, and emotional tenor, as well as their wives' personal happiness.[2] At the same time, lack of economic opportunities meant that most women had to marry in order to attain middle-class status. Marriage also denoted maturity, but even for those women eager to wed, the stakes were high; disappointed and deluded brides crowded literature, while women's private writings traced their tentative steps to the altar. Much as young men began diaries as they went off to war, women facing courtship took up their pens to chronicle their own life-or-death decisions. Mary Guion (1782–1871) of Westchester County, New York, spent 340 of the 387 pages of her 1800–1852 diary on her courtship years of 1800–1807, proportions that reflect the salience of that period. Similarly, Patty Rogers (1761–1840) of Exeter, New Hampshire, devoted the most deeply felt entries of her 1785 diary to the men she loved.[3] By contrast, men's losses in marriage were few and their gains many: in Mark Kann's estimation, the role of "Family Man" offered personal happiness, heirs, opportunity to demonstrate masculinity through spousal domination, public maturity, and "a familial stake in the community."[4]

For many young women, courtship was more a time of apprehension than enjoyment. In contemplating the often circuitous road to marriage, Mary Guion found that even the path "spread with roses . . . ends in a thicket wich often becomes a snare for the innocent and unsusp[e]cting who were allured by the pleas[a]ntness of the entrance—."[5] Female diarists of this period concurred on courtship's basic problem: men were not to be trusted. It seemed "contrary to the nature of things that a gentleman should speak his real sentiments to a lady," Eliza Southgate observed, while Elizabeth Cranch expostulated, "must flattery be a part in the composition of every young man who makes it his aim to please?"[6] Already at age fourteen, Lucy Sheldon of Litchfield Academy skeptically eyed a Mr. Stanley, whose "manners are genteel and agreeable, but I am afraid that beneath a form so beautiful is concealed a vile heart."[7] In the friendship albums which they inscribed upon leaving, Litchfield Academy students balanced odes to female friendship with verses on male deceit: "Ah ne'er let flatt'ry tempt you to believe; / For man is false, and flatters to deceive; / Adores those charms his falsehood would disdain / And laughs at confidence he strives to gain."[8] Women's fears reflected their vulnerability and the high price they paid if they did not accurately assess men's motives and character. They also show how women's emotional world reflected broader ideological currents. As Gordon Wood has pointed out, the eighteenth century was "the great era of conspiratorial fears and imagined intrigues." During the Revolutionary crisis, the British ministry had claimed good intentions while harming colonial interests, and throughout the early republic, Americans distrusted motives of those in power and remained obsessed with deception. Such fears bore a class aspect; while average folk were presumably honest, "the gentlemanly elite," which America's own elite understood to be the Old World's aristocracy, were well schooled in duplicity.[9] The commercial world also feared deceit: merchants employed a language of deception and misrepresentation to characterize their competitors, creditors, and villainous partners.[10] In anticipating male duplicity, women applied such Whiggish and mercantile analysis to men, the most powerful figures in their own lives, and in that sense made the personal political. The largely feminine world of sensibility only increased their apprehensions. As sensibility valorized the heartfelt, its opposite, the fear of deceit, was magnified, and duplicity was most dangerous in courtship, when the stakes were highest.

Such fears both heightened the significance of emotion work and created new tasks. To some extent, courtship employed surface and deep acting; Patty Rogers engaged in both forms and felt that her beloved would find her sentimental emoting attractive. But courtship demanded an additional emotional task to which sociologists have been less attentive: discernment. Women needed to not just produce or suppress their own emotions, but accurately determine other people's feelings: in this case, who loved them and whom they might love in return. Mary Guion's journal is especially revealing in this regard, because it chronicles whom she did *not* marry as well as whom she did. In that sense, unlike most surviving love letters, which spring from courtships that ended in marriage, her diary provides a more complete emotional history. Such emotional judgment entailed shrewdness as well as feeling and married rationality to emotion. In light of this, it seems particularly appropriate that village balls, in which young people sought their true love, were often held in the town academy, that local temple to reason.[11] For women navigating the perils of courtship, the skills of discernment were especially valuable in that they provided a tool to counter male duplicity and thereby promised power during this critical period. They would find that wages for courtship's extensive emotion work were both personal and monetary: successful marriage not only promised personal happiness but determined wives' economic status for life.

The imagined community of sensibility influenced courtship, but as young men and women paired off, they contended with an immediate audience that formed a larger stage than families or schools: a curious and observant village culture which made up the physically bounded and real-life emotional community in which they lived. While Litchfield Female Academy comprised an institutional community whose membership school officials limited, the village was a geographical community which included everyone in residence, regardless of age, gender, or class. And while overt strictures governed the Academy, village residents established courtship's feeling rules through informal gossip and visits within a vibrant peer culture. Both Patty Rogers and Mary Guion lived in towns small enough to encourage such village talk: Exeter, New Hampshire, a busy shipbuilding town of about seventeen hundred, and North Castle, New York, a farming community of about a thousand.[12] On this broader town stage, Rogers and Guion offered dramatically different performances. Rogers lived exclusively in a world of sensibility, much like Sarah Connell, and she suffused her relations with men with the sentimental feelings she learned from books, a devotion that rendered her dangerously oblivious to her neighbors. Guion, too, was well read in sentimental literature, but she lived in multiple emotional communities: through her reading, she also shared Sarah Pierce's regard for rationality and absorbed political ideology's concept of the republican wife, while her everyday experiences kept her feet firmly planted in the realities of small-town life. These two women also approached their parts with opposite motivations: Patty Rogers feared that no one would love her, while Mary Guion feared that she would love the wrong man. As a result, their diaries played strikingly different roles in their lives, they expressed opposite feelings about men, and their stories had divergent endings, but the same moral: without emotional discernment, marriage invited "misery" rather than "happiness."

Sensibility dwelt in the heart, and would seem to find its apotheosis in courtship, but Patty Rogers's journal casts new light on unrestrained sentiment: young girls such as Sarah Connell might safely enjoy the pleasures of this imagined world, but they proved delusive for a woman in her twenties seeking a husband. Rogers unwittingly characterized her diary's contents in her January 2, 1785, entry: "read in the evening in the history of the human heart—was pleased with the sentiment."[13] Daughter of a minister, comfortably off, and enjoying easy access to the latest books through Exeter's tidewater river, by her early twenties Rogers was steeped in the language and behavior of sentimentality. Feelings were her main subject, and her greatest fear was to be "disconsolate & friendless."[14] Repeatedly Rogers described "agreeable scenes," sentimental tableaux of poignant partings, retiring "to Bed with a tender heart," meetings in which "each bosom glowed with friendship," and, above all, much weeping.[15] Nursing her ill father, she "*felt those tender emotions* which excited a flood of tears!—I loved to have it in my power to do good to somebody or other!—," she effused one summer's day. "Can I by any thing, said I, relieve my fellow creatures!—I was dissolved in tears, I *felt* emotion I would not have exchanged for all the gaieties in Life!"[16] In this entry she combined the exclamation points and dashes, tears, rhetoric of tenderness, expressions of benevolence, and pleasure in emotion, especially sadness, common to sentimental writings. Throughout her diary, Rogers, like Mary B. Howell, also used Latin cognomens for her most significant friends: her beloved William Woodbridge appeared as "Portius," and Samuel Tenney as "Philammon."

Patty Rogers was unusual in her extreme emotions, but sensibility's influence was pervasive enough that by the mid-eighteenth century, most Northerners viewed marriage as a joining of hearts rather than a familial alliance or commercial transaction. It is initially puzzling that the middle and upper classes were increasingly tied to consumption culture and yet criticized marriage for money, but several reasons account for this. One of the main objects these young women consumed was British novels, which dramatized and deplored mercenary alliances. Such marriages had never been that prominent in their own American society, but this fictional rhetoric provided a compelling image of what marriage should not be. Americans also associated marriage for money with the very wealthy, and regarded it as an extension of the emotional coldness Whigs found so repulsive in the corrupt British aristocracy, so that Revolutionary ideology as well as fiction argued for nuptial ties based on love. But because Americans argued against marriage for money does not mean that they were inattentive to class. By the late eighteenth century, the cult of sensibility made the feeling heart a new mark of superior class status, so that class conveyed far more than property or lineage. This meant that class considerations lingered not just despite, but through, sentimental rhetoric. Since economic advancement expressed itself in gentility as well as possessions, a person's manner revealed not only their individual character but their class affiliation or, at least, aspirations, so that women might discern men's hearts and prospective incomes simultaneously. That Americans had come to understand marriage in these new affective terms was itself a statement of gentility. In real life (just as in the novel), the "man of feeling" was, then, preeminently a suitor. At the same time, men's talk of love conveniently obscured the inequality and power dynamics still central to marriage and cloaked male economic purpose, should there be one.[17] In matters of sexuality, if not love, however, economic metaphors persisted. The words "intercourse" and "commerce" were laden with double meanings while, inversely, merchants described commercial misdeeds as if they were seductions and cuckoldings culminating in sexual/financial "ruin."[18] Men, rather than women, used such words, and in doing so crudely recognized women's continuing economic need for marriage and the resulting exchange of sex for marital status.

Despite these economic overtones, one thing is clear: the language of the heart had become essential to courtship, although whether "love" meant high romance or steady affection varied from diarist to diarist. Moreover, much as they enjoyed greater latitude and access to reading and education than their mothers, daughters also denied their parents oversight of their courtships or say in their choice. By the late eighteenth century, betrothed Yankee couples' proclivity for premarital sex had long since trumped parental efforts at mercenary match-making.[19] In that sense, the village courtship community was largely a culture of peers, just as was the imagined world of sensibility. When Rogers declaimed the centrality of feeling to marriage, she expressed in heightened terms what her middle-class contemporaries had come to widely acknowledge: "Can such a state [as marriage] *fraught* with *feelings* the *most exquisitly* tender *be entered upon by the person of sensibility without the tear of soft distress?*" she wrote. "If so, I have done,—This I know was I making a *connexion* of the kind! every *bitter thought!—keen sensation!* which *ever entered* the *heart* of *Man would be mine!*"[20] Such attitudes transformed courtship and made it a process during which men and women discerned their own and each other's hearts and thereby assured an affectionate *"connexion."*

At the same time that sensibility's influence transformed the purpose of courtship, it made both controlling and accurately discerning feelings difficult. Sensibility might caution moderation and incorporate rationality in theory, but in practice it so valorized emotion that once sentimentalists began emoting, it was often difficult to stop, and feelings took on their own momentum. Like Sarah Connell, Patty Rogers sought to modulate her emotions, but she had little success. Even when praising contentment and tranquility, her words were passionate: "O! for an *easy temper,*" she wrote. "O! may all my days be tranquil!" and "O! my *sensations*! But *Stop! forbare* to *mention* them—."[21] In her 1785 diary, Rogers's references to reason are notably scarce. Her contemporaries recognized her difficulty controlling her feelings: as an embarrassed

William Woodbridge said, "some persons had *too* much *sensibility!*"²²
Even Rogers occasionally criticized her own effervescence. "O! I wish I might learn to be *silent*—," she chided herself after an "*unguarded* Moment." "But take care *little fond foolish Heart*—. . . drive from thee *thy too great susceptibility!*" she resolved on another occasion.²³ Such determination to contain her feelings rarely lasted more than a few days.

Patty Rogers's inability to modulate her feelings shaped her relationship with William Woodbridge, the Phillips Exeter Academy principal whom she loved and called Portius. At her diary's outset, Woodbridge had already jilted Rogers and was engaged to Elizabeth Brooks.²⁴ Not only could Rogers not stop loving Portius, but she was blind to how meanly he toyed with her affections. Woodbridge seems to have wanted to both marry Brooks and keep Rogers's love and attention. Each time he flirted with her, she accepted his protestations of sincerity and friendship uncritically and lapsed into adoration of her "angel." In a striking scene on January 11, Woodbridge systematically exposed her feelings for him. First, he asked her whose hair was in her locket, almost cer-

William Woodbridge, whom Patty Rogers called "Portius," and enthusiastically pursued, but failed to win, served as the first principal of Phillips Exeter Academy. Portrait by Alfred A. Smith. (Courtesy of Phillips Exeter Academy)

tainly knowing it was his. Then "he took my Pocket Book and read my papers," despite her protestations. Having availed himself of the items representing her love, he "pressed me to his *Bosom* with a *fondness* I thought expressive of approbation!" Patty kissed his hand "with *trembling* lips!" and "dropt a *graitful tear*!! *I felt!*"[25] When Woodbridge was not fanning her feelings, Rogers used her own methods to keep them aglow. Rereading their correspondence and writing letters to him served as a form of deep acting; they revived her affections and stimulated a *"torrent* of tears," setting in motion a cycle of grief and love. "Yes! I dare to love him!" Rogers declared in mid-February after exchanging letters and handclasps.[26] On March 27, Woodbridge and Brooks announced their marriage banns and, as was the custom, planned marriage within two weeks. Portius callously asked Rogers if it would pain her if her father married them at the Rogers home, and she acceded to show her "love and friendship."[27] Even then, their relationship continued: the following summer Woodbridge visited Rogers and the two exchanged letters once more, and on August 4, Portius kissed her. As late as September 18, he visited her and "took my hand. 'O! Patty,' says he, 'This seems like old times.' I returned a *gentle* squeeze—O! *virtuous* friendship! without thee what is Life!" Rogers exclaimed.[28] At diary's end, Rogers had renamed her feelings for Woodbridge, but their content had changed little.

Throughout these months, Rogers was not only unable to see through Woodbridge's behavior, but often oblivious to how curious neighbors might regard her, while her widowed father was too ill to take notice. If sensibility were theater, she was remarkably indifferent to her audience; much like Sarah Connell, her emotions focused her attention on her self, while her diary provided a mirror for self-admiration. Even when aware of public opinion, she could not contain her emotions. On August 23, Portius and his wife unexpectedly met Rogers at a neighbor's. "In vain was the trial to *suppress* those *painful feelings*!" Rogers wrote. "I urged the necessity of my behaving with the *greatest circomspection* well knowing *one* would observe every *motion* but *alas*! this did but augment my feelings, & throw me into great embarissments! how often will a sense of what one *ought* to do drive from us the very *capacity* of doing it!" Half fainting, her heart "almost ready to *burst* from its seat," Rogers fled in confusion.[29]

In short, Patty Rogers failed to set firm bounds on either Woodbridge's behavior or her own. Caught up in the imagined community of sensibility, she ignored the mores of Exeter, New Hampshire, her real-life community. The day after Rogers publicly fled Portius, her confidante Sally Thurston told her "all the Company" had remarked her behavior, and that a Mr. Gorham advised her, "it wont do—." Patty replied that she "was not *ignorant* how much I *exposed* myself," but that she still "could not *command my feelings!*"[30] Not only did she learn nothing from male behavior, but she was equally oblivious to her female friends' experience. Patty's "sweet friend Sally" suffered an extremely unhappy marriage that appalled Rogers, yet it did not teach her caution with men.[31] Patty Rogers enjoyed a lively homosocial world which complemented her heterosexual enthusiasms: she made frequent visits, occasionally weeklong, to Sally Thurston; slept with Sally (*sans* Mr. Thurston), although Sally was married; and indulged in odes to friendship, "Where the inmost recipes of the soul are known to each other."[32] At the same time, Rogers used her female friendships to bolster her sentimental illusions about men, which remained her main focus. Sally passed information on her to Woodbridge, obliged her by "conversing on that dear *object*," and let Patty meet her next suitor at her house, while Mrs. Gilman, another friend, supported her cause by telling men "very handsome things" about Patty.[33]

Rogers tried to regain emotional command in her relationship with Samuel Tenney. "I think my heart is not so susceptable either—It knows too much to be *caught* again. *it never shall be!*" she declared. "I hope I never shall be *ungarded* in my *behaviour* or *conversation* But I fear he thinks me a *silly* girl."[34] But her relationship with the thirty-seven-year-old doctor demonstrated the same naiveté and indifference to public opinion. They began courting in March, but Rogers did not call him *"Philammon"* until after Woodbridge married.[35] That name change signaled Tenney's entry into a sentimental sphere of heightened and unexamined emotions; by May she called him "a man of *judgement* and *taste* & *sentiment.*"[36] Much as Portius assured Patty of his sincerity and tender feeling for her even as he wed another, Philammon convinced her that his sexual advances were innocent. On August 4, he "took some liberties that would not have been *strictly* decent had they come to light—It gave me *pain*—," she recorded. "Surely, thought I, he must have mistaken my character—." On asking Tenney if he considered her a "bad girl," he replied, "You know we judge of the merit or *demerit* of an activity by the intention—," and since he never intended her ill, "he put his hand on my Bosom." Although Rogers "with avidity attempted to snatch it away," she failed and fell back on "intreaties," finally letting him put his hand on her handkerchief, then worn around the neck. After all this, she still "esteem[ed]" him and characterized her feelings as "an *ardent friendship* for him, *but not love!*"[37] Tenney might well have been confused, since the same day he was taking "liberties," Rogers had let "lovely *Portius*" kiss her, and her continued love for Woodbridge was public knowledge. Later in the month she was shocked and outraged to discover her neighbors said she enjoyed "such *obscene converse.*"[38] By fall, Tenney treated her with open disrespect: pretending ignorance, he quizzed her on why Portius now acted coldly, and he openly courted her rival, Tabitha Gilman. Yet Rogers again allowed Philammon to take "some little *liberties*," which, she insisted, "were *perfectly innocent* in themselves."[39]

Even more than Sarah Connell, Patty Rogers occupied the extremes of sensibility. As Jane Austen observed in *Sense and Sensibility*, exaggerated feeling was produced by being "voluntarily renewed," "sought for," and "created again and again" in a cycle of emotion producing emotion.[40] Like her letters to Portius, Rogers's diary kept her emotions pitched to the highest level, but did not elucidate her own or others' feelings. Sensibility provided a language to stimulate, admire, and describe emotions, but without control or reason, it obscured rather than revealed the heart and failed to do the essential emotional task of courtship: discern reality. Nor did sensibility help Rogers understand herself; instead, she mistook herself for a sentimental heroine, and even in the privacy of her journal, she sounded like someone in a book rather than a distinctive self. Ironically, Tabitha Gilman, whom Philammon married, went on to write the novel *Female Quixotism*, which features a foolish heroine very much like Rogers.[41] As a result of her total immersion in sentimentalism, Patty Rogers could neither see herself as others saw her, nor could she recognize Portius and Philammon for what they were. Her alternately silly and tragic behavior both discouraged future suitors and prevented her from considering better men.[42] At the same time, Rogers's fear that no one would love her prevented her from seeing how others might use her. In courtship, a time when good judgment was crucial, sensibility increased her vulnerability. Ironically, she was so immersed in sentimentality that she lost the ease and delicacy required of gentility and ultimately embarrassed her friends.[43] Patty Rogers's courtship journal ended unhappily, not because she married neither Portius nor Philammon and remained a spinster, but because unalloyed sensibility prevented her from understanding and protecting herself.

If Patty Rogers's courtship failed because she was too immersed in performing sensibility, Mary Guion's courtship succeeded because she recognized that often emotion was no more than a performance, especially for men. What distinguished Guion was her effort to examine every evidence of authentic and false feeling. Beginning her diary at age seventeen in 1800, Mary Guion began courting naively, but soon developed into a cautious realist who devoted 340 pages to determine what she felt, what her suitors meant, and what friends, family, and townspeople knew. While Patty Rogers mirrors Jane Austen's overly sentimental Marianne Dashwood, Mary Guion recalls her sister Elinor, a woman of wit and sense. Although well versed in sentimental literature and willing to weep over novels, Guion remained anchored in reality: while Sarah Connell visited the poor to share her feelings, Mary Guion brought an old woman "two smart pieces of porck."[44] Guion approached her courtship with a similar combination of the head and the heart: her task was to unmask the flatterers and deceivers who vied for her hand and to find the man to whom she could safely reveal her true feelings.

Mary Guion's family did not possess the wealth Sarah Connell enjoyed in high-toned Newburyport, but within the small world of North Castle, New York, where her family farmed for the market, the Guions were upper-middle-class.[45] Her journal makes clear how comfortably Mary, her parents, and seven siblings lived. They could afford to buy the latest fashions, obtain books, repeatedly shop in New York City, and provide hospitality to an almost continuous stream of visitors.[46] Most importantly, prosperity meant considerable free time. Guion recorded much more domestic labor than Connell or Rogers, including spinning, wool carding, milking, candle making, butchering, knitting, and sewing, yet she regularly spent nights at balls and days immersed in reading or writing, without any suggestion they interfered with important tasks. Undoubtedly, the fact that she had several sisters still living at home lightened her housework, much as servants did for Sarah Connell and Patty Rogers; moreover, like many families of that period, the Guions employed dressmakers and hired hands and relied on neighbors for quilting and other tasks. Guion's family "sircumstances" had limited her education, as her diary's misspellings and uneven hand attest, and she felt quite outclassed by the "Ladies of the firs[t] quality in Town," but she proudly recalled that she had been "envied by all the little misses at school" for her public exhibition prize.[47] That pleasure in learning, combined with her easy family life, enabled her to seek time for reflection and writing in her much-loved journal.

Mary Guion's class status provided freedom to read as well as to write. Like Sarah Pierce, she was an enthusiastic proponent of "improvement," a word which she employed repeatedly. Reading was an integral part of Guion's social life and her efforts at improvement: she and her brother regularly read out loud to each other, and Guion delighted in a lively conversation over books with her suitors. "I wish it was as customary for every family to hav a good library as it is to have a bed in their house—," she wrote.[48] Her father and brothers regularly borrowed volumes for her from the nearby Bedford Circulating Library, and literary friends lent books as well.[49] Between 1800 and 1807 Mary Guion quoted from, bought, read, or had read to her sixty different works, many of them sentimental classics that Patty Rogers and Sarah Connell enjoyed.[50] But if Rogers, Connell, and Guion perused similar literature, they did not find the same things in what they read. From their books, Connell and Rogers borrowed sentimental language and poses, as well as inspiration to write diaries in which they figured as heroines. In their journals, they omitted the mundane household labor that interfered with their preferred work: producing refined feelings rather than domestic objects. By contrast, in her diary, Guion reported both housework and reading, a balance that reflected the dual role that sentimentality and realism would play in her life. Unlike Rogers, she did not so much use reading to produce emotions in herself, as to draw warnings which prevented those feelings which might endanger her. This was especially true in reading novels, which comprised twenty of the sixty works she mentioned. For her emotional life, the plots of these novels were key: in them fictional heroines were variously subjected to handsome rakes, money-hungry parents, and nasty husbands, before finally meeting a fate of seduction and death or virtue and bliss. As Laurel Thatcher Ulrich has argued, young American women were unlikely to be so "strangely disconnected from their communities" and end up abandoned in some tavern, but these far-fetched plots accurately captured women's feelings of vulnerability in dealing with men.[51]

Most importantly, sentimental novels echoed the experience of Guion's favorite sister, Sally. Three years older than Guion and closely watched by her younger sister, Sally represented the real-life dangers of a wrong choice in marriage. Mary's awareness that Sally's husband had originally come to court her, but had found Sally home instead, undoubtedly sharpened her sense of danger.[52] Married in 1803 after a brief courtship to Isaac Sarles, Sally bore four children in six years and endured a husband who not only neglected her when she was sick and ridiculed her before others, but was a drunkard and a thief who impoverished his family.[53] Unlike Patty Rogers, who deplored her friend Sally Thurston's miserable marriage but did not learn from it, Mary Guion took her sister's experience to heart. "Oh! my Sister my poor Sister Sally has met with such a misfortune in marrying it wounds us all," she lamented; "he was to all appearance a fine man, too, but Alas! we are too often deceived by appearances and nothing now could make his character much worse than it at preasant appears." "Oh! how much do I pity her hard lot—!" Guion reflected later, ". . . much sooner would I meet with Death than live with a person of that description."[54] This merging of fictional and real-life plots colored how Mary Guion perceived her suitors, heightened her fears of making a mistake, and formed her determination to choose a husband well.

Mary Guion's diary recalls sentimental fiction in its plot—whom will she marry?—characters, and themes. Immediately recognizable to any novel reader was the man to whom she devoted many entries: Captain Jasup, a wealthy, middle-aged widower who, despite protestations of innocence, turned out to be a shameless rake.[55] They met at a wedding in 1804 where, Guion breathlessly reported, Jasup "seamed to wish to be very familiar took his seat next me & even ventured to put his arm round me wich quite ambaresed me for by his looks he was nearly forty and I knew not but he was a maried man." On meeting again, Jasup shocked Guion by openly embracing her, "teling me at the same time he wanted me to know him next time I seen him. what must I thinck of his fredom. did he not behave thus to se if I had wit suficient to resent it?" Significantly, Guion's reaction drew on a favorite sentimental novel: "I thot of it several times of makeing the same speach to him as Evelina did to Clement [in Frances Burney's 1778 novel] 'Your fredom Sir w[h]ere you are more acquainted may perhaps be better accepted' but did not speak it—."[56]

Despite these reservations, like Patty Rogers and the heroines of many seduction and betrayal novels, Mary Guion was quite taken with Jasup. She danced with him, went sleighing, allowed him to visit her, and flirted. But having recently read *Charlotte Temple,* she decided to investigate his character. Guion discovered that Jasup drank, gambled, had "strange transactions" with his housekeeper, and "had contracted an acquaintance with a fashionable tho despisable disorder," apparently venereal disease. He was, in short, a villain. "I believe the Gentlemen thinck it an honour to the[m] to tell as many Fictious stories to the Ladies as their imagination can invent, but I shall take it as a lesson and hope to profit by it for the future but I must learn to suspect all. . . . Adieu! Adieu! for ever, I will endevour to never write, speak, and even thinck, of him more—."[57] In this account, Guion cast herself in the role of innocent heroine, a potential victim to the villainous fictional males over whose escapades she had wept. But in her diary, she had an opportunity to rewrite the often unhappy endings of sentimental novels. Here novel reading and diary writing intersect; at first they parallel each other, but her familiarity with novels warned Mary Guion away from her seducer, and she became the author of her fate in a way Patty Rogers could never be.[58]

Throughout her diary, the question of whom Mary Guion will marry was intimately related to a theme prominent in sentimental fiction: whom can a woman trust? At a time when aspiring classes studied guides to manners and strove to appear genteel, it was difficult to discern the reality behind male appearance. Repeatedly, Guion felt that the least trustworthy men were from the upper classes. The theme that men's words were false appeared on the first surviving page of Guion's journal in spring 1800. There a Mr. J. S. promised to take her to a ball but never came for her. This may have been John Sutherland, but the behavior is more typical of Jotham Smith, an ambitious young man launching a very succesful mercantile career, who, much like the rich Captain Jasup, played with her emotions and deceived her. This "inconstant young Sycopha[n]t," as she derided him, repeatedly promised to visit Guion at certain appointed times but failed to appear. Occasionally she retaliated by snubbing him, but more typically she fell into his trap: "after all this I once more concented for him to come again wich I hartily repent of," Guion wrote in wonderment, "how strange it is I shoul[d] act so different to my Reason but what shal I do?"[59] By the time Guion met Captain Jasup in 1804, she had concluded that "two fac[e]d Gentlemen are quite common now a day," and wondered, "can an inocent female account for the meaning of so much discimulation in the other sex—?" Even before she investigated Jasup's character, she suspected his intentions. When Jasup proposed that they write to each other, Guion knowingly reported, "to that I would not consent for I am very sensible it is an easy matter for the pen to write expresions that the heart never experienced or at least not more at that time than any other and as I detest flattery so much I would not with my own consent indulge him with so fair an oportunity of that kind." In looking back at their relationship, Guion concluded that it was only Jasup's age which had lent credibility to "the reality of his words": "had he a been twenty years yonger perhaps his wishful looks Devilish flattery, lies, and feigned heart rending Sighs would not a found free access—."[60]

Mary Guion was no more sure of the reality of her own feelings than that of her suitors'. She repeatedly used her diary to puzzle over whom she loved best and therefore should marry. Here she drew on another literature, one that Sarah Connell, Mary Howell, and Patty Rogers rarely acknowledged, but which was important to Sarah Pierce and her students: the political philosophy of the early national period, which endowed not only education and motherhood but courtship with republican meaning. In their duplicity coquettes were "the antitype of republican virtue," much as were male seducers; Americans associated both with European corruption and aristocracy. Once wed, both husband and wife were to exemplify the disinterest, moderation, and harmony necessary for the republic's success. In particular, as wives, women were to inspire their husbands to virtue, even as "republican mothers" inculcated morality in the next generation. This politicization of family relationships by no means set men and women on an equal plane. As Elizabeth Maddock Dillon points out in *The Gender of Freedom*, romantic language inevitably emphasized differences between the sexes—the lovers' manliness or womanliness—and in that such language predominated in courtship, marriage was what she calls "a gendering machine."[61] Yet even if republicanism kept traditional expectations of female deference, it applied similar political standards to both male and female behavior. In that regard, it narrowed the gap between male and female ideals, much as gentility blurred expectations of masculine and feminine feeling.[62]

Guion was well versed in these political concepts, many of which she read in the *New York Magazine* and *Lady's Magazine,* whose language and ideals her diary echoed.[63] "Fops" and seducers were the main villains of her journal, and her concept of male-female relations mirrored republican fear of power. She was very pleased when a suitor presented her with a verse which saluted Guion as not just a lady of sensibility but in a more political guise as "a young Columbian fair." In keeping with both political and sentimental precepts, he emphasized her internal beauties: "modesty, Delicacy, Truth, Decency, Honor, Chastity, Discretion, softness, [and] prudence." "Tho brilliant outward charms display, they soon will fade and die away," he wrote. "The worth of Females is the mind accomplish'd virtuous & refind."[64] Guion's reflections on her sister Sally's unhappy marriage further show her incorporation of Revolutionary rhetoric into marriage: "those who list in the conjugal state are designed as help mates for each other not as tirants."[65]

Much as sensibility demanded that genteel young women feel, but not too much, and Litchfield Academy expected academic excellence without forfeiture of ladylike feeling, Mary Guion found herself prevaricating between contradictory impulses: "reason," which political discourse emphasized, and "fancy," which sensibility advocated. Of the books she cited, twenty may have been novels, but twelve were essays and philosophy, and in philosophical moments she usually favored reason and fell back upon the truism that reason should be her guide.[66] Reason told her that Jasup was too old for her and that no "sober woman" wanted a rake. "I have another companion that I call Fancy wich is apt to intrude itself unless I keep a wachful eye—," she realized. "Fancy" represented her heart and seemed to have had a strong sexual component: her entries on Jotham Smith and Captain Jasup, the men to whom fancy drew her, emphasized the former's looks and the latter's outrageous advances.[67] With both Smith and Jasup she had allowed fancy to momentarily triumph, only to be deceived and ill-treated. Not unlike the heroines of sentimental fiction, she found unalloyed romance and sexual passion left her a victim.

Guion rejected and feared passion, but was reluctant to jettison "fancy" entirely. Here she turned to sensibility to find the components that would best fit her desire for both security and affection. While seduction and betrayal novels warned her away from men, Henry Mackenzie's 1771 *The Man of Feeling* promised a male she could trust. Guion noted approvingly that the book's hero "very Justly deserves the name, for he was particularly fealing to the poor Pilgrims that by chance [he] met in the streets and at last died for love, or rather for joy when he found his love was returned." But the man who read Mackenzie's novel to her was the Rev. Grant, who turned out to be "as dexterous in pleasing the Ladies [at,] as some term the word kissing, as he was affluent in oratory," and in that regard one more deceitful male. Moreover, the man of feeling's demise at the novel's end suggested he had no place in Guion's society.⁶⁸ To determine how to incorporate Mackenzie's tender feelings into social reality, Mary Guion turned to another text, which offered a new model of marriage: Johann von Zimmermann's popular eighteenth-century treatise, *Solitude Considered, In Regard to Its Influence upon the Mind and the Heart*. For Zimmermann, marriage was above all the union of empathetic souls, and happiness was to be achieved within the domestic circle. Like many other diarists of this period, Guion often copied passages from Zimmermann which praised the marriage in which, "if the tear of affliction steal down the cheak of the one, the other with affection wipes it tenderly away. The sorrows of the one are felt with sensibility by the other. . . . Day after day they communicate to each other all that they have seen, all that they have heard, and every thing that they k[n]ow." Guion rhapsodized, with Zimmermann's words, "They are never tired of each others company and conversation. The only misfortune they fear, the greatest indeed they possibly experience is the misfortune of being seperated by occational absence or untimely death—."⁶⁹ In sum, Mary Guion resolved her conflict between fancy and reason by deciding that the proper basis for marriage was loving friendship, a relationship that both sensibility and republican rhetoric valorized.⁷⁰ This incorporated the warm, affective element of fancy without its sexual dangers and recognized the good sense of reason without its cold heart. Such a union promised both safety and love.

As always, Guion made sense of literature through the people she knew. She witnessed Zimmermann's ideal relationship in her older brother James's idyllic marriage to Tabitha Lyon, a union which suggested that reality might confirm both fiction and philosophy. James, who became a pillar of the community, married Tabitha Lyon in 1802; they would have nine children. Mary recognized that theirs was an unusually happy marriage, but believed that she could learn from them "how it will perhaps one day be with me—." She included a touching picture of the couple which recalled Zimmermann's ideal and which, significantly, took place over a book: "James & his wife paid us a visit. I believe their Affection for each other increases with their days. as he was reading several Love letters in the Spectator I saw him very loveingly press his lips to hers as a token of what he himself felt in it."⁷¹

Yet as Mary Guion discovered during her courtship, even when she had determined her true feelings, it was not always possible to express them. She was acutely aware that the entire community scrutinized her courtships. If women enjoyed the greatest agency of their lives in courtship, by no means did they enjoy a free hand. Unlike Patty Rogers, Guion was extremely attentive to her audience, especially her peers, and frequently reported false rumors about her intentions toward male visitors, a practice that made her reluctant to open her heart to anyone. A too-frank preference for one man might also endanger her reputation. The customs of the period similarly set limits to honesty in courtship. After entertaining an unwanted suitor, Guion complained, "the Gentlemen have much the advantage of the Ladies for they need only go w[h]ere they choose but we must stay at home and pretend to be pleased with the company of such persons whose absence would be a releif to us—."[72]

Guion also felt obliged to entertain Benjamin Smith, the man whom her parents preferred, although she did not want to marry him. Twelve years her senior and a longstanding neighbor, Smith would have supported her very handsomely, but Guion refused to allow material gain to be a consideration. "I know the lofty house and gilded Chariot attracts the eyes of all, and perhaps the envy of some, But real happiness I believe as often resides in more inferior stations and I am lead to believe as often takes its origin from the hut as out of Palaces," she insisted. But much as her parents did not interfere with her reading or diary keeping, they were too "indulgent" to force a match by "harsh argument's," and Guion made it clear to them that she would not marry Smith. All the same, she wrote, to differ with her mother on whom to marry "may then truly be said to make a conflict in the heart between love and duty," while "it is indeed a severe trial for me to thinck of crossing in the least the inclinations of a Father who not since my remembrance ever spoke to me in anger, but to me he is entirely silent on the subject."[73] To complicate matters, Smith was extremely persistent in his suit: from the late 1790s until Guion's wedding in 1807, he regularly visited her and pleaded his case with a tearful and abject devotion that recalled Mackenzie's "man of feeling." But much like Elizabeth Cranch, Mary Guion may have admired sensitive men in theory, but found them irritating in practice. Nevertheless, to oblige her parents, she continued to receive his visits, and in that sense simulated an interest she did not feel.

Appalled by her sister's miserable life, caught between reason and fancy, pressured by her parents, how did Mary Guion ever wed? The answer lies not just in reading her diary but in listening to it. Much like

Litchfield Female Academy's schoolroom of reciting voices, her journal is filled with talk: a cacaphony of "he saids" and "she saids" that reminds us that she lived in an oral culture. Even when Guion read books, she often read them aloud rather than silently, or she listened to a friend or family member read from them. In fact, the novels she read, which focused on women's lives, "often arouse the kind of intense interest in personal detail that gossip generates" (as Patricia Meyer Spacks puts it), and sharpened both her listening and storytelling abilities. Guion herself never used the word "gossip," but her description of conversations mirrors the spectrum that Spacks attributes to gossip: from malicious rumor, which Guion condemned, to intimate conversation in which people "use talk about others to reflect about themselves, to express wonder and uncertainty and locate certainties, to enlarge their knowledge of one another."[74] Guion's prose, which veered from imitations of published literature to colloquial expressions, illustrates the overlapping influence of oral and print culture. We can hear Guion's own voice in

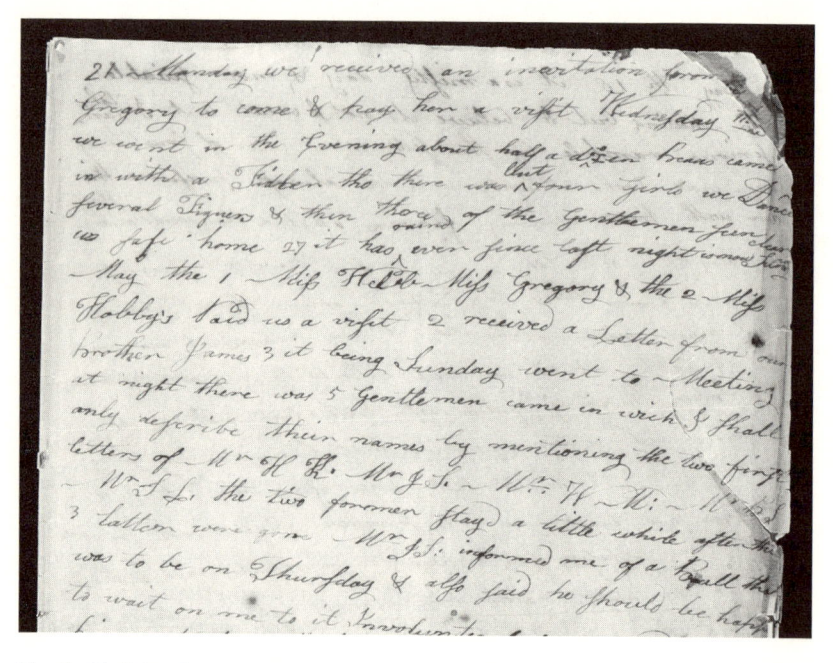

Top half of the first surviving page of Mary Guion's diary introduces the manuscript's leading characteristics: accounts of continuous visiting, puzzlement over emotions, and idiosyncratic spelling and punctuation. (Collection of The New-York Historical Society)

her idiosyncratic spelling: when she wrote "Mashel" for "Marshall," we detect her southern New York accent.[75]

This chorus of voices reflects the prominent role visiting and conversation played both in courtship and in the construction and performance of emotion.[76] The first surviving entry of Guion's diary, April 21, 1800, stated, "we received an invitation from [Polly] Gregory to come & pay her a visit," and during the course of her journal she mentioned over one hundred different female acquaintances. Many visits began spontaneously with one or two women stopping by, others joined, conversation and walks outside followed, with much teasing about potential suitors, Guion produced coffee and cake, while some guests moved on, and those who stayed piled into a single bed. Other occasions were quite formal: when Abigail Haight had Guion and some others to tea, refreshments were served by "a couple of black boys," and the ladies amused themselves by walking in "an elegant and beautiful flowr garden," which reminded her of James Hervey's writings.[77] More commonly, weaving, quilting, sewing, picking berries, and other women's jobs were lightened by conversation, which focused, in turn, on who was visiting whom. But while Guion might visit another woman freely and by herself, she hesitated to visit a man, especially alone. Instead, she took a friend or sibling along and visited the family, especially the sister, of the young man in whom she was interested. Men, however, could visit Guion without pretending interest in her siblings.[78] If they found a group of women had already gathered, a party would ensue with parlor games and singing. This informal gathering was only one of the many opportunities for men and women to meet without necessarily pairing off: balls, frolics, singing schools, and going to meeting all provided opportunities for interaction. Guion distinguished these occasions from those in which a lone male visited her and her family withdrew to allow them a private and lengthy conversation. Although a single woman was not expected to visit a man, she controlled who could visit her. The mere fact of allowing a man to visit signaled interest, and Guion often debated whether to allow a young man to enjoy that privilege, analyzed her suitor's words and tone, and was outraged if a suitor failed to show. Repeated visits implied commitment, and early American culture linked talk and courtship by calling an engaged person "bespoken."[79]

For Mary Guion, the conversations of both female friends and male suitors played a crucial role in choosing a good husband. How men talked suggested their character and intelligence: significantly, her contempt for Isaac Sarles focused on his "unbounded" talk and "unpleasant and passionate expressions."[80] In reaction, she sought men whose conversation was respectful and "candid" and judged their talk by the feelings it expressed and evoked. When several male visitors began to quote Alexander Pope's most "vulgar blackgardly" comments on women, for example, Guion excoriated them as "woman haters" and refused to participate in their conversation. Aware that men thought women liked flattery, she made it clear that she preferred serious conversation, writing of one suitor: "he b[e]gan his Discourse, as the comon run [of] Beaus do with no small share of flattery but finding I had no taste for such conversation he very artfully cha[n]g'd the subject & to that wich much more hit my fancy. the hed of his discourse was upon good manners from which I geathered some very good advice." With amusement, Guion dismissed the conversation of her more insipid visitors: "O Polly how happy we should always live togather said the conceited fop, and added he I should make you a good husband. doubtless said I—." Alternatively, she appreciated another man's delicacy in omitting words that would make her blush as he read out loud.[81]

Other men's conversation proved harder to judge. Jotham Smith of Bedford was an accomplished flirt who repeatedly expressed interest in Guion but then ignored her. He excused himself so adeptly that Guion did not know what to think: "he said so much he had allmost convincd me to disbelieve my own eyes," she marveled in mid-April, 1802. Guion devoted many pages to puzzling over the handsome Smith; in almost every encounter he bested her verbally, until she finally resolved to retaliate with silence.[82] Much as she condemned Isaac Sarles's "unbounded" talk, she criticized the "unbounded" confidence that enabled Smith to slight her. In Smith's case, she understood his behavior in terms of class. "I am entirely unacquainted withe high life if those are theire customs for he does of course think himself Superior to me," Guion complained, "but I only wich then I had never seen him."[83] Echoing republican political tracts and the sentimental preference for rusticity, Guion repeatedly contrasted her rural simplicity and candid speech to the urban sophistication and duplicity of the wealthy. This must be taken with a grain of salt; on one occasion, Guion voiced her rural identity on returning from a shopping spree in New York City, and she was quite attentive to fashion. Nonetheless, she felt that the Smith family trumped hers economically, and republican ideology provided a language for expressing that class difference.[84] Smith secured his niche in that elite world: he married Abigail Haight (who had invited Guion to her elegant garden party) and became a prosperous dry goods merchant in New York City.[85]

Conscious that men could disguise their characters with words, Mary Guion overtly sought information that would help her accurately judge them and was wary of entertaining unfamiliar suitors. For example, while she approved of the conversation and "refind Company" of a Mr. Pixley and found him "very well informd in books," she worried that as a newcomer his "Character" was "unknown" to her. Pixley replied that his character could be had "in writing" at Bedford, and "realy appeared pleased to see me have so much regard to that particulaur wich I think a very a Material one." Unsatisfied, she declared, "I do not expect him any more."[86] In using such methods as she maneuvered her way through the marriage market, Guion acted much like contemporary merchants, who were equally wary of unknown and potentially threatening competitors; like her, they feared deceit and employed family connections and recommendations to protect their credit.[87]

In another case, Guion found that fancy interfered with truth gathering. When Jonathan Jasup, the smooth-talking, middle-aged sea captain from Connecticut, protested his love and honorable intentions, she visited friends and family members to ascertain his character. Jasup's friendship with Isaac Sarles should have forewarned her, but she was still shocked when a male friend reported that he gambled and drank. "The discovery was both a pleasure and a pain," Guion wrote. "I was pleased that I had heard it soon enough to escape the snare spread for me, but sorry to thinck I had been so much deceived in a person I had so favourable an opinion of—." Reluctant to believe the worst, later that month she consulted with Mrs. Smith, Jasup's sister-in-law and a frequent visitor. But Mrs. Smith "almost convinced me it was only a fictious story for had that a been the case I should said she most likely a heard of it before now—." Guion then asked her brother James, but he only knew Jasup's brothers rather than the captain himself. At this point, Guion realized that infatuation was preventing her from accurately assessing information: "Oh thot I, it would a been quite a satisfaction to me if [James] had but a known him to, for then I could [have] had his opinion of him which had it a been simular to my own I should a valued, but if the reverse I must a thot he had a rong idea, so of course it would have answered no purpose at last—." Only when she received definitive proof did Guion conclude that Jasup was a liar and a rake.[88]

The reports that Guion and her friends exchanged were crucial not only in warning them away from dangerous men but in controlling their own reputations. In this sense, gossip built her public self; in Erving Goffman's terms, people play "discrepant roles" that influence communal information about public performance.[89] Mary Guion's relationship with Jotham Smith illustrates this. At an 1802 ball, Smith drew his wet finger across Guion's face to see if her rosy cheeks were "Artificial." "Vexd," Guion did not know how to judge his behavior. Was Smith playful or was he implying that she was sexually loose? Guion had reason for concern: women's sexual reputations were fragile and a major factor in their marriageability, while cosmetics were associated with corrupt court culture and compromised women.[90] Guion quickly discovered community interest in their relationship. At a quilting, a friend told Guion "she had a secret to tell me. I was Impatient to know it so she wispered to me that she heard Mr J S was comeing very soon to pay me a visit. how did this word at once please & shock me. Good heaven thot I after Such treatment as I received at the Ball what can he come for but to afront me again & if he does I shall be very carefull what I say."[91] When she confronted Smith the next day, he showed his awareness of the importance of reputation by immediately asking if she had told anyone about his behavior. Guion had, and later made a point of complaining to the woman who had initially recommended Smith, confident that she would spread her negative report.[92] In doing so, Guion influenced the public interpretation of Smith's behavior and protected her reputation.

As important as "Town talk" was in helping her judge men, Guion knew that it was not completely dependable. When false reports circulated about her brother James, she recognized community members' propensity to "vent their fury" on innocent people. Guion deplored such malicious, covert talk and distinguished it from an accurate and open exchange of community information. But even that was problematic. Mrs. Smith, Jasup's sister-in-law, so prided herself on her knowledge that she had proved reluctant to accept contrary reports. And as competitors for male attention, the young women in Guion's circle occasionally became "tattlers," and, despite her efforts, they spread rumors that she "used a cosmetit wash" and "painted." In deference to community opinion, however false, Guion limited a suitor's visits rather than let her "Loquiatious young friends" ruin her reputation. As she realized, many conversations "might be compared to a heep of feathers in a hard wind for words flew out very fast but without any substance or weight belonging to them."[93]

Mary Guion was willing to turn to female friends for information on her suitors, but she did not treat them as confidantes. Unlike Sarah Connell, Patty Rogers, and the Litchfield Academy diarists, she offered no odes to female friendship and seems to have had an extremely practical approach to other women: they were useful, they might be entertaining, but they did not figure among the most important people in her life. Since she related to women as a group more than as individuals, Guion was quite willing to share in the general speculation about future husbands which was rampant in her circle. At one point, Guion and a friend spent an evening "trying som tricks to know who were to marry." Their centuries-old method involved "placeing a key at the second chapter of Psalms tye it fast and then it must be held by two persons till they name a couple and repeat the first six verses then if the Bible turns they are to marry." In a frank recognition of both their prospects and the entertainment courtship offered, Guion and another friend laid bets on the possibility of their marriage within the year.[94] But Guion did not go beyond such lighthearted speculation and single out a friend with whom to discuss her deepest feelings or her marital choice. Typically, one day Guion went for "a long walck on the beach" with Debby Lounsbury. "[A]s friends we were talcking of what we did not wish every one to know," Guion wrote, as if she were about to reveal her heart. Instead, she let Debby do most of the talking, and even when Lounsbury guessed correctly which suitor Guion preferred, Mary would not admit it.[95]

Like Patty Rogers, Mary Guion demonstrates that the early republic was not neatly divided into homosocial and heterosocial communities. Rather, Guion reveals a universe that had elements of Carroll Smith-Rosenberg's homosocial world, but which lacked the intense feeling historians have associated with women's relations. Mary Guion's work world was heavily female—her chores aligned her with her mother, sisters, hired women, and female friends—and her social life included much joking with other women. But most of her life mixed men and women and fell into the sphere that Catherine Kelly terms "society."[96] She read novels, which were associated with women, but her father and brothers obtained the books for her; attended religious services numerically dominated by women but flirted with men over her hymn book; and visited her female friends, but hoped their brothers were at home. Guion was equally fond of her sister Sally and her brother James, although they played very different roles in her life. She wrote more warmly of her father than her mother, but seems to have been largely oriented to her peers, who were far more significant in her courtship than either parent.

Although men and books inspired her most intense emotions, Mary Guion did not dislike or resent women. We might expect the economic and social necessity of marriage to pit women against each other, but multiple factors mitigated such competition. Guion identified her rivals for men's affections, but none of them raised her ire, and who paired off with whom seems more a part of general gossip than personal animosity. Caty Holly and Abigail Haight competed with her for Jotham Smith's affections, but she found the former "so well accomplished" and the latter so elegant, that she could not criticize Smith for his preference.[97] She discovered that another of her suitors, a Dr. Minor, was visiting Betsy Lounsbury secretly, but rather than feeling resentful, Guion gained the valuable information that Minor was duplicitous and therefore unworthy of Guion's love.[98] Because Mary Guion believed men were untrustworthy flatterers, she never expressed envy of beautiful women; beauty only attracted "a parsel of Coxcomical young fellows" with "adulateing tongues" who increased women's peril.[99] As a result, young women's criticism of their bodies, so common in the twentieth century, was rare and mild in these early diaries; their authors continually monitored their emotional temperatures, not their physical appearance.[100] And since courting customs gave men rather than women the initiative, it made little sense to blame women for men's choices. Guion was interested enough in consumption to list her purchases from local peddlers and stores in Bedford and New York City, but she expressed no envy toward better-dressed women.[101] Although Guion's diary was much more revealing than the official stories that Litchfield Female Academy students produced, it disclosed a similar reluctance to voice resentment against the competition. Like them, she did not take it personally. Instead, these women seem to have accepted constant comparisons and public watching as a given. This, in turn, suggests that they saw themselves within a social context, whether in the Academy's institutional community or North Castle's village culture. In Mary Guion's case, this did not signify any sacrifice of individuality, since her distinctive voice resounds throughout her courtship diary, but an understanding of self-in-society seems to have modulated divisions among women.

Yet Guion clearly needed a confidante to whom she could speak freely. Throughout her diary she characterized herself as "partial to plain dealing" and worried a great deal that she might seem coquettish.[102] During her years of courtship, she became more and more desperate in her search for a man she could trust, at the same time that she lacked the close female friendships which sustained many women in her position. As she suffered repeated disappointments, her affection grew for her one trusted confidante: her diary. During the years from 1800 to 1807, Guion increasingly recognized the role her journal played in her life: "wen I amuse myself with my pen or a book I always find that I have very agreeable & entertaining company & that wich never Cloys," she wrote in 1804, undoubtedly thinking of the tedious young gentlemen she had been compelled to entertain. The following year, during which she struggled with her feelings for Captain Jasup, she repeatedly praised her diary. "I believe my pen will always expose my thots, what a tell tale has it ever been and still continues to be to me by placing them in so external a point of vieu that I can read them at leisure, wich tho simple as they are often afford me real pleasure." "I conseal nothing from this paper," she maintained on another occasion, and wrote yet again: "so different am I from many others that I find a real pleasure in it when my mind is animated, and a sympathising friend when dejected—." "[M]y two reall friends," Guion concluded in 1805, were "my boock & pen."[103]

Many scholars of diaries have regarded this narrative form as an extension of the writer's self, and on one level it served that function for Mary Guion. As Cecile Jagodzinski has suggested, early modern journals often used "'private speech,' speech directed to the interior self," a complex talking to oneself that "promote[s] self-clarification and self-definition for both reader and author."[104] We can see Guion doing this as she ruminated over her feelings. Such interior conversations presuppose an internal self distinct from the external. That Guion saw herself in these terms also appears in her caution in letting others read her diary, much as she was careful about revealing her feelings to her suitors: clearly, her diary was her private self, and she guarded its boundaries carefully. But Mary Guion's journal served an additional and equally important function. With her journal, she created the affectionate, confiding, egalitarian relationship she idealized in husbands and wives. If novels had warned her away from villains, her journal embodied the ideal alternative. In that sense, she anticipated the relationship she finally developed with the man she would marry: Samuel Brown. Brown first appeared in Guion's diary in December 1800, and by 1802 she reported rumors that they would marry. At this point she was drawn to him, but Jotham Smith, Jasup, and others caught her fancy. When she relinquished Jasup in 1805, her attention returned to Brown. In him she at last found "candid speach" and "a reasonable and a constant heart."[105] But by then she was herself reluctant to speak frankly. Much like other young women of the time, for two years she temporized, unable to either refuse or accept Brown.[106] In a striking metaphor, she felt she stood "upon a precipice," hardly knowing "which path to chuse." Unsure which way to turn, she "artfully . . . disguised my fealings and every emotion of my heart when in [Brown's] company," and confided her feelings to her faithful journal.[107]

Mary Guion's fears delayed her choice for two years, but her regard for reason enabled her to overcome them. Unlike Sally and Isaac, who had courted for only six months, Mary was determined to take her time. And unlike Isaac, whose Pound Ridge family was unfamiliar to the Guions, Brown was a near neighbor and his sister a good friend. Brown was also Guion's independent choice, a man whose modest economic standing made clear her commitment to marrying for love; ironically, he was Benjamin Smith's poorer cousin.[108] Most importantly, he was the polar opposite of the flattering suitors she distrusted. A man of few and plain words, Brown talked little in company, and in his visits bluntly declared his intentions: "he said he should look no farther until I said I would never have him. a coquet would laugh at such a plain & candid speach but I prefer it to all the unmeaning adulation my ears ever heard," Guion reported in 1805.[109] Unlike Jotham Smith's glib talk, which rendered her silent, Brown's quietness helped Mary Guion find her own voice. As their relationship deepened, she devoted more and more journal pages to analyzing her own feelings instead of puzzling over male conversation. At the same time, Guion set about gathering information on Brown. Samuel himself encouraged her: recognizing Mary's anxiety, he gave her a newspaper article which emphasized the need to "examine critically the character of the person with whom you propose forming this [marriage] connection."[110] Guion did just that. She marked his reserve in company but decided his eyes showed his love more than words, noted his modest finances, investigated what it would be like to live with his parents, repeatedly remarked on his faithfulness, candor, and tenderness, and contrasted Samuel's kindness to Isaac Sarles's meanness.[111] Bit by bit, Brown broke down her reticence, and in March 1807 Guion "at last determined [to] marry none but him for he has all my esteem, & I am all ashured of his."[112]

Neither a colonial alliance of households nor a Victorian romance, Mary Guion's courtship was distinctive to the early republic and to her personal circumstances. Much like the Victorian lovers Karen Lystra has described, Mary Guion tested Brown's affections, in this case whether he would persist despite her continuous stalling.[113] "[I]f he really loves me hee'l put up with it," she matter-of-factly declared. In testing him, she knew she was taking chances; as she put it, her delays would "either tire his patience or increase his amity." If they failed, Guion felt that she could not love again and that "a good settlement" was all she could hope for, a declaration which suggests her expectation that marriage was inevitable, even one without deep feeling.[114] But republican fears of power, her sister's unhappiness, fiction's emphasis on women's vulnerability, and earlier flirtations with untrustworthy swains impelled that test more than romantic ideology: "if ever I marry I shall be very cautious that I do not get blind in love as I once was," she had vowed in 1802.[115] In Victorian courtships, testing intensified after the couple had committed themselves to each other, and in that sense, they probed the depth and endurance of an already declared love. By contrast, Guion tested Brown before she made any commitment to him, a maneuver which reveals Guion's greater preoccupation with safety.[116] Historians have tended to see a rising trajectory of romantic love proceeding from the late eighteenth century into the Victorian period, yet Patty Rogers's highly romantic diary preceded Mary Guion's more cautious journal by twenty years. Individual experience accounts for that difference, but an alternative explanation suggests itself: that we need to look at not just the spread of romantic ideology, but the attention women gave to their fears. It was no accident that Patty Rogers was not only romantic but unafraid—of her reputation, of her chances, and of men's designs—while Mary Guion was her opposite. The contrast between the two suggests that one of the functions of romance is to divert women from their fears, even though those fears were well grounded in economic, legal, and political realities. Fortunately for Mary Guion, republicanism provided a counter-narrative to romantic ideology, not because it imagined that men and women could be equal (which it did not), but because its obsession with tyranny and deceit provided a vocabulary that enabled her to acknowledge her fears and protect herself. Sensibility was less consistently useful: while novels had warned her away from predatory men, fiction also made romance hard to resist.

Mary Guion's relationship with Brown also shows subtle differences from the Victorian practice of courting lovers revealing their inner souls to each other, crossing gender boundaries, and merging into a new and single self.[117] Guion was far more interested in self-protection than in self-revelation, a stance that again reflected the anxiety surrounding marriage. For much of their courtship, rather than speaking heart to heart, Guion confided her innermost thoughts to her journal, while Brown brought books to speak his love for him. Even in the months before their wedding, Mary Guion's idea of self-revelation was to simply admit the fact of her love, rather than to reveal details of her innermost self. Furthermore, although Mary loved Samuel, before their wedding that love seems not to have changed her sense of self, although marriage would later have that effect. Rather, she had quite simply found what she wanted, an honest man to whom she could reveal her love without fear. In her description of their final pledge, love and safety run together: "Oh Polly said he how well do I love you. I then laid all formality aside in my answer and said if you love me as well as I do you I dare say we shall live agreeable together. . . . here I have roat words that I cannot read without a blush but to no other did I ever talck thus and with him it is safe." To her joy, Brown emerged as both a model of republican virtue and a man of considerable feeling. On asking friends his true intentions, Guion was gratified to learn, "its you and only you, that he wants."[118]

Despite all her caution, Mary Guion's courtship was predicated on love, and once assured of safety, she acceded to fancy. Unlike Patty Rogers, who permitted Philammon liberties without his commitment, Guion knew her community regarded them as a couple, and in keeping with the colonial tradition that allowed the betrothed greater physical intimacy, she felt free to sit with him in her bedroom and to allow his visits when no one else was home. Calling him "my Sammy," "my expected Beau," and, above all, "my Friend," the two engaged in modest sexual banter. Guion recorded that Brown walked in on her when she was getting dressed, and although she told him to "march out" once she noticed his presence, she was more "confused" than offended, as she was when he tossed seeds down her unpinned neckerchief and offered to retrieve them. Such "tender pashions of virtuous love" might seem a far cry from romance, but they were grounded in "the strongest ties of love and affections," as Guion herself characterized them.[119] Catherine E. Kelly has argued that provincial New Englanders of the early nineteenth century placed "little stock in romantic love" and sought "to establish a household and reproduce the social order in marriage" rather than find "personal fulfillment." Similarly, Ellen Rothman maintains that "the ideology of romantic love made friendship between men and women into a consolation prize of sorts."[120] While I agree with Kelly's placement of courtship in a communal context, I find that Guion's desire to avoid her sister's fate made her prudent, not cold; she sought to make "the Nuptial ties of love" safe and expressed no interest in her economic standing as a married woman. If she had wanted money, a "man of feeling," faithful friendship, and her parents' approval, she could have gotten all four by marrying Benjamin Smith; instead, she chose Samuel Brown, a choice that only love's idiosyncrasies can explain. In her own republican context, if not within our own, calling Samuel her "friend" conveyed warmth and offered a "personal fulfillment" far beyond anything romance alone could offer. Clearly, he had won her heart as well as her head. Mary Guion revealed the extent to which she had let Samuel into her heart by characterizing him in exactly the same terms she had described her journal in 1805. Brown was, she felt, "a Sympathsi[zing] friend." Guion now had not two but three friends: "my book my Pen and my Lover."[121]

Guion's grouping of her book, pen, and lover captures for us the intertwining of reading, writing, and courtship that was crucial for her diary. As I have shown, there are many parallels between the plots, themes, and subjects of novels and diaries. But the relationship between reading and writing can be understood in a different, more ironic sense if we focus on the process common to both: the interplay of fiction and reality. The novels Guion read were fictional constructs of reality. That was part of their appeal: from the safety of her seat by the fire, Guion could analyze imagined aspects of her own life. She could also choose what messages to take from her reading: while Patty Rogers lifted romantic dreams from her books, Mary Guion (although not immune to a bold and handsome sea captain) borrowed warnings against certain types of behavior and men. In this sense, sentimental fiction was a reading of and a guide to reality. But throughout her diary, Guion understood fiction in another sense: the "Fictious" words of men whose intentions were dishonorable. This type of fiction had portended ruin for her sister Sally. Sally had mistaken "appearances" (fiction) for reality, and disaster ensued. Throughout her years of courtship, it was Mary Guion's aim to avoid a similar fate. To do so, she must distinguish the fictions around her and accurately read men's behavior.

Guion solved this problem of reading through listening, but above all through writing. In turning to a diary, she in a sense created yet another fiction, in that her journal was a partial vision of reality and often an echo of sentimental literature. But she recognized that her journal placed her thoughts "in so external a point of view," that she could read them "at leisure." Her diary helped distance her from life, from reality—even as it made sense of her reality—much as novels did, so that she could safely analyze its meaning and choose how to act. By making her simultaneously author and audience, writer and reader, her journal enabled her to both vent her emotions and explore them, be the subject of an often unmanageable life and control that life, recognize her fancies and counter them with reason.[122] Her creation of that partial fiction, that rereading of her life, helped bring her courtship to a happy conclusion.

Mary Guion's story might seem to be about living happily ever after, but it is really about work. For sentimentalists such as Sarah Connell, Mary Howell, and Patty Rogers, emotion work meant the surface and deep acting which produced the emotions sensibility prized. They worked up certain feelings appropriate to their class and gender and used their diaries to admire those feelings. Patty Rogers's profuse tears and florid prose appear undisciplined, but reflected her effort to maintain a certain emotional pitch. Mary Guion's emotion work was very different: she tried to dampen down feelings that might endanger her, such as her yen for Captain Jasup. She also labored to accurately identify the emotions she and others felt, so appearances would not deceive her. At the same time, she employed emotional relationships, such as friendships, to do work for her, especially to find and convey information essential to successful courtship. For Rogers, emotion work was an end in itself, but for Guion, it served a larger purpose: preventing the wrong choice in courtship.

Mary Guion sought authentic feeling, but she respected appearances and was quite willing to disguise her emotions and engage in surface acting if that served her interests. But while Sarah Connell disguised her emotions to please her father, Guion disguised hers to protect herself. In this regard, Guion had a remarkable sense of her self as an individual, and hers is a story of increasing agency; she was, in a sense, self-employed. Yet she still understood her self in relation to others, and her empowerment stemmed from her attention to them. If she was a rather cool friend, she filtered her feelings through the experience of her family, whom she deeply loved: her indulgent parents, who enabled her to read and write; and her siblings, especially her happily married brother James, who sparked her yearning for an affectionate and equal marriage, and her miserable sister Sally, whose fate enraged her. Neither was she a free agent within her community: she recognized the power of village culture, although she tried to use it to protect herself. She also understood her feelings in relationship to her favorite books, whether sentimental novels or republican essays. But unlike Connell and Rogers, she was an active reader who reflected on what she read and did not just repeat literary rhetoric. Instead, she developed a distinctive voice; while Rogers's and Connell's diaries sound like the sentimental heroines they read about, Mary Guion sounds like no one but herself. This peculiar combination of self and others suggests that we can draw no easy lines between an "I self" and a "we self." Instead, the self was a fluid entity negotiated as emotion was constructed. Neither can we separate the public and the private, which formed a continuously influential loop in the village courtship community, much as did diaries and novels within the world of sensibility.

The courtships of Patty Rogers and Mary Guion were grounded in the early republic's particularities, but the way in which these women experienced and used their culture shows unexpected similarities with twentieth-century Americans' construction of feeling. Eva Illouz's *Consuming the Romantic Utopia: Love and the Cultural Contradictions of Capitalism* reminds us how consumption dominates American culture and especially the experience of love. Since a two-income family is the contemporary means to affluence (just as marriage was essential to women's middle-class status in the past), romance retains economic implications. Illouz argues that since the early twentieth century's development of dating "relocated the romantic encounter to the public sphere of consumption," romance has become commercialized (and commerce romanticized) in America's market-driven culture. In the 1920s, advertisements offered products as a direct means to increase sexual attraction, but by the century's end, they more subtly depicted both men and women experiencing intimacy within the context of consumption and invited viewers to partake of that emotion and associate it with buying. As she puts it, "the concrete, specific materiality of the products has vanished into the impalpable realm of feeling."[123] The appeal of such ads is not to reason, but entirely to emotion: it in fact sells feeling, and since emotions feed on each other, a never-ending demand is created. In such a scenario, consumer choice is weakened, and discernment is difficult. During the early republic, courtship entailed few objects to buy; community get-togethers and visits featuring word games and toss-the-handkerchief required only imagination and everyday objects. Nevertheless, Patty Rogers functioned much like the viewers of modern advertisements that Illouz describes. She experienced feeling not through advertisements, but through the literature of sensibility. Through books, she entered into the feelings she read about and hoped that by having the feelings, she would have the reward: not a material object, but her loved one's heart. In short, she became a consumer of feelings, and much like consumers today, she found that her self became derivative and that she could not choose rationally.

Mary Guion was a very different consumer than Patty Rogers. In her *Talk of Love: How Culture Matters,* sociologist Ann Swidler argues that we should understand culture "less as a great stream in which we are all immersed, and more as a bag of tricks or an oddly assorted tool kit." In her interviews on Californians' experience with love, she found that men and women enjoyed enough distance from their culture to employ it in their own interests. Through its symbols, values, and lessons, people pick and choose their response and feelings, often in a "piecemeal" fashion which reflects both their individual needs and the diverse choices contemporary culture offers. In the process, she maintains, "people use culture to learn how to be, or become, particular kinds of people" and construct the self. This process is most clear in "unsettled" lives where, Swidler argues, "culture is more visible—indeed, there appears to be 'more' culture—because people actively use culture to learn new ways of being."[124] Swidler's metaphor of tools seems oddly old-fashioned for a study of twentieth-century Californians, who live in a thoroughly commercialized culture. Unlike Illouz, Swidler depicts her subjects not so much as emotional players as rational decision makers, who deal in ideas rather than feelings. Nonetheless, Swidler illuminates past as well as present behavior. American culture in the early republic offered far fewer choices than late-twentieth-century culture, especially for women, and their choices were fraught with much greater danger. But despite these differences, commerce played a role in courtship through providing a "cultural repertoire" of books and magazines from which women drew ideas and feelings, and learned who to be. In that sense, commerce and feeling are linked to courtship in both the early republic and modern America. If we apply Swidler's insights to the courtships of Patty Rogers and Mary Guion, we can see that their different uses of cultural tools influenced their fates. Through print culture, Mary Guion encountered and utilized both republicanism and sentimentality to interpret her suitors and construct her response, while she found further cautions and advice in oral culture. While Patty Rogers's immersion in the single world of sensibility increased her vulnerability, Guion's ability to fully use her society's cultural market empowered her, much as it has contemporary Americans. During the early republic, such active negotiation emerged most clearly (and was most necessary) in the "unsettled" time of courtship, but it could be found in everyday behavior as well. Neither did Mary Guion stand alone in her resourceful use of her culture. This is most apparent in the willingness of her contemporary diarists to choose when and how to express that most "unfeminine" of emotions, anger.

4

LOSING IT

Anger and the Boundaries of Female Behavior

J. Bowers seated himself by me. "how is it Miss May that when I make my best bow to you and ask you, so, you put on such a scornful look and a 'very well' is all I can get from you[?"] "I will tell you Mr Bowers—there are some Gentlemen whom the less we know of them the better. you happen to be one of that description.[" "]the devil! I knew you hated me but I think highly of *you* notwithstanding. tell me what tis I have done, what have you ever seen amiss in my conduct to yourself that should make you despise me for I see you do" I did not deny say [*sic*] that I *despised* him but in *downright* terms told him what I thought of him. would you believe it, he asked me to dance the next dance and would take no denial—after the dressing I had given him I did not expect it nor could I desire it but as a reprisal [refusal?] might have made him angry I danced with him two dances but the most pleasant partner I had was Mr. Cockrun . . . oh! with how different sensations do we give our hand to such a man in the dance. to Bowers. I hate, I detest him, and if I am wrong! why then I am sorry—.

—*Abigail May, Journal, August 1800*

Abigail May's forthright attack on Mr. Bowers, to his face and in her diary, initially confounds our expectations of feminine feeling during the early republic. In her study of emotion among eighteenth-century colonial Pennsylvanians, Nicole Eustace could find "no direct expression" of anger by women in either personal or published sources, and only one recorded incident in which a woman voiced resentment. By the Revolutionary era, she argues, anger found at best "equivocal and qualified acceptance" among elite men, while "anger avoidance was being redefined as a feminine emotional task, the crowning attribute of admirable women."[1] Robert Ferguson similarly argues that sanctions against anger imposed "tonal controls" on women in public and forbade them the right to "language in their own cause," while Peter Stearns and Carol Zisowitz Stearns perceive a new cultural deterrence against expressing anger during the eighteenth century, one both men and women shared. Premodern Americans, they argue, allowed considerable freedom in voicing anger, especially by the elite toward inferiors, and employed communal constraints emphasizing obedience. But by the mid-1700s, Western society developed a new concern for curbing anger, especially in the family and through individual self-control. They impute this to a variety of factors: valorization of love in courtship and marriage; new tenderness toward children, wives, and elders; increased comfort within the home, leading to greater sentimentality about domesticity as well as fewer occasions for argument; Enlightenment heightening of rationality and therefore the means for control; a desire to be well bred and eliminate "unattractive" characteristics; and a variety of economic factors. They emphasize that this cultural shift was incomplete and uneven and extended to the mid-nineteenth century, but given that Americans deemed anger most offensive within the family and by inferiors, we would expect women to actively avoid expressing it.[2]

For the later nineteenth century, historians find both a public/private and a male/female dichotomy in Victorian emotionology for anger. As Linda Grasso has argued in her study of women's published literature, to be angry is to judge, to question things as they are. Moreover, "for women, the expression of anger and the creation of an autonomous self are integrally linked."[3] According to Grasso, direct expression of such "unfeminine" attitudes was dangerous for women. Privately, women, especially mothers, suppressed anger within themselves or deflected it onto social inferiors; publicly, writers such as Louisa May Alcott wrote "behind a mask" and employed dissembling, indirection, and disguise in an effort to both conceal and express their outrage.[4] Other historians emphasize that although for both sexes anger represented irrationality and was to be controlled within the home, men enjoyed the right to possess angry feelings and could channel them into positive public purposes such as nation building and military heroics. By contrast, Victorians regarded anger as antithetical to womanhood itself, denied women the right to even feel angry, and demanded that females control their anger in both private and public spheres.⁵ Jane Hunter agrees that for Victorian girls, controlling anger defined goodness. In controlling such unacceptable feelings, she maintains, Victorian diaries acted as an early version of the "talking cure," in which women could censor themselves, vow to do better, "and then harness, the runaway fantasies of the id."⁶

Building on the eighteenth century's desire to curb anger, but not yet embracing the antebellum period's full-blown suppression of "unwomanly" feeling, the early republic devised its own constraints on female rage. Since women were legally, economically, and politically dependent on men, and others controlled and obscured their boundaries of self, assertion of self and expression of anger were, presumably, difficult. Female academies propounded rules limiting emotional expression, including anger, and republican mothers and wives won stature from what they did for others, not for themselves. Sensibility also inhibited anger: its key emotion was sympathy and its impulse toward contentment and harmony rather than rage. Similarly, gentility expressed itself in ease and complaisance; angry confrontation was its antithesis and called into question the class status which gentility sought to establish. Although in earlier eras the upper classes enjoyed the right to express anger at their social inferiors, late-eighteenth-century gentility demanded kindly condescension, especially from women. In their diaries, young women showed considerable deftness in emotion management, and we might expect them to extend this control to anger. Instead, their journals displayed a highly ambivalent attitude toward this volatile emotion. As their culture demanded, women expressed anger infrequently, often hedged it with qualifications, and were reluctant to reveal such feelings publicly. Nevertheless, among young single women I had no problem finding diarists who vented anger in a variety of antagonistic feelings, ranging from criticism to biting sarcasm to occasional fury, regardless of the emotional community in which they lived.⁷ To shift Ann Swidler's terminology from love to anger, they chose the cultural tools that permitted them to express and own this ostensibly unfeminine emotion.

This chapter examines how two different groups of young women approached and articulated anger. One group—sentimentalists and Litchfield Female Academy students—found that ideology and audience compelled them to voice anger tentatively and reluctantly, while a second group—Mary Guion, Abigail May, Susan Heath, and Rachel Van Dyke—raged and criticized with relish and at length. In that these women displayed anger their culture expected them to suppress, they could be said to "lose it": to lose emotional control and the ability to suppress anger, and to thereby withdraw their consent from cultural demands. Yet their diaries show that young women of both these groups rarely lost control completely: even when angry, they carefully eyed their effect on others, remained aware of social expectations, and maneuvered around them with extraordinary deftness. The phrase "losing it," however, remains telling, in that almost invariably the same concerns precipitated anger in these young women: issues of identity for both themselves and others, and in that sense, fear of losing the self. Anxiety over male deceit and preoccupation with their reputations in courtship occupied only part of this larger concern for accurate self-representation. During the early republic, that feeling was heightened by sensibility's idolization of the "feeling heart" and the self-admiration it allowed, the possibility of a new self through academy education, but above all by the process of emotion work itself. Those diarists with the strongest sense of self—Guion, May, Heath, and Van Dyke—felt the freedom to express the greatest outrage. In articulating their anger, or "losing it," they were in fact finding who they were.

By and large, the imagined world of sensibility discouraged anger: its language offered few words, poses, or values that facilitated anger, which it deflected into tears. As Sarah Connell "participated" in others' experiences and wept with sympathy, her boundaries of self eroded, and with them the assertiveness anger required. Sensibility recognized self by encouraging self-admiration, but the self that Connell admired was sympathetic, not confrontational. Unlike sentimental sadness, which society could indulge since it resulted in tears and offered no challenge to feminine roles, anger expanded the self in potentially dangerous ways: it suggested action, was based on entitlement, and implicated power. Precisely because of these qualities, although American culture ascribed emotion to women and reason to men, it saw anger, like sexual passion, as masculine, as if it were not a feeling but a right.[8] Sarah Connell recognized this when she invoked sensibility to avoid anger and called on what her culture regarded as safe, feminine feelings: "Let no angry thoughts, or words this day destroy my peace," she prayed in 1808. "May sweet serenity diffuse itself over my mind. Come, mild content and Heavenly innocence take up your residence in Sarah's breast, assist her in her journey through life."[9]

When sentimentalists gave way to "angry thoughts, or words" despite such prayers, they castigated themselves, especially if their anger was over a personal affront. Initially, Mary B. Howell could not resist recording her outrage when her purported friends treated her poorly, but she quickly backed off by seeking excuses for them and criticizing herself. When her "gallant" Alcandor dropped her arm and let her walk on while he stopped to talk with Mary's friend Agnes, Howell wrote, "I was not *vex'd*, yet I *did not like it*. I knew it was not from *ignorance*, for he seems (as Agnes says) Perfect master of *etiquette*." Mary and Alcandor reconciled, yet a few days later he and Agnes "exultingly" swept past her, and Mary went home *"beauless."* Reporting "I *never* was more hurt at any neglect in my life, to receive it from those we love, is doubly cutting," Howell was gratified to receive Agnes's explanatory letter and decided that her own behavior was wrong: she "had been passionate" and impulsive, and her "*feelings* had far outstripped [her] *reason*—." Howell identified her feelings as both "envy" and "'*swoln malice*,'" which she hoped her love for Agnes would overcome.[10] At the heart of her anger was her conviction that Alcandor and Agnes had not acted as who she thought they were: her friends.

Nevertheless, even within the world of sensibility, diarists found room for voicing anger, provided they could link their feelings to some larger sentimental ideal. For example, since sensibility praised sympathy, women felt entitled to express anger on behalf of others. When a deceptive lover seduced and abandoned her close companion, for example, Sarah Connell clearly thought wrong had been done: "how many have fallen victims to the baseness of those who call themselves lords of the Creation," she expostulated with uncharacteristic sarcasm. It was the responsibility of "every virtuous female [to] show her detestation of the libertine by wholly renouncing his society." But having derided male behavior, Connell, like Howell, drew back from such unwomanly outrage. She concluded by accepting a male acquaintance's judgment that through associating with these men, women "seemed to encourage such conduct" and were themselves at fault.[11] Sympathy also led Connell to periodically enter male territory by criticizing Federalists, but she clearly spoke on behalf of her Jeffersonian father. When Federalists "assaulted" and "abused [him] in a shameful manner," she reported, "It was with difficulty that I could suppress the resentment I felt at the base treatment my Father had received."[12]

In a more active expansion of their emotional repertoire, women became angry at those challenging sensibility itself. In doing so, they simultaneously asserted their identity as women of sensibility, challenged proscriptions against anger, and claimed their right to judge others.

Since their purpose, if not their feelings, remained sentimental, they felt entitled to upend the usual feeling rules. For example, a "vulgar, indelicate" speech on divorce "disgusted" Sarah Connell. Similarly, a Mr. Burnside, who had previously won her favor by noticing her "literary acquirements," made her "very angry" and his "foolish behavior nearly disgusted" her, when he proved not to be the gentleman she had thought him to be.[13] For Patty Rogers, sensibility limited her anger at men, but freed her to criticize women, who were supposed to embody sentiment. She could not bring herself to fault either Portius or Philammon; anger would have disrupted her sentimental idyll of love and friendship. By concluding that these men were "*never* designed" for her, she absolved them of all responsibility and undercut her right to anger.[14] Rogers also refrained from expressing any hostility to Elizabeth Brooks, whom Portius had chosen over her, but she dropped all pretext to tranquil sensibility when faced with Philammon's choice, Tabitha Gilman. Even then, she sought sentimental high ground by criticizing Gilman for her lack of gentility rather than for her romantic triumph. She called Tabitha "a person peculiarly disagreeable to me—not from any injury she ever did me, but there is a certain something in her manners with which I am ever disgusted—."[15] By using the word "disgust," Rogers and Connell identified their feelings as an expression of class superiority, of which sensibility was a part, and thereby asserted their own gentility.

So strong was Patty Rogers's desire to appear as a woman of sensibility, that she turned her anger on herself when other women revealed her own sentimental failings and literally outclassed her. These rivals disturbed her fully as much as Elizabeth and Tabitha. At a July 1785 dinner, a Mrs. Gilman exemplified the "ease" sentimentalists admired; with Mrs. Fisher, they comprised "two of the *Sweetest Women* in the World." "Never did I feel so *little* and *insignificant*, I felt less than the *least* of all beings—. . . . I could not have placed myself at a greater disadvantage than with two such *angelic forms & minds*—." Having combined reluctant admiration and envy, Rogers went on to attack herself for not appearing as she would wish herself to be: "O! this cruel diffidence of mine, which so much embarrasses me! & renders me contemptable in the eyes of others!" Wishing the dinner had been at her own home, where she might have appeared to better advantage, Rogers expressed her chagrin with a remarkable image: "I could have bit my finger ends off—," she wrote.[16] Later, Rogers again used this phrase when she "reflect[ed] on a little *manuvere*" with Philammon and his new love.[17] In this metaphor of self-mutilation, we finally hear Patty Rogers's distinctive voice rather than an echo of sentimental literature; that voice was angry, and its concern was identity.

Audience also discouraged expression of anger, but just as diarists found room within sensibility for outrage, Litchfield Female Academy students worked hard to assert themselves without directly challenging school rules. Open to instructors and classmates, student diaries comprised an official story of allowable student feelings, which were not to include anger. "Avoid anger, Wrath and evil speaking," declared the 1814 "Rules of the School and [Boardinghouse] Family," which established the identifying emotions for proper young ladies.[18] For girls such as Mary Wilbor, this meant that they criticized boardinghouse companions in their journals, but then offered soft words or refused to name names, an oblique practice which enabled them to vent their feelings without losing credit marks. Caroline Chester proved unexpectedly skilled in devising ways to skirt Academy feeling rules. Besides facing her usual academic humiliations, she found herself accused of "improper" behavior when she and some friends spent a holiday at Little Island; when her companions got wet from wading they removed their shifts to dry them, and then hurriedly dressed when they saw some men a quarter mile off. Caroline, who had remained clothed, endured a visit from Sarah Pierce, a stiff note from John Brace, and the knowledge that her behavior was "represented by some as a most flagrant breach of propriety & delicacy." Although Brace assured them they "had been *careless* only & not improper," he couched his forgiveness with so many warnings and intimations that they needed to "restore themselves" to his good opinion, that Caroline swore she would never go near the island for the next century. In describing this incident, Caroline expressed no resentment or anger, but she asserted herself in the length of her entries, her persistent deflection of accusation, and her concluding declaration, "I rejoice yes heartily rejoice that we all possess *clear consciences*."[19] In doing so, she subtly conveyed her outrage at the Academy's misrepresentation of her self.

In far more direct prose, Laura Maria Wolcott cheerfully admitted that "the up[s] + downs in my temper are as frequent + precipitous as the hills between Litchfield + Hartford." She was easily the most angry of Litchfield Academy diarists and as such anticipates the outrage Mary Guion, Rachel Van Dyke, Susan Heath, and Abigail May expressed.

Declaring herself "not in the habit of saying what I do not feel," she indulged "'the great *I*'" and ignored the audience that constrained Caroline Chester.[20] Wolcott vented her anger against three groups: those who misrepresented themselves, those who misrepresented women generally, and those who misrepresented her. Laura devoted her sharpest language to the classmate who apparently cheated on her exams, and who in that sense had represented herself as "a good scholar" when she was not. Laura was "provoked" at "Misses M. B. + B" who "reflect[ed] a dishonour on the whole sex," but she also "despise[d] . . . from the bottom of my heart" the *"contemptible puppy"* who wrote "against young ladies" in the paper. Already sensitive to the nuances of male-female relations, she ridiculed Litchfield's local balls: "how foolish it seems to have a parcel of young men + women *dress* + look as *amiable* + *pretty* as they can, go into a room + as soon as a man draws a stick across some strings all hop up + caper as if for their *very* life. . . . there they stay half tired to death + jump up + down for 8 hours. *How perfectly absurd."*[21] Wolcott was equally capable of outrage at how others perceived her. In her favorite phrase, she "despise[d] from the bottom of my heart" the girl who broke into a trunk to read Laura's notes, and in another canine metaphor she dismissed as "impudent *dogs*" the men watching her undignified attempt to struggle through the snow.[22] Yet like other Litchfield Academy girls, Laura often used initials or asterisks to mask the names of those she criticized, and, as she admitted, she was never angry long.[23]

The anger of sentimentalists and academy girls was compromised in that they shaped it to fit their audience or justified it with an ideological ideal. In that sense they did not feel their own needs entitled them to anger. But Mary Guion, Abigail May, Rachel Van Dyke, and Susan Heath had little patience with such limitations and engaged in criticism, sarcasm, and invective with much greater freedom. Yet all four were extensively exposed to sensibility and could recite sentimental phrases on appropriate occasions, such as when gazing at the moon or contemplating suffering. Moreover, all four wrote with an audience in mind, although it varied with each diarist. Unlike the case at Litchfield Academy, peers or near-peers, rather than supervisory figures, comprised their readers. Susan Heath's mother and two sisters kept diaries, borrowed and read out loud from friends' diaries, and took turns composing segments of family letters; given her family's enthusiastic exchange of manuscripts, Heath surely expected that relatives would someday read her own voluminous journals.²⁴ Mary Guion alternately feared that someone would read her diary, and hoped that it would find an audience. She went to great lengths to assure that no one would see her diary and typically wrote when her family was asleep: "am siting by the fire all a lone writing expecting every moment some intruder to discover me & expose my work adieu," she scribbled nervously. Yet she frequently prefaced entries with "if ever there was a reader to this," and occasionally invited the reader to guess her dance partner or her feelings. These references seem not to have been solely literary devices, for she allowed her adored older brother James to read her journal and was gratified that he "seemd to aplaud it."²⁵ While Guion's audience was only occasional, Abigail May began her diary as a letter to "my dear Lucretia [Goddard]," the friend she left in Boston as May traveled to Ballston Springs. May repeatedly referred to it as her "journal" and employed regular entries, but she also addressed Lucretia, and toward its end May joked about publishing her diary because her friends said it was *"too good to be lost."*²⁶ Rachel Van Dyke of New Brunswick, New Jersey, wrote even more publicly; she shared her 1810–11 diary with not only a female friend but a young male teacher who was a peer in that he shared his own journal with her.²⁷ But despite the limits implicit in sensibility and an audience, Guion, May, Van Dyke, and Heath lambasted those they disliked and seem to have taken a certain pleasure in choosing cutting words.

What Mary Guion, Abigail May, Rachel Van Dyke, and Susan Heath shared was a distinctive voice and a heightened sense of self. Each used sentimental language, but that language never dominated them. Each acknowledged a potential audience, but that audience did not limit them—and in Van Dyke's case invited her to overcome limitations. Each struggled to develop the greater autonomy which Linda Grasso has associated with anger. Most importantly, each felt a sense of entitlement to her feelings and used those feelings to challenge the status quo and the disposition of power. Without this voice and sense of self, unassertive sentimentalists such as Sarah Connell literally spoke a different language than these four women. Her friend seduced and abandoned, Connell briefly expostulated against men as "Lords of creation," a sarcasm that she borrowed from her reading. May employed the same phrase, but added her own vivid words: "those high and mighty Lords of the Creation as they call themselves will pick their teeth and stare confidently in your face not heeding the confusion it occasions— —."²⁸

With this pithy insult, Abigail May asserted ownership of both her language and her anger, but turned them against others, rather than herself, as Patty Rogers had done.

Mary Guion's diary illustrates her struggles to develop the self-assertion and confident deployment of language which accompanied expression of anger. As we have seen, Guion was mainly concerned with discerning whom she loved and who loved her, a process that required her to distinguish true feeling from duplicity and assert her judgment of others. During the early years of her courtship, she found this extremely difficult to do; her diary conveys this initial uncertainty in its language and reluctance to identify her mounting outrage. Between 1800 and 1805, as men deceived her, Guion reported herself "offended," mortified, resentful, "exasperated," disappointed, "vex'd," "perplexd," "displeas'd," and "mad," and regularly called men deceivers and sycophants, but she did not engage in the vivid insults May relished and could not bring herself to attack her objects in person at all.[29] Often she could not face her own feelings, excused duplicitous men, left the room, or refused to talk to them.[30] The less entitled she felt, the more difficult it was for her to express anger. Upset that Jotham Smith had teased her about her complexion, toyed with her affections, and repeatedly misled her, she used her diary to equivocate over what to feel and do:

> It hurt my pride to much to [tell] him know that I thout myself neglected by him & I [thought] it might perhaps hurt his [pride] as much to let him know I thot no more of him, so I said I had not thot mu[ch] about it for my part; well he said he had but that b[usiness] intruded. he made a many apology of that kind—but [he] waited on me very Genteally. we had a fine Ball—he began to talk of another fortnight [for his visit]. I told him I thot hed much better say a month. then I should not think [it] so strange if he did forget to come [as he had before]. I know not what to th[ink] of him weathere to believe his tales or not. I had realy a great mind to be even In the neglect of his visit but as I went with him [to the ball] that would no way answer but why should I blame him who I dare Say acted according to the Dictates of his passions & why should I blame him for his honesty?[31]

Mary Guion's initial reluctance to express her own angry "passions" sprang from several sources. Her tendency to see herself within a group context defused personal animosity, especially with women, while her identity as simple, rustic, and honest, in contrast to male flatterers, seems to have temporarily cast her in the role of unwitting dupe to men. Guion's acceptance of conventional sex roles also inhibited her anger: she criticized a woman who "seemd very talkative and much redier to give her Opinion than any one were to ask it," and, like other women, she worried that men might judge all females by one. As late as 1804, she wrote, "I often have unpleasant reflections from my free way in discourse."[32] Guion may have been proud of her public exhibition prize, but she was more often embarrassed by her limited education, and as her entry on Smith reveals, her spelling and punctuation were poor, despite her extensive reading. Especially in her early years of diary keeping, she criticized her journal repeatedly as "Silly Simple nonsence" which gave "but a very imperfec't idea to what I should wish it might be." "I really wish I was in possession of an education or a geniues sufficient to inscribe something that would afford if to no one els' to myself a real pleasure and satisfaction, but for those two or three last sheets I can find no sense in them, and they serve only to expose my ignorance but the less I practice the worse I write and of late I have been very littl in the habit of it," she lamented in 1805.[33] Without verbal authority, she found it difficult to articulate anger either in person or in writing.

As Mary Guion became a more experienced diarist, she overcame these inhibitions and used language as a tool to assert her anger. The more she wrote, and the more men deceived her, the more self-confident she became in her prerogative to judge others and define her own feelings. Just as her sister Sally's tragedy helped Mary choose well in courtship, it enabled her to voice anger authoritatively. Mary Guion's suspicions of Isaac Sarles appeared early in her sister's marriage. Soon after their 1803 wedding, Isaac wrote Mary a letter in which he praised his new sister-in-law's beauty. Guion was "highly displas'd," sent a hot tempered rebuke, and fumed, "I hope there is young men enough left yet to write love letters without putting Married Men to that trouble."[34] Over the next few years, Mary realized how appearances had deceived Sally. The combination of Isaac's meanness toward her sister, her own experience of male duplicity, and her growth as a diarist made possible the outrage Mary Guion finally voiced in her June 14, 1807, entry. A neighbor had laid "violent hands" upon Sally, who was then well advanced in her third pregnancy. True to form, Isaac blamed Sally for the attempted rape. In a fury, Guion wrote: "How can he be so stupidly ignorant as to wish to wound the fealings [of] the only woman that ever loved him, and on one of the most delicate Subjects, that of honour. indeed he has so little to boast of himself that he would willingly bring her upon a level with him, but, God forbid, for she is a most Virtuous woman and Oh! how much do I pity her hard lot—!" Guion quickly moved from compassion for her sister to a general attack on husbands who wielded power over their wives rather than being loving friends:

> is it possible that People should wish to render their lives uncomfortable by finding fault with a mere nothing, or does human nature act so contrary to reason as that Man should be pleased to se the person who his better Judgment chose from all others, dayly grieving and dragging out a miserable existance merely to show that power he has over her by useing unpleasant and passionate expressions that he would not to any other person. even that proves them cowards, for being well ashured that their wife is too much their friend to seek for any revenge it is only to her he dares talk thus unbounded. much sooner would I meet with Death than live with a person of that description.[35]

This passage is as extraordinary for its masterly prose as it is for its rage; both stand in contrast to her awkward equivocations over Jotham Smith. By 1807, Guion had attained the self-definition and confidence that enabled her to put anger into words and question male power. At the same time, she deftly met her culture's expectations of womanly behavior by couching her critique as an attack on Isaac's anger, "unpleasant and passionate expressions" and "unbounded" talk, while Guion herself observed boundaries in expressing her rage. That this was her sister's tragedy enabled her to maintain feminine concern for others while voicing her own fears. Moreover, Mary Guion was not out of control like the "passionate" Sarles. Aware that public revelation of her feelings would further endanger Sally, she apparently confined her animosity to her journal. But there is no mistaking either her rage or her moral and verbal authority as she denounced Isaac Sarles, and her confidence in expressing that anger bolstered her judgment in choosing a better man to marry.

While Mary Guion gained self-understanding through the dangers of courtship, Abigail May probed her character as she struggled with illness, a process that led her to express rage with less hesitancy than any other diarist in this study. To do so, she had to overcome not lack of verbal authority, but her training in sensibility. Abigail May quoted Mrs. Radcliffe and Oliver Goldsmith, admired men of feeling, found melancholy "pleasurable," and, much like Sarah Connell, mused on rustic happiness: "I could be happy in these secluded shades—with this proviso—let me have *those I love* with me the rest of the world I could abandon without a sigh." May aspired to sensibility's feminine ideal and greatly admired women who possessed both "a highly cultivated mind and a most feeling heart" and who were "unaffect'd," "well bred and accomplished." Like Elizabeth Cranch, May felt it was her duty to believe that whatever was, "tis best. tis certainly our duty to endeavour to think so—."[36] Yet in the midst of sentimental rhetoric, a subversive note surfaced. As a patient at Ballston Springs, with an unknown disorder that would soon kill her, the twenty-four-year-old May found both sensibility and rationalism inadequate, much like Sarah Connell facing her family's economic collapse. "I am dissatisfied with myself," she complained; "you will say that is nothing new but I find I am less able to bear affliction with fortitude at a time when I expected to shew the most. it has till now been my opinion that a good mind well stor'd was equal to every calamity—either my theory, or my mind is deficient." Typically, she indulged in a good cry and then derided it as "a pretty stupid employment."[37] Buffeted by worries, she found contentment elusive. "[Y]esterday morn was a severe trial for me," she wrote. "I however undertook to curb my feelings. I determined to get them under command, but they revenged themselves, by giving me a most distressing head ache."[38]

Residence at a spa full of strangers, many of them vacationing rather than ill, made May's situation worse and impelled the anger behind her entries: just as Guion worried that Jotham Smith had misrepresented her, May yearned to be understood as she really was but found herself repeatedly misread. May first described herself as "downright angry" over a false rumor that a Mr. H. was her "intended," and that they were pitied because her illness prevented marriage; "every one is on the look out for something to tell—," she complained, not for the last time.[39] In another instance, people gossiped that she and her doctor were romantically linked, robbing their friendship of its innocence and freedom. "I am ready to quarrel with the world, or rather its inhabitants, some of them, for making it necessary for us to act a part foreign to our hearts," she expostulated, in words that echoed Sarah Connell's, but which moved only May to anger. She found the springs "a censorious place," in which women were either "complemented with the credit of speeches we never made" or "severely . . . criticized by the Beaux." "[I]f a Lady is reserved she is no company, they 'had as leave set by a mile stone,'" she derided them, "if chatty and social, why 'how dearly she loves the men'—these very words have been used."[40] May felt they not only misrepresented her but treated her as a fool: "buz, buz, on every side our ears are assailed with compliments—addressed equally to the old young ugly or handsome—tis the *ladies must be flatter'd.* tis the part of the gentlemen to administer the *soothing essence.*"[41]

May resolved this misrepresentation by trying to associate herself with the most genteel people at Ballston Springs, but discovered that many presented a false front. Just as Mary Guion raged over misleading suitors, May's anger mounted as she experienced repeated deceptions and disappointments. "[P]ermit me to introduce to your notice Mr. Oliver Pain—tall finely shaped, good eyes, and teeth—a very handsome man—what would you have more. alas! what a pity it is so fine a casket should be empty—or filld only with trifles as if that nature claped on the cover and forgot to put in the brains— he however is very polite to the ladies, has great discernment in finding taste and elegance (in himself)," she wrote with relish. "[H]e walks and dances well and pretends to any quantity of sentiment—I got engaged in a most ludicrous conversation with him in the aft[ernoon] and had I been ill natur'd I might have gratified my propensity for ridicule to advantage, the 'sublime and beautiful' passed in review before us of which he apparently thought himself the epitome—." May had indeed been "ill natur'd" enough to ridicule him and admitted to having "confute[d]" him, although she felt "ashamed of a victory over so weak an opponent."[42] May was equally savage in her critique of Mr. Fell, whom she found so disgusting that she would not sit by him. She was kinder to a Mr. C., who quoted Thomson's *Seasons* to her "with much theatric gesture and *killing* glances" and was amused when he forgot his lines, but declared she "disliked his freedom" with other women.[43]

Unlike Mary Guion, who confined her aspersions to men, Abigail May did not spare the women at Ballston Springs. She aimed her angry expostulations at females who presented themselves as genteel, yet whose vulgar physicality undercut their sensibility: Miss Kissam, who was too voluptuous and indelicate, and a Mrs. Amory, whose "riding dress shew[ed] her shape to all possible advantage. . . . nothing was quite good enough to go down her delicate throat at dinner. . . . adding to all that, a supercilious and contemptuous dropping of the eye when any one pass'd, effectually disgusted our social party—."[44] May enjoyed a warm and loving relationship with Lucretia Goddard, her diary's reader, but that did not deter her from attacking women she did not like.

Above all, Abigail May's fierce unmasking of her contemporaries paralleled her struggle to assert and protect her dying self. An earlier 1796 travel diary, which May wrote when she was confident her health would improve, is on the whole sunny and lacks the edges she showed four years later, when she sensed her imminent erasure. By 1800, May found her thoughts "invariably revert back, either to scenes of distress, or past pleasures, which never more must be mine." She longed "to feel myself oh! my God—I was saying *as I used to* but that cannot be—."[45] In some ways, May felt she was already gone: she reflected on her "own *dead* heart which uninterested and uninspir'd is frequently wandering far from the gay scene, and takes no share in the profusion of fine speeches." Mortality instigated impatience with those who misunderstood her and impelled her search for genuine friends: "what a strange animal am I—how much the sport of others . . . here all I say is *laugh'd* at."[46] When the genteel and loving Mrs. Western befriended her, May found it gave her "considerable consequence in the eyes of all," a consequence she judged "pathetic . . . but better than none."[47] Expressing anger was one way to preserve her self. May repeatedly recognized that she was losing control of both her emotions and her life: "my heart frequently runs away with my pen—," she wrote. She knew she had "worked" herself "into a pet with men," and admitted "I cannot when alone command my thoughts."[48] In calling herself "your fond faithful, but foolishly and often wrongfully thinking and acting Abby," May came close to apologizing for her behavior, yet she also wrote, "'no power on earth can effectually subdue or even repress the feelings of a heart like mine—.'"[49] Almost invariably, her need to express anger took precedence over any considerations of emotional control.

Abigail May's diary displayed an unusual degree of anger, but was her public face as angry as her private writing? The occasion on which she recorded openly insulting someone—the quotation which heads this chapter—presents an ambiguous case. In this incident, Bowers was sufficiently aware of May's dislike to ask why she "hated" and "despise[d]" him. The fact that "all the ladies" regarded Bowers "coolly," may have freed May to speak her mind "in *downright* terms," but it is difficult to say what thoughts she expressed, for she wrote, "I did not deny say [*sic*] that I despised him." Did she not deny that she despised him or did she not say that she despised him? That slip of the pen both obscures her behavior toward Bowers and captures women's ambivalence toward the public expression of anger. Yet he disbelieved May enough to ask her to dance, and, despite her dislike, she complied lest she anger him. Throughout her diary, May expressed the desire to speak her heart, but here she recognized society's limits on female anger in public and feared going too far. She made up for this by asserting her true feelings in writing: "I hate, I detest him, and if I am wrong! why then I am sorry—."[50] As a "transcript of [her] feelings," her journal provided a private place where she could express her least "feminine" emotions and in doing so helped her behave more circumspectly in public. The written self she left us may well express greater rage than did May's public persona. In that sense, her diary operated as a backstage, where she could indulge emotions she could not fully voice before the people she despised. Nonetheless, she went farther than any other diarist in this study in publicly conveying her animosity.

If Abigail May was reluctant to insult people to their face, she did not hesitate to deride them behind their backs: she mailed her journal to her friends in Boston, who seem to have delighted in her angry wit. In this regard, May was like Rachel Van Dyke (1793–?) of New Brunswick, New Jersey, who also shared her diary with readers. Beginning her diary at age seventeen, Rachel Van Dyke was no longer a schoolgirl but not quite on the marriage market and rarely attended the balls that entertained courting couples. For her diary, this meant that she was not preoccupied with either marital choice or duplicitous men. Instead, she understood herself as a young woman pursuing intellectual "improvement" beyond the recitations she had endured at Miss Sophia Hay's Young Ladies' School. As her journal began in May, 1810, she was just finishing additional academy work and beginning daily Latin lessons with her teacher, twenty-two-year-old Ebenezer Grosvenor or "Mr. G—," as Rachel called him.[51] In agreeing to this special tutorial, he allowed her into the classics, the archetypal male intellectual domain. Her Latin class also initiated a process of self-revelation: that Van Dyke sought a skill supposedly beyond women's ability, and that Mr. G— thought she could and should learn Latin. A second level of intimacy soon followed. Rachel and her teacher exchanged and wrote comments in each other's journals. As Lucia McMahon has argued,

Rachel and Mr. G— conducted a "romantic readership" in which they established a flirtatious intimacy through exchanging verse, favorite books, and their diaries.[52] In her emotional development, he was far more important than her father, who played a minor role, or her mother, whom she rarely mentioned.

Like Litchfield Academy students, Rachel Van Dyke undoubtedly composed her diary with an eye to her instructor. But while Sarah Pierce sought to vindicate women's minds by teaching intellectual skills but enforcing femininity, Mr. G— seems to have been quite a different audience. As her Latin teacher and a man representing reason, Mr. G— signaled that the usual bounds of female behavior did not apply to Rachel, and he fostered the intellectual seriousness she could not find elsewhere: Mr. G—'s "sentiments on the female sex," she noted, were "generous in the extreme, and he is respectful, lively, and unassuming."[53] He joined her in deploring those who did not understand her desire to learn, compared her writing to Addison and Sterne, read her diary carefully enough that he was able to compose several entries in her own style (a dead-on imitation), and asked her to judge his own journals.[54] With this audience, Rachel felt free to acknowledge sensibility, express her love of learning, and be critical and sarcastic. In sociological terms, she created a "scene" backstage that few saw except her teacher. Her select group of readers witnessed her integrated self: simultaneously a woman and an intellectual.[55]

For a female of the early republic, these identities inherently clashed. Van Dyke repeatedly conveyed her sense of this: although her parents apparently supported her pursuit of a masculine education, she knew that men scorned female intellectuality. "[Men] should converse with us as if we were *conversable* beings, blessed with abilities to reflect and acquire knowledge as well as themselves—," she complained, and "not consider us as pretty, fashionable simpletons."[56] Female friends sneered at her ambitions as well. Like all the women in this study, Van Dyke was well aware that gossip flourished about her.[57] She felt "surrounded by friends who are but little acquainted with your studies, who think you waste your time in attending to them and who take but little trouble about your improvement."[58] When Van Dyke found a Greek book at her friend Maria's house and asked her if she were studying Greek, Maria "walked away from me with a scornful lip—turning it up as if she tasted something disagreeable—and said very emphatically, 'No—I have not *genius* enough to study any other language but my own,'" a comment which Rachel decided "was evidently meant for me."[59] When Rachel tried to teach her cousin Betsy, much as Mr. G— taught her, Rachel's sister Lydia made fun of her by posting on her door: "Reading and sprigging *teached* here at fourteen pence a week—Young Ladies who learn *manners* must pay two pence more." To avoid such animosity, Van Dyke did not tell her friend Susan Wallace that she was studying Latin "lest it should look like pedantry," and hesitated to reveal her botanical and chemical studies.[60]

With Mr. G—'s support, Rachel Van Dyke persisted in her efforts to integrate her identities as a woman and an intellectual. In juxtaposing studying and visiting, she contrasted typical male and female activities, and unhesitatingly opted for her books. "I declare going to school is far more pleasant than visiting," she wrote, and pronounced herself "supremely happy" during her tutorial. As for visiting, Rachel deplored "talking nonsense" and felt "vexed to be obliged to waste so much time" with others. "I have a better opportunity to improve now than it is likely I shall ever have again and I don't wish to spend it in visiting or amusements."[61] Throughout her diary, Van Dyke cherished having a room of her own, where she could study, think, and above all be herself.[62]

As a woman on the boundaries of acceptable female behavior, Rachel Van Dyke was acutely sensitive to issues of integrity and misrepresentation. Her ideal was Mr. G—, since "he certainly is what he appears to be." With him, she felt the freedom to "talk to him with less restraint—with less fear that what I say should be repeated—than to any other friend I have—and I believe—nay I am sure he does the same to me."[63] Her diary charts her continuous search for a female friend with whom she could enjoy similar freedom. As a woman not yet contemplating marriage but seeking entrance to male intellectual preserves and writing for a man's eyes, Van Dyke rarely criticized men. Instead, her diary is striking for the frequency with which she attacked women. Moreover, unlike most Litchfield Academy students whom school rules constrained, she criticized women as individuals; in particular, she criticized women who pretended to be who they were not instead of being true to themselves, as Rachel tried to be. Should she mistake her female friends and reveal herself to them, she feared exposure, ridicule, and rejection; she knew her true self was unacceptable to many people. In time, Van Dyke would come to trust her friend Maria Smith and let Maria read her diaries as well, but Rachel's response to those who disappointed her was an anger which she articulated with verbal finesse learned from books.

Van Dyke despised affectation in women. She dismissed half the girls in her boarding school as "conceited or so affected they can scarcely move," and singled out a Mrs. Linn, formerly "a shabby, ignorant little school girl" who now pretended to a gentility and education she did not possess. "There is nothing provokes me so much as ignorance, affectation and vanity combined," Rachel wrote. "When she talks, she lisps—winks to make her black eyes look sparkling—twists her mouth—and draws herself into so many various positions that she really makes herself ridiculous. . . . I seated myself by her and entered into conversation with her to see if she had taken as much pains with her mind as her dress—I verily believe she has no mind. When she expressed herself to me in language and ideas which you could plainly see had been acquired by conversation only—not by reading—and in that lisping, formal affected manner—I could have quarreled with her most willingly."[64] Mr. G—'s importance in establishing her ideals is apparent in her dismissal of Frances Deare: "A pretty face and an affected delicacy and refinement is all I know that she has to boast of, and I join with Mr. G— and say, I hate the face, however fair That carries an affected air."[65] With a nastiness Abigail May would have appreciated, Van Dyke laughed at a Miss Gault, "a pretty piece of affectation or awkwardness. I don't know what it is, or she twists and turns herself in so strange a manner that brother Augustus might well observe as he once did—'That girl has been to the school of Deformity.'"[66]

Rachel Van Dyke's contempt for affectation was linked with her desire to be a learned woman. Mrs. Linn had "no mind," she complained, and Miss Gault attended "the school of Deformity" rather than of true learning. Van Dyke voiced this same concern with Jane Dumont, a promising friend who conversed "unreservedly" and "possesses a fine understanding and a heart generous, noble, and tender." "She is scientific, indeed, as Mr. G— says and I say, she is an honor to her sex," Rachel initially wrote, "I hope I may be her equal one day or other."[67] Jane professed great love for her, and Rachel dreamed that they would "together, *climb the hill of science*," spent the night exchanging confidences with Dumont, and "showed her my books, opened my desk to her and let her read some of my papers," as if Jane were Mr. G—.[68] But Van Dyke also felt that Dumont was not the "scientific," well-educated woman she hoped for: "the *learned* Miss J[ane] D[umont] . . . will talk to you of her various studies—as long as she thinks you ignorant of them, but as soon as you begin to converse with her on the very subjects of which she boasted a knowledge she will gradually draw herself off and change the topic of conversation."[69] Jane neither studied hard nor made allowances for other girls, like Rachel, who lacked her opportunities for education. Envy may have colored Rachel's reaction: at one point she complained that Jane "should not talk so much of her studies—it makes her look so ostentatious."[70]

Van Dyke also questioned whether Jane Dumont was a woman of true sensibility. Although her identity centered on intellectuality, as a well-brought-up young woman, Rachel was well versed in the sentimental standards: the poems of Edward Young, James Thomson, and William Cowper; Zimmermann's essays, which she cited repeatedly; and Goethe's *The Sorrows of Young Werther*, over which she wept.[71] Van Dyke herself composed sentimental poetry which was published in a local newspaper; using the pen name "Augusta," she appeared publicly as a versifying woman of sensibility. But in her diary she also deprecated novel reading and favored "instructive books" such as history and science; unlike Sarah Connell, she infrequently used sentimental language or immersed herself in sentimental tableaux, and the excesses of sensibility offended her love of reason.[72] Rachel attacked Jane Dumont for writing her just such "flowery stuff, apologies for neglect, and protestations of eternal love and friendship." Even worse was the fact that Jane "is the same *true and faithful friend* to nearly half the girls she meets." "I detest deceit, and I begin to think all her friendship for me is mere deception," Rachel wrote angrily.[73] Van Dyke intuited that Jane's sensibility was really a performance: "She dazzles, she flatters me by her romantic expressions—she knows how to lull prudence to rest, to wind the feelings to the highest pitch of sensibility, to touch the unsuspecting chord of the soul, to steal your confidence and then leave you to regret it. Yes to regret it—for most sincerely do I regret some things that I have told her."[74] Rachel came to suspect Jane's letters were "downright flattery" and, while she found she "could not help admiring her compliments, how well they were *turn'd*—composed—how high she soared—," she doubted their sincerity.[75]

Rachel Van Dyke knew that her angry feelings were socially unacceptable. Her "dear*est*" brother Augustus, older by five years, told her "that some of my remarks on characters were rather unnecessary and too severe." Since she respected him, we might expect her to defer to him, but she did not. "If I thought that my remarks would ever do anyone—the least injury—my pen nor my tongue should never reveal them—," she wrote, "but as it is my intention to keep my journal as sacred as my thoughts, I see no hurt in writing what I think. And if I am severe on those whom I dislike, I trust that I do equal justice to the opposite characters."[76] Rachel respected her brother enough to let him read her journal, but did not allow him to limit what she wrote. It would be interesting to see her reaction if Mr. G— had corrected her penchant for invective, but he never did. Instead, he usually did not respond to her sarcastic portrayals of women at all. At one point, he agreed with her criticism of Abby Condict's deceit and imputed Condict's faults to her efforts to be feminine, as if he and Rachel were males discussing another sex.[77] With this encouragement, Van Dyke showed no hesitation or shame in expressing anger, especially at women, in her journal's pages. When she finally exchanged diaries with Maria, and Maria read what Rachel had written about her, Maria "unjustly accused me of cruelty of wounding her feelings purposely, when in reality such a thing was far from my thoughts," Van Dyke reported, but remained unperturbed. "But—the dear girl—I forgive her this injustice, for perhaps had I been in her situation, I should have thought exactly as she did."[78] However, that freedom in expressing anger may have stopped with her diary; like Mary Guion, Van Dyke apparently did not directly convey her angry feelings to any of the people she disliked.

In expressing their anger, Mary Guion, Abigail May, and Rachel Van Dyke all aimed their fire at those outside their immediate families: Guion criticized deceitful suitors and her brother-in-law, May raged against Ballston Springs' visitors, and Van Dyke sneered at female friends and acquaintances. Susan Heath (1795–1874) of Brookline, Massachusetts, went further: she dared to direct her fury at her own father and brother. Her voluminous diaries, running from 1812 to 1874, contain more intrafamilial vituperation than any other in this sample. In voicing this anger, Susan Heath charts the far boundaries of allowable feminine feeling for her time.

In a society in which God and George Washington figured as fathers, anger toward a male parent was deemed blasphemous, a verbal form of patricide. But just as sentimentalists justified their anger by appealing to sensibility's ideals, Heath couched her feelings in the language of social convention. Living in Brookline, a small town bordering mercantile Boston, she recognized that consumption reflected the class status of the head of household and established him as a good provider. Heath began her diary in 1812 on her seventeenth birthday with traditional hopes for "improving" herself, but soon turned to improving Ebenezer Heath by sarcastically contrasting the father he should be with who he in fact was: a wealthy but mean-spirited tightwad.[79] "I asked my *kind, affectionate* Father for *one dollar* before I went from home—of his generous heart [he] refused me," she taunted in 1813. Sometimes he indulged his children, she admitted, but "if a trifling want is expressed—like a necessary article of cloathing—it seems at once to banish to an *immeasurable distance* all his good humour & affection," she observed on another occasion.[80] A shopping trip to Boston only reminded her of what her father would not allow: "to have our eyes pained with beholding articles innumerable, cheap & absolutely indispensable & yet through Pa's extreme & unheard of parsimony [to] be utterly unable to purchase any thing. People with such inconsistent dispositions ought to live single in some remote corner of the earth & never associate but with people of their own cast & not involve a large family in the mortification of appearing so mean."[81] Susan Heath's father repeatedly lectured the family on "Poverty—extravagance—waste—economy" to her derision.

> While we are blessed with life & health we have the comfortable prospect of the frequent recurrence of *such scenes*—for while we live we must have wants—& *that* is the *tremendous evil* here—O the ingratitude of man! it is incredible what flinty hearts some people have! nothing but a miracle can effect any change—.... Oh! that [God] would see fit to exercise his power upon one—who is sadly unpardonably deficient in performing the Sacred duties devolving upon the Father of a family—upon one whom by the *excessive parsimony* of his disposition embitters the lives of his family— — — — —.[82]

To add insult to injury, despite his insistence on economy, Heath was himself a lazy and poor manager.[83]

Ebenezer Heath challenged the family's gentility not just through his refusal to purchase appropriate goods, but through a far worse failing, his lack of kindness. While no advocate of "excessive sensibility," Susan Heath was an avid reader who admired the tenderness, ease, and benevolence associated with the genteel, qualities notably absent in her father.[84] He was as cheap with feelings as with things, and rendered the entire family miserable through his "inflexible fits," "*loud* reprimand[s]" for complete silence, and creation of *"perpetual anxiety."*[85] "How can any man like to make himself so disagreeable & make his family so uncomfortable—for nothing at all?" his daughter mused. "Strange—unaccountable perversion! such people have their reward however. It is not with the *love* & *affection* of their fellow creatures—but with the opposite feelings!!"[86] Faced with "the inhuman cruelty of the man we call Father," she "tryed to banish painful reflection by reading of the benevolent [novelist Samuel] Richardson—What a father & friend was he!"[87] Fiction, she found, provided a better and truer parent than her own father.

Most painful for Susan Heath was her father's mistreatment of her mother; she found he misrepresented himself as a husband as well as a father. Hannah Heath's "loving & amiable partner," as she derided him, cancelled his wife's pleasure trips, indulged a well-known "predelection for young ladies," and refused his wife delicacies necessary to her health. "[S]he is subject continuously to trials of this kind—not knowing the happiness of having her *spouse* agree with her in opinion or even consult her feelings or wishes upon any occasion—," Heath observed.[88] Like Mary Guion, Susan Heath analyzed the power structure of marriage in republican terms: "Ma was very much disappointed not to go to Boston in the snow—& there was nothing to prevent but the imperious will of her tyrannical spouse. It is surprising how some people like to exercise their power! But such conduct cannot bring them happiness—their conscience upon reflection must sting like an adder—& they are truly more deserving of pity than indignation—. . . instead of securing the esteem & affection of those by whom they are surrounded—they excite the worst feelings of our nature—& are our very abhorrence!"[89]

Susan Heath pushed the boundaries of female feeling not just by despising her father, but by making those feelings known to others. Unlike Mary Guion and Rachel Van Dyke, who largely confined their anger to their diaries, Susan Heath's contempt for her father was obvious to her family—or, at least, to her mother and sisters, since she reported no direct confrontations with her father. In 1817 at age twenty-one, Heath made clear that she was not only much more vocal than these other diarists, but that she yearned to go farther: "I can talk & wish & deplore—but alas! my power extends no farther—it is painfully limited," she observed.[90] Faced with open rebellion, her mother attempted to dissipate Susan's anger through direct and indirect methods. Hannah Heath's own diary reveals her to be a highly religious woman who strove for unquestioning resignation; not once did she express anger in its pages.[91] Susan Heath longed to imitate the "heavenly temper" that her mother modeled for her daughters: "Ma is always the same—always polite—even when her heart is sad & her mind perplexed, sewing & singing all the morning—," she marveled.[92] Recognizing how much her husband had alienated Susan, Hannah Heath actively redirected her daughter's feelings into more acceptable channels. Throughout her diary, Susan Heath described her rage at her father and her mother's subsequent efforts to foster submission. "Pa's behaviour cap'd the climax this eve," Susan Heath wrote after a typical incident in 1827:

> he was in particularly bad humour—& it seemd to be his aim to render us all as uncomfortable as possible—I had my indignation excited till I thought I could not bear it! How I longed for the power of inflicting some punishment for such unheard of ingratitude!! But Ma reasoned me into resignation & calmness by her good sense & pious conversation—She reminded me that if God can bear with such sinful, ungrateful—guilty creatures—we ought certainly to have patience—O the goodness of God! who can understand it? To us in particular he is continually showering down his mercies—& what returns do we make![93]

Despite these efforts, Hannah Heath was not successful in eliminating her daughter's anger; at the time of this account, Susan Heath was thirty-one years old and still struggling with her fury. Well into middle age, she recorded her anger, and although she appended resigned admonitions to each account, they only temporarily dissipated her righteous indignation, which invariably boiled over at the next opportunity. Over time, her contempt included her oldest brother John, a drunken liar who ruined his family; for him, Susan Heath recorded few efforts to control her feelings. Since she believed Ebenezer Heath had mismanaged John, Susan's criticisms of her brother allowed her to express indignation toward their father without regret or apology.[94] Susan Heath's clearest deference to social conventions appears in her practice of couching criticisms of her brother and father in terms of the "indescribable wretchedness" they caused her mother.[95] Although Susan Heath repeatedly attempted the emotion work required to accept her lot, early on she concluded that feelings could not be denied: "when I looked at Ma I felt ashamed—I wondered & admired! but could not imitate!"[96] More shrewdly, she recognized that Hannah's pious feelings provided no solution; her mother "feels—acutely feels—without the power of achieving—," she observed on several occasions.[97] In the calculus of emotion, women's feelings could not make up for the fact that men like John and Ebenezer Heath were unfeeling. Discerning women's essential powerlessness in marriage and determined to support her mother, Susan Heath remained single. With her sisters, she retreated from family problems into what she called a "magic ring," a feminine circle, free of male misbehavior, within which she read, sewed, and pondered her feelings.[98]

In vivid, forthright prose, Mary Guion, Abigail May, Rachel Van Dyke, and Susan Heath demonstrate women's willingness to voice their anger during the early republic. May excoriated both males and females, Guion lambasted duplicitous men, Van Dyke dissected insincere and stupid women, and Heath attacked her father and brother. Unlike the antebellum women writers whom Linda Grasso studied, each faced not an unsympathetic public, but a small, select, and private audience of peers with whom they felt free to break the rules and voice their discontent and judgment of others. Nonetheless, even the most verbally unbuttoned of these women experienced some limitations on their anger. They admired the contentment that sensibility idealized and the ease that gentility encouraged, while consideration for others intruded, even when they expressed anger. All four were reluctant to express their anger to the faces of those they disliked, and, excepting Abigail May's outburst with Mr. Bowers, their diaries seem to have provided a substitute for the angry exchanges they never had. As such, their journals are as much a testament to the public limitations on women's anger as to the freedom they experienced in private.[99]

Women's expression of anger might have been equivocal, but their targets were clear: those who challenged the diarists' identity or misrepresented themselves.[100] Rather than displacing their anger on social inferiors, these female diarists focused on the peers or superiors whose behavior directly challenged them.[101] Since they were single and marriageable, they regularly castigated flattering men, whose false words presented substantial danger. Mary B. Howell was also perturbed by those who presented themselves as her friends and yet treated her poorly, while Rachel Van Dyke had no patience with Jane Dumont's sentimental poses or silly females who aped learning. All these were not who they seemed. Susan Heath concentrated her fire on a more specific target: her father, who represented patriarchy and the well off, but whose behavior was neither paternal nor genteel. These young women were equally concerned with how gossip misrepresented them. Such concerns reveal that these women understood themselves as simultaneously individual and collective. On the one hand, they wanted people to accurately understand who they were as individuals: Abigail May's diary is a cry of pain that people know her as she was, not as they casually assumed, while Mary Guion wanted her neighbors to understand that she was not the kind of woman who used paint. On the other hand, these diarists could not separate themselves from other women; hence, their repeated frustration over how other women behaved.[102] When Abigail May and Rachel Van Dyke expressed anger at other females, they often made fun of them physically, as if women literally embodied their faults, while they located men's faults in words, which men could change at will. In these regards, women's anger, like their sense of self, was ambiguous: it both voiced individual assertion and recognized shared identity.[103]

To assert anger or themselves, women needed a language that allowed emotion full range. If words were cultural tools which women might employ to construct themselves, all words were by no means equally useful to their employers. At a time when the most advanced education depended on memorization and recital, and women copied others' verses into friendship albums and commonplace books, finding words of one's own was difficult. As the language associated with women, sensibility failed to provide a clear rhetoric of anger and individuality. Sarah Connell and Patty Rogers, the most sentimental of these diarists, expressed the least anger and also had the least distinctive voices. To express her fury, Mary Guion had to reject the vocabulary of sensibility and turn to republican ideology, a male discourse, as did Susan Heath. Of these diarists, Abigail May developed the most distinctive language, a mixture of witty invective and bitter reflection that, significantly, was the most explosive.[104] Once they found these words, diarists such as Abigail May and Rachel Van Dyke enjoyed cutting their contemporaries down to size. Carol Zisowitz Stearns and Peter Stearns have speculated that "growing literacy may have played a role in shaping new emotional standards" for anger. They note that Walter Ong saw "oral societies as verbally aggressive" and argue that, inversely, perhaps literacy "produces a new sense of and desire for control, including a new interest in controlling anger and a new vocabulary to put this interest into effect."[105] On the contrary, these four diarists suggest that literacy and familiarity with print culture encouraged a delight in wit and words that enabled women to express rather than suppress their anger. In fact, their chief pay for their emotion work seems to have been the sheer pleasure of using words as weapons without risking retaliation. How women would choose to use that ability, however, was an individual decision: Susan Heath and her sisters read the same books, were apparently equally well-educated, and all suffered from their father's meanness, but Susan alone made contempt for him her diary's major theme.[106] At the least, we can say that print culture cut both ways: the content of books might teach humility, but the process of reading also provided the verbal agility to voice dangerous emotions.

Like language, emotion work played an ambiguous role in expressing anger and constructing the self. Women's anger over issues of identity reflected their frustrations with the surface and deep acting expected of them during a time of contradictory gender expectations. During the early republic, women were to appear rational but remain sentimental, gain an education but not become bluestockings, and display gentility but not affectation. Demands for emotion work pervaded all aspects of life: at balls, promenades, and the family tea table, in school, and before the gossiping village community. In all these areas, women often wanted to successfully act their expected parts. Gentility was one of the few ways women could influence their class status, many women genuinely admired sensibility, successful courtship demanded attention to gossip, and ladylike behavior was the price of academy education. The rewards and punishments of expected emotional expression were clear, but however much women gained socially, they lost individually in pretending to be what they were not. Some women achieved congruence of self: this seems to have been the case for Sarah Connell, and her early diary is correspondingly even-tempered. The women who most deeply felt that their true selves were unrecognized or disrespected displayed the most anger. For them, anger provided a momentary and private way to subvert socially expected emotion work, and they seized every cultural pretext to justify their outrage.

Emotion work not only instigated women's anger but provided the means to control such passions. Mary Guion talked herself out of hating Jotham Smith, Sarah Connell evoked sentimentality to tranquillize her feelings, Abigail May tried to "command" her thoughts, as did

Susan Heath (usually unsuccessfully), and Mary B. Howell attempted to keep her feelings from "outstripp[ing her] *reason.*" But the stringent suppression, deflection, and disguise of anger that historians have found in the later nineteenth century appeared infrequently in these earlier diaries. Unlike Victorian girls, these young single women of the early republic did not use their diaries primarily as a "talking cure" in which they censored themselves, repented, and reformed. Although as single women May, Guion, and Van Dyke occasionally faulted themselves for negative feelings, none expressed more than fleeting shame over such emotions. Susan Heath was unusual in providing evidence of systematic parental effort to supervise her emotional expression and for berating herself for her lack of resignation—a practice, however, that was quite ineffective and never stopped her from lambasting her father at the next opportunity. Even when Sarah Connell evoked contentment to banish anger, her tone was mild and unperturbed. Mary Guion criticized Isaac Sarles for his anger, and Abigail May feared Mr. Bower's anger, but these diarists rarely reported other women's anger, and when they did, seem not to have regarded it as particularly upsetting.

Contemporary reactions to Abigail May's vitriolic diary suggest the considerable equanimity with which many women regarded each other's outrage. During the spring after May's September 1800 death, her sister copied her diary, but did not expurgate Abigail's angry entries. "In compliance, with the wishes of my honor'd Mother and many other *dear* friends," her sister resolved to "retrace these lines her hands have pen'd not with any idea of improving (for that is beyond my power), but merely to preserve what is to her friends an inestimable treasure; she wrote from the warm and genuine impulses of her feeling heart; the ever-varying emotions of which may be traced throughout the whole!"[107] May's diary circulated among family and friends for years afterwards; amazingly, it turned up in Susan Heath's 1817 Brookline, Massachusetts, household through her Goddard relatives. Susan Heath's reaction suggests how little she absorbed her mother's strictures against anger. Upon reading May's journal, Heath expressed only admiration for it in her own diary and praised the "superiour & exalted mind" and "feeling heart" of "that dear, amiable & accomplished woman." The repetition of "feeling heart" suggests that, like May's sister, she regarded all of Abigail's feelings as good. "We can think & talk of nothing but Abby May. what a sweet name is Abby—," Heath wrote, as she and her sisters paged through her 1800 journal, apparently untroubled by May's biting remarks and perhaps recognizing a sister in anger.[108]

Above all, young women's lack of concern over anger exemplified their success in turning emotional skills to their own purposes. If emotion work created women's concern for identity, it also produced the ability to finesse the rules governing feeling, limit themselves to surface acting, and wield the cultural tools available to them. To varying degrees, these women understood the distinction between what anthropologist Melford E. Spiro calls "learning a culture and becoming enculturated. To learn a culture is to acquire its propositions; to become enculturated is, in addition, to 'internalize' them as personal beliefs, that is, as propositions that are thought to be true."[109] Their culture's emphasis on the "feeling heart" typically directed young women into sentimental emoting over the moon, the poor, and the delicacy of their own feelings, but it also offered a subversive subtext: that feeling itself was to be valued, whatever it might be. That is surely one reason why sentimentalists found controlling their emotions so difficult: control contradicted the heart's expression. As that distinctly out-of-control academy student Laura Wolcott wrote, in what appears to have been her motto, "ANYTHING BUT INDIFFERENCE."[110] The combination of the "feeling heart" and emotion work skills meant that young women often learned what their culture expected and produced it, but did not completely internalize cultural scripts, so that they retained entitlement to their feelings, even to anger. Instead, many women recognized and articulated anger, encouraged and were entertained by other women's expostulations (so long as their audience was their peer group), and incorporated a right to outrage in their sense of themselves. Safely backstage and facing no retaliation for her opinions, Rachel Van Dyke spoke for many diarists when she declared, "I see no hurt in writing what I think."[111] But the fact that Van Dyke's anger stayed on paper and that Wolcott penned her motto in code meant that their emotions could change little in their external world. Although women seem to have revealed their anger to each other, they rarely displayed it to those who caused their rage. Unlike sentimental sadness, anger invites action and challenges power, but unless it becomes public and purposeful, it, too, becomes a feeling that can only produce more feeling. At best, sharing those feelings with other women produced recognition of a common plight, but without further avenues, anger, like sensibility, provided few solutions to real-life problems. As Susan Heath realized, "I can talk & wish & deplore—but alas! my power extends no farther—." Moreover, these diarists wrote as single and religiously uncommitted women. As they entered marriage, considered religious conversion, and experienced motherhood, women faced new feeling rules, reordered their priorities, and adopted new emotional tasks. That emotional reconstruction would substantially curtail both women's expression of anger and their developing sense of self.

5

RECONSTRUCTING THE HEART
Religion, Marriage, and Motherhood

> Miss S S & Mr Porter there—this gentleman is a young Clergyman who is now paying his address to Miss S S & is next Spring to transform her from the gay sprightly young lady to the grave matronly Madam of the Parish—.
> —*Elizabeth Cranch, Journal, 9 February 1786*

Until adulthood, young women of the early republic experienced multiple emotional communities, and their movement between them was fluid. Women might shift residence by changing what they read: sentimentalists lived primarily in an imagined emotional community available to them in books and often signaled abandonment of that dream world by giving up novels. In the physical world, young women's locality influenced where they resided emotionally. On visiting her wealthy relatives, Elizabeth Cranch shifted her language and feelings to suit that social occasion. When girls attended schools such as Litchfield Female Academy, they entered a distinct emotional sphere: an institutional community bound by school rules and watchful peers who demanded that rationality balance sensibility. Young women might occupy several emotional communities at once: even within their school, Academy girls expressed themselves one way with teachers and another with friends, and knew that John Brace allowed an individualistic competition that Sarah Pierce abhorred. When she read novels, Mary Guion visited the imagined community of sensibility, but most days she lived in the gossiping community of her New York neighbors. Sometimes young women stumbled as they moved from one emotional community to another: Abigail May's anger during her visit to Ballston Springs sprang partly from her frustration with trying to fit into a social set she alternately despised and longed to join, and Patty Rogers failed to understand that sensibility's imagined community rendered her ridiculous in her home town. But by and large, young women seem to have negotiated the transitions to new emotional communities with self-awareness and skill.

As girls grew up, they figuratively packed their bags and moved to new emotional communities, but this migration to maturity was different in kind. Unlike the fluid shifting of their girlhood, irrevocable events marked the world of mature womanhood. Four paths led to that new emotional terrain: religious commitment, marriage, motherhood, and traumatic encounters with death. Some women such as Sarah Connell experienced all four of these events in close proximity, a wrenching process which tore her from sensibility's pleasantries and deposited her in a new emotional world. For others, this was an extended process which might take as much as ten years. For still other women, this transit was partial; they might experience only intensified religious commitment, but even without husbands or children, they found themselves "born again" emotionally as well as religiously. Despite these variations, maturing girls commonly found that previous emotional patterns and expectations of emotion work shifted: as they grew up, their culture demanded not just surface acting—disguising anger, displaying genteel manners, or saying the expected—but the deep acting of submissive mothers, wives, and church members who had internalized their culture's values. Resigned gratitude replaced anger, and the always precarious balance between individuated expression and social regulation tipped definitively toward the latter. The transition from girlhood to womanhood also marked a period during which the cultural repertoire from which they drew narrowed; young women began to employ cultural tools fewer in number, blunter, and requiring more work on their parts.

Young women were well aware that life-altering changes awaited them, and many regarded the successive stages of this prospect eagerly. At Litchfield Female Academy, age sixteen denoted new maturity: Sarah Pierce allowed only girls over sixteen to attend parties, while student songs put courtship's start at that age. This also seems to have been the age close to menarche.[1] Lucy Sheldon's 1801–3 Music Book shows that Litchfield students trilled "the day that we were married O sweetest day of all the year," and undoubtedly some of them, like Mary Guion, eagerly laid bets on whom they would marry.[2] By age eighteen, Susan Heath expected "sense & judgment according to my years," and she located the boundary between childhood and womanhood at twenty. For that latter birthday, she "ardently wish[ed] for the feelings and capacity of a woman," which for her meant "exert[ing] all my time and talents to some good purpose" and imitating her mother.[3] Like her contemporaries, during these years Heath began attending balls as courtships began. Elizabeth Cranch illustrates young women's happy musings about adulthood: "P[egg]y & I sat and chatted by ourselves & amused ourselves with forming imaginary schemes of future pleasure—," she wrote, "in planning scenes in which our hearts felt interested we promised to remember the evening & when time shall have rolled years over our heads to recollect it—."[4] For most New England women during the early republic, the path to adulthood culminated with marriage at about age twenty-two and religious conversion in the late twenties.[5]

But much evidence suggests that diarists also found adulthood intimidating, associated marriage with gloom, and dreaded the future. Still happily misbehaving, fifteen-year-old Laura Maria Wolcott was glad she was not yet old enough to attend balls and clearly planned to delay growing up. Criticizing two schoolmates for being too "sober," she complained, "They are in their manners at least 25. Pshw, for such premature maturity. they are afraid by smiling they will over set their dignity."[6] As she grew up, Susan Heath saw each birthday as a test that she failed. Facing age eighteen, her "so long dreaded birthday," she derided herself as a "complete ignoramus," while at twenty, "the pleasing delusion" of childhood over, she felt wholly lacking in the accomplishments expected: "how different ought I to be from what I am. the thought has pained me more than I can express," she mourned.[7] Herself nervously contemplating marriage, Elizabeth Cranch in 1786 expected wedlock "to transform [her friend] from the gay sprightly young lady to the grave matronly Madam of the Parish—." In writing that "*Sukey Seargent* is no more—," once her friend had married, Cranch spoke as if Sukey had died.[8] Ten years later, Abigail May used much the same language in describing her visit with "the gay sprightly Miriam Fullerton that was—but oh! how alter'd—she looks dull, dejected, in short like a *married woman*. I'll say with Solus—'oh, I'll never be married' if such sower looks come of matrimony—."[9] Once her sister was married, Mary Guion expected Sally to give up single pleasures, however innocent; when Sally and Isaac Sarles planned to attend a ball, despite the fact they were married and parents, Guion told them to stay home.[10] Whether promisingly pleasant or unduly serious, adulthood appeared as a foreign country, with different rules and expectations and no way back. In that sense, young women recognized it as a distinct emotional community. How did they make the transition to that world, and what did it mean for them? Each of these diarists responded differently to expectations as they grew up, but all of them labored intensively to develop identities and emotions that made sense of their new reality.

While still housed within Litchfield Academy's tightly constructed community, young women sensed impending shifts in their emotional world. This feeling was especially strong among the Academy's older girls. They alone enjoyed the privilege of attending balls, their first step into the ranks of courting women. At the same time, as Sarah Pierce pointed out, prizes at the Public Exhibition were "generally beyond the reach of any but the oldest and best informed pupils," who faced heightened intellectual expectations as their formal education ended with weeks of drilling and tense competition. To these academic and social demands, Sarah Pierce added another: that they choose Jesus as their savior and enter the ranks of the saints, a process that would bring them into a new emotional world just as surely as marriage and their education's conclusion. Religious language, in fact, echoed many of the concerns which preoccupied young women choosing a husband. Just as young women cautioned each other against men's deceit, calls to conversion warned them against spiritual self-deception: as John Brace reminded students, "deception is a great sin, particularly concerning religion, for a person to pretend they are something when they are nothing."[11] Both marriage and conversion also denoted increased seriousness; sermons of this period conventionally contrasted youth's gaiety with the "gloomy concerns" of religion, and assumed that conversion required a definitive break with youthful pastimes.[12]

As founder of a school for young women on the boundary between youth and maturity, Sarah Pierce demanded attention to religion and supported the efforts of Lyman Beecher, Litchfield's resident Congregational minister. Students might choose to attend the town's Episcopal church, but Beecher regularly visited the Academy regardless of students' denominational affiliation. He preached an evangelical Calvinism that maintained the complete moral government of God, but which insisted that humans could choose Jesus as their savior, and, indeed, must do so in order to be saved. More a pastor than a theologian, Beecher did not regard Calvinist depravity as an excuse for passivity and energetically demanded complete transformation of the religious affections, as seekers spurned their identity as sinners and were "born again" as new, redeemed selves. His revival methods centered on the emotions, just as did his theology; Beecher was confident that the right combination of circumstances and pressures would help sinners make the right choice. His first wife, Roxana, modeled his expectations for academy girls. She had been a young, well-off, and learned novel reader, but upon marriage to Lyman, she experienced religious conversion and submitted to her husband's dominance.[13] John Brace experienced such a "change of heart" under Beecher's preaching during the winter of 1815. In that conversion, Brace reported, "my understanding was first convinced and then my heart affected."[14] In a similar manner, he and Pierce addressed both the head and the heart in persuading academy students to choose Jesus as their savior.

Caroline Chester's 1815 and 1816 diaries chronicled the methods Litchfield Female Academy employed to induce religious conversions.

Litchfield Female Academy's architecture echoed the appearance of churches and meetinghouses, and in that sense reflected its religious role during revivals. "View of the Litchfield Academy," attributed to Napoleon Gimbrede, ca. 1830. (Collection of the Litchfield Historical Society, Litchfield, Connecticut)

In the winter 1815 term, she experienced religion in an academic guise. Brace typically began the day by reading the Bible and offering prayers, and Caroline often reported that she recited lessons in Sacred History, a curricular staple.[15] School rules demanded that students keep the Sabbath by attending services every Sunday, "doing good to others," and avoiding "sloth, frivolous conversation, light reading, or vain employment."[16] But when she returned to classes in spring 1816, Caroline found that a revival which had begun the previous summer was in full swing, and she faced systematic pressures to convert which focused on her heart. As an institutional emotional community, Litchfield Female Academy easily adapted to such religious purposes. In the academic setting, teachers dominated the classroom, challenged individual students, announced scholarly wins and misses, and compelled students to examine their failings weekly. During the religious revival of 1816, ministers assumed these roles. Sarah Pierce stepped aside, and Reverend Beecher preached from the schoolroom on Acts 16 and concluded by asking the students, "I hope e'er long to hear you my dear young friends asking with the same earnestness, 'What shall I do to be saved.'" One day Chester heard two sermons at school; on another occasion, a prayer meeting began at 5 a.m. in the schoolhouse as sermons and prayer replaced class lectures.[17] Ministers and teachers challenged students directly and individually to choose their identity: at one point, Sarah Pierce stepped in and graphically separated the sheep from the goats by dividing Academy students into two groups, "those that had obtained a hope and those that had not."[18]

Much as Litchfield Academy life extended into the boardinghouse, the revival followed students into their homes. Caroline stayed at Miss Edwards's home, where on her second day back she discovered four ministers conducting a prayer meeting in the parlor. Chester, who had long struggled academically and rarely knew the correct answer, now faced a similar challenge in her boardinghouse, as visiting ministers quizzed her on her religious state. One Saturday morning in June, Reverend Beecher "called at Miss Edward's and conversed & prayed with me in the most solemn manner, . . . he wished to know what idol was between me and God. I did not answer though I well knew it was the *World*—."[19] On another occasion, a visiting minister called at Caroline's boardinghouse, assembled the students, and "told us he should ask each one of us this question *'Have you ever repented'* and we must answer it as in the presence of God," Chester wrote, as she described a spiritual public exhibition:

> never in my life did I feel so much fear in the presence of a MAN.... he asked five and all answered NO. is it possible cried he that five immortal souls will perish forever? is it possible that my coming here this afternoon will be a 'savor of death' unto any of these never dying souls? but I must do my duty.... If I should at the judgment day see any of you at the left hand I shall remember that I warned beg'd & intreated you to repent and I will wash my hands of your blood; oh! What depraved and vile hearts must you possess who though invited to come to Christ that you may live *still still* remain stupid refusing to ever repent choosing death rather than life.[20]

In using the word "stupid," this clergyman drew on traditional Calvinist language for spiritual dullness, but the word seems freighted with additional meaning, given the revival's parallels with Litchfield pedagogy and Caroline Chester's persistent feelings of academic failure.

Friendship and family as well as academic competition provided the context for religious decision making. Initially, Caroline took comfort that her friends also remained unsaved, but as others converted, she felt increasingly left out. "[M]y dear room-mates appear much more concerned for their precious immortal souls," especially her good friend Nancy, she reported.[21] Litchfield Female Academy's students support historians' assertion that while men perceived God as a sovereign during early-nineteenth-century conversions, women understood the deity as "a family member or personal friend" rather than as a king. Revival hymns invited Academy students to make Christ their new friend, one they would never lose, unlike the school friendships that often ended with the term. The hymn "Christ knocking at the door of the heart" pictured Jesus as a sentimental man of feeling: with his "melting heart" and "matchless kindness," the verses reassured them, "He will [be] the very friend you need." In his sermons, Beecher extended the metaphor by preaching that they should tell others about God just as they would recommend an "amiable" friend.[22] During this same period, church members began to call the meetinghouse itself a "friend," and to associate that structure with emotional and warm imagery unknown to the colonial period.[23] By using a highly charged term for the deepest relationships among young women as well as for the ideal husband, this new theological language bridged students' single and future married states. Theological and personal relationships entangled further as parental figures pressed conversion upon Academy students. When Miss Edwards, Caroline's beloved boardinghouse mother, spoke to her individually about her soul, Caroline wrote, "I would give the whole world were it in my power to be a Christian but oh! My wicked heart prevents." Her own mother, usually more concerned about her daughter's academic and social life, advised Caroline that "the *Spirit of God* can alone give that deep sense of error which will make you more anxious to correct your faults than to justify them & to feel the value of the affection which aids you to understand your own character."[24]

The Academy's highly regimented life also supported evangelicalism's call to conversion. Sarah Pierce regularly emphasized the need to "improve" time in one's studies: in a typical closing address, she urged "the constant improvement of each hour" as students accumulated knowledge.[25] School rules governed every hour of the day and reminded students that they must "account to God" for how they employed their time; in letters from home, parents reiterated the importance of a "just sense" of time's value.[26] Calls to conversion also emphasized time's scarcity: that time passed quickly, and once lost was never retrieved, that each day should be used well, and that sinners needed to seize the moment and choose Jesus. During the 1816 Litchfield revival, Caroline Chester summarized these truisms in her essay, "Upon the Right Improvement of Time."[27] For Litchfield Academy students, especially the older girls, this message had special meaning: in an academy education that was intense but brief, time passed quickly indeed, such schooling was a once-in-a-lifetime opportunity, and the approaching exhibition reminded them that time was running out. The conclusion of academy life also meant the breakup of school friendships, which often proved difficult to maintain afterwards.[28] Taking the role of minister, Miss Pierce lectured that habits of indolence and sin would only increase after graduation. "Will God be more merciful hereafter, when you have sinned longer against him—But will that hereafter arrive?" she asked. As classes ended, Sarah Pierce typically turned from her demands for scholarly excellence and asserted that education would no longer suffice. "Can intellect stay the dart [of death]? . . . the time of our control over you has elapsed & we send you from us with . . . hopes that we all shall meet in that world where those who assemble 'meet to part no more.'" As at the end of every term, ministers also reminded students that death threatened to part them from each other forever. Lyman Beecher was perhaps excessively frank in making this point: during the 1815–16 revival, he preached that of former Academy students, five went insane, five turned to drink, and two died.[29] Together, the academy and the revival reminded students that as they left one world they needed to prepare for another.

Sarah Pierce's demands that her students convert were closely tied to her assumption that they would become mothers. Anticipating Victorian visions of maternal influence, she insisted that mothers would "plant the seeds of vice or virtue" in their children, create a home more appealing than a vicious world, and entice their husbands to religion.[30] John Brace concurred: in his 1819 concluding address, he reminded his students that they would not be able to "discharge the duties of life, without religion. . . . Is it not dreadful to reflect, that without religion, you may instill into the youthful mind the bitterest hatred to the God of heaven; that, from the state of your own feelings you may produce in the mind of others, that spark of evil, that may eventually convert the heart into a perfect volcano of mischief."[31] However well-trained their minds, women's hearts decided their family's fate.

Not every Litchfield student responded to revival pressures by choosing Jesus as her savior. Academy revivals exposed them to evangelical demands, but many young women required more drastic life changes than leaving school before they reconstructed their spiritual lives. Much as she tried to do well in her academic work but somehow could not, sixteen-year-old Caroline Chester struggled to convert and failed there as well. She could do the surface work of salvation—hear sermons, attend conferences, desire a new heart—but the deeper changes which conversion required eluded her. Perhaps the public nature of religious demands and conversion repelled her, as it did many young women later in the nineteenth century. Privacy was always scarce at Litchfield Academy, but its religious revivals invaded even the heart.[32] Alternatively, we can see Caroline's reluctance as refusal to do the intensive emotion work required for conversion and acceptance of adult womanhood. Instead, Caroline opted for the daughter's role: genteel benevolence, serving others, if not God. She decided she would be "kind and obliging to *all* around me (according to my dear mama's request) consulting the happiness & care of my companions giving up my own wishes to theirs—."[33] But an estimated half of Academy students became "'subjects of unerring grace'" by fall 1815, presumably more during spring 1816, and the revival's pressures prepared Caroline for future evangelical demands.[34] Even for resistant sinners, the call to conversion clearly reminded them that their lives were about to change. Young women could glimpse their future in the motto penned in a friendship album during the Academy's 1815 revival: "Trust God—suspect yourself."[35]

Once their formal education ended, young women entered a transitional period during which they lost their identity as students, continued as daughters at home, and anticipated a future of marriage. As an unusually serious scholar, Rachel Van Dyke experienced an extreme form of the emotional confusion that engulfed some young women as they left academy life and approached the emotional community of mature women. Unlike Caroline Chester, she was a highly successful student who loved learning and prolonged her education by continuing Latin studies with Mr. G—, who acted as both her tutor and her friend, with intimations of romance. Her unusual exposure to the male academic world anticipated the late Victorian world of competitive coeducational high schools which Jane Hunter has described, but which did not exist during the early republic. When Mr. G— ended her lessons and left town in December 1810, seventeen-year-old Rachel was pitched into a serious depression: she lost not only her intellectual life, which had been an important component of her identity, but Mr. G—, and, by the end of her diary, her father and her beloved pastor, Reverend Ira Condict.[36] Unlike Litchfield Academy students, she faced these traumas without the aid of a tightly constructed community to shape her choices. Hesitant and anxious, she began to turn from intellectuality and anger to religion and melancholy.

In her journal's early pages, Rachel Van Dyke recorded periodic tears and sentimental musings, but the later, cumulative losses of her studies and loved ones deepened these into sadness.[37] Elements of her previous self persisted: she exchanged letters with Mr. G— and kept up her journal, even if he no longer read it. But her tongue lost its tartness, and she wept frequently, copiously, and often without knowing why. Depression initially caught her unawares. "I could scarcely compel myself to talk this morning—it is hard work—it is a painful task to talk about trifles—& to appear cheerful when your heart is sad and filled with gloomy thoughts," she wrote in mid-November 1810, as she anticipated her lessons' end. "It must be the dull weather that takes away my spirits. . . . I fancy I shall never attend school again."[38] Acutely lonely, she called her pillow her "only friend" and wet it with tears; while she had earlier retreated to her room to think, now she fled there to "weep for hours." Without the sense of purpose her studies provided, she felt she wasted time and did nothing "worth mentioning."[39] Van Dyke initially turned to sensibility to understand, shape, and dignify her feelings. "The most exquisite pleasures which I enjoy are those of my imagination," she wrote, echoing Sarah Connell. "Sometimes I lay for hours indulging the most extravagant flights of fancy—nay, sometimes I forget myself. I seem to realize what I only imagine, and then my heart in reality throbs with all the emotion of enjoyment."[40] At the same time, Rachel retained enough rationality to criticize her own emoting. She called herself "a weak romantic foolish girl" and "a mere baby" and feared that she "indulge[d] too much in a kind of weak sensibility. I know not what to call it. It certainly is a weakness. I reflect upon the miseries of human life—I feel unhappily situated—My heart aches—My tears flow—I wish I was in a convent—I wish I was good—I wish I was fit for Death—."[41]

Since "weak sensibility" stimulated her feelings but provided no solutions, Van Dyke turned to religion as an alternative avenue to adulthood. Initially, her churchgoing was social rather than devout. Early in her diary, she admitted that she skipped church three Sundays in a row because her old hat was shabby, she could not find a more pleasing one, and she knew that it would go out of fashion in a month anyway.[42] But her friend Ruth Condict, who had also studied Latin with her, was her pastor's daughter, and Van Dyke found his sermons increasingly appealing: "he appears to know and feel what he preaches" rather than engaging in "raptures, gestures, metaphors, etc.," she wrote, an observation which suggests her awareness of sensibility's failings and need for emotional congruity and honesty. "Except I am converted—except I am born again—I cannot enter into the kingdom of God," she recited from a Sunday sermon.[43] Without the studies that had given purpose to her life, she became keenly aware of time's flight and, much like the Litchfield Academy students, worried that "days, weeks, months, years roll away" while her evil heart remained cold.[44] Rachel still wept, but as she substituted spiritual for academic improvement, she gained new purpose. The deaths of Reverend Condict and her father within weeks of each other reiterated the importance of religion. "But cease my heart. Put thy trust in God, and be resigned to his will," she cautioned.[45] By the end of her journal, at age eighteen, Rachel Van Dyke had left her studies behind, begun to record her friends' marriages, and taken the first steps toward a more serious spirituality.

As young women moved into their twenties, their shift away from the youthful world of sensibility and school became definitive. The majority of young women, unlike Rachel Van Dyke or Litchfield students, did not attend academies; for them, maturation was inextricably entwined with courtship and marriage. As we have seen in the cases of Patty Rogers and Mary Guion, courtship presented opportunities for women to exercise discernment. Once their marital choice was made, however, and even before their wedding, women experienced intimations of a new order. Elizabeth Cranch kept her diaries in fits and starts, and what survives tells us relatively little about her courtships, but her writings are exceptionally revealing of her emotions as an already affianced woman. In her case, she was engaged twice: at age nineteen to "Corydon," as she called Thomas Perkins, who then left to seek his fortune in the West; and, after Perkins's early death, to Jacob Norton.[46]

Each of Elizabeth Cranch's engagements presented different emotional tasks. From her first relationship, she struggled to cope with loss and an unclear future. Much as Rachel did not know what to do when her studies ended, Mr. G— left, and her father died, Cranch did not know what to do while she waited for her fiancé to return from the frontier. She had dispensed with her most important decision, choosing a spouse, but because of his absence, the expected conjugal life did not ensue. Seeking diversion, she experimented with sensibility when she visited genteel relatives in 1785–86, where she enjoyed the leisure and class setting conducive to gentility. When she returned home in March 1786, she continued to construct her feelings along sentimental lines; much like Sarah Connell, she lingered at twilight and "felt a kind of *mild* Sadness—in my heart—not wholly unpleasing—and tho the Tears fell from my eyes profusely—they were not those of distress—."[47] But such playacting could not substitute for the very real grief she felt for her absent fiancé. Insomnia alternated with troubling dreams, while farewells to dying or departing friends and news of an unexpected deception heightened her anxiety. Cranch repeatedly sought to master her emotions through her earlier practice of stringent control and cultivated indifference, and vowed to "reason myself into calmness," but found the task almost impossible.[48] Once she heard of her fiancé's death, Cranch's resolution to "hold my happiness in readiness to part with it" deepened: "tis my fortune—from the most important to the most trifling occurrences to have them disappointed, if I am ardent in my desires of them—," she wrote. "Indifference is to be sought for, but I can not acquire it in so great a degree as perhaps is my duty—however I shall be taught it—."[49]

In search of the emotional tools to cope with this loss, Elizabeth turned first to her mother, Mary Cranch, and then to a second relationship, this time with Jacob Norton, a neighboring Congregationalist minister, whom she would eventually marry. They became her overt teachers in the emotion work required for contentment and adult womanhood. Unlike many diarists in this study, who were closer to peers and siblings than parents, Elizabeth Cranch and her mother were lovingly attentive to each other. In 1788, as Elizabeth nervously contemplated her second engagement, Mary Cranch repeatedly reassured Elizabeth that she had little to fear, "talked me into a rational calmness of mind—" and "used all the tender perswasions of affection, and all the rational motives of religion to compose me—and drive from my mind the thick clouds which overcast my happiness—and spread a temporary gloom over every future scene—."[50] The "rational motives of religion" proved especially important: the belief that God commanded her to count her blessings and leave the future in divine hands became a mantra in Cranch's letters and remaining diary. But more help was needed: as Cranch put it, in words similar to Abigail May's, "I can theorise—but not practice." Jacob Norton, the young, liberal minister who replaced Perkins, also offered religious reassurances, but as her future husband, played a more expansive and overt role. Cranch realized that when she was sad, she "made *my friend* [Jacob] unhappy—and in that moment I felt how strong a motive his happiness was in inducing me to strive to conquer every feeling that made me anxious—."[51] Not only did consideration for Jacob's feelings influence her own demeanor, but she granted him the right to supervise her emotions. As her wedding approached, Cranch increasingly turned to him. "The gloomy weather depresses my spirits—what shall I do to raise them?" she asked; "tis not always in my power to preserve the Soul's calm sunshine—externals have too great an effect upon the intellectual system—cannot you teach me to regulate it better—." Cranch expected this emotional supervision during marriage, and in writing Norton, referred to herself in the third person, as if she had already become another being, while her dashes suggest her trembling voice. "You will have many Se[a]sons to instruct me in my good friend—to point out the path of duty—and guide me thro' it—& I trust your Eliza will not be untractable. . . . The loss of a—Husbands—Love—appears to *her*—the only *utterly insupportable evil*—."[52]

As eager as she was for guidance, Elizabeth Cranch feared that her prospective husband might dominate her emotions under the guise of helping her. Norton's casual suggestion that she might be deceived in his character intensified fears common to courting women, and made her wonder about the entire relationship.[53] Echoing her aunt Abigail Adams's famous warning to her Revolutionary spouse, Elizabeth anticipated emotional monarchy and cautioned Jacob: "I will not tell you what influence your presence may have upon my mind—You ought not to be too sensible of your power— —those who *can govern*—*may* tyrannise—." Cranch tried to equalize their relationship by repeatedly addressing him as her "friend" and by offering to bear his feelings, while he advised hers: "deposit as many as you can with your Eliza—they cannot burthen her, whilst they relieve you—," she wrote, but found Norton rarely asked her to do this for him.[54] In a highly equivocal last letter before their wedding, she struggled to assert the independence of her emotions and her self: "*You* must be chearful if you would have me so—," she wrote, suggesting that she would become his mirror, but also flung out, "You told me I must inform you how I *felt*—That is impossible; and unless you could exchange characters and circumstances with me you can never know—." Her last diary entries before the wedding were equally anxious: "O my heart! Shall I wish it less sensible?—Shall I not be happy unless I am unfeeling?" she exclaimed. Finally lapsing into resignation, she wondered if she would ever write again, prayed she would be "useful," and concluded, "Here then I leave the unfinished page—."[55] With these mixed feelings, she married him.

Elizabeth Cranch's image of an "unfinished page" provides an apt symbol for her own sense of self after marriage. In a pattern common to women's diaries, once wed, she became much less prominent a figure in her journal, until then a significant vehicle for self-expression.[56] Silence was her initial response to marriage; at the bottom of that last "unfinished page" of February 7, 1789, her next entry was dated September 15, 1797, which recalled her wedding and first days of marriage. Separate journals, which may also have been written retroactively, began in 1794, so that her silence extended five rather than eight years and obscures how she and Jacob initially negotiated emotion management.

But her remaining diaries suggest the outlines of her emotional life as a wife and mother. Between 1794 and 1809, Elizabeth Cranch Norton returned to periodic efforts to keep up her diaries; that she, an overworked minister's wife, wrote at all suggests a determination to articulate and preserve her self, as did her brief efforts to keep up her reading into the mid-1790s, when she was a new wife and mother. But her entries quickly fell into a pattern of housework, visiting, and formulaic expressions of gratitude, especially on Thanksgiving and New Year's days. Her proficiency at housework suggests that sentimental writers possessed substantial domestic skills, but as single women had chosen not to write about such tasks. In contrast, once married, Elizabeth Cranch Norton had little to say about her emotional interior, but much about the physical work accompanying eight children, an often absent husband, constant visitors, students to board, and clerical meetings entailing twenty-four to dinner. In a rare moment of introspection, she recognized the relationship of housework and feeling: "I employd myself in domestic business in order to prevent my self from indulging in too tender feelings!—they must be reserved for a solitary hour!" she wrote.[57] She and Jacob fell quickly into their respective duties, and on their anniversary she often expressed affection for him, as she did toward her children on their birthdays, but her reported emotions were far less volatile than as a single woman, her tone dutiful, and her orientation outward to her family and her tasks rather than inward to her self.

As a single woman, Elizabeth Cranch had sought emotional containment by reasoning herself into indifference. As a married woman, she finally attained that state, but the sources were exhaustion and gratitude rather than reason. She knew she was lucky that her children, parents, and husband remained healthy, and that she had survived eight pregnancies. But by her forties, her diaries skipped over months, her handwriting deteriorated, and Elizabeth Cranch Norton moved beyond feeling as she slid "down the declivity of life," finally dying in 1811 at age forty-eight.[58] Ironically, her page had indeed turned out to be "unfinished": although funeral orations had by then begun to detail the life of the deceased, Jacob Norton devoted scarcely one page of it to his wife; instead, he replaced her individuality with a generic type for the Christian. Norton did, however, show some general understanding of her labors by casting heaven as a place of rest.[59]

Of all these diarists, Mary Guion was the most resourceful and showed the greatest agency in managing her courtship, yet even though her adult life was easier than Elizabeth Cranch Norton's, she, too, underwent a major transformation through religion, marriage, and motherhood. Much as her courtship occupied over seven years, her postnuptial emotional transition was gradual. After much doubt, Guion wed Samuel Brown in October 1807 at age twenty-five. Suffering from the same marriage panic as Elizabeth Cranch, she almost fainted during the ceremony, but quickly found that Brown was "the best of husbands."[60] Since she did not have her first child until 1811, Mary and Samuel enjoyed several years during which they delighted in each other's company, and through the mid-1810s, her diary struck a positive note. But even without children or religious conversion, her life had changed: with marriage to her "Lover," Guion would never again keep her diary with the faithfulness that had characterized her single years. Much like Elizabeth Cranch Norton, Mary Guion Brown found that marriage induced silence: on the same page on which she described her wedding, she skipped to spring 1808 and reached January 1, 1809, by the bottom of the page.[61] After devoting 340 pages to her courtship years from 1800 to 1807, she penned only 47 pages for the years 1807 to 1852. Marriage ended the circumstances of daily life which had initially encouraged Mary Guion to write: her need for a confidante, the influence of novels, and free time. Her love for Samuel was itself an impediment. Before marriage, her diary had substituted for the ideal man she sought, but afterwards she found Samuel's company "far preferable t[o] writing"; at the same time, Samuel so loved her that he was rarely gone; reluctant to pen entries in his presence, she lost the privacy on which she had built her sense of self as a single woman.[62] On one occasion, he returned unexpectedly, found her writing, and "laughingly insisted on seeing what I was writing," Mary wrote. "I really did not want him to see it."[63] Both seem to have felt her diary an intruder in their marriage, a remnant of an earlier self that could not continue.

After marriage, Mary Guion Brown also lost the plot that had governed her diary since 1800. The question of whom to marry was settled, her true feelings determined, and novels seem to have no longer spoken to her. Only a year after her marriage, even before she had children, she wrote, "Novels are for the most part lain aside. I wish the biblle had a cauld my attention when I was young as much as Alusive stories did."[64] When she became a mother, Guion Brown had even less time or inclination to write. After three years of childlessness, she gave birth to her first daughter in 1811; a second followed in 1814 and twin girls were born in 1817. "I write now of no Parties nor any thing but domestic affairs but I visit and am visited," she wrote as early as 1813, with one child born and another on the way; her language suggests she did not believe "domestic affairs" deserved recording.[65] Much as it did for Elizabeth Cranch Norton, work for others overwhelmed both reading and writing. Samuel tried farming and a distillery and finally turned to making ladies' shoes for the New York market, which meant the addition of several apprentices. By 1820, she cared for a household of ten.[66]

While sentiment served as a religious conduit for Rachel Van Dyke, children brought Mary Guion Brown new spiritual seriousness and a change in self-conception. Unlike Elizabeth Cranch Norton, who maintained the same mild piety throughout her life, when single, Mary Guion had been indifferent to religion. She had erratically attended services, experimenting with Baptist, Presbyterian, Methodist, Episcopal, and even Catholic worship, largely out of curiosity, and she preferred novel reading to attending services of any kind.[67] Her most pressing concern, courtship, dominated religious considerations: her most detailed account of religion concerned the preacher who cornered her in the parlor and tried to kiss her.[68] Guion's brother had suggested that as she grew older, she should drop fiction for scripture, but she shrugged off his entreaties until after marriage.[69]

Yet by the mid-1810s, religious language dominated her diary. In fall 1815, as the mother of two, weakened by work and childbirth, Mary Guion Brown began to attend St. Matthew's Church in Bedford. Although Episcopal theology did not demand conversion as Lyman Beecher had, she described her new religious feelings in much the same evangelical language. Episcopal churches had been among the first denominations to reflect sensibility, and by the turn of the century had redesigned their interiors to encourage heartfelt but refined emotion.[70] For her, the key emotional event was not owning Jesus in a revival, but coming forward to the communion table. Watching others take the sacrament, she could not "pretend to describe my feelings. the tears flowed in streams from my eyes and it appeared to me that now was the acceptable time and now was the day of Salvation and ye[t] I durst not venture to be a pertaker at the alter."[71] In October 1816, she had her first two children baptized, which "relieved my mind a little," but she continued yearning for the privilege of being a communicant. Pregnant with twins and fearing death in childbirth, she was so heavy with child that she could scarcely walk to church. Her diary entries at this time speak in a scarcely recognizable voice: "my distress of boath body and mind were very great for scarcely a night but I was awoke from my sleep with extreme pain. . . . I became dejected melancholy and very low sperited. all the consolation I did receive was from the Scriptures and some good books—." Her twin girls were born in late January 1817, and although she almost died, her faith in God was renewed, and five months later, she finally became a communicant herself.[72]

From then on, Mary Guion Brown's emotional and social life centered on her church. Compared to the highly eclectic and constant reading of her youth, she rarely picked up a book, and when she did, it was the Bible or other religious tomes. Between 1807 and 1852, she mentioned reading only four books besides Scripture. While as a young woman she had sewn while listening to a novel, now she stitched with the missionary society while hearing Mrs. Judson's memoir of religious work in Burma and Calcutta, and expressed her commitment in newly submissive tones: "how often have I prayed to our Heavenly Father that he would make me an instrument in his hands of bringin[g] one Soul to repentance but cause me first to thouroughly rep[en]t myself and that we may all be blessd with more of the out pourings of thy holy spirit is my consta[n]t Prayer—."[73] Convinced that affliction proved God's love, she recorded every kind of disaster: her much-loved brother James's opposition in a land dispute, the deaths of his daughters from consumption, the illness of her own daughter, death of a son-in-law, loss of her parents and in-laws, her house struck by lightning, and a cholera epidemic in New York City.[74] Mary Guion Brown's life was by no means unremittingly bleak: her love for Samuel radiated throughout her married life, and she took great pleasure in raising her "dear Children" as good Christians. She knew she was lucky, but her tone in these later entries was often resigned, and she perceived the considerable good in her life as God's arbitrary blessing. Resigned gratitude became the hallmark of her diary as a married woman, much as it did for Elizabeth Cranch Norton. Most notably, the sense of agency Mary Guion Brown had felt as a young woman was entirely absent in these later years.

Equally striking is her later diary's lack of anger, sarcasm, and wit. As a young woman, Mary Guion had enjoyed making fun of her suitors and was distinctly unwilling to suffer fools gladly, while her rage over injustice prompted sympathy for her sister Sally and attacks against Isaac Sarles. All these qualities made her writing voice distinctive, and all disappeared with marriage. As a wife, mother, and devout churchgoer, she borrowed her language of resigned gratitude from religious texts; much like diarists who imitated their sentimental reading, the more derivative her writing became, the less she could express anger. While she had earlier dissected Isaac Sarles's meanness with articulate fury, her final report on his marriage employs muted tones. In spring 1832, she wrote of Isaac: "for this number of years he had led a very Disipated life and reduced his family to poverty. in the month of d[e]cember he was home and abused his family all that words [c]ould do telling his hartbroken wife she was the whole cause of all their trouble and that now he was going to leave her. he went to New York and in about three weeks his lifeless body was brot up for interment—."[75]

Mary Guion Brown did not entirely lose her younger self after marriage, motherhood, and religious commitment. Since she had four daughters and joined female benevolent societies, more of her life was spent with women, but much as in her single years, her most intense feel-

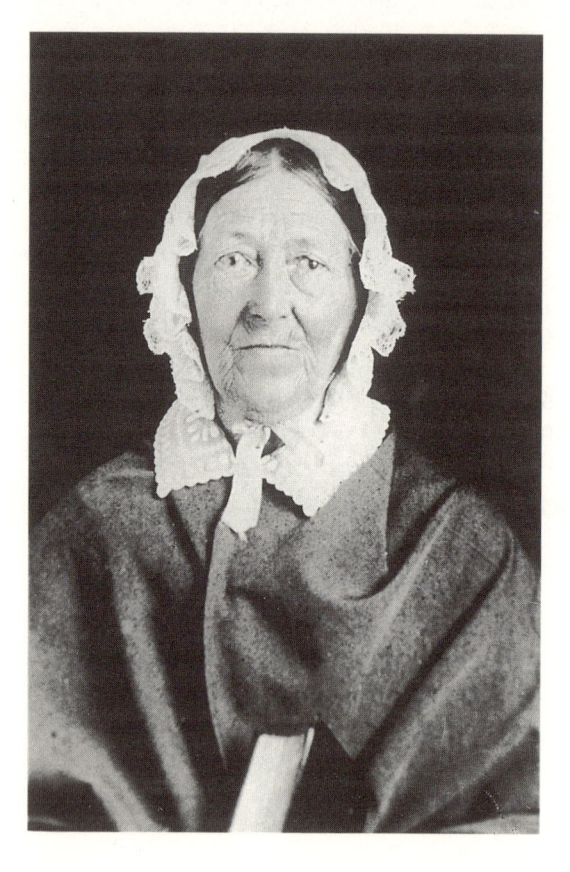

Mary Guion Brown, photograph. (Office of the Town Historian, Bedford Hills, New York)

ings stayed within her family, and she recorded no close female friends. Although she controlled her daughters much more than her parents had controlled her, nurture rather than breaking the will governed her child-raising methods, as was true for Elizabeth Cranch Norton. In keeping with her earlier love of "improvement," she sent several daughters to boarding school, so that they enjoyed the academy education she had lacked. Her descriptions of her daughters focused on their love of books, although she was relieved that they preferred "Pious books" and history to novels.[76] In her old age Mary Guion Brown had her photograph taken: it shows a weary woman wearing an old-fashioned cap and rough shawl, but holding a book in her hand—undoubtedly a Bible, but a book nonetheless, suggesting that her identity as a reader remained.

Mary Guion Brown's reaction to rereading her courtship journal at age forty-one illustrates how her sense of self had changed. Initially, she was appalled: "when I look at the former part of my writings they appear so light and trifling so much levity & nonscense I am tempted to commit them all to the flames as I have done a number of pages," she wrote. "O! that I had turned my mind to something of a more serious nature in my youthful days, when I had much leisure time and no cares of a family. I am well asshured that youth Is the fittest season to serve the lord but Oh how did I neglect that season. Heavenly Father forgive me."[77] Mary Guion Brown did burn part of her diary; the first surviving page is dated April 21, 1800, and since the original manuscript probably began the first day of the new century, she may have burned almost four months of entries. In that her early diary represented her younger self, this act suggests a form of self-mutilation. Not only her actions, but her language dismissed her needs as a young woman: she repeatedly disdained them as "Light and trifling so much levity & nonscence" and not "serious" compared to serving God. Using evangelicalism's discourse of time scarcity, she felt her youth was a waste, and in burning her diary, she intimated that her days belonged to God, not to her, and that her unsanctified moments did not deserve to be part of recorded time. Yet Mary Guion Brown could not bring herself to destroy the entire manuscript. Although writing would never again occupy a central place in her development, she seems to have recognized that her journal was more "precious" than "worthless," and that it had once been a source of power in her life.[78] But in her later years, its role was marginal: erratically kept, it functioned as a testament to God's mercies, and Mary Guion's voice was reduced to murmurs of gratitude.

In her journal, Sarah Connell chronicled an even more disturbing tale of not just emotional reconstruction through marriage and motherhood, but self-erasure. During the first years of her diary, as a single girl she had happily admired her emotions in the imagined world of sensibility. Connell's academy education seems to have caused her neither Caroline Chester's sense of failure nor Rachel Van Dyke's dedication to learning; rather, it created an abiding love for her female friends. But as Sarah's family lost its Newburyport home during the Embargo and sank in class status, she began to shift her emotional center from herself to others: she hid her disappointment from her father, and for the first time hesitated to reveal her heart to her friends. Other than encouraging further tears, sensibility offered no solutions to her problems. Physical distance from her friends, combined with class difference, cautioned that her "feeling should no longer run away with my judgment." While not entirely rejecting sensibility, she began to restrain her previously impulsive behavior and prepared to enter a new emotional community. In the next few years, she would marry, undergo religious conversion, and become a mother, experiences that would first break and then reconstruct her heart.

Connell's turn from sensibility intensified when she met her future husband, Samuel Ayer, and entered the community of courting couples. In contrast to Guion's voluminous courtship diary, this part of Connell's journal is brief and suggests how unsuspectingly she entered into this relationship. A Dartmouth graduate five years older than Sarah, Samuel had turned to medicine when they met in the summer of 1809.[79] At first he seemed a man of feeling and fellow resident of the imagined community of sensibility: Connell found him "Amiable, sensible, and polite. His countenance is but the index of his heart," she declared, paying him sensibility's highest compliment. "It is expressive of all that is good, and exhibits the smile of complacency." She believed she could share all her feelings "with unbounded confidence," and abandoned the caution she had begun to develop with women. "Many would call this enthusiasm," she remonstrated. "But it is only the unfeeling, and such as never felt their hearts warmed by the pure emotions of affection."[80] But Ayer dominated her feelings as no single female friend had: "Absent from the *Man*, who possesses my undivided heart, nothing interests me," she wrote. "I am alone in a crowd. I pass through life in a kind of stupid indifference to all around me."[81] For the first time, she reported her feelings deadened rather than stimulated.

Until Sarah's marriage at age nineteen in October 1810, sentimental literature and gender expectations had tempered her emotions, but no single individual had overtly directed them; Sarah tried to please her father, not obey him. Yet within a month of their marriage, Samuel Ayer asserted mastery of her feelings. While Elizabeth Cranch had asked Jacob Norton to guide her feelings, Ayer apparently took control on his own volition. Separated from her oldest female friends and with her family life in disarray, Sarah Connell Ayer was particularly vulnerable. He pointed out "a fault, which, if not corrected, must eventually have depreciated me in his esteem, and tended to my ruin." Hers was an error common to sensibility: "colouring, and enlarging, which was in the end one, and the same thing, since it tended to deceive." Stung by Samuel's rebuke, Sarah decided that her heart was essentially deceptive and that she must "deliberate" before speaking. Submitting to his wishes, she prayed that Ayer would "ever point out and teach me to correct everything he sees amiss in me, and thus I may in time become worthy."[82]

In May, 1811, seven months after her wedding, Sarah Connell Ayer yielded further control of her emotional world by making a Calvinist profession of faith before Congregationalist Reverend Asa McFarland.[83] This did not mark a complete break with her sentimental principles. As a girl in Andover and Newburyport, she showed some of Mary Guion's religious eclecticism: she had attended Congregational meeting and periodically copied sermons into her diary, but she was equally willing to attend Episcopal services or none at all. Influenced by eighteenth-century cultural currents, many religious denominations incorporated sentimental concepts. As she observed, "religious subjects [were] subjects, interesting to every heart of sensibility." By the 1810s, even conservative Congregational churches had combined the Scottish Enlightenment's belief that aesthetics influenced the moral sense with Calvinism's doctrine of preparation, and redesigned their meetinghouses with material comforts and refinements meant to positively influence the "religious affections."[84] But unlike Elizabeth Cranch Norton's liberal Protestant husband or Mary Guion Brown's Episcopal priest, Reverend McFarland was a strict Calvinist, and his theology's feeling rules were distinctly different from sensibility. Above all, they insisted that the heart and its effusions were naturally depraved rather than good, only God could save her, and she could do nothing to redeem herself.[85] This conviction made sense of Sarah Connell Ayer's new reality, a clustering of life changes that impelled religious resolution: as a daughter, she was unable to stop her parents' quarrels, financial decline, or drinking, and as a wife, she found Samuel judged her duplicitous. At the same time, her role as a married woman demanded that she set aside the trappings of girlhood, of which sensibility was a part. Chief among these were novels, which had been so important in shaping her identity and her prose. Although still finding *Clarissa* "inimitable," she praised it chiefly for its understanding of "the depravity of the passions," declared herself "an enemy to the generality of novels," and, like Mary Guion Brown, began to employ the Scripture-based language of devotional tracts.[86]

Sarah Connell Ayer's spring 1811 conversion marked the transition from single to married life, sensibility to Calvinism. It also anticipated the most crucial event in her emotional development: motherhood. At the time of her conversion, Sarah was probably in the initial months of her first pregnancy. That volume of her diary ended October 26, 1811, as she awaited childbirth. The next volume began September 29, 1815. During the intervening years she experienced the tragedy that assured she would fully embrace the emotional world of Calvinism. She wrote:

> Since closing my last journal, I have been the mother of four children, which now lay side by side in the grave-yard. The first was born in *1811, Dec. 10th*. The second the *10th of Oct. 1812.* and lived only two days, the third the *4th of Sept. 1813,* and the *4th. the 25th of Nov. 1814*. This last was a sweet, Interesting boy, and lived to be six months old. He was a lovely flower, and I trust he is now transplanted in the garden of Heaven. Though the death of this child was a great trial, yet I hope I was made to bow submissive to the will of my Heavenly Father.[87]

This catastrophic loss established the feeling rules Sarah Connell Ayer observed for the rest of her life: to be insensible to the world and sensible only to God. This was an emotional task so demanding that at first Connell Ayer found it difficult to express her self at all. Between 1811 and 1815 she did not write in her diary, and for some years thereafter, she used her journal to transcribe clerical sermons rather than her own feelings. In contrast to Mary Guion Brown and Elizabeth Cranch Norton, trauma rather than exhaustion stopped her pen. By the late 1810s, she had found her voice, but used it to whip her feelings into the shape that church and family demanded.

Between 1811 and 1822, Sarah Connell Ayer belonged to the Congregational Church in Portland, Maine, where her "beloved pastor" Edward Payson succeeded her non-churchgoing husband as the prime influence on her emotional expression. Their relationship seems to have been unusual: in her study of nineteenth-century women and their ministers, Karin E. Gedge has argued that female parishioners were critical, theologically self-reliant, and rarely close to pastors, but Connell Ayer's loss of her children seems to have made her especially dependent on clerical guidance.[88] Unlike Samuel Ayer, who expected his wife to be more rational, or Asa McFarland, her uncharismatic Concord minister, Payson prized the heart over dogma. As a clerical version of the sentimental man of feeling, he simultaneously provided continuity with Sarah Connell Ayer's youth, bridged the gulf between male and female emotions, and eased her heartache.[89] Payson's memoirist compared him to William Cowper, Sarah Connell Ayer's favorite poet, and Payson acknowledged that prayer was "a form of devout poetry." "As in poetry, so in prayer, the whole subject matter should be furnished by the heart," he maintained, "and the understanding should be allowed only to shape and arrange the effusions of the heart in the manner best adapted to answer the end designed." Nationally famous for his spontaneous public prayers and emotionally charged voice, Payson believed they conveyed his congregation's "own desires and emotions . . . more fully and perspicuously than they could express them themselves."[90] Such prayers preserved elements of Sarah Connell Ayer's earlier love of sensibility, as did her admiration for rural life. In the years following her children's deaths, visits to the countryside comprised the one occasion that elicited sentimental language. As late as 1831, she enthused over "a neat little cottage" which exemplified "retirement, rural-life, domestic happiness." But in keeping with her new values, she quickly turned her eyes from nature to a churchyard and recast the scene into a Christian idyll that "breathe[d] the spirit of devotion."[91]

While Reverend Payson intensified the passions of his parishioners toward God, as a Calvinist he expected them to keep a tight rein on their feelings toward others and expected women to submit to male emotional control. His church enforced this belief by disciplining members not only for sins of behavior, such as intemperance and failure to attend services, but for unacceptable emotions expressed in "unbecoming" or "passionate and improper language" and in "manifesting an improper temper" in conversation. Punishment was equally attentive to feeling. Surface acting was not enough: members were to show the "sincerity" of their "professed penitence," condemn and "acknowledge" their fault, and display "tokens of penitence." With one accused member, the church "labor[ed] with him to bring him to a right tempor" before he gained forgiveness and re-admittance.[92] Through church discipline, Payson established a distinct emotional community whose clear feeling rules recall Litchfield Academy's disciplinary system and oral culture.

Sarah Connell Ayer's family obligations demanded a "right tempor" much as did her church. Concepts of republican motherhood had expected women to play a key role in the religious education of their children, but Victorian ideology heightened the association of femininity and piety and made women fully responsible for the spiritual state of their families.[93] This belief vastly increased emotion work's significance: the emotions women were to model were the same tractable traits that sensibility had prized, but their results were recast in religious terms. Sarah Connell Ayer clearly believed that if only she controlled her feelings, she would not just please her loved ones (which she had felt as a sentimentalist), but that they would come to Jesus and be saved. When her father, who lived with the Ayers, died without repenting, for example, she wrote, "Perhaps had I been more mild and affectionate, he would have been less fretful—but ah! How often have I been irritated—and spoken to him in a hasty and undutiful manner! . . . had I loved more as becomes one professing godliness, he might have thought more favourably of Christianity and its professors."[94] Sarah Connell Ayer had no more success with her husband, who left religious duties to his wife, refused to lead family prayers, and infrequently attended church. Unlike Samuel Brown, who ultimately joined Mary Guion's Episcopal parish and became a church officer, Samuel Ayer seems to have enjoyed frustrating his wife's hopes for his conversion. When he had corrected her sensibility shortly after marriage, Sarah had written, "I shall love him the better as long as I live," but she rarely mentioned him affectionately thereafter. Ayer not only resisted her evangelical attempts, but occasionally attended Unitarian meetings, perhaps as an intentional slight, since his wife believed Unitarians were depraved.[95] But Sarah's resources for changing him were limited: while Samuel Ayer had not hesitated to instruct his wife on proper feeling, she as a woman could influence him only indirectly, through controlling herself.

Most important for Sarah Connell Ayer was the conversion of her children, for whom she was directly responsible. After the deaths of her first four children, three more lived to maturity: a son born in 1819 and two daughters in 1817 and 1823, the last named after her academy friend Harriot.⁹⁶ While she had described her deceased son as a "flower" in the heavenly garden, Connell Ayer perceived her last three children as naturally wicked, making the task of winning them to Christ even more difficult. At the same time, loss of her firstborn children increased her efforts' urgency. As a result, she became far more intrusive a mother than her own parents had been, and her child-raising practices combined Calvinist breaking the will with early Victorian emphasis on the mother.

As a Calvinist, Sarah Connell Ayer sought to break her children's will by criticizing any displays of temper, reminding them God saw all they did, and exhorting them to beg God's forgiveness. But as a woman, she employed "the emotionology of motherhood": through controlling her thoughts, feelings, even her countenance, she tried to model the characteristics her children should acquire.⁹⁷ John Brace had anticipated this approach at Litchfield Female Academy, when he admonished students at term's end, "from the state of your own feelings you may produce in the mind of others, that spark of evil, that may eventually convert the heart into a perfect volcano of mischief."⁹⁸ Preventing that volcano required not only surface acting, but a deep acting far more difficult than any she had known as a sentimentalist. As a young girl, Sarah Connell Ayer had induced emotions by entering into others' feelings and drawing on the goodness of her own heart, but as a Calvinist and a mother, she believed she had to suppress her depraved heart and model not her self, but Christ. Here Calvinist theology was key. Mary Guion Brown and Elizabeth Cranch Norton had also tried to shape their children, but since their theologies retained more positive views of human nature, their maternal emotion work was much less strenuous: they could draw out rather than suppress the best characteristics of both their own and their children's hearts. Even though "born again," Sarah Connell Ayer lacked the confidence that her heart had really changed. When her pastor first examined her religious experiences in 1811, she had repeatedly voiced the caveat, "if I kn[o]w my own heart," and, like other Calvinists, she never lost that doubt.⁹⁹ Popular culture, in contrast, created a different problem: as American society moved into the Victorian period, it set expectations of maternal behavior so high, that Connell Ayer felt that she could not meet them.¹⁰⁰ Whether the perfect mother or a reborn Christian, she had to be what she was not. To do this, she repeatedly castigated any assertions of her will, exhorted herself to be "strict in the duty of self-examination," and begged God to "'Lay me low, and keep me there.'"[101] In praying that her children "be led to avoid their Mother's faults, and to follow her only, as they may hope she follow'd Christ," she based her hopes on her own perceived failings. Not surprisingly, she almost despaired of success: "Ah! how insufficient do I feel to bring up my children as I ought."[102]

As a Calvinist mother, Sarah Connell Ayer experienced not just frustration and extensive emotion work, but two specific feelings: shame and guilt. In his study of seventeenth-century Puritans, John Demos characterized shame as a sense of failure resulting from an audience which rejects the core self. In contrast, guilt emanates from internal values, requires transgression of one's own ideals, and results from hurting others. As a Calvinist, Connell Ayer experienced the shame common to Puritans: her theology required self-loathing, her language of abasement echoed theirs, and she felt her inherent worthlessness exposed to all. But as a mother, she felt guilty: unlike Calvinism, maternal ideology argued that women were naturally Christ-like, so that any but perfect actions seemed sinful and threatened her children's salvation. Demos found that shame predominated in New England from 1650 to 1750, followed by a transitional period which was succeeded by a culture of guilt between 1800 and 1850.[103] Sarah Connell Ayer's case suggests that Calvinist motherhood managed to combine the worst of both worlds.

Despite these strenuous emotional demands and subsequent feelings of inadequacy, Sarah Connell Ayer felt that she should appear and actually be cheerful. God is "our friend," she wrote; "this belief will make us cheerful and happy." Conversely, failure to be happy suggested lack of belief in God. In this sense, sadness denoted religious doubt, which in turn obligated a mask of good cheer.[104] Connell Ayer repeatedly described the women she most admired as "cheerful and pleasant" and "mild and pleasant." They were also "submissive and patient under sufferings," qualities she continually prayed for.[105] These beliefs were not new: Jonathan Edwards had admired his wife for "continual, uninterrupted cheerfulness" and regarded it as a sign of her authentic conversion.[106] Yet in trying to be cheerful, Sarah Connell Ayer had to be careful not to fall into levity or gaiety. As a contemporary diarist noted, "the mirth which was perfectly innocent in a gay girl of sixteen, would ill become a wife of six and twenty . . . there is a difference between chearfulness and gaiety; I prefer the former; it is most steady and renders us most pleasant to others," and in that sense was a "christian virtue." Not only was levity self-centered, but it misused time, which "flies fast enough without our shortening it by useless conversation," as another dour Calvinist put it.[107] Since time belonged to God, wasting it was a religious affront. Proper cheerfulness, in contrast, improved time by serving others.

Far from showing signs of levity, Sarah Connell Ayer's maternal diary was almost unremittingly sad. Such Calvinist grief differed markedly from sensibility's melancholy. As a sentimentalist, Sarah had often remarked that she enjoyed pensive moments and relished tears; sadness was one of sensibility's chief pleasures and fed into its self-referencing tendencies. But Calvinists found sadness as problematic as good cheer. Sadness showed that a sinner realized depravity, but once that sinner was saved, sadness implicitly challenged the justice of God's moral government, which in turn elicited feelings of failure and more sadness. Throughout her religious diary, Sarah Connell Ayer was caught in this cycle. Ironically, expressing sadness allowed her some relief from Calvinism's stringent demands. Modern psychologists have suggested that sadness is a "'me' emotion rather than an 'it' emotion; they reason that the focus is on the consequences to the self," turning the sad person inward.[108] In that sense, sadness allowed an attention to the self that Calvinism otherwise condemned and created a minimal self-acknowledgment, if not sensibility's self-admiration. As Sarah Connell Ayer expressed this problematic emotion, she also discovered a means to convert her children, which was the great task of her adult life. By conveying sadness in her journal, she hoped to bring them to Christ. "O if when the hand that now writes is cold in death, when their Mother is laid in the grave," she pointedly wrote, "if then, this manuscript should fall into their hands, may they remember, may they see recorded in her diary, how often she has wept and pray'd for them in secret."[109]

In her efforts to be a good mother, Sarah Connell Ayer also turned to female friends for support. Especially important to her were the meetings of the Portland maternal association (founded by Mrs. Payson), where women discussed their obligations as mothers, and cultivated a "teachable, affectionate and humble temper" in themselves.[110] She became increasingly active in women's groups in Eastport, Maine, where she and Samuel moved in 1822. Moving to such a small, newly settled fishing village suggests that Samuel Ayer's economic prospects had declined, removing his wife further from the upper-class world of her youth and increasing her household labor. Yet Eastport offered advantages to her. With a tiny group of Calvinists desperate for lay support, it drew her into six different societies: a "*fragment and reading* society," Sabbath School, another maternal association, a female missionary society, a female charitable society, and a female benevolent society, in addition to numerous prayer meetings and church services which women numerically dominated.[111] These circles provided a sphere in which she could unburden her feelings. Sarah Connell Ayer repeatedly praised her "many dear Christian friends" who supported her, provided "sympathy, and council" and to whom she could "open [her] heart unreservedly." "I do love Christian society above all others," she concluded.[112]

But the friendships she gained through these associations did not occupy the same place in her emotional world as friendships had when Sarah Connell Ayer was a girl. Although they enabled her to share her feelings "unreservedly," since these organizations accepted the emotional demands of both Calvinism and motherhood, they provided at best temporary respite from their burdens. Maternal associations in effect taught the "emotionology of motherhood," and in doing so turned this vehicle of female friendship into a powerful enforcer of society's feeling rules, unlike the friendships of single women, which allowed anger as well as sensibility. Sarah's high Calvinist standards also obliged her to criticize her friends' perceived failings and to exhort them to reform, much as she did her children. As these religious tasks extended into friendships, peer relationships offered less freedom of expression and more work. For example, when her Unitarian neighbor Mrs. Rice visited, Connell Ayer felt obliged to provide spiritual advice as well as Calvinist books on divine sovereignty and Unitarian errors, a gesture unlikely to create cordial relations. She also visited her friends in their last illnesses to "speak peace to [their] troubled mind," an effort which expressed both her affection and her Christian duty.[113] Perhaps because adult friendships carried these additional tasks, Sarah Connell Ayer experienced them as less satisfying. When her childhood friend Harriot Osgood died in 1832, Connell Ayer contrasted "the coldness and indifference, the inconstancy of some whom I have considered friends" in Eastport, with Harriot's unchanging "sisterly affection."[114]

As a result, Sarah Connell Ayer's diary as an adult woman lacked the pleasure in self which balanced her empathy for others in her sentimental journal. Virginia Lieson Brereton has argued that the Calvinist narrative's incessant talk of sin "elevated sinners to the very center of the cosmic drama," and provided "drama and a starring role of sorts [that] may have been particularly attractive to women, who usually led protected and sometimes dull and restricted existences within the domestic confines."[115] But however much Connell Ayer talked about herself, the content was unremittingly negative and obsessed with failure. Preoccupation with her own sinfulness elicited not the satisfaction of a starring role, but an emotion new to her journal: a fierce anger directed mainly at herself for her imperfections, and a barely concealed anger at others. If "anger, not sadness, maintains selfhood," these new feelings comprised an attempt to break out of her narrative, assert her self, and protest the sinfulness that bound her.[116] As was true for all these diarists, Sarah Connell Ayer's anger focused on identity and misrepresentation. As she attempted to be a good mother but felt herself failing, and tried to be submissive but succumbed to resentment, her outrage sought expression. Anger at her self seemed acceptable, since Calvinism sought to destroy the sinful self. But anger at others was more problematic: much as she could convert others only indirectly, she felt compelled to express her anger indirectly. By repeatedly chastising herself for not being able to bear "neglect and unkindness," she managed to both protest such treatment and seek moral high ground, but this solution proved only briefly satisfying and ultimately demonstrated her sinfulness.[117] Instead, under the pressure of a culture in which she felt accountable "for every idle word" she uttered, Sarah Connell Ayer's sense of self disintegrated.[118] With every year, her self-criticism increased in virulence, culminating in 1830 with the wish to do away with herself entirely. "I do feel weary of living at this wretched dying rate—so occupied with worldly cares, so careless in regard to the honour of God, to my own eternal good—and to the spiritual welfare of my husband, children, and those around me.... It seems sometimes as though I should eventually destroy myself," she wrote.[119]

Sarah Connell Ayer's high Calvinism, unhappy marriage, and loss of children, culminating in resentment and depression, seem extreme and unrepresentative, but they capture basic changes in women's lives as they matured. Not everyone struggled with her burdens: the deaths of four children in four years were unusual even in the nineteenth century, and women were increasingly likely to prefer the free will of evangelicalism to Calvinism. While she experienced the full force of the elements demanding emotional reordering—marriage, motherhood, religious commitment, and transforming encounters with death—other women underwent only a few of these, felt them to a lesser degree, or enjoyed mitigating circumstances. Yet Sarah Connell Ayer's experience was well within the mainstream in both her youthful delight in sensibility and in her efforts to be a good mother by molding her emotions. Her simultaneous self-condemnation and barely suppressed resentment were not peculiar to her, but could be found in the published diaries of religious contemporaries such as Harriet Newell, and would become major themes in best-selling Victorian novels such as *Elsie Dinsmore*.[120] Moreover, the variations among these diarists seem different in degree rather than kind, and, whatever their individual circumstances, they faced a general cultural expectation that they revise their feelings as they grew up. While this book is primarily a study of young, unmarried women's lives, their experiences as matrons suggest a new understanding of the relationship between emotion work and the life cycle.

These journals indicate that for many women, childhood alone did not determine temperament; instead, emotions were literally a work-in-progress in response to adult experience.[121] For Sarah Connell Ayer, marriage and the death of her children broke her will as her parents never had, enabling this child of gentility to become a Calvinist parent herself. Motherhood may not have broken Mary Guion Brown's spirit, but it transformed her into a very different person, while it sank Elizabeth Cranch Norton into such exhaustion that she could barely hold her pen. In her study of early-nineteenth-century religion, Susan Juster has argued that through conversion "women were empowered by recovering their sense of self through the assertion of independence from others," but the fact that spiritual rebirth was often conjoined to marriage and motherhood considerably reduced its empowering possibilities.[122] The greater impact of marriage and child raising on women seems to have created emotional discontinuity and necessitated a reshuffling of emotional tasks in their lives. This indicates not just that women expressed emotions differently than men, but that they constructed those emotions at different points and through different processes in their lives.

Such emotional reordering often accompanied changes in both reading and writing. Not every young woman immersed herself in sensibility or employed its language, but sentimental literature and language were far more common among young single women than their matronly sisters. Religious conversion called for many acts of renunciation, and rejecting fiction was often, although not invariably, one of them. Sarah Pierce forbade reading novels on Sunday, which implied that they were at odds with holiness, and as devout matrons, both Mary Guion Brown and Sarah Connell Ayer spurned fiction.¹²³ What religion did not end, physical exhaustion finished. If we remember that reading was often done out loud, we see how pressed these women were; apparently even finding the time to listen to someone read was difficult.¹²⁴ Historians have speculated that early American reading was intensive and focused on the Bible and almanacs, but that by the early republic, reading had become extensive and drew on many diverse texts rather than a few.¹²⁵ The spread of fiction was an important part of that transition, and as prime novel readers, women facilitated this new type of reading, but these diaries suggest that the relationship of women to books shifted with their life stages, with women moving in reverse order, from extensive to intensive reading, as they became adults. That change in reading, in turn, shaped women's writing and the language with which they described their emotions. Of course, when newly religious diarists gave up novels, they did not completely forfeit sensibility; many continued to read the "plaintive poetry" which Mark Twain effectively parodied in *Huckleberry Finn*. But their participation in the imagined world of sensibility was much more limited, and they often lost the freedom of movement between emotional communities which characterized their youth. Instead, many matrons dwelt in a reinforcing universe of marriage, motherhood, and religion. Negotiating between fact and fiction and conflicting emotional communities had challenged young women, but had also encouraged the authority and dexterity which had earlier enabled them to express anger confidently and in that sense assert the self. In the diaries of these married women, such angry language is typically muted, absent, or turned against the self.

Women's emotional lives after marriage suggest that although American men may have moved from a collective to an individualistic identity during the early nineteenth century, women's sense of self varied with their life cycle, just as did their reading and writing. When young and single, many women enjoyed a sense of self-distinction and agency that often plummeted after marriage, regardless of broader American patterns. If books provided cultural tools from which women constructed the self, the decline or greater narrowness of their reading as wives and mothers meant far less choice in who they imagined themselves to be. As Ann Swidler has argued, in "settled" as opposed to "unsettled" lives, people are much less engaged in active cultural choice, and how to live seems predetermined or natural.¹²⁶ In the perhaps extreme case of Sarah Connell Ayer, she was left with the single tool of Calvinist religion, while Elizabeth Cranch Norton had a greater range of tools at her disposal, but less time and energy to use them. In selfhood, as in reading, women's life experiences seem to have operated in reverse order from men's and from the larger patterns which men controlled. Catherine Kelly has argued that "marriage offered their best chance to claim adult status—a status comprised of the interlocking roles of wife, mistress, and mother," and that women took pride in the self marriage created, but for a woman to be adult in that culture was to contain her individual self and accept that containment. Undoubtedly elements of pleasure and satisfaction accompanied women's mature roles, but their pride sprang from a context quite different from their single years.[127] This is apparent in late-nineteenth-century Midwestern diaries: after marriage women used "aggregate language" and employed "we" to talk about their own lives, while men used "I" even when speaking of experiences common to their spouses.[128]

Changes in reading influenced women's vocabulary and conceptual framework, but religion apparently played a special role in the emotion work that guided women to adulthood. Intensification of religious commitment, whether expressed in conversion, church membership, or taking the sacraments, signified not just surface acting but deep interior changes which in turn anchored other emotional shifts. Such commitment directly addressed issues of identity and the construction of self, as converts were transformed from sinners to saints, and congregations divided the sheep from the goats. Identity change figured most prominently in evangelical and Calvinist theologies, although even Episcopalians like Mary Guion experienced a similar transformation through the medium of sacramental piety, and liberal Congregationalist churches had absorbed elements of sensibility's preoccupation with the heart. As young women changed their identities, religion grounded in the affections or requiring rebirth echoed and reconfigured problems central to youthful sensibility. In theological terms, such religious expectations confronted a major paradox in women's lives: society, conduct books, and sensibility expected them to perform certain emotions, even as prescriptive works insisted feelings be heartfelt. Young women felt this conundrum most acutely, since the world of sentiment was presumably their province: hence, their early effort to produce the emotions expected. Religions emphasizing conversion demanded an alignment of heart and behavior by arguing that the surface acting of good works was insufficient to salvation without an inner change. Sensibility, of course, had sought this as well, but was willing to settle for class markers of a feeling heart: graceful gestures, delicate language, refined appearance, and an indefinable ease.

What religious conversion offered was congruence between the surface and the interior, so that the do-ing of emotion work was transmuted into emotional be-ing. Aspiring young women might perform sensibility from the outside in, but the converted needed to experience piety from the inside out. Part of evangelicalism's and Calvinism's appeal to young women lay in directly addressing issues of identity just when these women moved from girlhood to maturity, so that their hearts fit their new roles in life. At the same time, such theologies simultaneously explained a new reality of loss and provided the "new heart" to cope with that loss. The congruence that conversion promised also addressed society's pervasive fear of deception: that men were flatterers, sentimentalists were *poseurs,* and churchgoers were unsaved. To "rest" in Jesus was to rest from emotion work, an evangelical form of sensibility's "ease," as women finally became who they presumably were and should be. Having settled their own selves, women were then to devote themselves to others' needs.

In fact, religion provided no lasting assurance of emotional congruity, as Sarah Connell Ayer's journal attests. For her, as for other Calvinist diarists, conversion inaugurated a lifetime of emotion work rather than the ease in identity they sought. To some extent, this problem diminished during the nineteenth century, as evangelical religion increasingly turned to Arminian theology: free will promised resolution of self-doubt and correspondingly less striving, as sinners chose and settled their own spiritual fates. But religion remained prominent in women's path to maturity, for it not only addressed issues of identity, but explained death.

During the early republic, death was peculiarly women's task: whether as wives, daughters, mothers, or neighbors, females nursed the sick, watched the dying, and prepared the corpse. Accompanying this intimate physical labor was an emotional task which reflected larger cultural themes: women were to express grief over death, but not give way to intense feeling. This emotional containment echoed concern that sentimental women not become irrational, but it also taught them to accept God's disposition of events, anticipate the afterlife, and prepare for their own demise.[129] In that sense, personal loss could transmute into religious gain, as "the desire to replace a severed relationship with another, more fulfilling one, drove women to convert."[130] All these diaries make clear that although their authors were young, encounters with death were frequent and typically served as a religious warning. The death of classmates reminded Litchfield Academy students that life could end at any moment, a theme Sarah Pierce routinely proclaimed at graduation; Rachel Van Dyke's experience of her father's and pastor's deaths pitched her into depression; Abigail May's anticipation of her own passing roused her to anger and rejection of youthful sensibility; Patty Rogers attended her dying father, as she moved from fruitless courtship to single piety; Sarah Connell Ayer's loss of her first four children shaped her entire adult life; Elizabeth Cranch Norton anticipated death with every family illness; and Mary Guion Brown's loss of several family members and fears of death in childbirth anchored her religious life. In her extensive survey across cultures and centuries, Susan Starr Sered found that mothers who suffered death of children invariably turned to religion, whether organized or of their own making, to understand this calamity.[131] For these diarists, not death alone, but death combined with the other forces changing their lives, all clustered around the transit from youth to maturity, signaled the need for emotional reordering: school's end, courtship, marriage, and motherhood,

By preserving the hair of their loved ones, young women memorialized their friends and reflected on the importance of preparing for the hereafter. Hair Memorial to Sarah, in Mary Wallace Peck's Friendship Album, 1825. (Collection of the Litchfield Historical Society, Litchfield, Connecticut)

as well as death, reminded young women that time was passing, as did the journal itself, as diarists marked off each day.

Anticipation of death, combined with religious conversion, a narrowed universe, and an eroded sense of self, all contributed to the prevailing tone of many married women's diaries: resigned gratitude. Producing that emotion was a major task of their adult lives and built on life-long demands for contentment. As sentimentalists, young women had cultivated contentment through borrowing the feelings of rustics. At Litchfield Female Academy, Sarah Pierce had maintained that contentment should be taught "as soon as a child begins to desire [others'] playthings," a sentiment her students had dutifully echoed. "I cannot but think that a contented mind is one of the greatest blessings which we can possess," Caroline Chester had written, while her classmates had practiced penmanship by writing "Contentment without wealth is better than wealth without contentment."[132] But resigned gratitude demanded far more than girlhood's often superficial contentment. On the eve of her marriage, Elizabeth Cranch quailed before the formidable task facing her: "O my heart! Shall I wish it less sensible?—Shall I not be happy unless I am unfeeling?" she had exclaimed before abandoning her "unfinished page." These three wives would all answer, yes, feeling less—in particular, not feeling resentment or anger—helped them through married, maternal, and religious life.[133] A certain degree of resignation had prevailed even before marriage: Elizabeth Cranch, Mary Guion, and Sarah Connell all faced their weddings with a sense of the irrevocable. Even during her courtship, Mary Guion, that most resourceful of diarists, had expressed a certain fatalism: "my future lot I long to know," she had written, aware that despite all her efforts, once cast, her lot could not be changed. Adult women's gratitude embodied their perception that not only could they not change much, but that they deserved little, a sentiment these three women shared despite their distinctly different theologies. This feeling echoed their reduced sense of self; as the self took up less space emotionally and on their journals' pages, it demanded and expected less. Moreover, these women knew that their lot could always be worse: Sally's miserable marriage persistently reminded Guion of the fate she had escaped, while the deaths of Sarah Connell Ayer's first four children impelled gratitude for the offspring who survived. In practicing resigned gratitude, women prepared for death, which demanded those exact same emotions: resignation to death and gratitude for the life that had been and that remained. As young women, these diarists had evoked contentment as a class and gender marker, but as matrons, their problem was to create resigned gratitude in the face of limited lives, and to accept their world as right and good. The difference between those emotional tasks charts the distance they had traveled since their youth.

The contrast between those emotional tasks also charts a difference between many adult women who were single and those who were married. The emotional community of matrons was not entirely closed to single women: of the four experiences most likely to reconstruct women's hearts, traumatic confrontations with sickness and death and overwhelming religious commitment provided entrance to this community's outer circles for many single women, even without marriage and motherhood. In particular, single women who underwent Calvinist conversion experienced a submissive relationship with God and a self-lacerating language that gave them much in common with matrons, with the deity standing in for a husband. But unlike Sarah Connell Ayer, who experienced the full force of all these events, Susan Heath managed to evade or mitigate every one of them. In doing so, she provides an instructive example of how individual circumstances intersect with broader social forces.

From her seventeenth birthday, when she wrote her first entry, into middle age, Heath's voluminous diary changed little in its language, expression of anger, love for her mother, and contempt for her father. Unlike many spinsters who did not marry because their romantic ideals were so high, she participated in the village courtship community only briefly and seems to have had little interest in marriage.[134] Heath also showed considerable continuity in her reading patterns: well into her thirties, she read extensively in history, philosophy, and fiction, as well as in the Bible, much as she did in her teens. While many single women were at their family's beck and call, those who could share duties with sisters enjoyed better lives, and Heath fell into that more fortunate category.[135] A faithful churchgoer all her life, she enjoyed the ministry of Brookline's John Pierce, a Congregationalist uninterested in controversy and sympathetic to liberalism. His theology emphasized continuity in life rather than conversion's transformation, and in that regard reinforced Heath's broader emotional development.[136] In 1824, when she was twenty-nine, Susan Heath lost her sister Mary to a sudden illness, an event which led Susan to realize that "real grief was a sensation new to us untill we lost our lovely Mary—but now how changed are our feelings—every thing wears a different aspect—& I wonder at my former feelings—my thoughtlessness—my indifference upon subjects so *all important*—."[137] Had those reflections affected her more and led to religious rebirth, Susan Heath's emotions would have become more like her married sisters'. But her feelings returned to their previous channels, as she was absorbed into the usual family pleasures and squabbles. In all these areas, Heath sidestepped the forces must significant in changing women's adult sense of self. Even then, her life as a single woman was by no means without emotion work: Susan Heath's mother, Hannah, continued efforts to teach her daughter the resigned gratitude essential to mature womanhood, and in that Susan recorded self-admonitions after every angry outburst against her father, she toiled at the emotional tasks common to married women. But Susan Heath never entirely lost her anger, and she seems to have regarded resigned gratitude as her mother's task, although she might occasionally share it. In this regard, she understood her culture well: she was a daughter, not a wife and mother, and in that sense she lived in a different emotional world.

CONCLUSION

> Mrs. Hasket Derby... continually pleases and delights you; she appears to live for others, nor ever bestows a thought upon herself, yet [is] so perfectly unconscious of it, that it seems inherent in her disposition, and to flow without any effort.
> —*Eliza Southgate Bowne, Journal, 11 July 1802*

The story of young women's emotions during the early republic comprises many small, intimate moments: their diaries variously record teary eyes, outraged exclamations, yearning for love, skeptical rejoinders, and pious submission, as emotion work entered every aspect of their lives. But if we look at the context of such emotional minutiae, we can see that these young women performed on a broad stage, and that their performances had political, economic, social, and ideological meaning. Above all, young women's feelings reflected their culture's contradictory expectations, each of which created work: to feel spontaneously, but not too much; to assert female intellect, but not forfeit ladylike feeling; to consult the heart in courtship, but not neglect the head; to value the "feeling heart" but not express anger; and to suppress the self upon marriage and religious commitment, but do it gladly. Through their emotional balancing acts, young women performed important tasks as they constructed both themselves and society, but their wages and benefits varied widely, their employers remained often unaware of their labors, and their working conditions were peculiarly feminine.

In shaping their feelings, women worked for themselves as well as their culture, and in that sense emotion work offered empowering possibilities. Emotion work was highly skilled labor, and as they grew up, females became increasingly adept at employing emotions to their advantage, especially to protect themselves from those who threatened them. As sentimental readers, they cultivated refinement that they used to attract respectful treatment, condemn the "disgusting," and judge suitors by the books they proffered. Even the mild-mannered Sarah Connell used her sentimental skills to reject unwanted men. At female academies, young women's adroit balance of head and heart helped them deflect criticisms of female education and provided young intellectuals like Rachel Van Dyke with a daring sense of freedom. Women deployed their cumulative skills to the greatest effect in courtship, when they assessed men, determined when to reveal their own feelings, oversaw public understanding of their emotional commitments, and employed their friends as detectives and defenders. As a result, courtship was the period in which women potentially possessed (and needed) the greatest agency.

Although ultimately expecting women to bend to cultural currents, emotion work entailed an initial individuation of self, as these young, well-off women examined their feelings and considered who they were. Reading and writing were the means through which that articulation took place and comprised their most empowering cultural tools, rather than dreams, which guided some colonial- and Revolutionary-era Americans.[1] Development of the diary of feeling—whether employed as backstage, mirror, official story, or confidante—invited women to ponder their hearts and in that regard distinguish their emotions. Reading had much the same effect: although familiarity with print culture always threatened to produce a derivative voice, sentimental fascination with the self encouraged young women to compare themselves to fictional heroines. We can see the difference reading made when we compare these journals to what Marilyn Ferris Motz calls "folk diaries": written by literate but not literary farm women, they not only jettisoned feelings for lists of chores and climatic change, but rarely used the pronoun "I". Unlike "self-conscious attempts at literary production," folk diaries did not "attempt to differentiate the self from society." "The focus is not inward to the self, but outward to the environment" in these journals, she argues. Their writing was "intensive," much as was their reading, in that both were concentrated and limited.[2] By contrast, reading and writing enabled women such as Elizabeth Cranch to become assertively and literally "self-conscious": "You told me I must inform you how I *felt*—," she wrote Jacob Norton. "That is impossible, and unless you could exchange characters and circumstances with me you can never know—."[3] This heightened sense of a distinctive self became the loose cannon of emotion work; in some cases, it encouraged women to express their anger and to rage over those who presumed to misrepresent them. Even when sporadic and tentative, it chose when, how, and if to respect the conventions Erving Goffman saw as necessary to social status. The fact that these young women rarely apologized for their emotions suggests they felt a right to them; their self-possession seems grounded on ownership of their feelings.

As young single women created this self, they gained satisfaction from themselves and approbation from others. Sensibility invited women to admire themselves with a freedom rare in the earlier years of the eighteenth century and transgressive to Calvinists of any era. It is difficult to read these often spirited diaries without sensing that their authors admired their own writing ability; as chapter 4 suggests, pleasure in self-expression periodically took priority over behaving well, at least in their journals. Among female friends, women felt especially free in expressing the self that they developed within those private pages. Carroll Smith-Rosenberg has interpreted female friendship as a warm and supportive retreat from an oppressive outer society, and these diaries provide much evidence to support her. Such relationships were part of a wider orientation to peers that was both experiential and ideological. Enjoying access to an academy education and books not available to their mothers, many well-off young women seem to have sought emotional acceptance more among their contemporaries than from their parents. Siblings, whether brothers or sisters, provided an arena of emotional freedom, as did friends. The increased use of the word "friend" for peers, husbands, and even Jesus is emblematic of the new and hopeful emphasis on more egalitarian relations, as was this period's enthusiasm for "sympathy."[4]

In more public arenas, women gained as well: the teas and assemblies which proliferated during the eighteenth century provided occasions for the public to admire the results (if not the process) of women's emotion work. At Litchfield Female Academy, young women accrued overt, verbalized, and public recognition for emotion work from both peers and elders. For most, this comprised the one occasion in their lives in which they stood individually before a substantial crowd of both men and women and received prizes for emotional and intellectual tasks. The social esteem women gained might take concrete form in a marriage proposal from an ambitious, sensitive, and honest suitor, who was friend as well as lover. In all these regards, young single women earned the currency of respect for their extensive emotion work.

Women as a group took this public recognition further. Although possessing neither the vote nor financial independence, well-off young women employed emotions to interpret and assert both their class and their republican citizenship. As daughters of aspiring classes, they displayed the "baubles of Britain," but they also modeled gentility, a way of being as refined as their imported linens. In this regard, young women were central in redefining class to include not just money or occupation but feelings, and high sensibility appeared as a form of emotional conspicuous consumption. Their emotion work also played a political role for both themselves and the republic at large. By assuring that however many baubles their families bought, their feelings did not possess aristocratic selfishness and coldness, women's sensibility bridged the gap between men's materialism and republican values. In that sense, long before what Barbara Welter has called the "Cult of True Womanhood," men depended on women's roles to allow them to pursue their own self-interest, and men's economic labor was posited on women's emotion work. But such female toil benefited not just men, but women as well. Ostensibly private, women's diary entries echoed the public sphere's political values and language and reveal women's own position within that larger sphere. In the carefully calibrated balance of rationality and tenderness which young ladies learned in academies, prosperous daughters used their emotions to secure not only the republic's success but an education for themselves. Women's simultaneous immersion in political, economic, and emotional issues is most clear in their courtships, as republican men's fear of conspiring tyrants found its parallel in republican women's fear of deceitful suitors. When Mary Guion wrote, "those who list in the conjugal state are designed as help mates for each other not as tyrants," she declared her citizenship in the republic.[5]

As much as women gained public respect and private self-confidence from emotion work, it also hindered them. By participating in the republic's maintenance and class formation largely through performing emotion, women could do little to change society's structure. Sensibility seemed to grant membership in the upper classes, but in fact relationships to powerful men determined rank and wealth, and no amount of refined feeling changed women's basic economic dependence. Catherine Allgor has vividly illustrated the important role women played in Washington's "parlor politics" at this time, but Louisa Adams would have had few opportunities to use her skills without marriage to John Quincy Adams, and such efforts served his political career, not hers.[6] Similarly, young women's successful balance of intellectuality and ladylike traits might reassure nervous fathers and win their daughters an academy education, but could not vindicate the female intellect enough to allow opportunities equal to men's. Although women incorporated republican rhetoric in their fears of duplicitous males, emotions provided only a temporary and personal solution to female inequality: courting women might ascertain and avoid rakes, but they could not change the society that made females vulnerable to tyrannical males. Again, men admired women's piety, but displays of feminine spirituality rarely convinced men to allow women to become recognized ministers. Even within the family domain, the prospects emotion work offered were often illusory; as philosopher Sandra Lee Bartky has argued, "The *feeling* of out-flowing personal power so characteristic of the caregiving woman is quite different from the *having* of any actual power in the world."[7]

These limits are not surprising. During the early republic, American culture not only feared women's selfhood, but remained apprehensive of men's. That self signaled an interest potentially at odds with the greater good; all the more disconcerting because it was unseen, it inspired fear of the unknown and reflected every imagined anxiety. In assuming an interior at odds with external appearance, charges of duplicity provide a measure of early republican perceptions that the private self had become pervasive. Such fears ran through every aspect of their society, whether political, commercial, or religious, and both men and women shared them, as witness Sarah Pierce's extraordinary comparison of ambitious schoolgirls to Alexander the Great. Such anxiety intensified during the later nineteenth century, as cities increased anonymity, social mobility obscured class identification, and "confidence men" and "painted women" came to embody Victorian society's seemingly pervasive hypocrisy.[8] American culture resolved these concerns through gender politics, as expressed in feelings: reluctant to curtail their individuated self and the power it promised, men placed increased emphasis on women's nature, in the hope that women actually were who men wanted them to be. As we have seen in the reconstruction of women's hearts at marriage and motherhood, emotion work was the medium through which that congruence took place, and essentialism was its ideological result.

As spirited and perceptive as these diaries are, and as deftly as their young authors negotiated their way through society, their victories seem compromised, even before marriage. Their greatest emotional freedom occurred among their female peers, but even that domain reflected constraining societal conventions. Rachel Van Dyke felt compelled to hide her true self from women who shared their broader culture's contempt for female intellectuals; Sarah Connell hesitated to open her heart to her prosperous friends, as her class status sank; the ties that nourished women emotionally also bound them to other women's behavior and fate, for good and ill; and in maternal associations women encouraged their friends to embody the self-control expected of mothers. Female friendship may have encouraged sharing, but it was not wholly tolerant of difference. Siblings, too, set bounds to their sisters' emotional freedom. As young women moved toward maturity, previously encouraging brothers began to enforce societal strictures; Mary Guion's adored brother James suggested the time had come to give up novels, and Rachel Van Dyke's brother judged her diary entries too severe. When dealing with social superiors rather than peers, women's hearts were even less free, as witness Sarah Connell Ayer's relationships with her father and husband, Elizabeth Cranch Norton's submission to her fiancé's emotional direction, and Mary Guion Brown's reluctance to reveal her diary to Samuel, even though she loved him. At best, emotion work entailed a continually negotiated balance between self and society, a negotiation that recognized a private and distinct self, but which could only delay or deflect gendered expectations. Marriage often marked a definitive decline in women's ability to negotiate on their own behalf. In striking contrast to courtship, once wed, women used their emotional skills to suppress rather than to protect the self. In doing so, the always precarious balance between the individuated self and social demands tipped decisively in favor of the latter. Ironically, in courtship women enjoyed an agency which they forfeited in marriage, its direct result.

Moreover, the means through which both single and married women were most likely to articulate a distinctive self was essentially private: their diaries. In political scientist James C. Scott's terms, journals (like gossip) were "hidden transcripts," "discourse [by subordinate groups] that takes place 'offstage,' beyond direct observation by power holders." Such oral or written transcripts "confirm, contradict, or inflect what appears in the public transcript" of the powerful, which defines and controls them.[9] The difference between the hidden and public transcript reveals the degree to which subordinates reject hegemonic discourse. In these journals, that difference appeared most strongly in women's single years, during which they articulated the "great *I*," sought to protect that I, and expressed anger at those who threatened and deceived them. In all these ways, they used emotion work to their own ends or refused to do the emotion work society had assigned them. However, these acts were private in that they had a very limited audience, were individual and hence lacked force, and aimed at protecting themselves rather than changing their world. Thus, Abigail May denigrated Mr. Bowers to the few readers of her diary and to some extent to his face, but in front of others, she danced not one but two dances with him, even though she hated him.

Women's weakness was most pronounced in public policy. While public literature infused women's writings and private lives, and women shaped public perception of themselves in village social life, females influenced public policy at best symbolically. To the degree that women's dissent remained private, public transcripts resisted change. The early republic's public prints included a lively discussion of women's place, but quickly determined that for men, rights meant opportunities, while for women, rights signified duties, with their opportunities translating into personal choice of a husband, who then defined those duties.[10] This meant that for all the emotion work women did in determining their husbands, their status changed very little. As Scott writes, "No matter how elaborate the hidden transcript may become, it always remains a substitute for an act of assertion directly in the face of power."[11] In the early national period, even the public organizations women were most likely to join were Sabbath Schools and mothers' groups, which reinforced traditional religious and maternal scripts. Not until the rise of antebellum organizations aimed at reforming society would women's voices move beyond hidden transcripts to decisively and collectively challenge the public sphere. However, those later reform efforts drew on women's private experiences by making emotional appeals key elements in their protests against slavery and drunkenness. At that point, women such as Harriet Beecher Stowe shifted emotion work from themselves to others, and played a significant role in constructing national feeling about these moral and political issues.

In contrast, men's emotion work was tied more firmly to the outer world, less hidden, promised more power, intruded less on their private selves, and offered wages in different currency than did women's. Nineteenth-century urban male clerks perused sentimental fiction, much as did women; moreover, the desire to establish gentility through reading was common to both genders. But young men had an additional and overriding reason for such reading: to develop the "mercantile character" that would bring them success in the marketplace.[12] A future as competitors in the marketplace also changed the context of men's education. Men attended single-sex academies, like women, but unlike their sisters, they might continue to college, and neither form of men's education created the intense conflict between intellectual competition and gentility which women experienced. While society expected neither men nor women to express anger within the home, it accepted and even admired public male anger in politics, economic competition, and war. Lastly, both men and women experienced the oversight of their gossiping village community during courtship, but poor discernment of suitors exacted a higher price for women than for men, and men gained far greater wages and benefits from marriage than did women, for less emotional investment. In such circumstances, men might well seek marriage more eagerly than women, and a romantic veneer served men's interests more than women's.

The cumulative effect of these differences meant that men experienced emotional transformation not so much through the more private events of marriage and parenthood as at their political and economic majority, when they fully entered into public life. At that point, men's and women's emotional tasks diverged most clearly, as men faced economic and social demands to assert the individuality women were to suppress. For women, intimate, familial events rebuilt their emotional world, but work in the marketplace, rather than affection within the home, established nineteenth-century men's mature identity. Marriage might have had economic implications for women, just as good incomes qualified men for marriage, but the relative place of each in their respective lives made coming of age highly gendered. The process of growing up was, however, emotionally wrenching for both men and women. Finding their way in the wage-earning world entailed a loss of the parental home, and intensified economic competition caused such emotional upheaval that many young men sought the consolation of intense same-sex friendships. Within those bonds, men in their teens and twenties could express affection, gain confidence, establish useful alliances, joke about women and marital prospects, and prepare themselves for their future as men rather than boys. Once they established their economic future, however, men were able to marry, and at that point many set aside the intimate same-sex relationships which had helped them through this traumatic transition. Like women, they settled into a new life and emotional community which seemed strikingly different in priorities and feelings from their youth, but which directed men toward the marketplace and women toward the family.[13] Even in their familial role, men's sense of self was different from women's: nineteenth-century fatherhood was praised for "what it could do for men, rather than what fathers should do for their children."[14] Moreover, while women possessed only indirect power, men enjoyed what Laura Maria Wolcott as a wife called "the daily direct influence under the title of 'husband.'"[15] Yet if men's and women's emotion work after marriage was different, it was related, for men's public role was predicated on women's private emotional tasks. As Gillian Brown has argued, men's individualism was, in fact, a "domestic individualism" dependent upon the home.[16]

Given the "hidden" character of women's transcripts and the different trajectory of men's emotional lives, society not only changed little, but showed fitful awareness of the effort women's emotion work required. True, some people, especially women, recognized that emotion work was work, and hard work at that. As Eliza Southgate Bowne wrote in 1802 of a Mr. Hasket Derby, "an easy unassuming politeness . . . is not the acquirement of a day."[17] Litchfield Academy's instructors were clearly aware of their students' struggles: John Brace noted in his diary when a girl had "mend[ed] her temper" enough to win an exhibition prize, and in the Academy's hothouse atmosphere, it is difficult to believe that any student's efforts escaped Sarah Pierce's all-seeing eyes.[18] Emotion work was most clearly displayed during courtship: within an observant and gossiping village culture, women's efforts to attract the right kind of man, express their own feelings, and to discern and reject rakes were public knowledge. Similarly, ministers drew upon a vast literature of pastoral counseling in guiding sinners through the emotion work demanded for salvation, and women's published conversion narratives and memoirs detailed their efforts to be good Christians.

But other forces undercut recognition of the work women put into emotion. Eliza Southgate Bowne admitted the difficulties of acquiring "easy unassuming politeness" for Mr. Hasket Derby, but took quite a different tack with his wife, whom she found "the most agreeable, fascinating woman I ever saw. She continually pleases and delights you; she appears to live for others, nor ever bestows a thought upon herself, yet [is] so perfectly unconscious of it, that it seems inherent in her disposition, and to flow without any effort."[19] As Sarah Connell found, the more skilled she was at producing sensibility, the less apparent her work was; instead, like Mrs. Derby, her feelings appeared effortless. Arlie

Russell Hochschild points out that the expectation that women follow feeling rules requires them to engage in more "emotion managing" than men. Since effective emotion managing looks spontaneous, this reinforces the belief women are naturally emotional, effectively conceals the work that women put into shaping their feelings, and prevents them from being paid for their work.[20] In that sense, the very nature of emotion work assures its invisibility.

In light of this extensive emotional toil, we need to reconsider the prevailing understanding that women's household productive work declined beginning in the late eighteenth century.[21] In a material sense, this transition began, although Elizabeth Cranch Norton's mind-numbing recital of cooking, sewing, and cleaning tasks, besides raising eight children, reminds us how much physical productivity continued for wives. But leisure and consumption did not simply replace such physical work. Instead, women's emotional production not only continued, but increased. Even before marriage, young women engaged in the manufacture of emotion; especially for wealthy women, this form of work rapidly overtook making candles and textiles. Nonetheless, women's emotion work was relatively light during their single years: academies put intensive demands on them for only a short period, and the stakes were high during courtship, but self-admiration and agency lightened these burdens. In that sense, women's pay compensated for their effort. After marriage, women's emotion work increased, but their wages and benefits decreased: expectations were so high that few women felt satisfied with their performance, society regarded the most stringent self-suppression as unremarkable and normal, and indirect influence promised little agency.

Increased gendering of emotions after 1830 further obscured and deepened women's emotional labors. During the early years of the republic, shared class status meant that prosperous men and women also shared considerable emotional ground: even though Americans expected women to be more sentimental and men more rational, gentility was a common ideal for both genders and potentially narrowed the feeling gap between them. A generation later, even within the same class, Americans expected significantly different emotions from men and women and enshrined their expectations in the middle-class norm of "True Womanhood."[22] In both the early republic and the Victorian period, emotional prescriptions reflected the mutual operation of gender and class, but during the earlier years, class tended to trump gender in the expression of feelings, while later in the nineteenth century, gender appears to have trumped class. In the process, the emotional distance between men and women widened, even within the same social rank. At the same time, the way in which gender was constructed shifted. During the early republic, ideologues employed essentialist arguments in constructing womanhood, but allowed some role for the environment. This situation enabled Sarah Pierce to justify and expand female education, an arena in which women worked to overcome supposedly natural limits and displayed the acquired results in public exhibitions. But as society's gender ideals became more essentialist during the nineteenth century, society perceived women's most admired attributes—maternity, piety, compassion, chastity—as the result of nature rather than work. To recognize these traits as work, men had to admit that women were naturally someone other than who men wanted them to be, and that "true" womanhood was dissimulation, a prospect that would have ignited broader cultural fears of duplicity. Women not only had to hide how they changed themselves, but their efforts to change others, and confine themselves to indirect influence. At the same time, men's work became largely paid work, and in the process came to define work itself, with women's household labor coming to represent an Eden seemingly "without the curse of labor."[23] The implications for emotion work in these interlocking developments were wholly to women's disadvantage. In simultaneously distinguishing women's emotions from men's, heightening standards of women's emotional contributions, and attributing their feelings to nature, antebellum prescriptive literature devalued, obscured, and increased the work demanded of women.

Not only does the history of emotion challenge the idea that women's productive labor decreased beginning in the late eighteenth century, but it questions the usefulness of the conventional divisions between male/female and public/private spheres in understanding how men and women "do" and experience gender. The more scholars have examined everyday life, especially using first-person narratives with all of their texture, complexity, and ambiguity, the more difficult it has been to sustain such general dichotomies. As a result, although historians of women initially emphasized how men's and women's spaces and lives differed, many now repudiate "binary thinking," and maintain that even in the dualistic nineteenth century, shared experiences transcended separate spheres.[24] Similarly, the more historians have studied the public and private spheres, the more boundaries have blurred. The meaning of public and private has varied so much within and across periods, that determining how these spheres changed over time has proven very difficult, while the "multidimensionality" of everyday life has left scholars suggesting that we replace dualism with multiple spheres, although they have not agreed on what those spheres should be.[25] The felt need for new approaches is apparent in historians' experimentation with Charles Taylor's concept of the "social imaginary" and Pierre Bourdieu's reconfiguring of "habitus" as ways to ground personal experience without losing the power of generalization.[26] Clearly, we need more useful conceptual tools to understand history as men and women actually experienced it. I suggest that instead of asking about locality and behavior, which have been the prime subjects of the spheres debate, we ask, rather, what women and men feel, how and where emotions are created, and what those feelings and that process mean. Emotion work provides a distinctive touchstone to women's (and men's) status which helps explain a modern paradox that the spheres debate has not been able to resolve: in the twenty-first century, we often *see* changes in women's sphere, and, by implication, their status—in where they are, and what they are doing—but *feel* that somehow little has changed. That is the point: the emotional dimension of women's lives seems to have proven singularly resistant to change. In a sense, the experiences of their hearts have not shifted as much as other circumstances. Emotion work provides a new way to understand public/private, male/female experience, and, indeed, to provide a new conceptualization that goes beyond those distinct but related dualisms. It illuminates not only how the individual constructs the self, but how communal cultures of feeling are created. Emotional communities do not assume male/female or public/private boundaries, but subsume them within worlds of feeling that may or may not include the same sexes, the public or the private, or even a real as opposed to an imaginary locality. Immediate to people's lives, flexible to the life cycle, manageable in size, and responsive to transitional and conflicting circumstances, emotional communities embrace multidimensionality rather than make it problematic. As the site where people do gender, class, and race and build the self, they combine the highly personal world of feelings with larger ideological and economic factors, without abstracting them from everyday experience and individual agency. In joining emotional communities to emotion work, we gain a new means to determine the wages and worth of men's and women's labor, find common ground for studying men as well as women, and re-integrate the long-missing component of power dynamics into gender studies.[27]

Using this new conceptualization and extrapolating from the historiography of modern America, I find some variations, but many striking parallels between women's emotion work in the early republic and the twentieth century. During the 1910s and '20s, visual media succeeded print culture as a prime influence, young women learned to imitate movie actresses rather than fictional heroines and separated themselves from dominating Victorian mothers, and companionate marriage denoted passion more than friendship. Class remained important in this culture of materialism, but buying began to stand in for emotional production, as the purchase of feelings through objects effectively replaced personal embodiments of gentility. The appearance of freer sexual behavior seemed to conflate the experiences of young men and women, but diaries show that the transition from flapper to "flapper wife" still entailed self-suppression. "I am struggling to conquer myself," a young bride wrote in her 1926 journal, using language Sarah Connell Ayer would have recognized. Two years later, struggling to make her marriage work, she vowed, "I must deny my very self. I must not only learn rigid surface control; I must suffer a complete inner negation."[28]

While we are surprised to find such self-suppression in the 1920s, we expect it from 1950s housewives, but that later decade raises a different question: what cultural reach do different emotional communities have, and why, and how does that affect the emotion work of individuals? The contrasts between single and married women's lives impelled more emotion work at marriage, just as it had during the early republic, but the colonial period, Victorian era, and the 1950s seem to have had similar expectations of young women and matrons, so that emotion work did not so much intensify at marriage, as continue. Despite some tolerance for high-spirited girls (as witness Jo March in Alcott's *Little Women*), Victorian society seems to have offered fewer and less distinct emotional communities for women to negotiate. Gender considerations impelled this undifferentiated demand, but other cultural institutions reinforced it: during the Victorian period, for example, the spread of mourning made death a more central cultural focus for all ages, evangelicalism's growth through revivals and reform exposed young women to more insistent demands for conversion, mothers were more dominant in their daughters' lives, and novels gave new prominence to mothers and children. Charles Taylor has argued that "the inability to imagine the self outside of a particular context" creates an "embeddedness" that limits the self.[29] In that sense, women during the nineteenth century and 1950s had less occasion to develop the self-articulation and skill in deflecting cultural demands which characterized the more fluid early republic. Ironically, multiplicity of emotional communities seems to have created more emotion work for women but also a stronger sense of self and more skills in coping with societal demands. The challenge for historians is to understand which emotional communities exist and dominate in some eras and not others, and why. If that task is complex, it also provides a means to compare the influence and development of emotional communities and women's emotion work over time.

Late-twentieth-century feminism would seem to have changed or reduced women's emotion work, but also illustrates American culture's ability to make feeling a central component in resisting change. On the one hand, consciousness-raising groups provided new emotional communities in which women reconstructed their feelings as they applied radical feminist analysis to their lives. On the other, just when feminism advocated that women free themselves from domestic labor, American culture raised expectations for women's physical appearance, especially for young women. This has not only added physical work, as women produce muscles, but created a new and sometimes lethal kind of emotion work, as adolescents berate themselves into diets and exercise. The eighteenth century's erasure of the physical, initiated with its reconceptualization of pregnancy as feeling, reversed itself, and in the twentieth century, emotions have been used to produce a desired physical form. Once these young women grow up, they labor at additional emotional duties. Expectations that women should work at controlling their feelings as mothers has continued: as late as 1987, books on child raising warned against the effects of maternal emotion on children, but regarded fathers' feelings with little concern.[30] In her work after *The Managed Heart*, Arlie Russell Hochschild has gone on to chronicle women's struggles balancing professional and familial commitments in two-career marriages, an effort she has characterized as a "second shift" which continues after their wage-earning "first shift." That second shift entails not just doing the dishes, but trying to persuade husbands to contribute to cleaning and childcare. She found that contemporary wives see themselves as "lucky" if their husbands contribute to household tasks, however minimally, an attitude I find reminiscent of their early republican predecessors who regarded marriage with resigned gratitude and diminished entitlement.[31] If emotion work raises issues of identity and contributes to anger, as it did in the early republic, we might expect this ever-expanding toil to influence the character of women's outrage. Ann M. Kring's study of the psychological literature on gender and anger shows that although men and women often become angry for the same reasons, within relationships, women become angry over "betrayal, condescension, rebuff, unwarranted criticism, or negligence; whereas, men report more anger than women if their partner is moody or self-absorbed."[32] In short, much like the early republic, issues of identity still promote female anger.

In her shrewd *Oprah Winfrey and the Glamour of Misery: An Essay on Popular Culture*, Eva Illouz illuminates the startling changes and persistent continuities of women's emotion and self-construction. She argues that Winfrey has built a self-help culture oriented not to making money, as Horatio Alger's novels for boys were, but to mental health, a special concern of women, who are far more likely to go to therapists and in that sense engage in a peculiarly modern form of emotion work. What is good for the self is an important component of that effort, and suggests Winfrey's break with the past, as does the fact that as a celebrity, she, not just fathers or husbands, directs women's emotions. Most importantly, she is African American, and her emotional community carries distinct tones of the Southern Black, oral, improvisational, call-and-response tradition that embodies the revival's demand for a rejuvenated heart, while her popularity suggests that a Black woman has become an arbiter for what women of every ethnicity should feel. This stands in striking contrast to eighteenth-century sentimentalists and their Victorian successors who equated whiteness with genteel feeling, although Garrisonian abolitionists would extend feeling across the racial line, and even Mary Guion suggested that despite his black skin, her slave Harry might still have a human heart.[33] In that African Americans have long practiced the emotion work required to cope with oppression, Winfrey is an experienced teacher whose lessons reflect both race and gender.[34]

If, as I have argued, emotion work may be understood as a vehicle through which women create a negotiated self, Oprah Winfrey's show represents a complex negotiation between therapeutic culture, women's individual needs, traditional gendered expectations, and a new acceptance of African American emotional expression. The goals and process of that emotion work and the structure of its emotional community, however, recall many traditional elements of the seemingly distant world of Sarah Connell and her sentimental friends. Much as women of sensibility occupied both real and imaginary emotional communities, Winfrey's fans can join face-to-face communities through attending her show, joining a book club, or talking to friends, or they can participate in the imaginary community emanating from television. While eighteenth-century women constructed emotions through novel reading and journaling, Oprah's followers receive her views from a new electronic medium, but they also read her recommended novels and advice books and search them for clues to their own emotional development. As Illouz writes, "Emotions are 'the glue' binding members together; more specifically, the group comes into existence through a particular shared way of narrating emotions."[35] And while Sarah Connell enjoyed weeping, Oprah's audience relishes the spectacle of other people's struggles, tears up in response, and admires their own therapeutically developed sensitivity, if not their gentility. Talk shows put the audience as well as Oprah in the eye of the public, so this "transcript" is not completely "hidden," yet much as mainly women read novels or each others' diaries in the past, mainly women watch the Oprah Winfrey show, buy the books she recommends, and discuss the resulting emotional labor with each other. Their efforts to implement her directives remain hidden and highly individual, and the solution to their problems is typically to change their own feelings rather than to change the society in which they live. Taking care of themselves has a new priority, and women may choose a modern solution—divorce—as they examine their feelings, but that only inaugurates their next emotional task: to forge new and ever healthier relationships and produce yet more feeling.

From the eighteenth century to the present, I find that women's emotion work, especially after marriage, has entailed a remarkable number of characteristics that have become associated with archetypal women's work. Like housework, emotion work tended to be invisible: society maintained that women were naturally emotional, just as it regarded the needle as women's natural instrument, and child raising as an inherent rather than acquired skill. Much as middle-class husbands noticed the results of women's household labors—fresh bread, clean shirts—but did not often view the process that produced them, they appreciated their wives' submission without always fully understanding the work behind it. Yet men remained the employers of women's invisible work through defining the feeling rules which women followed and determining the sphere within which they expressed emotion, just as they set expectations for their favorite dinner. Like its physical parallel, married women's emotion work was done for others, rather than to express women's individuality. This is why the more emotion work Sarah Connell Ayer, Elizabeth Cranch Norton, and Mary Guion Brown did, the less they were able to express themselves; hence, the silences and tendency to quote sermons and prayers so characteristic of married women's diaries, as the lifelong struggle to find words of their own became even more difficult. The wages of housework and emotion work alike were paid in feeling—a father's happiness, a husband's approval, her children's love—providing, of course, family members noticed such labors. Shaped by these longstanding cultural practices, even in today's society, women's emotion work in the wage-earning world, especially in female-dominated jobs, has remained simultaneously expected, unappreciated, and underpaid. As a result, despite their extensive training in emotion work, the airline attendants Arlie Russell Hochschild studied found that their passengers regarded cheerfulness as their due rather than a cultivated skill.[36]

Lastly, emotion work remains distinctive in that it invaded women's lives, especially the lives of married women, in a way no purely physical labor could. Sarah Connell Ayer, Elizabeth Cranch Norton, and Mary Guion Brown might employ servants to help with housework, but they could not hire out emotion work—as, indeed, they could not as single women, although that work seems to have been more gratifying. Over time, the duties of wife and mother fueled an increasingly demanding spiral of emotional expectations, as women struggled to both disguise their own emotions and model the emotions others were to feel. Much like late-twentieth-century service workers, during their life cycle, women experienced a "speed up" of higher emotional (and, often, physical) productivity, but lower wages and less control of working conditions. But wives and mothers could not go home from work and rebuild themselves; their homes *were* their workplace. Ironically, many contemporary wage-earning women report that they prefer the office to the home, because the office places fewer and less difficult demands on them. As more and more women become wage-earners, the home has simultaneously become a place of less work, in that activities there are unpaid and therefore not considered "work" at all, and more work, in that physical tasks remain while the emotion work of adjusting to modern roles has escalated.[37] If the exemplar of early republican womanhood was a young woman gazing tearfully at the moon, wondering what her future would be, the modern equivalent is the woman pondering how she can feel and do all that is expected of her. Since the eighteenth century, the minutiae of everyday life have changed in their particulars, but these diarists would recognize the tasks they still elicit: women's efforts to examine their hearts, fulfill or defy cultural expectations, protect themselves, love well, rage, and construct their identities. We should not be surprised if, then or now, it was difficult to make this look easy. In the labor of their hearts, even more than of their hands, women's work was never done.

NOTES

Introduction

1. Burstein, *Sentimental Democracy*, xiv.
2. P. Stearns with C. Stearns, "Emotionology," 813. For a brief review of emotion history's historiography, see Stearns, "History of Emotions."
3. Peter N. Stearns has been a major contributor to emotion history. See especially C. Stearns and P. Stearns, *Anger*; and, by Peter N. Stearns, *Jealousy*; *American Cool*; *Battleground of Desire*; and *Anxious Parents*.
4. P. Stearns and C. Stearns, "Emotionology," 814.
5. Lutz, "Engendered Emotion," 69–70, 77.
6. Smith-Rosenberg, "Female World of Love and Ritual"; E. Rothman, *Hands and Hearts*; Lystra, *Searching the Heart*; Kelly, *In the New England Fashion*; and J. Hunter, *How Young Ladies Became Girls*. Of these approaches, mine is closest to Jane Hunter's, although she covers the late Victorian rather than early national period.
7. Rodney Hessinger emphasizes the early republic's concern for youth, but focuses on the adult reaction more than youth's own role. See *Seduced, Abandoned, and Reborn*.
8. Perlmann, Siddali, and Whitescarver, "Literacy, Schooling, and Teaching"; Wittmann, "Was There a Reading Revolution?"; Davidson, *Revolution and the Word*; Lehuu, *Carnival on the Page*, chap. 1; Bushman, *Refinement of America*; Kerber, "Daughters of Columbia"; E. Rothman, *Hands and Hearts*; Lystra, *Searching the Heart*; and Butler, *Awash in a Sea of Faith*.
9. Rosaldo, "Toward an Anthropology of Self," 143.
10. Rose, *Intellectual Life*, 4.
11. Goffman, *Presentation of Self*, 75.
12. Branaman, "Goffman's Social Theory," xlvii (quotation), xlvi–xlvii, lxxiv–lxxx; Goffman, *Presentation of Self*, chap. 3.
13. Branaman, "Goffman's Social Theory," xlix; Halttunen, *Confidence Men and Painted Women*, 40, 42, 104–5, 186. Carl Elliott points out that the idea that we are only masks makes no sense. "The very concept of mask presupposes that there is something underneath. Otherwise a mask is not a mask. It is a face." *Better Than Well*, 50.

14. Hochschild, "Emotion Work," 566. For overviews of this sociological field, see Thoits, "Sociology of Emotions," and Steinberg and Figart, "Emotional Labor since *The Managed Heart*."

15. Hochschild, *Managed Heart*, 7, 35. She has collected her essays on emotion work in the anthology, *Commercialization of Intimate Life*.

16. Hochschild, "Emotion Work," 567.

17. Kaledin, *Mothers and More*; Jensen, *Loosening the Bonds*; Apple and Golden, *Mothers and Motherhood*; Bowlby, *Carried Away*; Scanlon, *Inarticulate Longings*; and Ginzberg, *Women and the Work of Benevolence*. Boris and Kleinberg's "Mothers and Other Workers" provides a historiographical overview.

18. Boydston, *Home and Work*, chap. 7.

19. Hochschild, *Managed Heart*, 30.

20. Jagodzinski, *Privacy and Print*, 4, 6.

21. Campbell, *Romantic Ethic*, 73.

22. Spacks, *Privacy*.

23. Sobel, *Teach Me Dreams*, 4. Nicole E. Eustace takes a similar point of view, but without Sobel's emphasis on dreams, in "'Passion Is the Gale.'"

24. West and Zimmerman, "Doing Gender," 129, 127.

25. S. Shields, *Speaking from the Heart*, 111. Shields, however, has much less to say about class than gender.

26. Stabile, *Memory's Daughters*, chap. 2.

27. *Jemima Condict Her Book*, 41.

28. Reddy, *Navigation of Feeling*, 104. Reddy links emotives to sentimentalism on 161–72.

29. Hunt, Diary, vol. 1, 46.

30. Guion, Diary, 235.

31. S. Shields, *Speaking from the Heart*, 30.

32. Anthony Giddens and feminist theorists advocate this approach; see Klein, "Gender and the Public/Private Distinction," 101.

33. The core diarists are Sarah Connell Ayer, Mary Guion, Susan Heath, Mary B. Howell, Abigail May, Elizabeth Cranch Norton, Martha (Patty) Rogers, and Rachel Van Dyke. The Litchfield Female Academy diarists are Mary Ann Bacon, Sarah Beekman, Henrietta Cornelia Bevier, Caroline M. Boardman, Mary G. Camp, Caroline Chester, Mary A. Child, Julia Cowles, Jane Lewis, Adeline Mitchell, Eliza A. Ogden, Betsey Reynolds, Charlotte Sheldon, Lucy Sheldon, Charlotte Maria Smith, Catherine Van Schaack, Mary L. Wilbor, and Laura Maria Wolcott. The remaining diarists informed my general understanding. Of them, I cite Abigail Foote, Elizabeth Foote, Ann Eliza Heath, Mary Heath, Lucinda Read, and Candace Roberts in endnotes and, therefore, the bibliography. Other, uncited, diarists who rounded out my sample I list here with the archives that hold their journals: Elizabeth Bancroft, American Antiquarian Society, Worcester, Mass.; Samantha Barrett, Zeloda Barrett, Julia Churchill, Nancy Thompson Hunt, Ann Francis Johnson, and Lucinda Howe Storrs, The Connecticut Historical Society Museum, Hartford;

Amanda Elliott and Eliza Ann Hull Staples, Connecticut State Library/State Archives, Hartford; Hannah Bliss, Henrietta M. Goddard, Betsy Graves Johnson, and Anna Cabot Lowell, Massachusetts Historical Society, Boston; Esther W. T. Grout and Jerusha Leonard, Pocumtuck Valley Memorial Association Library, Deerfield, Mass.; Sarah Thomson, Rutgers University Special Collections, New Brunswick, New Jersey; and Eunice Callender and Sarah Ripley Stearns, Schlesinger Library, Radcliffe Institute for Advanced Study, Harvard University.

34. Brereton, *From Sin to Salvation*, xiii. Brereton, however, used mainly published conversion narratives.

35. Fineman, "Organizations as Emotional Arenas," 12–13.

36. Rosenwein, "Worrying about Emotions," 842–43.

37. Lutz, "Engendered Emotion," 70.

38. Bartky, *Femininity and Domination*, 119.

39. De Sousa, *Rationality of Emotion*, 19.

40. Carlson and Hatfield, *Psychology of Emotion*, 5.

41. P. Stearns and C. Stearns, "Emotionology," 813. Psychologist James R. Averill, a social constructionist, distinguishes emotional syndromes, states, and reactions, with a syndrome being similar to feeling rules or emotionology. Averill, "Emotions Unbecoming and Becoming," 265.

42. Hochschild, *Managed Heart*, 29, 17, 220, 27.

43. Antonio R. Damasio sees most feelings springing from emotions, but not all emotions producing feelings, and adds the additional category of "background feelings." However, the physiology of feeling/emotions is more difficult for the cultural historian to probe than emotion's verbal expression. Damasio, *Descartes' Error*, 143. Gesa Stedman notes that "'Feeling' meaning the emotions, susceptibilities, and sympathies in a collective sense only comes to prominence in the late eighteenth century," while "emotion as a *synonym for feeling and passion*" goes back to the seventeenth century and became common in the nineteenth century. Stedman, *Stemming the Torrent*, 35, 36.

1. The Work of the Heart

1. Caroline Chester defined sensibility as part of a school assignment. She added, "It may very easily be distinguished from false as the former has effect upon the heart while the latter only effects the nerves." "Caroline Chester's [1816] Journal," in Vanderpoel, *More Chronicles*, 193. For a brief overview of sensibility, see Todd, *Sensibility*. Gesa Stedman found that not until the mid-1700s did sensibility come to mean "*emotional consciousness*" and class-associated "capacity for *refined* emotion." She notes that "sentiment" "could also refer to a *thought or reflection coloured by or proceeding from emotion*," and that by the late eighteenth century it suggested excessive emotional refinement. *Stemming the Torrent*, 40, 39, 44. Lacking a better alternative and despite its pejorative connotation, I use

"sentimental" as the adjectival form of sensibility. For elite women's expressions of sensibility in the colonial period, see Ousterhout, *Most Learned Woman in America*, 12–13, 26, 57–58, 136, 278. In contrast to women of the later period, Elizabeth Graeme Ferguson, the subject of Ousterhout's book, expressed sentimental ideas more than feelings, with a much more restrained tone.

2. For birth/death dates, Whipple Website; *Diary of Sarah Connell Ayer*, 377; Nagel, *Adams Women*, 2. Sarah Connell Ayer's journal ran from 1805 to 1835, but in this chapter I only consider the entries to late 1810, which comprise her journal's sentimental portion. Similarly, in this chapter, I only treat Elizabeth Cranch's sentimental 1785–86 journal, while I treat Abigail May's 1800 diary in chapter 4.

3. Howell, 1799–1805 Journals, 60. On this association, see Skinner, *Sensibility and Economics in the Novel*.

4. Chambers, "Seduction and Sensibility," 245–50; Nagel, *Adams Women*, 29–31, 86–91.

5. Howell, 1799–1805 Journals, 9. Bushman, *Refinement of America;* Breen, *Marketplace of Revolution*, part 1; Carson, "Consumer Revolution"; and Clemens, "Consumer Culture of the Middle Atlantic," all detail consumption's growth.

6. Small, *Beauty and Convenience*.

7. Carson, "Consumer Revolution," 662. In his detailed study of Windsor district, Vermont, William J. Gilmore finds this commercial revolution reaching well into rural New England during the early republic and terms it "a radical transformation of life." *Reading Becomes a Necessity*, chap. 2; quotation, 55.

8. Breen, "Meaning of 'Likeness,'" 329. In his "Sensibility of Comfort," John E. Crowley maintains that initially class, manners, and health were far more important than comfort in inspiring this consumer revolution, but that comfort gained prominence over the eighteenth century.

9. Elizabeth Heath Howe, Penmanship Copybook, 1781.

10. Franklin, *Autobiography*, intro. by Lewis Leary (1962), 80, quoted in Breen, *Marketplace of Revolution*, 154; on the pre-Revolutionary role of women and consumption generally, see 172–82.

11. On the role of the tea table in manners and display of goods, which dated from the early eighteenth century for the elite, see D. Shields, *Civil Tongues and Polite Letters*, chap. 4; Breen, *Marketplace of Revolution*, 170–72; and Kowaleski-Wallace, *Consuming Subjects*, 19–69.

12. Breen, *Marketplace of Revolution*, 158–62.

13. Earle, *Diary of Anna Green Winslow*, 7, 14.

14. Harriet Trumbull to Governor Jonathan Trumbull, 10 January 1801, in Morgan, *Season in New York*, 87–88.

15. May, Journal, 33.

16. Hemphill, *Bowing to Necessities*, 72. Richard Bushman emphasizes the traditional, courtly orientation of conduct books; *Refinement of America*, chap. 2.

17. Howell, 1799–1805 Journals, 59. On Chesterfield's popularity, Hemphill, *Bowing to Necessities*, 70–72; and Bushman, *Refinement of America*, 36–38.

Thomas A. Chambers believes Americans regarded Chesterfield very critically, but even at Litchfield Female Academy, students maintained that "every young Lady" should read Chesterfield. Chambers, "Seduction and Sensibility," 263–64; Lucy Sheldon, 1801–3 Journal, 17.

18. Eliza Southgate used this phrase in referring to an older woman displaying the manners of fifty years past. Eliza Southgate to Octavia Southgate, October [1800?], in *Girl's Life Eighty Years Ago*, 33.

19. Bushman, *Refinement of America*, 80–83; quotation, 81.

20. A. Shippen to Nancy Shippen, 22 Sept. 1777, in Armes, *Nancy Shippen*, 41.

21. Mary Way to Eliza Way Champlain, Dec. 1816, in MacMullan, *Sisters of the Brush*, 59.

22. May, Journal, 30.

23. Ibid., 49. Karen Halttunen found a similar emphasis on ease in the later Victorian period; *Confidence Men and Painted Women*, 93.

24. May, Journal, 43, 44.

25. Ibid., 40.

26. Guion, Diary, 229, 271, 197, 310 (quotation).

27. This theme runs through all their works, but see, for example, Number 24 of *Cato's Letters* in Jacobson, *English Libertarian Heritage*, 61–67. Although eighteenth-century dramatists presented the Roman hero Cato as stoic, they used this archetypal figure to create sympathy essential to republican communal feeling. Ellison, *Cato's Tears*, chap. 2.

28. Merish, *Sentimental Materialism*, chap. 1; quotation, 33.

29. Of the 376 social libraries that were established in America between 1731 and 1800, 266 were founded in the 1790s. Shera, "Beginnings of Systematic Bibliography," 274.

30. By contrast, Jane Hunter found that late Victorian parents often monitored their daughters' reading and writing, including of diaries. However, she also maintains that mothers did not always appear in their daughters' diaries, and seems to be arguing for both maternal absence and presence. *How Young Ladies Became Girls*, 40, 64–66, 103–4.

31. *Diary of Sarah Connell Ayer*, 14, 5.

32. Ibid., 64, 79. The book Mr. Gleason gave Sarah was probably Vicesimus Knox's *Elegant Extracts*, an extremely popular poetry anthology which influenced Jane Austen's writing. Benedict, *Making the Modern Reader*, 215–17.

33. A gentleman offered Sterne's and Smollett's works, but one of her landlady's "girls" offered Goldsmith; it is difficult to tell if this was a daughter or a servant. If it were the latter, this is an example of the lower classes trying to join the higher-class culture of sensibility. May, Journal, 11, 12. On how reading expressed one's taste, see Bushman, *Refinement of America*, chap. 9, and J. Hunter, *How Young Ladies Became Girls*, chap. 3.

34. J. Hunter, *How Young Ladies Became Girls*, 38, 11. The rise of genteel consumption reduced women's economic opportunities outside the home, as impor-

tation and international trade dependent on contracts and credit succeeded the local barter economy. Crane, *Ebb Tide in New England*, 135–38.

35. *Diary of Sarah Connell Ayer*, 44.

36. Howell, 1799–1805 Journals, 32, 61.

37. Easton, *Passionate Spinster*, 44; Susan Heath, Diary, 19 Jan. 1819. The only journals of Abigail May to survive are from visits, so we have no way of knowing what housework she did at home. Cranch, in contrast, kept diaries of her life at home as well as visiting, and in doing so, showed how sensibility and housework shifted according to the setting.

38. Ulrich, *Age of Homespun*, 5.

39. Boydston, *Home and Work*, 44; Klepp, "Revolutionary Bodies." Southern gentry's tendency to hide the outbuildings where work was performed from the lives of the master's family provides a visual parallel to this verbal erasure. K. Brown, *Good Wives, Nasty Wenches*, 262–63.

40. For examples of diaries devoted almost entirely to work, see Abigail Foote and Elizabeth Foote, "Journals."

41. *Diary of Sarah Connell Ayer*, 3–30.

42. As Robert B. Winans points out, some books occupied multiple categories, and in that regard, this breakdown of Connell's reading is artificial. He points out that the four most popular novels in the late eighteenth century were novels of sensibility, but that many others of his list of twenty-four were not; "Bibliography and the Cultural Historian," 184. I argue, however, that women obtained sensibility from a variety of formats, and that novels' unique function was to train them in the first-person narrative.

43. On the development of extensive reading and the lingering of intensive style, see Hall, "Uses of Literacy in New England"; Richard D. Brown associates extensive reading with class and status in his "Afterword" in Joyce, *Printing and Society in Early America*.

44. William Gilmore maintains that after 1800, of the books available in Windsor district, Vermont, "two-thirds of all law books, four-fifths of all medical books, and seven-tenths of all works in modern literature had British authors." This British dominance declined after the 1820s or so. Often, British novels were reprinted in American editions within months of their first appearance. Gilmore, *Reading Becomes a Necessity*, 212. The same merchants who imported teapots and textiles also imported books and newspapers. P. Hunter, *Purchasing Identity in the Atlantic World*, 141.

45. S. Heath, Diary, 3 and 5 Oct. 1814, 16 Oct. 1816, 14 March 1817.

46. Studies of the proportion of novels sold, borrowed, and owned provide a varied picture, with William Gilmore, *Reading Becomes a Necessity*, emphasizing their pervasiveness, especially in commercial, well-off communities; and Robert B. Winans finding their numbers largest in the inexpensive circulating libraries and in frequency of borrowing; "Growth of a Novel-Reading Public," 270–71; a situation affirmed by Sears, "Libraries and Reading Habits In Early

Portland," 158. Concord, Massachusetts's Charitable Library Society, however, had relatively few novels compared to religious works, suggesting that, as Gilmore finds, prosperity influenced reading; Gross, "Reconstructing Early American Libraries," 343–69. However, even prosperous professionals sometimes preferred nonfiction works; Larkin, "Merriams of Brookfield," 39–73. Kett and McClung caution that estate inventories of books underrepresent women's reading; "Book Culture in Post-Revolutionary Virginia," 106. Another source for fiction was magazines: David Paul Nord notes that in 1790, almost 47 percent of *The New York Magazine*'s items dealt with what he calls "manners and morals," and, in turn, 24.3 percent of this category included romances; "Republican Literature," 52–53. Robert Darnton questions if there was a "reading revolution" during the early republic, but puts it best when he writes that reading "assumed many different forms among different social groups during different eras"; "Toward a History of Reading," 92.

47. Cranch devoted over two pages to describing one novel, which I have not been able to identify. She also read *Benignus*, which I believe to be Mr. Pratt's *Liberal Opinions, or, the History of Benignus*. WorldCat describes this as "fiction" and Cranch records a moralistic fictional plot. Cranch, 1786 Journal, 61–63; and 1787 Journal, 26 July 1787. Candace Roberts summarized Ann Radcliffe's *The Romance of the Forest* in detail; 1801–6 Diary, 3 March 1804.

48. *Diary of Sarah Connell Ayer*, 8, 46, 79, 87, 126, 133, 136, 153, 162. Of course, many other sentimental novels had heroines without putting their names in the title.

49. Henderson, "Imperfect Dead," 497–502.

50. This "fictionalization" occurred occasionally during the colonial period but much more frequently thereafter; Kagle and Gramegna, "Rewriting Her Life"; Kelley, "Reading Women/Women Reading."

51. Mullan, "Feelings and Novels," 127, 131. After studying a Victorian friendship album, Mary Louise Kete argued that in the nineteenth century, verse was more significant than fiction and was widely revered and practiced. I found that these diarists often fell back on verse to express themselves, but maintain that the novel provided a narrative form in addition to a language of emotion, and in that sense was doubly significant. Kete, *Sentimental Collaborations*, 25.

52. J. Hunter, *How Young Ladies Became Girls*, 89.

53. S. Heath, Diary, 11 April 1817; see also the 3 Nov. 1817 entry in which she compares a visitor to a character in *Evelina*. Heath was exceptional in criticizing books other than novels; see Diary, 2 and 21 May 1817.

54. Kelley, *Power of Her Sympathy*, 92. Earle, *Diary of Anna Green Winslow*, 70, 13.

55. Wolcott, 1826–27 Journal, 65. In this case, she commented on a story called "The Rainbow" in John Wilson's *Lights and Shadows of Scottish Life*, a fictional representation of Scottish society.

56. Chambers, "Seduction and Sensibility," 263 n40.

57. Mary B. Howell read or quoted from forty-six different works between 1799 and 1805. Of these, twelve, or about a quarter, were novels. Howell, 1799–1805 Journals, 47, 49, and throughout.

58. Michaelson, "Women in the Reading Circle."

59. Rosenwein, "Worrying about Emotions," 842–43.

60. For examples of mid-eighteenth-century women (and occasionally their husbands) reading novels, see Hayes, *Colonial Woman's Bookshelf*, 115–16, 105, 108, 113.

61. Anderson, *Imagined Communities*, 15, chap. 4. Marilyn Ferris Motz has written that diarists "used that most private form, the diary, to establish themselves as citizens of the world." "Private Alibi," 191. This practice extended into the late Victorian period; J. Hunter, *How Young Ladies Became Girls*, 68.

62. Armstrong and Tennenhouse, *Imaginary Puritan*, chaps. 6 and 7.

63. Habermas, *Structural Transformation*, part 2.

64. G. Brown, *Consent of the Governed*, 153, 123. For many insights on this point, see Brooke, "Consent, Civil Society, and the Public Sphere."

65. Lewis, "Politics and the Ambivalence of the Private Sphere," 146–48.

66. *Diary of Sarah Connell Ayer*, 103.

67. Howell, 1799–1805 Journals, 62.

68. Hochschild, *Managed Heart*, 7, chap. 3.

69. Among the many scholars who have observed this are Benedict, *Framing Feeling*; Chambers, "Seduction and Sensibility"; Spacks, *Privacy*, chap. 3; Halttunen, *Confidence Men and Painted Women*, 93; and Barker-Benfield, *Culture of Sensibility*, chap. 6.

70. *Diary of Sarah Connell Ayer*, 118. Abigail May made the same observation; Journal, 46.

71. *Diary of Sarah Connell Ayer*, 93–4.

72. Howell, 1799–1805 Journals, 48. This was probably Robert Bloomfield's 1800 *The Farmer's Boy: A Rural Poem*.

73. *Diary of Sarah Connell Ayer*, 13.

74. Howell, 1799–1805 Journals, 51. Similarly, Denis Diderot used "Richardson's novels as a means of testing his friends in order to evaluate their hearts." Van Sant, *Eighteenth-Century Sensibility and the Novel*, 53.

75. Mary Cranch to Betsy Cranch, 29 January 1774. 1773–79 folder, Jacob Norton Papers (hereafter JNP). A similar sartorial metaphor appears in Sarah Eve's Dec. 12, 1774, obituary in the *Pennsylvania Packet:* "her manners were polished: They were not put on, and laid aside, like a part of dress." Jones, ed., "Extracts from the Journal of Miss Sarah Eve," 21.

76. K. Brown, *Good Wives, Nasty Wenches*, 291–95; and Barker-Benfield, *Culture of Sensibility*, 173–87.

77. Howell, 1799–1805 Journals, 40, 8; *Diary of Sarah Connell Ayer*, 51, 84, 88, 89, 90, 91; Connell Ayer, Diary, vol. 1, 16 August 1809.

78. *Diary of Sarah Connell Ayer*, 7; Elizabeth Cranch to Jacob Norton, 13 May 1788, 1788 folder, JNP.

79. "Students Known to Have Attended the Litchfield Female Academy," in Fields and Kightlinger, *To Ornament Their Minds*, 114–31.

80. D. Shields, *Civil Tongues and Polite Letters*, 263–66, and Bushman, *Refinement of America*, 296–98. Nicole Eustace suggests that these names were used for privacy, but that does not explain the particular cognomens that were chosen; although any code name would have worked, people often chose names with literary antecedents. Eustace, "'Cornerstone of a Copious Work,'" 519–20.

81. Whipple Website. Patty Rogers often called the two men she loved "Portius" and "Philammon," and Elizabeth Cranch employed cognomens even in her earlier, less sentimental journal; Easton, *Passionate Spinster*, 72; and Cranch, 1781–82 Journal, 20 June and 19 Nov. 1781, and 18 April 1782.

82. Todd, *Sensibility*, 5–6.

83. On the profusion of tears in sentimental literature, see Vincent-Buffault, *History of Tears*. Jane Hunter suggests that Victorian sensationalist fiction "both stimulated and relieved excitement," producing a nineteenth-century equivalent of exercise's endorphin rush. *How Young Ladies Became Girls*, 79.

84. Mullan, "Feelings and Novels," 123, 120.

85. *Diary of Sarah Connell Ayer*, 128.

86. Howell, 1799–1805 Journals, 55. Occasionally even women of sensibility became impatient with tears. As Abigail May wrote in her diary after one emotional bender, "I found crying a pretty stupid employment." May, Journal, 8.

87. *Diary of Sarah Connell Ayer*, 20.

88. Hochschild, *Managed Heart*, 35.

89. *Diary of Sarah Connell Ayer*, 7. Mary Orne Tucker, a wife of twenty-six, used the word "participate" for a similar purpose; "Diary of Mary Orne Tucker," 334.

90. As David Shields points out, the countryside that sentimentalists visited was a tamed garden devoid of hard labor, not a wilderness. *Civil Tongues and Polite Letters*, 128–29. On the vogue of cottages representing rusticity, comfort, and sensibility, see Crowley, *Invention of Comfort*, chap. 7. Similar visits to the poor appear in "Diary of Mary Orne Tucker," 317–18.

91. Karen Halttunen sees this strategy continuing well into the nineteenth century; *Confidence Men and Painted Women*, 195.

92. *Diary of Sarah Connell Ayer*, 60, 11.

93. Todd, *Sensibility*, 143.

94. *Diary of Sarah Connell Ayer*, 11.

95. Ibid., 152. Dr. Johnson derided such feelings, as have subsequent historians: Kaplan, *Sacred Tears*, 51. Karen Halttunen calls this "spectatorial sympathy" in her "Humanitarianism and the Pornography of Pain," 307; and Patricia Meyer Spacks dismisses this as "emotional masturbation" and "cost-free suffering" in *Privacy*, 57, 61.

96. Howell, 1799–1805 Journals, 21, 17.

97. *Diary of Sarah Connell Ayer*, 83; see also May, Journal, 24, 47.

98. *Diary of Sarah Connell Ayer*, 56.

99. Greven, *Protestant Temperament*.

100. Lewis, *Pursuit of Happiness*, chap. 1; K. Brown, *Good Wives, Nasty Wenches*, chaps. 9 and 10.

101. *Diary of Sarah Connell Ayer*, 103.

102. Howell, 1799–1805 Journals, 13–14; see also May, Journal, 11, 31.

103. Mason and Phillips, "[1785-86] Journal of Elizabeth Cranch," 17–18, 10; Cranch, 1786 Journal, 21–22.

104. Mason and Phillips, "[1785-86] Journal of Elizabeth Cranch," 30, 17.

105. Ibid., 10, 17, 28; Cranch, 1786 Journal, 18.

106. Hemphill, *Bowing to Necessities*, part 2, especially chap. 6.

107. Laqueur, *Making Sex*, chap. 5; and Shapiro, "Sexuality."

108. Burstein, "Political Character of Sympathy," 625; Barnes, *States of Sympathy*, 2; Ellison, *Cato's Tears*, 19–20.

109. Waldstreicher, *In the Midst of Perpetual Fetes*, 73; Fliegelman, *Declaring Independence*, 40; Knott, "Sensibility."

110. Coviello, "Agonizing Affection," 452.

111. Carole Shammas also argues that despite the appearance of "Mr. Sensitive" in portraits, he remained very much the head of household, and this new image of masculinity declined by the late eighteenth century. Shammas, *History of Household Government*, 80–82; Greven, *Protestant Temperament*, 309–12.

112. Todd, *Sensibility*, chap. 6.

113. Crain, *American Sympathy*, chap. 1; Fea, "Way of Improvement."

114. Shalhope, *Tale of New England*, 86, 100–104.

115. May, Journal, 15, 13, 28, 31.

116. Ibid., 30, 49; McMahon and Schriver, *To Read My Heart*, 189; Guion, Diary, 181, 234; "The Tear," in Cook, 1813–15 Album.

117. Crain, *American Sympathy*, 32.

118. Stabile, *Memory's Daughters*, 109–10.

119. Chambers, "Seduction and Sensibility," 264; Hessinger, *Seduced, Abandoned, and Reborn*, chap. 1.

120. Fea, "Way of Improvement," 479, 484–87. Harwood, did, however, share *The Wild Irish Girl* with Sally. Shalhope, *Tale of New England*, 100–104.

121. Mason and Phillips, "[1785-86] Journal of Elizabeth Cranch," 33, 7, 17; Cranch, 1781–82 Journal, 27 April 1782; Cranch, 1786 Journal, 54. On "unmanly" tears, see also "Lucy Sheldon's Journal for the Winter 1803," in Vanderpoel and Buel, *Chronicles of a Pioneer School*, 51.

122. May, Journal, 15. Peter Coviello found that Jefferson described "agonizing affection" as "manly" in his first draft of the Declaration of Independence, but continued to find unrestrained feeling distasteful and lauded reason. In any event, Congress deleted his passage emphasizing the role of feeling in nationhood and replaced it with rationalistic justification, a choice suggesting the limits of feeling for late-eighteenth-century men. "Agonizing Affection," 459–60, 452–53.

123. While Jacquelyn C. Miller emphasizes the conflation of male/female expression of emotion in her "An 'Uncommon Tranquillity of Mind,'" most his-

torians of sensibility believe that it maintained gendered distinctions; Michaelson, *Speaking Volumes*, chap. 1; Brody, *Manly Writing;* and C. Johnson, *Equivocal Beings*, 14.

124. Juster, "'Neither Male nor Female,'" 367; Sturkenboom, "Historicizing the Gender of Emotions."

125. Davidson, *Revolution and the Word*, 136–50; Godbeer, *Sexual Revolution*, chap. 8; Hessinger, *Seduced, Anbandoned, and Reborn*, chap. 1. C. Dallett Hemphill has also found that conduct books of this time emphasized issues of sexuality for women; *Bowing to Necessities*, chap. 6.

126. Sarah Connell to Maria Kittredge, 13 March 1810, in *Diary of Sarah Connell Ayer*, 372–73.

127. Barker-Benfield, *Culture of Sensibility*, 299.

128. Greven, *Protestant Temperament*, part 4.

129. *Diary of Sarah Connell Ayer*, 87, 89, 138; Labaree, *Patriots and Partisans*, chap. 7.

130. Connell Ayer, Diary, vol. 2, 14 April 1810.

131. *Diary of Sarah Connell Ayer*, 85, 87, 88.

132. Mason and Phillips, "[1785-86] Journal of Elizabeth Cranch," 24; see also Eliza Southgate to Moses Porter, [1800/01], in *Girl's Life Eighty Years Ago*, 40.

133. Breen, "Meaning of 'Likeness,'" 329.

134. Mason and Phillips, "[1785-86] Journal of Elizabeth Cranch," 32.

135. Allen and others, *Diary of John Quincy Adams*, 1:345.

136. Goffman, *Presentation of Self*, chap. 3, 133.

137. Ibid., 15–16, 235–37.

138. "Diary of Mary Orne Tucker," 324.

139. *Diary of Sarah Connell Ayer*, 3, 39, 84, 43, 173.

140. Ibid., 330.

141. Ibid., 18; Connell Ayer, Diary, vol. 1, 16 August 1809.

142. Goffman lists female friends among those playing "discrepant roles" in which people understand a performance without themselves being the direct audience. He categorizes female friends as sympathizing "colleagues" with similar public roles who can relax with each other. By attributing to the backstage both preparatory work and relaxation from performance, Goffman confuses two functions and uses categories such as "discrepant roles" to bridge the gap. I suggest a distinction needs to be made between offstage and backstage; backstage suggests work for the performance, and offstage time off from performance, in this case with friends. *Presentation of Self*, 153, 160.

143. Although passages have been cut from the manuscript, obscuring the details, Sarah Connell's mother's drinking emerges in the July and August 1810 entries, especially 26 July 1810, Diary, vol. 2. Although close to her father, aunts, and female friends, she mentioned her mother infrequently.

144. Hochschild found that shifts in status and roles raised questions about appropriate feeling rules; *Managed Heart*, 75n.

145. *Diary of Sarah Connell Ayer*, 93.

146. Ibid., 92, 103.

147. Cox, 'The Stranger Within Thee', 63, finds sensibility caught between individualism and "social sympathy," as does Janet Todd, who believes that it enabled women to "exalt their own sensibility without appearing improperly self-centred"; *Sensibility*, 60.

148. *Diary of Sarah Connell Ayer*, 35.

149. Ibid., 77, 20; Howell, 1799–1805 Journals, 13, 10; see also the poem "Midnight" by the Gothic novelist M. G. Lewis, which Howell quoted on 44–45.

150. Brickley, "Sarah Pierce's Litchfield Female Academy," 63. Nancy Beadie came to much the same conclusions for almost five hundred New York state academies between 1835 and 1890; "Academy Students," 255, 257.

151. Hemphill, *Bowing to Necessities*, 106. Christie Anne Farnham has also pointed out that conservative antebellum Southerners felt comfortable sending daughters to college because that education was "emblematic of class, a means to a refinement that labeled one a lady worthy of protection, admiration, and chivalrous attention." *Education of the Southern Belle*, 3.

2. Schooling the Heart

1. *Diary of Sarah Connell Ayer*, 103; Howell, 1799–1805 Journals, 14, 2.

2. Cranch, Commonplace Book, 1787–88, 1.

3. Pearson, *Women's Reading in Britain*, chap. 3.

4. Howell, 1799–1805 Journals, 53.

5. Bloch, "Gendered Meanings of Virtue," 16; and Lord Kames, *Six Sketches* (1776), 220, quoted in Zagarri, "Morals," 199.

6. Hicks, "Portia and Marcia."

7. "Comparison of the Sexes," *American Museum* (Jan. 1789): 59.

8. Linda Kerber links the politicization of women specifically with education in "Daughters of Columbia," as does Kelley, "'Vindicating the Equality of the Female Intellect.'"

9. Brickley, "Litchfield Female Academy," 26–27, 29, 31.

10. Brickley, "Sarah Pierce's Litchfield Female Academy," 233; 29 August 1815 summary of academy rules, in Boardman, 1815 Journal, 2, 4, 5. In her 1806 diary, Betsey Reynolds noted that Mr. Brace read *The Vicar of Wakefield* to the class, justifying it with the argument that unlike most "pernicious" novels, it was not just a story but had a moral; Reynolds, 1806–7 Journal, 21. Refraining from reading novels on Sunday was not unusual. Susan Heath, who was mildly sentimental, was shocked when a neighbor tried to borrow a novel on the Sabbath; Diary, 25 Oct. 1812.

11. Pierce, "Address at the Close of the Summer 1820," in Vanderpoel and Buel, *Chronicles*, 208–9. The word "improvement" appears repeatedly in Academy student journals also. On the eighteenth-century understanding of the word, see Fliegelman, *Declaring Independence*, 183.

12. Pierce, "Address at the Close of School, October 29, 1818," in Vanderpoel and Buel, *Chronicles*, 178, 177. Fourteen years later, the Academy published a pamphlet making exactly the same argument; *By-laws*, 3.

13. Pierce, "Address at the Close of School, October 29, 1818," in Vanderpoel and Buel, *Chronicles*, 177–79.

14. Pierce, "A Fragment," in Vanderpoel and Buel, *Chronicles*, 211; Kerber, "Republican Mother." As Margaret A. Nash has explained in "Rethinking Republican Motherhood," other academies supported a concept of "republican womanhood" that was less narrow than Pierce's focus on maternity. John Brace, Pierce's nephew and assistant teacher, also emphasized women's indirect influence, especially as a mother, in his 25 Oct. 1819, "Address at the Close of the School," in Vanderpoel, *More Chronicles*, 206–11. In her "'Vindicating the Equality of Female Intellect,'" Mary Kelley finds this pattern of rigorous education and limited female roles in academy education generally at this time, as does Anya Jabour in William and Elizabeth Wirt's family; "'Grown Girls, Highly Cultivated.'"

15. These are the subjects listed on Litchfield Academy's earliest diploma; Vanderpoel and Buel, *Chronicles*, plate 21.

16. In "'Cultivating the Powers of *Human Beings*,'" Margaret A. Nash maintains that historians have exaggerated the "ornamental" aspects of women's academy educations during the early republic.

17. Pierce, quoted in Wolcott, 1826–27 Journal, 3.

18. "Caroline Chester's [1816] Journal," in Vanderpoel, *More Chronicles*, 177. For a general discussion of diary keeping at Litchfield Female Academy, see Brickley, "Sarah Pierce's Litchfield Female Academy," 214–22.

19. Camp, 1818–34 Diary, no pagination or dates.

20. "Caroline Chester's [1816] Journal," in Vanderpoel, *More Chronicles*, 184; Moseley, *Diaries of Julia Cowles*, 1–5.

21. "Caroline Chester's [1816] Journal," in Vanderpoel, *More Chronicles*, 179. What seem to be John Brace's comments appear in Wolcott, 1826–27 Journal, 36; see also her references to him, 50.

22. "1796. Charlotte Sheldon—Her Diary," in Vanderpoel and Buel, *Chronicles*, 12. Caroline Chester expressed relief when she had to read her journal to Pierce rather than Brace; "Caroline Chester's [1816] Journal," in Vanderpoel, *More Chronicles*, 168. Some students were not above flattering Miss Pierce in their journals, probably an unsuccessful maneuver; "1822. Mary L. Wilbor Diary," in Vanderpoel and Buel, *Chronicles*, 235, 237.

23. Camp, 1818–34 Diary. Mary A. Child also hoped that only her "kind preceptress" would see her journal, but had no control over this; Child, 1820 Journal, 21 May 1820.

24. Bevier, 1809 Diary, 19 August 1809.

25. According to Kathryn Kish Sklar, at Litchfield Female Academy, Catharine Beecher "learned to record her private thoughts for public perusal and to interpret her personal experience in socially acceptable terms." *Catharine Beecher,*

17. Unlike Beecher, students sometimes refused to submit their journals at term's end, even if that meant withdrawing from competition for the top prize. Brace, "Private Journal 1814," in Vanderpoel, *More Chronicles*, 94.

26. Gilmore, *Reading Becomes a Necessity*, 39, 38. Sandra M. Gustafson also emphasizes that oral and print culture were not opposites but linked; *Eloquence Is Power*, xvii.

27. Study of the past "soundscape" is just emerging: see Bruce Smith, *Acoustic World of Early Modern England*, who uses the word "soundscape" throughout; Classen, *World of Sense;* Schmidt, *Hearing Things;* Mark W. Smith, *Listening to Nineteenth-Century America;* Hoffer, *Sensory Worlds in Early America;* and Rath, *How Early America Sounded*. Recent historical studies of the senses have tended to neglect the role of gender; Mark W. Smith, "Making Sense of Social History," 177.

28. Knox, *Elegant Extracts* (1784), 1:191, quoted in Michaelson, *Speaking Volumes*, 143.

29. Gilmore, *Reading Becomes a Necessity*, 40; Fliegelman, *Declaring Independence*, 80; see also 28–35. Many schools were reluctant, however, to allow females to move from elocution to oratory; Nash, "'Cultivating the Powers of *Human Beings*,'" 244.

30. As a student at Litchfield in 1796, Charlotte Sheldon recorded reading novels and other works; this type of independent reading seems to have become less frequent as academy life became more structured. "1796. Charlotte Sheldon—Her Diary," in Vanderpoel and Buel, *Chronicles*, 10–17.

31. Sheldon, 1801–3 Journal, 8, 22.

32. Ogden, 1816–18 Journal, 14. Caroline Chester linked memorizing and reciting when she wrote, "As usual attended school my time was principally spent in committing to memory and reciting my lesson in Geography and writing—." "Caroline Chester's [1816] Journal," in Vanderpoel, *More Chronicles*, 169. On reciting, see Brickley, "Sarah Pierce's Litchfield Female Academy," 257. When Catharine Beecher left Litchfield to establish her own school, she made sure that students spoke in their own words rather than merely reciting; Kelley, "'Vindicating the Equality of Female Intellect,'" 17.

33. Ogden, 1816–18 Journal, 34.

34. Brickley, "Sarah Pierce's Litchfield Female Academy," 197, 198; Ogden, 1816–18 Journal, 38.

35. Bevier, Diary, 3 Sept. 1809.

36. Brickley, "Sarah Pierce's Litchfield Female Academy," 203–4.

37. *Autobiography of Lyman Beecher* (1961 ed.), 1:399, quoted in Hedrick, *Harriet Beecher Stowe*, 27; "Caroline Chester's [1816] Journal," in Vanderpoel, *More Chronicles*, 169.

38. Brickley, "Litchfield Female Academy," 27.

39. "Caroline Chester's [1816] Journal," in Vanderpoel, *More Chronicles*, 170.

40. "1796. Charlotte Sheldon—Her Diary," in Vanderpoel and Buel, *Chronicles*, 13; Ogden, 1816–18 Journal, 29.

41. *By-laws*, 9; on Sarah Pierce's credit system, see Brickley, "Sarah Pierce's Litchfield Female Academy," 130–46.
42. Ogden, 1816–18 Journal, 26.
43. Mary Chester to Edwin Chester, 29 May 1819, in Vanderpoel and Buel, *Chronicles*, 190; see also Sheldon, 1801–3 Journal, 21.
44. Ogden, 1816–18 Journal, 38, 40; "Caroline Chester's [1816] Journal," in Vanderpoel, *More Chronicles*, 174.
45. "1822. Mary L. Wilbor Diary," in Vanderpoel and Buel, *Chronicles*, 239.
46. Delia Storrs to Lucius Storrs, 3 Aug 1822, Sarah Pierce Collection, in Litchfield (Connecticut) Historical Society (hereafter LHS).
47. Brickley, "Sarah Pierce's Litchfield Female Academy," 133; "Caroline Chester's [1816] Journal," in Vanderpoel, *More Chronicles*, 179.
48. Reynolds, 1806–7 Journal, 29.
49. Brickley, "Sarah Pierce's Litchfield Female Academy," 133–35; "Caroline Chester's [1816] Journal," in Vanderpoel, *More Chronicles*, 171.
50. Sheldon, 1801–3 Journal, 9–10. Southern women's academies between 1825 and 1860 also supervised how their students held their bodies; Stowe, "Not-So-Cloistered Academy," 93.
51. Ogden, 1816–18 Journal, 39–40; Beekman, 1807 Journal. For other expressions of relief over Pierce's praise, see Sheldon, 1801–3 Journal, 5, 8, 11, 12; and Van Schaack, 1809–10 Journal (no dates and no pagination).
52. "Mary Ann Bacon—Her [1802] Journal," in Vanderpoel and Buel, *Chronicles*, 67; Reynolds, 1806–7 Journal, 3.
53. Brickley, "Sarah Pierce's Litchfield Female Academy," 130–46.
54. Ogden, 1816–18 Journal, 14.
55. On directing social performances, see Goffman, *Presentation of Self*, 97–100.
56. Wood, *Radicalism of the American Revolution*, 135.
57. Opal, "Exciting Emulation," 468. Opal primarily focuses on rural vs. town reactions rather than gender issues. On colleges' use of meritocratic systems, see Hessinger, *Seduced, Abandoned, and Reborn*, chap. 3.
58. Smith-Rosenberg, "Female World of Love and Ritual," 14; see also Lasser, "'Let Us Be Sisters Forever.'" For a multi-article and international retrospective of Smith-Rosenberg, see *Journal of Women's History* 12 (Autumn 2000).
59. This extension is apparent in Diggs, "Romantic Friends"; the essays in Duberman, Vicinus, and Chauncy, *Hidden from History*; and Rotundo, *American Manhood*.
60. Lystra, *Searching the Heart*, 42–46, 154–56, finds much common ground between men and women, as do E. Rothman, *Hands and Hearts*, 319n14 and 333n63, and Francis Minkema, "Hannah and Her Sisters." Kelly, *In the New England Fashion*, includes both chap. 3 on female friendship at academies, and chap. 7 on heterosociability in village culture.
61. Lynne Templeton Brickley emphasizes how students "internalized" Pierce's values through the credit/debit system; by contrast, I am interested in

how the external aspect of that system acted on their relationships with each other, especially in terms of competition; see her "Sarah Pierce's Litchfield Female Academy," 130–46. Gordon, "Young Ladies Academy of Philadelphia," 80–82, briefly describes "emulation" at this academy. Green, "Female Education and School Competition," maintains that schoolteachers did not regard competition between girls as a problem before the 1820s. A number of other historians have addressed women's competition in pre–Civil War education, often only in passing. Christie Ann Farnham briefly considers competition in Southern women's colleges in the antebellum period in *Education of the Southern Belle*, 141–43, 148–49, 152–53. Rosenzweig, *Another Self*, 30–33, very briefly discusses the possibility of conflict between female friends in the 1800s. For the late Victorian period, Jane Hunter emphasizes that while young women in that era competed in coeducational high schools, single-sex schools were largely noncompetitive; *How Young Ladies Became Girls*, 193, 440n74. On female competition in the working class, outside the academy, see Karen V. Hansen's brief treatment in *A Very Social Time*, 64–66. In his general study of jealousy, Peter N. Stearns found that jealousy was not a major issue in the 1800s; *Jealousy*, 22. Literary critics have been more attentive to women's competition as represented in short stories and novels; historians need to give equal attention to the social context of this literature. An excellent example is Reichardt, "'Friend of My Heart.'" Recently, a number of writers have addressed competition among women in late-twentieth-century America; Tavris, "Are Girls Really as Mean as Books Say They Are?"

62. Camp, 1818–34 Diary.

63. Reynolds, 1806–7 Journal, 23.

64. Ogden, 1816–18 Journal, 29, 38–39.

65. "1822. Mary L. Wilbor Diary," in Vanderpoel and Buel, *Chronicles*, 239.

66. "Caroline Chester's [1816] Journal," in Vanderpoel, *More Chronicles*, 174, 165, 176, 166.

67. Brace, "Private Journal 1814," in Vanderpoel, *More Chronicles*, 99. Unfortunately, no journals of Sarah Pierce have survived, so we do not know if she described exhibition competition in the same terms.

68. Ibid., 103–4. Graduation with diplomas was not incorporated into the semester's end until after 1814, and since so many points were required, only a very small minority graduated. However, many other students participated in the exhibition. Brickley, "Sarah Pierce's Litchfield Female Academy," 127–28, 138.

69. Brace, "Private Journal Vol. 2 [1815]," in Vanderpoel, *More Chronicles*, 117; Brace, "Private Journal 1814," ibid., 103, 104. The trustees of the Young Ladies' Academy in Philadelphia spoke of student competition at exhibitions in much the same terms; Nash, "Rethinking Republican Motherhood," 182. Christie Anne Farnham has found that the prod of public embarrassment pushed otherwise lackadaisical Southern belles to either study hard for exhibitions at female colleges or to drop out before graduation; in time, Southern colleges eliminated the exhibition entirely; *Education of the Southern Belle*, 141–42.

70. Sedgwick, *New-England Tale*, 54–55.

71. Brickley, "Sarah Pierce's Litchfield Female Academy," 133–35. For examples of rules in conduct books, see Bushman, *Refinement of America*, chap. 2.

72. "Alterations from Copy of Rules of Julia Seymour—1820," in Vanderpoel and Buel, *Chronicles*, 231.

73. "The Rules of Litchfield Academy. 1825," in Vanderpoel and Buel, *Chronicles*, 256.

74. Eliza Ann Mulford, "[1814] Rules for the School and Family," in Vanderpoel and Buel, *Chronicles*, 146; "Alterations from Copy of Rules of Julia Seymour—1820," ibid., 230.

75. "Rules of Miss Pierces School Litchfield, May 19, 1818," Litchfield Female Academy Collection (hereafter LFA).

76. *By-Laws*, 9; Pierce, "Moralistic Essay and anecdote," Sarah Pierce Collection, LHS.

77. Green, "Female Education and School Competition," emphasizes the concern for femininity which dominated schools in the antebellum period.

78. Wolcott, 1826–27 Journal, 4, 43, 71–72.

79. Beekman, 1807 Journal, contains undated essays or notes on time, envy, sisterly affection, patience, prosperity, pride, suspicion, education, and friendship.

80. Pierce, "A Fragment," in Vanderpoel and Buel, *Chronicles*, 212.

81. "Caroline Chester's [1816] Journal," in Vanderpoel, *More Chronicles*, 182. Sarah Pierce also took off thirty credit marks for homesickness; "Alterations from Copy of Rules of Julia Seymour—1820," in Vanderpoel and Buel, *Chronicles*, 231.

82. Buel, 1830 Penmanship Writing Book. Mary Bassett, who also attended the School for Young Ladies in Auburn, New York, similarly wrote aphorisms on slips of paper, including "Command your ruling passions." Bassett, 1829 Album. In addition, Caroline M. Boardman repeatedly wrote "contentment," along with her name, on the last page of her 1815 journal.

83. Clark, "Mechanical View of the Faculties of the Soul"; Bergengren, "Review Text."

84. "The Two Cousins," in Vanderpoel and Buel, *Chronicles*, 100–118. Such plays continued concerns in children's literature of this time; Murray, "Rational Thought and Republican Virtues."

85. Van Schaack, "On Politeness."

86. Eliza Ann Mulford, "[1814] Rules for the School and Family," in Vanderpoel and Buel, *Chronicles*, 147; 29 August 1815 school rules, Boardman, 1815 Journal, 5.

87. "The Rules of Litchfield Academy. 1825," in Vanderpoel and Buel, *Chronicles*, 256.

88. Eliza Ann Mulford, "[1814] Rules for the School and Family," in Vanderpoel and Buel, *Chronicles*, 146–47.

89. Pierce to Brace, 1 Feb. 1833, in Vanderpoel and Buel, *Chronicles*, 314.

90. "Caroline Chester's [1816] Journal," in Vanderpoel, *More Chronicles*, 172, 183, 172, 168, quoting her mother.

91. Ibid., 171; see also Mary Ann Bacon's essay on education in "Mary Ann Bacon—Her Journal," in Vanderpoel and Buel, *Chronicles*, 72. In the decades before the Civil War, Southern college women also connected academic success with pleasing parents and friends, as shown in Farnham, *Education of the Southern Belle*, 141; and Stowe, "Not-So-Cloistered Academy," 95.

92. J. Hunter, *How Young Ladies Became Girls*, 197–210. Ironically, late Victorian girls' schools lacked the competitive structure earlier academies had because they feared that such competition would hurt young women's health. I suggest that the difficulty at schools such as Litchfield Academy was not so much the physical effects of competition but that competition set in motion feelings at odds with the school's rules.

93. "Caroline Chester's [1816] Journal," in Vanderpoel, *More Chronicles*, 169.

94. Wolcott, 1825 Diary, 22 August 1825.

95. Sheldon, 1801–3 Journal, 22. Lucy also complained that she "was not placed as high in the dance, as I intend to be next time," but did not name any individuals who preceded her; 18 Jan. 1803 entry.

96. "Caroline Chester's [1816] Journal," in Vanderpoel, *More Chronicles*, 165. The 1825 rules stated, "You must write a letter to be corrected and sent home to your friends once in four weeks—except excused," but this was the minimum, and apparently instructors did not peruse all letters sent home; "The Rules of Litchfield Academy. 1825," in Vanderpoel and Buel, *Chronicles*, 256.

97. Ogden, 1816–18 Journal, 23, 32, 36.

98. Sheldon, 1801–3 Journal, 2; Brickley, "Sarah Pierce's Litchfield Female Academy," 212.

99. "Caroline Chester's [1816] Journal," in Vanderpoel, *More Chronicles*, 179.

100. Ibid., 187.

101. Brickley, "Sarah Pierce's Litchfield Female Academy," 374–77, 397–402. In these regards, I agree with Catherine Kelly that academies "provided girls an institutional setting in which to develop friendships." *In the New England Fashion*, 70.

102. Paraphrase of Sarah Pierce by Henrietta Bevier, quoted in Brickley, "Sarah Pierce's Litchfield Female Academy," 399–400. Pierce also had students write an essay "on the amiableness of sisterly affection" and also on friendship; Beekman, 1807 Journal.

103. Wolcott, 1826–27 Journal, 78–79, 7.

104. Wolcott, 1825 Diary, 13 Sept. 1825.

105. "Caroline Chester—Her [1815] Diary," in Vanderpoel and Buel, *Chronicles*, 152; "Caroline Chester's [1816] Journal," in Vanderpoel, *More Chronicles*, 171–72, 181.

106. Armstrong, "Mental and Moral Feast."

107. Peck, 1825–27 Album; this was also quoted in Bassett, 1829 Album. For similar lines on friendship, see Marian Lewis, 1814 Album; Cook, 1813–1815 Album; and, especially, "Written for a friend upon her departure—," in Hart, 1819 Album. For examples of friendship albums for a later period, see Jabour, "Albums of Affection."

108. See, for example, "Melancholy," in Hart, 1819 Album; "The Tear," in Jane R. Lewis, 1828 Common Place Book; and "Ode to Sympathy," in Marian Lewis, 1814 Album.

109. Brickley, "Sarah Pierce's Litchfield Female Academy," 403–4.

110. Child, 1820 Journal, 26 June, 1820; Bevier, 1809 Diary, 8 July 1809.

111. Eliza Ann Mulford, "[1814] Rules for the School and Family," in Vanderpoel and Buel, *Chronicles*, 146.

112. "A Definition of Politeness," in Vanderpoel and Buel, *Chronicles*, 233; "1821. Sarah Kingsbury's Copy of Rules of the Litchfield Academy," ibid., 232.

113. Wolcott, 1825 Diary, 18 August 1825.

114. Bevier, 1809 Diary, 12 August 1809.

115. "1822. Mary L. Wilbor Diary," in Vanderpoel and Buel, *Chronicles*, 236, 235, 234.

116. "Caroline Chester's [1816] Journal," in Vanderpoel and Buel, *Chronicles*, 178, 181, 176, 185, 192.

117. "1796. Charlotte Sheldon—Her Diary," in Vanderpoel and Buel, *Chronicles*, 12.

118. Lucy Sheldon to Mrs. Huldah Sheldon, 29 Nov. 1803, in Vanderpoel and Buel, *Chronicles*, 53–55; "1822. Mary L. Wilbor Diary," ibid., 237; "Litchfield at the Beginning of the Nineteenth Century," ibid., 20–40.

119. Sarah Pierce to Ruth (Pierce) Croswell, n.d., Sarah Pierce Collection, LHS; Reynolds, 1806–7 Journal, 7; Beekman, 1807 Journal, 28 May 1807.

120. August 29, 1815 school rules, in Boardman, 1815 Journal, 3.

121. Halttunen, *Confidence Men and Painted Women*, 73–75; "The Rules of Litchfield Academy. 1825," in Vanderpoel and Buel, *Chronicles*, 257.

122. *By-Laws*, 14.

123. Pierce to Brace, July 1833, in Vanderpoel and Buel, *Chronicles*, 314–15.

124. McGiffert, *Their Stories*, 6, 9–11. Laura referred to her mother and sisters as "friends" of John Brace; Wolcott, 1826–27 Journal, 70. According to the Litchfield Female Academy Student Biographies, Laura Wolcott attended between 1822 and 1827, as did her six siblings.

125. Wolcott, 1826–27 Journal, 3.

126. Ibid., front cover; on singing, 12; on Beecher, 76–77; on assignment, 7; on anger, 36, 38, 42, 52, 53, 64; on trunk, 30; on Byron, 13–14, 55; on sneers, 42. I analyze her feelings of anger in chap. 4.

127. Ibid., 5, 81, 85–86.

128. Ibid., 85.

129. Ibid., 19.

130. Ibid., 59–60.

131. Wolcott may have been quoting from the *Spectator* here, since her concluding remark's language differs from her previous lines. Wolcott, 1826–27 Journal, 67, 68.

132. Ibid., 30, 45.

133. See, for example, ibid., 83.

134. The phrase "emulative zeal" was used in a verse by John Pierpont in "Extracts from [Lucy Sheldon's] Commonplace Book," in Vanderpoel and Buel, *Chronicles*, 56.

135. Brace, "Address—Oct. 28, 1816," in Vanderpoel, *More Chronicles*, 204.

136. J. Hunter, *How Young Ladies Became Girls*, chaps. 9 and 10.

3. Discerning the Heart

1. Roberts, 1801–6 Diary, 23 Dec. 1804. Nineteen studies, taken together, show that the average age of marriage in New England in the latter half of the eighteenth century was 22.7; Shammas, *History of Household Government*, 184.

2. Guion, Diary, 190. On wives' legal position, see Grossberg, *Governing the Hearth*.

3. Easton, *Passionate Spinster*, 23, 123. For genealogical information on Mary Guion and her family throughout this chapter, I use Guion and Guion, *Descendants of Louis Guion*, 143–47.

4. Kann, *Republic of Men*, 79–84; quotations, 79 and 82.

5. Guion, Diary, 201–2.

6. Eliza Southgate to Moses Porter, 17 July 1801, in *Girl's Life Eighty Years Ago*, 67; Mason and Phillips, "[1785-86] Journal of Elizabeth Cranch," 11; see also 19–20. For similar expectations of male deceit, see S. Heath, Diary, 19 Feb. and 2 June 1817; and Roberts, 1801–6 Diary, 5 August 1806. In contrast, women depicted other females as deceitful much less often; "Diary of Mary Orne Tucker," 329, and my analysis of Rachel Van Dyke in chapter 4.

7. "Lucy Sheldon's Journal for the Winter 1803," in Vanderpoel and Buel, *Chronicles*, 53.

8. "Advice to a Young Lady," in Mitchell, 1820–21 Album; see also "The Broken Promise," in Seymour, 1822–27 Album.

9. Wood, "Conspiracy and the Paranoid Style," 407, 422. Jay Fliegelman emphasizes that "flattery and seduction" were the two major concerns of both fiction and politics in the eighteenth century, and Richard Godbeer finds an increase in images of predatory males during the late 1700s. Fliegelman, *Prodigals and Pilgrims*, 36; Godbeer, *Sexual Revolution*, chap. 8.

10. Ditz, "Shipwrecked," 59.

11. Bancroft, 1793–95 Diary, 2 Jan. 1794.

12. Easton, *Passionate Spinster*, 27; North Castle's population in 1800 was 1,178. "Federal Census, 1800," 116.

13. Easton, *Passionate Spinster*, 39.
14. Ibid., 67; on her family and class, see chaps. 1 and 2.
15. Ibid., 41, 48, 55.
16. Ibid., 86.
17. Nicole Eustace argues that at mid-eighteenth century, courtship simultaneously involved romantic love and establishing social position, with romantic talk obscuring substantial socioeconomic issues. Eustace, "'Cornerstone of a Copious Work,'" 537.
18. Bloch, "Changing Conceptions," 39; Ditz, "Shipwrecked," 63–65.
19. For a general discussion of lack of parental control over American marriages in the eighteenth century, see Shammas, *History of Household Government*, chap. 4. Historians take a variety of views on love as grounds for marriage in this period. Laurel Thatcher Ulrich argues that in turn-of-the-century frontier Maine, marriage was not about romance; *Midwife's Tale*, 138–47. For the early nineteenth century, Catherine E. Kelly stresses household alliances over romantic love; *In the New England Fashion*, 132. In contrast, other historians find love as the preeminent reason for marriage after 1800; E. Rothman, *Hands and Hearts*, chap. 1; Lewis, "Republican Wife," 693–95; and Lystra, *Searching the Heart*.
20. Easton, *Passionate Spinster*, 94.
21. Ibid., 55, 60, 45.
22. Ibid., 46.
23. Ibid., 74, 104.
24. Ibid., 42–43.
25. Ibid., 43.
26. Ibid., 46, 57, 51.
27. Ibid., 60, 135n64, 62.
28. Ibid., 81–82, 89, 101.
29. Ibid., 95.
30. Ibid., 97.
31. Ibid., 57, 83, 88.
32. Ibid., 50, 51, 45, 72; see also 69, 70, 100.
33. Ibid., 41, 83, 88, 107.
34. Ibid., 88.
35. Ibid., 59, 65. Nicole Eustace argues that codenames in courtship were for privacy, but Patty Rogers showed little interest in secrecy and her usage seems more closely associated with her desire to maintain a feeling of high sensibility. Eustace, "'Cornerstone of a Copious Work,'" 519–20.
36. Easton, *Passionate Spinster*, 73.
37. Ibid., 89–91.
38. Ibid., 89, 97.
39. Ibid., 105, 100, 102.
40. Austen, *Sense and Sensibility*, 5.
41. Davidson, *Revolution and the Word*, 191–92.

42. As Rogers told her sisters, she had "*feelings* which would prevent my marrying anybody [else] at present." Easton, *Passionate Spinster*, 47.

43. As Woodbridge said, "'I don't know how to act with regard to Patty! I *feel* embarrassed. I wish to treat her with tenderness! & yet I do not.'" Ibid., 41.

44. Guion, Diary, 153.

45. In 1803, Mary Guion's father Jonathan appeared among the top fifth of taxpayers; North Castle 1803 tax assessment roll. The diary says little about how Guion made his money, except for noting sale of some livestock in New York.

46. The Guion family illustrates how the commercial revolution reached into rural life; while Guion was often busy with farm chores at home, she also visited New York City five times during her single years and there purchased luxury items such as fabric, ribbons, and books. Guion, Diary, 9–11, 60–61, 94–96, 211–13, 317–21 for trips to New York City and purchases.

47. Ibid., 160, 218.

48. Ibid., 276.

49. Jonathan Guion, Mary's father, was among the shareholders of the Bedford Circulating Library; through him she had access to the basic sentimental and philosophical works of the time. *Principles of the Bedford Circulating Library, Catalogue*, 73. On her "ever indulgent Father" and her brother taking out books for her, see Guion, Diary, 119, 181. Of the sixty works she mentioned between 1800 and 1807, at least twenty-six were held by the Bedford Circulating Library.

50. Of the sixty works Guion mentioned, twenty were novels, nine religious works, eight books of essays, eight digests, often of prescriptive literature, five poetic works, four memoirs, four books of philosophy, and two school books. Both Connell and Guion read works by Oliver Goldsmith, Elizabeth Singer Rowe, M. G. Lewis, Johann von Zimmermann, Mary Hay, James Hervey, Alexander Pope, Maria Edgeworth, and Frances Burney. On Mary Guion's reading, see R. Brown, *Knowledge Is Power*, 170–72. Patty Rogers's diary is from her twenty-third year and lists few books she had read, but her prose is testimony to extensive reading in sentimental literature during her younger years. On Rogers's reading, see Davidson, *Revolution and the Word*, 74–75, 191–92.

51. Ulrich, *Midwife's Tale*, 158. Here I follow Davidson, *Revolution and the Word*, chap. 6. Ellen Rothman argues that fiction taught young women to act on their feelings in courtship, and in that sense endangered them, but as Patty Rogers and Mary Guion show, fiction offered more than one message to readers, who picked and chose among them; *Hands and Hearts*, 40–41. Sometimes literature influenced men's perceptions of courtship as well; see Lemay, *Robert Bolling Woos Anne Miller*, 30.

52. Guion, Diary, 54.

53. Ibid., 240, 196, 364.

54. Ibid., 196, 322.

55. Captain Jonathan Jasup (or Jessup; 1761–1826) was a middle-aged and childless widower when he met Mary Guion. His first wife had died in 1799

aged twenty-six. Jasup was a sea captain, carpenter, part owner, and master of the Greenwich sloop "Concord," built in 1797. Jessup, *Edward Jessup of West Farms*, 283–84; "Ship Registers and Enrollments of Bridgeport, Connecticut, c. 1789–1867," 58–59.

56. Guion, Diary, 158, 159. Here Mary Guion quotes, somewhat inaccurately, Letter XIII in Frances Burney's *Evelina: or The History of a Young Lady's Entrance into the World*, in which Evelina responds to Lord Orville's extravagant compliments.

57. Guion, Diary, 166–68, 173–74, 187–88, 156; quotations 189, 215, 194.

58. Rachel M. Brownstein offers a parallel example of the role of literature in real life as, in turn, depicted in fiction. She cites Thomas Hardy's *Tess of the D'Urbervilles*, in which Tess, after her seduction, says "Why didn't you tell me there was danger in menfolk? Why didn't you warn me? Ladies know what to find hands against, because they read novels that tell them of these tricks [of men]; but I never had the chance o' learning in that way." *Becoming a Heroine*, 241.

59. Guion, Diary, 1, 55, 72, 57. On Jotham Smith's class and career, Christopher Beal, e-mail to the author, 25 Nov. 2005.

60. Guion, Diary, 152, 203.

61. Dillon, *Gender of Freedom*, 130, 134.

62. On republican and Lockean disdain of coquetry, see G. Brown, *Consent of the Governed*, chap. 5.

63. On the republicanism of the magazines she read, see Nord, "Republican Literature," and List, "Magazine Portrayals of Women's Role."

64. Guion, Diary, 92.

65. Ibid., 241.

66. Ibid., 174, 84, 239. The same dichotomy appeared in novels of this period; Davidson, "Flirting with Destiny," 29.

67. Guion, Diary, 189, 174, 77, 158–59.

68. Ibid., 181.

69. Ibid., 180, quoting Johann von Zimmermann; see also 174–76 and 179 for further excerpts from Zimmermann. An English translation of this work from Zimmermann's German appeared as early as 1779; titles vary in wording. Other diarists read and quoted from Zimmermann, who deserves scholarly attention: Roberts, 1801–6 Diary, 1 April 1804; "Diary of Mary Orne Tucker," 315; *Diary of Sarah Connell Ayer*, 43; and 28 references scattered throughout Rachel Van Dyke's diary, McMahon and Schriver, *To Read My Heart*.

70. On this period's concept of marriage as friendship, see Lewis, "Republican Wife," 707–10.

71. Guion and Guion, *Descendants of Louis Guion*, 144; Guion, Diary, 203, 53.

72. Guion, Diary, 45, 58, 114, 247, 257 (quotation). Nicole Eustace emphasizes colonial women's reluctance to reveal their intentions in courtship; "'Cornerstone of a Copious Work,'" 529–30.

73. Guion, Diary, 202, 206. In contrast, Steven M. Stowe found that antebellum Southern women were closely tied to their parents' advice on whom to marry; "Not-So-Cloistered Academy," 101–3.

74. Spacks, *Gossip*, 10, 5. Because "gossip" is a value-laden word and sociologists have been unable to agree on its meaning, I have used the more neutral words "talk" and "conversation" in this chapter. Such talk in the early national period continued the community oversight common among women in the colonial period; Ulrich, *Good Wives*, chap. 3; K. Brown, *Good Wives, Nasty Wenches*, chap. 9; and Kamensky, *Governing the Tongue*.

75. Guion, Diary, 90.

76. An overview of studies of visiting among middle-class Americans is Macdonald and Hansen, "Sociability and Gendered Spheres." Karen V. Hansen's excellent study of visiting in the New England working class argues for gendered patterns, with women more likely to have guests for tea than men, who were more likely to visit than to be hosts; *Very Social Time*, 83. Catherine E. Kelly emphasizes "heterosociability" in nineteenth-century New England small-town life in her *In the New England Fashion*, 192–99. Elements of all of these aspects run through Guion's diary, depending on what Guion's immediate need was; clearly, visiting was a handy tool.

77. Guion, Diary, 1, 285.

78. Two themes in studies of middle-class visiting are "the increasing divergence in male and female visiting practices during the progression of the nineteenth century," and women visiting with other women; Macdonald and Hansen, "Sociability and Gendered Spheres," 540. Nancy Tomes found that Quaker single women largely visited other single women, although single men might come along; "Quaker Connection," 180.

79. Guion, Diary, 247–48. On "bespoke," see Cassidy, *Dictionary of American Regional English*, 1:223.

80. Guion, Diary, 322.

81. Ibid., 25–26, 8, 254, 181.

82. Ibid., 49 (quotation), 83, 72, 90.

83. Ibid., 57. Guion was well aware of class differences in her small community, although they do not seem to have prevented her from consorting with those above her.

84. Guion, Diary, 212–14. On fashion in provincial New England during the antebellum period, see Kelly, *In the New England Fashion*, chap. 8.

85. Smith died in 1825 after selling his city home to Philip Hone, the diarist. Edwin N. Moore to Donald W. Marshall, 28 June 1962, Jotham Smith file.

86. Guion, Diary, 65.

87. Ditz, "Formative Ventures."

88. Guion, Diary, 189, 191, 192.

89. Goffman, *Presentation of Self*, chap. 4.

90. Guion, Diary, 47; on sexual slander, see Ulrich, *Good Wives*, chap. 5; and K. Brown, *Good Wives, Nasty Wenches*, chap. 9 and 313–18; on cosmetics in the early republic and the Victorian period, see Stabile, *Memory's Daughters*, 136–47; and Halttunen, *Confidence Men and Painted Women*, 88–89.

91. Guion, Diary, 48.

92. Ibid., 49, 67.
93. Ibid., 64, 123, 83, 247, 155–56.
94. Ibid., 176, 49. She also used a "foreteller," and her friend Mr. Owen put a lock of hair under his pillow to determine his marital choice; see 33, 35–36, 39. Guion discovered the Bible and key method of soothsaying in Daldianus Artemidorus's *Interpretation of Dreams*, a much-published collection of ancient superstitions and rites written in the late second century. Opie and Tatem, *Dictionary of Superstitions*, 23–25, lists examples of divination using the Bible and key, ranging from the medieval to modern periods. Late Victorian girls also used such methods; J. Hunter, *How Young Ladies Became Girls*, 342–43.
95. Guion, Diary, 211.
96. Here I concur with Catherine Kelly's emphasis on "society" as well as on the primacy of peer relations; *In the New England Fashion*, 191, 66–67.
97. Guion, Diary, 76, 285.
98. Ibid., 151–52.
99. Ibid., 251.
100. Brumberg, *Body Project*, xx–xxvi, contrasts nineteenth-century girls' concern with character with twentieth-century girls' obsession with their bodies.
101. By comparison, see Matt, "Frocks, Finery, and Feelings."
102. Guion, Diary, 187 (quotation), 305, 224, 233–34, 228.
103. Ibid., 141, 175, 241, 235, 209.
104. Jagodzinski, *Privacy and Print*, 11.
105. Guion, Diary, 13, 45, 253, 247.
106. E. Rothman, *Hands and Hearts*, chap. 2, emphasizes women's fears facing marriage.
107. Guion, Diary, 201, 202, 329.
108. Ibid., 206. A comparison of tax records for 1803 shows that Daniel Brown, Samuel's father, held property worth less than half of Jonathan Guion's; North Castle 1803 tax assessment roll.
109. Ibid., 228.
110. Ibid., 219.
111. Ibid., 226, 202, 196, 211–12, 225, 238, 228, 275, 286, 292, 240.
112. Ibid., 308.
113. Lystra, *Searching the Heart*, chap. 6.
114. Guion, Diary, 208, 199, 259.
115. Ibid., 54.
116. Lystra, *Searching the Heart*, 166.
117. Ibid., chaps. 2, 5.
118. Guion, Diary, 334, 250.
119. Ibid., 324, 335, 316, 303, 314, 335, 286, 299, 332.
120. Kelly, *In the New England Fashion*, 132; E. Rothman, *Hands and Hearts*, 37.
121. Guion, Diary, 248, 331, 330.

122. Margo Culley also sees "a dislocation from the self, or a turning of subject into object" in diary keeping and characterizes this as a "double consciousness." Culley, *Day at a Time*, 10.

123. Illouz, *Consuming the Romantic Utopia*, 14, 84.

124. Swidler, *Talk of Love*, 24, 30, 71, 89.

4. Losing It

1. Eustace, "'Passion Is the Gale,'" 179, 173, 178.

2. Ferguson, *American Enlightenment*, 179; C. Stearns and P. Stearns, *Anger*, chap. 2. Gwynne Kennedy found that during the early modern period, men believed women were more prone to anger, and hence feminine anger lacked legitimacy; *Just Anger*, chap. 1.

3. Grasso, *Artistry of Anger*, 13.

4. Ibid., 47, 46, 30.

5. C. Stearns and P. Stearns, *Anger*, 36–50.

6. J. Hunter, *How Young Ladies Became Girls*, 51, 55–56.

7. Carol Zisowitz Stearns and Peter N. Stearns confine themselves to defining anger as a biological reaction to "antagonistic" situations, and avoid distinguishing degrees or types of anger; *Anger*, 15, 16.

8. S. Shields, *Speaking from the Heart*, 140, 11, 146.

9. *Diary of Sarah Connell Ayer*, 48; see also 49.

10. Howell, 1799–1805 Journals, 10, 12, 13, 14.

11. Sarah Connell to Maria Kittredge, 13 March 1810, in *Diary of Sarah Connell Ayer*, 372.

12. *Diary of Sarah Connell Ayer*, 146; see also 69, 131–32.

13. Ibid., 121, 136.

14. Easton, *Passionate Spinster*, 57.

15. Rogers never overtly criticized Elizabeth Brooks, but expressed puzzlement that "I was the *unfortunate* & she the *happy* Girl!" Ibid., 77, 70.

16. Ibid., 84; for her resentment over her perceived inferiority to others, see also 86.

17. Ibid., 100.

18. Eliza Ann Mulford, "[1814] Rules for the School and Family," in Vanderpoel and Buel, *Chronicles*, 146. Betsey Reynolds reported that "several things unexpected happened which rendered me unusually Angry," and made her fail to win a credit mark; 1806–7 Journal, 36.

19. "Caroline Chester's [1816] Journal," in Vanderpoel, *More Chronicles*, 190–191. As a Litchfield Academy student, Julia Cowles also expressed no criticism or sarcasm, but once she returned home and could compose her diary more freely, she wrote much more frankly; Moseley, *Diaries of Julia Cowles*, 48–50.

20. Wolcott, 1825 Diary, 22 August 1825; Wolcott, 1826–27 Journal, 77, front cover, 3.

21. Wolcott, 1826–27 Journal, 17, 42, 74.
22. Ibid., 30, 38–39.
23. Ibid., 53, 78, 42.
24. Susan Heath records reading friends' diaries in her own journal; see, for example, S. Heath, Diary, 9 July and 18 August 1817; 28 and 29 July 1818; and 8 and 9 January 1819.
25. Guion, Diary, 118, 126, 315, 25.
26. May, Journal, [1], 69. May called this semi-epistolary composition "my journal" several times; see 24 and 65.
27. McMahon and Schriver, *To Read My Heart*, 1–2, 216–17.
28. May, Journal, 12.
29. Guion, Diary, 11, 9, 49, 59, 55, 83, 63, 83.
30. Ibid., 2, 67, 26, 83, 72, 90.
31. Ibid., 52.
32. Ibid., 27, 26, 150.
33. Ibid., 14, 121, 217.
34. Ibid., 83.
35. Ibid., 321–22.
36. May, Journal, [3], [4], 24, [4], 51, 39, 15, [4].
37. Ibid., 9, 8.
38. Ibid., 31.
39. Ibid., 12.
40. Ibid., 46.
41. Ibid., 55; see also 11.
42. Ibid., 48–49.
43. Ibid., 50, 53.
44. Ibid., 26.
45. Ibid., 9, 56.
46. Ibid., 55, 13.
47. Ibid., 40, 65.
48. Ibid., 44, 55, 9.
49. Ibid., 65. May died ten days after her journal ended; Chambers, "Seduction and Sensibility," 272. Throughout his article, Chambers rightfully sees May's struggle to distinguish true from false sensibility, but does not analyze her breaking of rules concerning anger.
50. May, Journal, 50–52.
51. McMahon and Schriver, *To Read My Heart*, 5–6, 25. Quoted excerpts reprinted by permission of the University of Pennsylvania Press.
52. McMahon, "'We Would Share Equally,'" 310.
53. McMahon and Schriver, *To Read My Heart*, 81.
54. Ibid., 54, 116, 128–29, 77.
55. Goffman, *Presentation of Self*, 210.
56. McMahon and Schriver, *To Read My Heart*, 81.
57. Ibid., 50.

58. Ibid., 89.

59. Ibid., 54; Van Dyke reported a similar exchange with Maria concerning Latin, 62. Van Dyke's young friend Ruth Condict was also dedicated to studying Latin, and, Rachel believed, was envied by those who "'hate that excellence they cannot reach'," 36.

60. Ibid., 175, 110, 84.

61. Ibid., 86, 72, 85.

62. Ibid., 203, 90–91. Van Dyke's praise for her room is similar to those of later Victorian girls; J. Hunter, *How Young Ladies Became Girls*, 93–98.

63. McMahon and Schriver, *To Read My Heart*, 130, 125.

64. Ibid., 223, 80.

65. Ibid., 204.

66. Ibid., 202.

67. Ibid., 80, 202, 140, 141.

68. Ibid., 141, 153.

69. Ibid., 141, 84.

70. Ibid., 55.

71. Ibid., 340–42, 103.

72. Ibid., 354–59, 113, 66.

73. Ibid., 299, 211, 299.

74. Ibid., 190.

75. Ibid., 215.

76. Ibid., 249, 43. Without any sense of irony, Van Dyke professed her admiration for a female friend *"who never speaks ill of anyone,"* 67.

77. Rachel said Condict was *"very deceitful,"* and Mr. G— agreed, writing, "it somehow seems to me that she does not indulge this most detestable vice from vicious motives—but seems to think she must—in order to make her self a *woman*—seems to think there is a species of *importance* conferred by it." McMahon and Schriver, *To Read My Heart*, 78.

78. Ibid., 200.

79. S. Heath, Diary, 11 Sept 1812. Ebenezer Heath's wealth is clear from the pew rents based on 1806 calculations; see First Parish, Brookline, "Original Valuations of the Pews in the First Parish, Brookline." Heath's extensive Brookline landholdings in 1822 are listed in Jones, *Land Ownership in Brookline*, 28–34, 1822 map.

80. S. Heath, Diary, 10 Nov. 1813, 8 Feb. 1817.

81. Ibid., 8 July 1816.

82. Ibid., 19 Oct. 1817, 23 March 1825.

83. Ibid., 14 May 1824.

84. Ibid., 4 May 1825.

85. Ibid., 7 June 1818, 16 April 1820, 8 July 1823.

86. Ibid., 10 April 1827; see also 1 June 1826.

87. Ibid., 12 March 1827.

88. Ibid., 19 Sept. 1823, 13 July 1816, 14 Oct. 1827, 3 Sept. 1817, 26 August 1826.
89. Ibid., 9 June 1827.
90. Ibid., 3 Sept. 1817.
91. Hannah (Williams) Heath, 1805–12 Diary, and her 1819–32 Book of Prayers and Meditations and "Extract Book."
92. S. Heath, Diary, 8 March 1825 and 13 March 1818.
93. Ibid., 13 March 1827; see also 1 July 1825.
94. On John Heath's drinking, see ibid., 18 May 1818 and 6 August 1823; on his family's destitution, 23 Oct. 1818; on Susan Heath's rare efforts to feel sympathy or patience toward her brother, 15 March 1817 and 14 March 1818; and on her father's mismanagement of John, 19 July 1817 and 8 July 1823.
95. Ibid., 18 April 1817.
96. Ibid., 6 March 1821.
97. Ibid., 11 Feb. 1826; see also 23 Oct. 1818.
98. Ibid., 20 August 1825.
99. Rachel Van Dyke's published poem provides a striking contrast to her spirited diary; it is a vague and derivative ode to evening that even Sarah Connell would have been embarrassed to write, and suggests that her public face was much milder than her private one; McMahon and Schriver, *To Read My Heart*, 354–55. Carol Tavris has argued that speaking one's anger increases it, but these diarists suggest that writing one's anger reduces or displaces it; Tavris, *Anger*, 132–35. Lower-class urban women seem not to have hesitated to express anger publicly, as evidenced in Stansell, *City of Women*, 58–62.
100. Mary R. Reichardt also found that the antagonistic relations among women in Mary Wilkins Freeman's stories centered on "themes of cheating, theft, or false identity, all 'sins' committed by a woman to raise or protect her acceptance and esteem in her rival's eyes." "'Friend of My Heart,'" 56.
101. Linda Grasso and Nicole Eustace have theorized that it was culturally more acceptable for women to be angry at social inferiors, but these diarists were irked more with their social peers and superiors than with their subordinates. Both Rachel Van Dyke's and Mary Guion's families owned slaves, but neither woman expressed any anger toward them, nor were any of my core diarists more than irked at servants, and they tended to sentimentalize the poor. Grasso, *Artistry of Anger*, 46–47; Eustace, "'Passion Is the Gale,'" 40.
102. This concern runs through Van Dyke's journal; see, for example, McMahon and Schriver, *To Read My Heart*, 56, 68, 73.
103. Occasionally diarists reflected directly on their relationship between their individuality and collectivity as women; see "Diary of Mary Orne Tucker," 331–32.
104. As Steven Neuwirth pointed out in his study of Mary Rowlandson's seventeenth-century captivity narrative, an assertive, angry female voice takes on both distinctiveness and authenticity; "Her Master's Voice," 58.

105. C. Stearns and P. Stearns, *Anger*, 32.

106. Susan Heath's sisters Mary and Ann Eliza wrote mild-mannered diaries in which their father infrequently figures. The major exception is Ann Eliza Heath's 18 March 1825 entry which is very similar to Susan Heath's 23 March 1825 critique of family strife. Susan Heath's sisters kept their diaries for no more than a year; a longer span might have encouraged them to explore their relationships with their father. Mary Heath, 1824 Diary, and Ann Eliza Heath, 1825–26 Diary.

107. Introduction dated 10 March 1801, "Aunt Abby May's Ballstown Journal," [1]. I have compared May's angriest entries in the original with this copy, and except for minor slips of the pen, they are the same: May's sister left her criticisms of Oliver Pain, Mr. Bowers, and Miss Kissam intact.

108. S. Heath, Diary, 24–29 May 1817.

109. Spiro, "Some Reflections," 326.

110. Wolcott, 1826–27 Journal, 30, 45.

111. McMahon and Schriver, *To Read My Heart*, 43.

5. Reconstructing the Heart

1. Jane Hunter calculates the age of menarche in 1850 to be about fifteen, and it was probably a bit higher during the early republic; *How Young Ladies Became Girls*, 131.

2. "The Day of Marriage," in Lucy Sheldon Music Book.

3. S. Heath, Diary, 3 Sept. 1813 and 11 Sept. 1815. See also "Diary of Mary Orne Tucker," 320.

4. Mason and Phillips, "[1785-86] Journal of Elizabeth Cranch," 12.

5. Shammas, *History of Household Government*, 184. David Kling sets the mean age at conversion for Connecticut females during the Second Great Awakening at 28.8, with only 14 percent under twenty, but 23.4 percent between ages twenty and twenty-four, and 16.2 percent between twenty-five and twenty-nine. Fifty-five percent of the female converts were married; *Field of Divine Wonders*, 177.

6. Wolcott, 1826–27 Journal, 69.

7. S. Heath, Diary, 11 Sept. and 3 August 1813, 11 Sept. 1815.

8. Mason and Phillips, "[1785-86] Journal of Elizabeth Cranch," 31; Cranch, 1786 Journal, 48.

9. May, 1796 Journal, 19.

10. Guion, Diary, 178.

11. Boardman, 1815 Journal, 74. On evangelical concern for "dissimulation," see Juster, *Disorderly Women*, 177.

12. Boardman, 1815 Journal, 8–9. So common was the association of religion and gloom that in her 1802 diary, Mary Orne Tucker pointed out occasions when

religion was not gloomy, as if that were an exception; "Diary of Mary Orne Tucker," 308.

13. Harding, *Certain Magnificence*, 56–62; and Caskey, *Chariot of Fire*, chap. 2, 6–9. Beecher's ability to preach both divine sovereignty and free will is apparent in student diaries; Child, 1820 Journal, 11 June and 2 July 1820; and Ogden, 1816–18 Journal, 41.

14. Brace, "Private Journal Vol. 2 [1815]," in Vanderpoel, *More Chronicles*, 115.

15. "Caroline Chester—Her [1815] Diary," in Vanderpoel and Buel, *Chronicles*, 152, 153. Henrietta Cornelia Bevier's 1809 diary offers many parallels to Chester's account.

16. Eliza Ann Mulford, "[1814] Rules for the School and Family," in Vanderpoel and Buel, *Chronicles*, 146.

17. "Caroline Chester's [1816] Journal," in Vanderpoel, *More Chronicles*, 166–67, 171, 175.

18. Boardman, 1815 Journal, 38.

19. "Caroline Chester's [1816] Journal," in Vanderpoel, *More Chronicles*, 164, 175.

20. Ibid., 188.

21. Ibid., 172.

22. Juster, *Disorderly Women*, 185–89; Boardman, 1815 Journal, 12; Ogden, 1816–18 Journal, 30. In addition, a classmate depicted God as "The Friend of All" in her 18 Dec. 1822 contribution to Marian Lewis, 1814 Album; and Mary A. Child summed up a sermon depicting God as her friend in her 1820 Journal, 2 July 1820.

23. Buggeln, *Temples of Grace*, 159.

24. "Caroline Chester's [1816] Journal," in Vanderpoel, *More Chronicles*, 172.

25. Sarah Pierce, "Address at the Close of the Summer 1820," in Vanderpoel and Buel, *Chronicles*, 208.

26. Eliza Ann Mulford, "[1814] Rules for the School and Family," in Vanderpoel and Buel, *Chronicles*, 146; "Caroline Chester's [1816] Journal," ibid., 183.

27. "Caroline Chester's [1816] Journal," ibid., 166.

28. Farewells to friends were common in Litchfield Female Academy friendship albums. Catherine E. Kelly emphasizes the difficulty of extending academy friendships into maturity, an interpretation at odds with Carroll Smith-Rosenberg, who sees schoolgirl friendships continuing through life. Kelly, *In the New England Fashion*, 80–81; Smith-Rosenberg, "Female World of Love and Ritual," 4.

29. Pierce, "Address at the Close of the Summer 1820," in Vanderpoel and Buel, *Chronicles*, 209, 210. Beecher's statistics are in Boardman, 1815 Journal, 71.

30. "Dialogue between Miss Trusty and Her Pupils," in Vanderpoel and Buel, *Chronicles*, 214, 215.

31. Brace, "Address at the Close of the School Oct. 25, 1819," in Vanderpoel, *More Chronicles*, 211.

234 *Notes to Pages 154–159*

32. J. Hunter, *How Young Ladies Became Girls*, 148–49.

33. "Caroline Chester's [1816] Journal," in Vanderpoel, *More Chronicles*, 177. Caroline Boardman's and Eliza Ogden's journals also chronicle the 1815–16 revival, reporting the same religious methods as Chester did; they, too, did not convert.

34. Abigail Bradley to Eliza Nash, 15 Sept. 1815; Bradley-Hyde Papers, 1–66:2, Schlesinger Library, Radcliffe Institute for Advanced Study, Harvard University, quoted in Brickley, "Sarah Pierce's Litchfield Female Academy," 323.

35. Julia Parmalee wrote this, quoting Edward Young's "Jealousy," in Cook, 1813–1815 Album.

36. McMahon and Schriver, *To Read My Heart*, 200, 300–302, 290–91. Catherine Kelly points out the difficulty of young women continuing intellectual pursuits at home; *In the New England Fashion*, 84–90. Rachel Van Dyke's unusual intellectuality and her study with Mr. G— make her maturation process more like late Victorian girls' than like her contemporaries'; J. Hunter, *How Young Ladies Became Girls*, chap. 9.

37. McMahon and Schriver, *To Read My Heart*, 142, 151, 122, 171; Van Dyke's friend John Barker coined the word "solemncholy" to describe these feelings, 276.

38. Ibid., 185.

39. Ibid., 244, 259, 276.

40. Ibid., 206.

41. Ibid., 243, 289, 260.

42. Ibid., 65.

43. Ibid., 113, 276, 225.

44. Ibid., 228.

45. Ibid., 297.

46. Nagel, *Adams Women*, 87–95. Cranch's use of the name "Corydon" appears in her 1781–82 Journal.

47. Cranch, 1786 Journal, 9.

48. Ibid., 49.

49. Ibid., 45; 1787 Journal, 3 May 1787.

50. Cranch, 1788–89 Journal, 28 August, 27 Sept., and 11 Dec. 1788.

51. Elizabeth Cranch to Jacob Norton, 13 May 1788, 1788 folder, JNP; 1788–89 Journal, 30 Dec. 1788; see also 28 Jan. 1789 entry.

52. Elizabeth Cranch to Jacob Norton, 5 April and 13 May 1788, JNP.

53. Elizabeth Cranch to Jacob Norton, 17 April 1788, JNP. Norton's letter suggesting she was deceived in him has apparently not survived.

54. Elizabeth Cranch to Jacob Norton, 5 and 17 April 1788, JNP.

55. Elizabeth Cranch to Jacob Norton, 1 Feb. 1789, 1789–90 folder, JNP; 1788–89 Journal, 2 and 7 Feb. 1789.

56. See for example, the diary of Emily Hawley Gillespie, which Judy Nolte Lensink found "less emotionally rich" after marriage; *"A Secret to Be Burried,"* 180.

57. Cranch, 1807–9 Journal, 17 Oct. 1808.
58. Cranch, 1805–7 Journal, 21 Nov. 1807.
59. Norton, *Blessedness of Those Who Die*, 24–25. On changes in funeral sermons, see Henderson, "Imperfect Dead," 492.
60. Guion, Diary, 339–40; she uses the phrase "the best of husbands" on 341 and 343.
61. Ibid., 340.
62. Ibid., 341.
63. Ibid., 344. Eliza Southgate also discovered that her husband expected to read her letters after their 1803 marriage; Eliza Southgate Bowne to Octavia [Southgate], 30 May 1803, in *Girl's Life Eighty Years Ago*, 148.
64. Guion, Diary, 342.
65. Ibid., 344.
66. On Samuel Brown's different efforts to make a living, see Guion, Diary, 342, 345, 351. According to the North Castle, New York, manuscript census, in 1820 their household included three boys aged between sixteen and twenty-five, probably employees, as well as the four Brown girls and Harry, then a free male between fourteen and twenty-five, making ten with Samuel and Mary. North Castle 1820 census, 276.
67. Guion, Diary, 276; 290, 300, 301; 285; 319; 209. Her father Jonathan Guion belonged to the Bedford Presbyterian Church; Eardeley, "Bedford Presbyterian Church Record Book 1," 13, 37, 40.
68. Guion, Diary, 128, 181–82.
69. Ibid., 257.
70. Buggeln, *Temples of Grace*, 164.
71. Guion, Diary, 346.
72. Ibid., 347, 348. Most of the Guion and Brown families joined St. Matthew's Church of Bedford; see "General Records of the Baptisms, Marriages, Communicants and Deaths."
73. Guion read *Memoirs of the Late Mrs. Susan Huntington*, one of the Rev. Leigh Richmond's tracts, the *Memoirs of Mrs. Ann H. Judson, Late Missionary to Burma*, and one of her brother Alvah Guion's sermons; Guion, Diary, 356, 357, 363, 368, 367. Ironically, although she was a minister's wife, Elizabeth Cranch Norton was less hostile to "frivolous" literature after marriage than Mary Guion was.
74. Guion, Diary, 352–53, 357, 359–60, 362, 377, 349, 371, 346, 350–51, 365.
75. Ibid., 364.
76. Ibid., 352, 379.
77. Ibid., 350.
78. Ibid., 119.
79. *Diary of Sarah Connell Ayer*, 377, 101. This published version of the diary is dependable for the earlier period of her life, lacking only some entries concerning her mother, which have been excised. In the years after 1810, the editor sometimes deleted summaries of sermons and religious entries, occasionally

but not always marking these with asterisks. As a result, for the post-1810 period, the published diary presents a far more secular image of the author than does the manuscript. In quoting from the diary, I have used the published version where it is accurate and the manuscript version when it offers additional material.

80. *Diary of Sarah Connell Ayer*, 124–25.

81. Ibid., 143.

82. Ibid., 175, 177; Connell Ayer, Diary, vol. 2, [20 Oct.] 1810. Arlie Russell Hochschild states as a general principle that superiors possess the right to define inferiors' emotion work; *Managed Heart*, 84–85.

83. *Diary of Sarah Connell Ayer*, 196.

84. Ibid., 82; Buggeln, *Temples of Grace*, 128–29.

85. McFarland, *Historical View of Heresies;* on parallels between sentimental and Calvinist feeling, see Campbell, *Romantic Ethic,* 123–37.

86. *Diary of Sarah Connell Ayer*, 194. Samuel Ayer's animosity to her imagination suggests he approved of her move away from fiction.

87. Ibid., 209.

88. Ibid., 231; Gedge, *Without Benefit of Clergy*, chap. 7.

89. Although Payson was technically a Calvinist, Richard Rabinowitz characterizes his theology as "devotionalism . . . or sentimentalism, because it stressed so powerfully the role of emotions in one's religious consciousness." *Spiritual Self in Everyday Life*, 157.

90. Cummings, *Memoir of the Rev. Edward Payson*, 33, 246. The most thorough analysis of Payson is Rabinowitz, *Spiritual Self in Everyday Life*, chap. 12.

91. *Diary of Sarah Connell Ayer*, 320.

92. "Record of the Second Parish Church, Portland, Me.," 51, 34, 21, 33, 34, 43, 16. Susan Juster discovered that Baptist disciplinary records of this period focused on dissimulation, especially among women; this seems to be another version of the same concern, emotional congruence; *Disorderly Women*, chap. 5.

93. For the ideology that succeeded republican motherhood, see Welter, "Cult of True Womanhood" and "Feminization of American Religion, 1800–1860."

94. Connell Ayer, Diary, vol. 4, 29 Oct. 1827.

95. Ibid., vol. 2, [20 Oct.] 1810; *Diary of Sarah Connell Ayer*, 254, 260, 293, 242. Catherine Kelly discusses wives' efforts to convert their husbands; *In the New England Fashion*, 139–45.

96. *Diary of Sarah Connell Ayer*, 377–78.

97. Lewis, "Mother's Love," 59.

98. *Diary of Sarah Connell Ayer*, 231, 52–71; Brace, "Address at the Close of the School Oct. 25, 1819," in Vanderpoel, *More Chronicles*, 211.

99. Connell Ayer, Diary, vol. 2, [17 August] 1811.

100. By the Victorian period, ideologues argued that "the nature of woman was inherently Christlike"; Porterfield, *Feminine Spirituality in America*, 67; see also Kling, *Field of Divine Wonders*, 225.

101. Connell Ayer, Diary, vol. 3, 23 Mar. 1821; vol. 4, 5 Oct. 1829.

102. Connell Ayer, Diary, vol. 4, 30 Dec. 1827; *Diary of Sarah Connell Ayer*, 241.

103. Demos, "Shame and Guilt in Early New England."

104. Connell Ayer, Diary, vol. 2, [26 May] 1810. On one hand, seventeenth-century diarists admired sadness as evidence of spirituality; Barr-Zisowitz, "Sadness," 610. On the other, Jane Hunter found that an association of depression and unbelief lingered to the late 1800s; *How Young Ladies Became Girls*, 154.

105. *Diary of Sarah Connell Ayer*, 218, 275.

106. For Jonathan Edwards, see Karlsen and Crumpacker, *Journal of Esther Edwards Burr*, 12.

107. "Diary of Mary Orne Tucker," 320–21; Lucinda Read, 1815–16 Diary, 8 June 1815.

108. Carol Barr-Zisowitz cites Arlie Russell Hochschild, N. L. Stein, and J. L. Jewett as taking this position, in her overview, "Sadness," 609.

109. Connell Ayer, Diary, vol. 4, 22 August 1824. Invalid letter writer Deborah Vinal Fiske used similar tactics; S. Rothman, *Living in the Shadow of Death*, chap. 6.

110. "A Constitution for Maternal Associations," in *Mother's Manual*, 57. Such associations provided a sentimental and sororal solution to the Calvinist problem of depravity; Meckel, "Educating a Ministry of Mothers."

111. *Diary of Sarah Connell Ayer*, 231, 267, 293, 231, 237, 259, 294, 272, 280, 278.

112. Ibid., 233, 247, 266, 257.

113. Ibid., 289, 269; see also 234, 245, 250, 258. As Candy Gunther found in her study of Rachel Stearns's 1834–37 journal, conversion to a new denomination separated her from old friends who belonged to other churches; "Spiritual Pilgrimage of Rachel Stearns."

114. *Diary of Sarah Connell Ayer*, 330.

115. Brereton, *From Sin to Salvation*, 19–20; Rodger M. Payne maintains that religious conversion contributed to a modern self in his *Self and the Sacred*, 14.

116. Barr-Zisowitz, "Sadness," 613–14.

117. Connell Ayer, Diary, vol. 4, 6 Jan. 1828; see also *Diary of Sarah Connell Ayer*, 252. Linda Grasso suggests that theological evolution away from Calvinism's angry God did not facilitate women's expression of anger: although the image of a meek, suffering Christ validated women's suffering, it robbed them of the right to express anger. Moreover, since women's cultural power was tied to their Christ-like character, anger also robbed them of their one source of influence. Grasso, *Artistry of Anger*, 144.

118. Connell Ayer, Diary, vol. 3, 1 Jan. 1825.

119. Connell Ayer, Diary, vol. 5, 2 May 1830. Sarah Connell Ayer did not kill herself; she and her daughter Harriet died of scarlet fever in 1835. *Diary of Sarah Connell Ayer*, 377–78.

120. Noble, *Masochistic Pleasures*, 44–53, 86–93.

121. Philip Greven maintains his emphasis on childhood experience in his "Self Shaped and Misshaped."

122. Juster, *Disorderly Women*, 201. By contrast, David Kling emphasizes the importance of submission in women's conversions and argues that "female conversion signaled a preparedness for marriage and future maternal responsibilities." *Field of Divine Wonders*, 209.

123. For other diarists giving up novels, see Read, 1815–16 Journal, 31 Dec. 1816; and "Diary of Mary Orne Tucker," 314. On clerical animosity toward novels, see Kling, *Field of Divine Wonders*, 224.

124. Even in the unusually liberal Child family, the wife seldom read on her own, and at best listened to her husband read out loud; Zboray and Zboray, "Reading and Everyday Life," 290.

125. Hall, "Uses of Literacy in New England." Hall has more recently suggested that such patterns of intensive and extensive reading may have varied by group; see his "Books and Reading in Eighteenth-Century America."

126. Swidler, *Talk of Love*, 103–7. As a student of twentieth-century life, Swidler tends to assume a degree of choice broader than for any stage of life in the early republic, and perhaps also for contemporary life. She also tends to assume equal availability of cultural tools.

127. Kelly, *In the New England Fashion*, 122, 123.

128. Lensink, *'A Secret to Be Burried'*, 177.

129. Stabile, *Memory's Daughters*, chap. 4. Mary Louise Kete has maintained that by the Victorian period, mourning "replaced conversion as the primary spiritual and social event of the American life," but mourning's vision of meeting again built on religious commitment and reward. Kete, *Sentimental Collaborations*, 59.

130. Juster, *Disorderly Women*, 199.

131. Sered, "Mother Love, Child Death."

132. Pierce, "A Fragment," in Vanderpoel and Buel, *Chronicles*, 212; "Caroline Chester's [1816] Journal," in Vanderpoel, *More Chronicles*, 182; Buel, 1830 Penmanship Writing Book.

133. Cranch, 1788–89 Journal, 3 and 7 Feb. 1789. Unlike the nineteenth-century Virginia gentry Jan Lewis has studied, for these northern mothers, the home was a place of emotional control rather than free expression. Compare Lewis, *Pursuit of Happiness*, 81–82, 102–3.

134. Berend, "'The Best or None!'"

135. Chambers-Schiller, *Liberty, a Better Husband*, 112, chap. 7.

136. D. Johnson, *John Pierce IV.*

137. S. Heath, Diary, 20 Dec. 1824.

Conclusion

1. Sobel, *Teach Me Dreams*. My core diarists infrequently mentioned dreams.

2. Motz, "Folk Expression," 143, 138, 133, 132, 144, 138.

Notes to Pages 185–194   239

3. Elizabeth Cranch to Jacob Norton, 1 Feb. 1789, 1789–90 folder, JNP. I would not go quite as far as Linda Grasso, who compared Victorian women's reading and writing to "twentieth-century consciousness-raising groups." These diarists were more likely to debate women's place with their reading and themselves than with contemporaries who could challenge them. Grasso, *Artistry of Anger*, 195.

4. Eustace, "'Passion Is the Gale,'" 301–2. On the role of brothers and sisters, see Glover, *All Our Relations*, and Atkins, *We Grew Up Together*.

5. Guion, Diary, 241.

6. Allgor, *Parlor Politics*, chap. 4.

7. Bartky, *Femininity and Domination*, 116.

8. Halttunen, *Confidence Men and Painted Women*, xv–xvi.

9. Scott, *Domination and the Arts of Resistance*, 4–5; 140–52.

10. Zagarri, "Rights of Man and Woman," 203.

11. Scott, *Domination and the Arts of Resistance*, 115.

12. Augst, *Clerk's Tale*, chap. 4; quotation, 182; see also Zboray, "Reading Patterns in Antebellum America." Richard D. Brown emphasizes differences in male/female reading, but Augst and Zboray draw from a larger sample; Brown, *Knowledge Is Power*, 193–96.

13. Rotundo, *American Manhood*, chaps. 4 and 8. Such same-sex friendships also characterized eighteenth-century youths; Lombard, *Making Manhood*, 94–97. Participation in abolitionism's radical subculture paralleled the stresses of coming of age and as such also encouraged same-sex relationships, even after marriage; Yacovone, "Abolitionists and the 'Language of Fraternal Love.'"

14. Frank, *Life with Father*, 175.

15. Laura Wolcott Rankin to Robert Rankin, no date, quoted in McGiffert, *Their Stories*, 68.

16. G. Brown, *Domestic Individualism*, 1–10.

17. Bowne, 6 July 1802, Journal, in *Girl's Life Eighty Years Ago*, 110.

18. Brace, 16 Oct. 1814, "Private Journal 1814," in Vanderpoel, *More Chronicles*, 103.

19. Bowne, 11 July 1802, Journal, in *Girl's Life Eighty Years Ago*, 118.

20. Hochschild, *Managed Heart*, 164–65, 8. Similarly, Candace Clark argues that "A man's show of sympathy is a benefaction; a woman's sympathy is owed, expected," and in that sense, it is worth less, and the effort that went into it is ignored; *Misery and Company*, 78.

21. Woloch, *Women and the American Experience*, 3rd ed., 120–25, sums up the literature on this transition.

22. Welter, "Cult of True Womanhood," is the classic description of this ideology.

23. Boydston, *Home and Work*, chap. 7; quotation, 147.

24. Elbert, *Separate Spheres No More*, 3. See also McCall and Yacovone, *Shared Experience;* Vickery, "Golden Age to Separate Spheres?"; and Kerber, "Separate Spheres."

25. Klein, "Gender and the Public/Private Distinction," surveys the different definitions of these words. Karen V. Hansen suggests the four categories of "public, private, market, and social realms" as alternatives in "Rediscovering the Social," 269, 296; and Elizabeth Maddock Dillon suggests a third sphere of "sociality" in *Gender of Freedom*, 6–7, a concept similar to Catherine Kelly's emphasis on "society," *In the New England Fashion*, 191. Mary P. Ryan also supports a refining of categories in her "Public and the Private Good," 24.

26. On the meaning and uses of the "social imaginary," see Poovey, "Liberal Civil Subject and the Social"; on "habitus," see Bourdieu, *Outline of a Theory of Practice*, chap. 2.

27. Ditz, "New Men's History."

28. Winifred Willis, Diary, 22 July 1924 and 24 Feb. 1926, quoted in Spurlock and Magistro, *New and Improved*, 87, 88.

29. Taylor, *Modern Social Imaginaries*, 55.

30. Lutz, "Engendered Emotion," 74.

31. "The Economy of Gratitude," in Hochschild, *Commercialization of Intimate Life*, 117.

32. Kring, "Gender and Anger," 222.

33. Illouz, *Oprah Winfrey*, 136, chap. 7.

34. DeVault, "Comfort and Struggle," 55.

35. Illouz, *Oprah Winfrey*, 138.

36. Steinberg, "Emotional Labor since *The Managed Heart*," 13; see also Folbre, *Invisible Heart*.

37. Hochschild, *Time Bind*.

BIBLIOGRAPHY

Abbreviations

HFP Heath Family Papers. Massachusetts Historical Society, Boston.
LHS Collections of the Litchfield Historical Society, Litchfield, Connecticut.
JNP Jacob Norton Papers. Massachusetts Historical Society, Boston.

Manuscript Sources

Bancroft, Elizabeth. 1793–95 Diary. Typescript. Mss. Dept., Misc. mss. boxes "B." American Antiquarian Society, Worcester, Massachusetts.
Bassett, Mary. 1829 Album. LHS.
Beekman, Sarah. 1807 Journal. LHS.
Bevier, Henrietta Cornelia. 1809 June 10–Sept. 3 Diary. 1 vol. (ZL-236), Manuscripts and Archives Division, The New York Public Library, Astor, Lenox, and Tilden Foundations.
Boardman, Caroline M. 1815 Journal. Typescript. LHS.
Buel, Maria. 1830 Penmanship Writing Book. LHS.
Camp, Mary. 1818–34 Diary. 920 C1522 Main Vault. Connecticut State Library/State Archives, Hartford.
Child, Mary A. 1820 Journal. Typescript. LHS.
Clark, Betsey. "Mechanical View of the Faculties of the Soul." Drawing, 1800. LHS.
Connell Ayer, Sarah. 1805–35 Diaries. Accession number 1990-028, 5 vols. New Hampshire Historical Society, Concord.
Cook, Elizabeth M. (Catlin). 1813–15 Album. LHS.
Cranch Norton, Elizabeth. Commonplace Book, 1787–88. JNP.
———. Journals: 1781–82, 1786, 1787, 1788–89, 1805–7, 1807–9. JNP.
———. Letters: 1773–79, 1788, 1789–90 folders. JNP.
Eardeley, William A. "Bedford Presbyterian Church Record Book I 1786–1859." Typescript. Office of the Town Historian, Bedford Hills, New York.
First Parish, Brookline. "Original Valuations of the Pews in the First Parish, Brookline." Massachusetts Historical Society, Boston.

Foote, Abigail, and Elizabeth Foote. "Journals of Abigail Foote and Elizabeth Foote—1775." Typescript. The Connecticut Historical Society Museum, Hartford.
Guion, Mary. 1800–1852 Diary. Bound volume. The New-York Historical Society.
Hart, Jennette. 1819 Album. LHS.
Heath, Ann Eliza. 1825–26 Diary. HFP.
Heath, Hannah (Williams). 1805–12 Diary, 1819–32 Book of Prayers and Meditations, and "Extract Book." HFP.
Heath, Mary. 1824 Diary. HFP.
Heath, Susan. 1812–74 Diary. HFP.
Heath Howe, Elizabeth. Penmanship Copybook. 1781 Bound Vols. Box. HFP.
Howell, Mary B. 1799–1805 Journals. Typescript, MS 79282, item 8. The Connecticut Historical Society Museum, Hartford.
Hunt, Nancy Thompson. Diary, volume 1, 1809–14. Ms. Thompson, Nancy. The Connecticut Historical Society Museum, Hartford.
Lewis, Jane R. 1828 Common Place Book. LHS.
Lewis, Marian. 1814 Album. LHS.
May, Abigail. "Aunt Abby May's Ballstown Journal." Special Collections. New York State Historical Association Library, Cooperstown.
———. 1796 Diary. Collection S-964. Special Collections. Maine Historical Society, Portland, Maine.
———. Journal, 24 May–30 August 1800. Microfilm, May-Goddard Family Papers. Schlesinger Library, Radcliffe Institute for Advanced Study, Harvard University.
Mitchell, Adeline. 1820–21 Album. LHS.
North Castle 1803 tax assessment roll. Town of North Castle, Westchester County, New York. New York State Archives, Albany, New York.
Ogden, Eliza A. 1816–18 Journal. Typescript. LHS.
Peck, Mary. 1825–27 Album. LHS.
Pierce, Sarah. Letters; "Moralistic Essay and anecdote." Sarah Pierce Collection, LHS.
Read, Lucinda. 1815–16 Diary. Massachusetts Historical Society, Boston.
"Record of the Second Parish Church, Portland, Me. First Century. Copied from the Original." Collection—1234 MH Special Collections. Maine Historical Society, Portland, Maine.
Reynolds, Betsey. 1806–7 Journal. LHS.
Roberts, Candace. 1801–6 Diary. Typescript. Bristol Public Library, Bristol, Connecticut.
St. Matthew's Church, Bedford, New York. "General Records of the Baptisms, Marriages, Communicants and Deaths."
Seymour, Jane M. 1822–27 Album. LHS.
Sheldon, Lucy. 1801–3 Journal. LHS.
———. Music Book. LHS.

"Ship Registers and Enrollments of Bridgeport, Connecticut, c. 1789–1867." G. W. Blunt White Library, Mystic Seaport Museum, Mystic, Connecticut.
Smith, Charlotte Maria. 1816 Diary. The Connecticut Historical Society Museum, Hartford, Connecticut.
Smith, Jotham. Jotham Smith file. Office of the Town Historian, Bedford Hills, New York.
Van Schaack, Catherine. 1809–10 Journal and 26 Oct. 1809 essay, "On politeness." Catherine Van Schaack Papers, Misc. Mss. The New-York Historical Society.
Wolcott, Laura Maria. 1825 Diary. LHS.
———. 1826–27 Journal. Typescript. LHS.

Published Primary Sources

Allen, David Grayson, and others, eds. *Diary of John Quincy Adams.* Vol. 1, *November 1779–March 1786.* Cambridge, Mass.: Belknap Press of Harvard University Press, 1981.
Armes, Ethel, ed. *Nancy Shippen Her Journal Book: The International Romance of a Young Lady of Fashion of Colonial Philadelphia with Letters to Her and about Her.* Philadelphia: J. B. Lippincott, 1935.
Austen, Jane. *Sense and Sensibility.* In *The Complete Novels.* Oxford: Oxford University Press, 1994.
By-laws, Constitution [of Litchfield Female Academy]. [1832].
Cummings, Rev. Asa. *A Memoir of the Rev. Edward Payson, D.D., Late of Portland, Maine.* New York: American Tract Society, 1830.
"Diary Kept by Elizabeth Fuller, Daughter of Rev. Timothy Fuller of Princeton." In Francis Everett Blake, *History of the Town of Princeton in the County of Worcester and Commonwealth of Massachusetts 159?-1915.* Vol. 1, *Narrative*, 302–23. Princeton: by the town, 1915.
"Diary of Mary Orne Tucker." *Essex Institute Historical Collections* 77 (1941): 304–38.
Diary of Sarah Connell Ayer: Andover and Newburyport Massachusetts, Concord and Bow New Hampshire, Portland and Eastport Maine. Portland, Maine: Lefavor-Tower Company, 1910.
Earle, Alice Morse, ed. *Diary of Anna Green Winslow: A Boston School Girl of 1771.* 1894; repr. Williamstown, Mass.: Corner House Publishers, 1974.
Easton, Marilyn J., ed. *Passionate Spinster: The Diary of Patty Rogers: 1785.* Philadelphia: XLibris Corporation, 2001.
"Federal Census, 1800. Westchester County, New York." *New York Genealogical and Biographical Record* 57 (April 1926): 109–18.
A Girl's Life Eighty Years Ago: Selections from the Letters of Eliza Southgate Bowne. Women in America Series. New York: Arno Press, 1974. Reprint of 1887 edition.

Jacobson, David, ed. *The English Libertarian Heritage: From the Writings of John Trenchard and Thomas Gordon in "The Independent Whig" and "Cato's Letters."* The American Heritage Series. Indianapolis: Bobbs-Merrill Company, Inc., 1965.

Jemima Condict Her Book: Being a Transcript of the Diary of an Essex County Maid during the Revolutionary War. Newark: Carteret Book Club, 1930.

Jessup, Rev. Henry Griswold. *Edward Jessup of West Farms. Westchester Co., New York, and His Descendants.* Cambridge, Mass.: John Wilson and Sons, 1887.

Jones, Eva Eve, ed. "Extracts from the Journal of Miss Sarah Eve." *Pennsylvania Magazine of History and Biography* 5 (1881): 19–36, 191–205.

Karlsen, Carol, and Laurie Crumpacker, eds. *The Journal of Esther Edwards Burr, 1754–1757.* New Haven: Yale University Press, 1984.

Kelley, Mary, ed. *The Power of Her Sympathy: The Autobiography and Journal of Catharine Maria Sedgwick.* Boston: Massachusetts Historical Society, 1993.

Lensink, Judy Nolte, ed. *"A Secret to Be Buried": The Diary and Life of Emily Hawley Gillespie, 1858–1888.* Iowa City: University of Iowa Press, 1989.

MacMullan, Ramsay. *Sisters of the Brush: Their Family, Art, Life, and Letters 1797–1833.* New Haven: PastTimes Press, 1997.

Mason, Lizzie Norton, and James Duncan Phillips. "The [1785-86] Journal of Elizabeth Cranch." *Essex Institute Historical Collections* 80 (Jan. 1944): 1–36.

McFarland, Asa. *An Historical View of Heresies, and Vindication of the Primitive Faith.* Concord: George Hough, 1806.

McMahon, Lucia, and Deborah Schriver, eds. *To Read My Heart: The Journal of Rachel Van Dyke, 1810–1811.* Philadelphia: University of Pennsylvania Press, 2000.

Morgan, Helen M., ed. *A Season in New York: 1801 Letters of Harriet and Maria Trumbull.* Pittsburgh: University of Pittsburgh Press, 1969.

Moseley, Laura Hadley, ed. *The Diaries of Julia Cowles: A Connecticut Record, 1797–1803.* New Haven: Yale University Press, 1931.

The Mother's Manual Containing Practical Hints, By a Mother. Boston: Weeks, Jordan and Co., 1840.

North Castle, Westchester County, New York, 1820 Federal Census. M33 Roll: 75. HeritageQuest Online.

Norton, Jacob. *The Blessedness of Those Who Die in the Lord, . . . his Beloved Wife, Who Died Jan. 25, in the 48th Year of her Age . . . .* Boston: Lincoln and Edmands, 1811.

The Principles of the Bedford Circulating Library, Catalogue of Books, and Subscribers Names. Mount Pleasant: William Durrell, 1797.

Sedgwick, Catharine Maria. *A New-England Tale or, Sketches of New-England Character and Manners,* edited by Victoria Clements. Early American Women Writers. New York: Oxford University Press, 1995.

Vanderpoel, Emily Noyes. *More Chronicles of a Pioneer School from 1792 to 1833, Being Added History on the Litchfield Female Academy Kept by Miss Sarah Pierce* and Her Nephew, John Pierce Brace. New York: The Cadmus Book Shop; Printed at the University Press, Cambridge, Mass., 1927.

Vanderpoel, Emily Noyes, compiler, and Elizabeth C. Barney Buel, ed. *Chronicles of a Pioneer School from 1792 to 1833, Being the History of Miss Sarah Pierce and Her Litchfield School*. Cambridge, Mass.: University Press, 1903.

Secondary Sources

Allgor, Catherine. *Parlor Politics: In Which the Ladies of Washington Help Build a City and a Government*. Jeffersonian America. Charlottesville: University Press of Virginia, 2000.

Anderson, Benedict. *Imagined Communities: Reflections on the Origins and Spread of Nationalism*. London: Verso, 1983.

Apple, Rima D., and Janet Lynne Golden, eds. *Mothers and Motherhood: Readings in American History*. Women and Health Series. Columbus: Ohio State University Press, 1997.

Armstrong, Erica R. "A Mental and Moral Feast: Reading, Writing, and Sentimentality in Black Philadelphia." *Journal of Women's History* 16 (Spring 2004): 78–102.

Armstrong, Nancy, and Leonard Tennenhouse. *The Imaginary Puritan: Literature, Intellectual Labor, and the Origins of Personal Life*. The New Historicism: Studies in Cultural Poetics. Berkeley: University of California Press, 1992.

Atkins, Annette. *We Grew Up Together: Brothers and Sisters in Nineteenth-Century America*. Urbana: University of Illinois Press, 2001.

Augst, Thomas. *The Clerk's Tale: Young Men and Moral Life in Nineteenth-Century America*. Chicago: University of Chicago Press, 2003.

Averill, James R. "Emotions Unbecoming and Becoming." In *The Nature of Emotion: Fundamental Questions*, edited by Paul Ekman and Richard J. Davidson, Series in Affective Science, 265–69. New York: Oxford University Press, 1994.

Barker-Benfield, G. J. *The Culture of Sensibility: Sex and Society in Eighteenth-Century Britain*. Chicago: University of Chicago Press, 1992.

Barnes, Elizabeth. *States of Sympathy: Seduction and Democracy in the American Novel*. New York: Columbia University Press, 1997.

Barr-Zisowitz, Carol. "Sadness: Is There Such a Thing?" In *Handbook of Emotions*, 2d ed., edited by Michael Lewis and Jeannette M. Haviland-Jones, 607–22. New York: Guilford Press, 2000.

Bartky, Sandra Lee. *Femininity and Domination: Studies in the Phenomenology of Oppression*. Thinking Gender Series. New York: Routledge, 1990.

Beadie, Nancy. "Academy Students in the Mid-Nineteenth Century: Social Geography, Demography, and the Culture of Academy Attendance." *History of Education Quarterly* 41, no. 2 (2001): 251–62.

Benedict, Barbara M. *Framing Feeling: Sentiment and Style in English Prose Fiction 1745–1800*. New York: AMS Press, 1994.

———. *Making the Modern Reader: Cultural Mediation in Early Modern Literary Anthologies*. Princeton: Princeton University Press, 1996.

Berend, Zsuzsa. "'The Best or None!': Spinsterhood in Nineteenth-Century New England." *Journal of Social History* 33 (Summer 2000): 935–57.

Bergengren, Charles. "Review Text: Scientific Revolution." Fall 2004. http://gate.cia.edu/cbergengren/arthistory/sr/sr.htm

Bloch, Ruth H. "Changing Conceptions of Sexuality and Romance in Eighteenth-Century America." *William and Mary Quarterly* 60 (Jan. 2003): 13–42.

———. "The Gendered Meanings of Virtue in Revolutionary America." In *Rethinking the Political: Gender, Resistance, and the State*, edited by Barbara Laslett, Johanna Brenner, and Yesim Arat, 11–32. Chicago: University of Chicago Press, 1995.

Boris, Eileen, and S. J. Kleinberg. "Mothers and Other Workers: (Re)Conceiving Labor, Maternalism, and the State." *Journal of Women's History* 15 (Autumn 2003): 90–117.

Bourdieu, Pierre. *Outline of a Theory of Practice*. Translated by Richard Nice. Cambridge Studies in Social Anthropology 16. Cambridge: Cambridge University Press, 1977.

Bowlby, Rachel. *Carried Away: The Invention of Modern Shopping*. New York: Columbia University Press, 2001.

Boydston, Jeanne. *Home and Work: Housework, Wages, and the Ideology of Labor in the Early Republic*. New York: Oxford University Press, 1990.

Branaman, Ann. "Goffman's Social Theory." In *The Goffman Reader*, edited by Charles C. Lemert and Ann Branaman, xlv–lxxxii. Cambridge: Blackwell, 1997.

Breen, T. H. *The Marketplace of Revolution: How Consumer Politics Shaped American Independence*. New York: Oxford University Press, 2004.

———. "The Meaning of 'Likeness': American Portrait Painting in an Eighteenth-Century Consumer Society." *Word and Image* 6 (Oct.-Dec. 1990): 325–50.

Brereton, Virginia Lieson. *From Sin to Salvation: Stories of Women's Conversions, 1800 to the Present*. Bloomington: Indiana University Press, 1991.

Brickley, Lynne Templeton. "The Litchfield Female Academy." In *To Ornament Their Minds: Sarah Pierce's Litchfield Female Academy 1792–1833*, edited by Catherine Keene Fields and Lisa C. Kightlinger, 20–81. Litchfield: Litchfield Historical Society, 1993.

———. "Sarah Pierce's Litchfield Female Academy, 1792–1833." Ed.D. dissertation, Harvard University, 1985.

Brody, Miriam. *Manly Writing: Gender, Rhetoric, and the Rise of Composition*. Carbondale: Southern Illinois University Press, 1993.

Brooke, John L. "Consent, Civil Society, and the Public Sphere in the Age of Revolution and the Early American Republic." In *Beyond the Founders: New Approaches to the Political History of the Early American Republic*, edited by Jeffrey L. Pasley, Andrew W. Robertson, and David Waldstreicher, 207–50. Chapel Hill: University of North Carolina Press, 2004.

Brown, Gillian. *The Consent of the Governed: The Lockean Legacy in Early American Culture*. Cambridge, Mass.: Harvard University Press, 2001.

———. *Domestic Individualism: Imagining a Self in Nineteenth-Century America*. The New Historicism: Studies in Cultural Poetics. Berkeley: University of California Press, 1990.

Brown, Kathleen M. *Good Wives, Nasty Wenches, and Anxious Patriarchs: Gender, Race, and Power in Colonial Virginia*. Chapel Hill: University of North Carolina Press, 1996.

Brown, Richard D. "Afterword: From Cohesion to Competition." In *Printing and Society in Early America*, edited by William L. Joyce, et al., 300–309. Worcester: American Antiquarian Society, 1983.

———. *Knowledge Is Power: Diffusion of Information in Early America, 1700–1865*. New York: Oxford University Press, 1989.

Brownstein, Rachel M. *Becoming a Heroine: Reading about Women in Novels*. New York: Viking Press, 1982.

Brumberg, Joan Jacobs. *The Body Project: An Intimate History of American Girls*. New York: Random House, 1997.

Buggeln, Gretchen Townsend. *Temples of Grace: The Material Transformation of Connecticut's Churches, 1790–1840*. Hanover, N.H.: University Press of New England, 2003.

Bunkers, Suzanne L., and Cynthia A. Huff, eds. *Inscribing the Daily: Critical Essays on Women's Diaries*. Amherst: University of Massachusetts Press, 1996.

Burstein, Andrew. "The Political Character of Sympathy." *Journal of the Early Republic* 21 (Winter 2001): 601–32.

———. *Sentimental Democracy: The Evolution of America's Romantic Self-Image*. New York: Hill and Wang, 1999.

Bushman, Richard L. *The Refinement of America: Persons, Houses, Cities*. New York: Alfred A. Knopf, 1992.

Butler, Jon. *Awash in a Sea of Faith: Christianizing the American People*. Cambridge, Mass.: Harvard University Press, 1990.

Campbell, Colin. *The Romantic Ethic and the Spirit of Modern Consumerism*. Ideas. Oxford: Basil Blackwell, 1987.

Carlson, John G., and Elaine Hatfield. *Psychology of Emotion*. Fort Worth: Harcourt Brace Jovanovich, 1992.

Carson, Cary. "The Consumer Revolution in Colonial British America: Why Demand?" In *Of Consuming Interests: The Style of Life in the Eighteenth Century*, edited by Cary Carson, Ronald Hoffman, and Peter J. Albert, 483–700. Perspectives on the American Revolution Series. Charlottesville: Published for the United States Capitol Historical Society by the University Press of Virginia, 1994.

Caskey, Marie. *Chariot of Fire: Religion and the Beecher Family.* Yale Historical Publications, Miscellany 117. New Haven: Yale University Press, 1978.

Cassidy, Frederick G., ed. *Dictionary of American Regional English.* Vol. 1, Introduction and A-C. Cambridge, Mass.: Harvard University Press, 1985.

Chambers, Thomas A. "Seduction and Sensibility: The Refined Society of Ballston, New York, 1800." *New York History* 78 (July 1997): 244–72.

Chambers-Schiller, Lee. *Liberty, a Better Husband: Single Women in America, The Generations of 1780–1840.* New Haven: Yale University Press, 1984.

Clark, Candace. *Misery and Company: Sympathy in Everyday Life.* Chicago: University of Chicago Press, 1997.

Classen, Constance. *World of Sense: Exploring the Senses in History and across Cultures.* London: Routledge, 1993.

Clemens, Paul G. E. "The Consumer Culture of the Middle Atlantic, 1760–1820." *William and Mary Quarterly* 62 (Oct. 2005): 577–624.

Coviello, Peter. "Agonizing Affection: Affect and Nation in Early America." *Early American Literature* 37, no. 3 (2002): 439–68.

Cox, Stephen D. *'The Stranger Within Thee': Concepts of the Self in Late-Eighteenth-Century Literature.* Pittsburgh: University of Pittsburgh Press, 1980.

Crain, Caleb. *American Sympathy: Men, Friendship, and Literature in the New Nation.* New Haven: Yale University Press, 2001.

Crane, Elaine Forman. *Ebb Tide in New England: Women, Seaports, and Social Change, 1630–1800.* Boston: Northeastern University Press, 1998.

Crowley, John E. *The Invention of Comfort: Sensibilities and Design in Early Modern Britain and Early America.* Baltimore: Johns Hopkins University Press, 2001.

———. "The Sensibility of Comfort." *American Historical Review* 104 (June 1999): 749–82.

Culley, Margo, ed. *A Day at a Time: The Diary Literature of American Women from 1764 to the Present.* New York: The Feminist Press, 1985.

Damasio, Antonio R. *Descartes' Error: Emotion, Reason, and the Human Brain.* New York: G. P. Putnam's Sons, 1994.

Darnton, Robert. "Toward a History of Reading." *Wilson Quarterly* 13 (Fall 1989): 86–102.

Davidson, Cathy N. "Flirting with Destiny: Ambivalence and Form in the Early American Sentimental Novel." *Studies in American Fiction* 10 (Spring 1982): 17–39.

———. *Revolution and the Word: The Rise of the Novel in America.* New York: Oxford University Press, 1986.

Demos, John. "Shame and Guilt in Early New England." In *The Emotions: Social, Cultural and Biological Dimensions,* edited by Rom Harre, and W. Gerrod Parrott, 74–88. London: SAGE Publications, 1996.

de Sousa, Ronald. *The Rationality of Emotion.* Cambridge, Mass.: MIT Press, 1987.

DeVault, Marjorie L. "Comfort and Struggle: Emotion Work in Family Life." *Annals AAPSS* 561 (Jan. 1999): 52–63.

Diggs, Marylynne. "Romantic Friends or a 'Different Race of Creatures'? The Representation of Lesbian Pathology in Nineteenth-Century America." *Feminist Studies* 21 (Summer 1995): 317–40.

Dillon, Elizabeth Maddock. *The Gender of Freedom: Fictions of Liberalism and the Literary Public Sphere*. Stanford: Stanford University Press, 2004.

Ditz, Toby. "Formative Ventures: Eighteenth-Century Commercial Letters and the Articulation of Experience." In *Epistolary Selves: Letters and Letter-Writers, 1600–1945*, edited by Rebecca Earle, 59–78. Aldershot, England: Ashgate, 1999.

———. "The New Men's History and the Peculiar Absence of Gendered Power: Some Remedies from Early American Gender History." *Gender and History* 16 (April 2004): 1–35.

———. "Shipwrecked; or, Masculinity Imperiled: Mercantile Representations of Failure and the Gendered Self in Eighteenth-Century Philadelphia." *Journal of American History* 81 (June 1994): 51–80.

Duberman, Martin Bauml, Martha Vicinus, and George Chauncy Jr., eds. *Hidden from History: Reclaiming the Gay and Lesbian Past*. New York: New American Library, 1989.

Elbert, Monika M., ed. *Separate Spheres No More: Gender Convergence in American Literature, 1830–1930*. Tuscaloosa: University of Alabama Press, 2000.

Elliott, Carl. *Better Than Well: American Medicine Meets the American Dream*. New York: W. W. Norton, 2003.

Ellison, Julie. *Cato's Tears and the Making of Anglo-American Emotion*. Chicago: University of Chicago Press, 1999.

Eustace, Nicole. "'The Cornerstone of a Copious Work': Love and Power in Eighteenth-Century Courtship." *Journal of Social History* 34 (Spring 2001): 517–46.

———. "'Passion Is the Gale': Emotion and Power on the Eve of the American Revolution." Ph.D. dissertation, University of Pennsylvania, 2001.

Farnham, Christie Anne. *The Education of the Southern Belle: Higher Education and Student Socialization in the Antebellum South*. New York: New York University Press, 1994.

Fea, John. "The Way of Improvement Leads Home: Philip Vickers Fithian's Rural Enlightenment." *Journal of American History* 90 (Sept. 2003): 462–90.

Ferguson, Robert A. *The American Enlightenment, 1750–1820*. Cambridge, Mass.: Harvard University Press, 1997.

Fields, Catherine Keene, and Lisa C. Kightlinger, eds. *To Ornament Their Minds: Sarah Pierce's Litchfield Female Academy 1792–1833*. Litchfield: Litchfield Historical Society, 1993.

Fineman, Stephen. "Organizations as Emotional Arenas." In *Emotion in Organizations*, edited by Stephen Fineman, 9–35. London: SAGE Publications, 1993.

Fliegelman, Jay. *Declaring Independence: Jefferson, Natural Language and the Culture of Performance*. Stanford: Stanford University Press, 1993.

———. *Prodigals and Pilgrims: The American Revolution against Patriarchal Authority, 1750–1800*. Cambridge: Cambridge University Press, 1982.

Folbre, Nancy. *The Invisible Heart: Economics and Family Values*. New York: New Press, 2001.

Frank, Stephen M. *Life with Father: Parenthood and Masculinity in the Nineteenth-Century American North*. Gender Relations in the American Experience. Baltimore: Johns Hopkins University Press, 1998.

Gedge, Karin E. *Without Benefit of Clergy: Women and the Pastoral Relationship in Nineteenth-Century American Culture*. Religion in America Series. New York: Oxford University Press, 2003.

Gilmore, William J. *Reading Becomes a Necessity of Life: Material and Cultural Life in Rural New England, 1780–1835*. Knoxville: University of Tennessee Press, 1989.

Ginzberg, Lori D. *Women and the Work of Benevolence: Morality, Politics, and Class in the Nineteenth-Century United States*. Yale Historical Publications. New Haven: Yale University Press, 1990.

Glover, Lorri. *All Our Relations: Blood Ties and Emotional Bonds among the Early South Carolina Gentry*. Baltimore: Johns Hopkins University Press, 2000.

Godbeer, Richard. *Sexual Revolution in Early America*. Baltimore: Johns Hopkins University Press, 2002.

Goffman, Erving. *The Presentation of Self in Everyday Life*. Garden City, N.Y.: Doubleday Anchor Books, 1959.

Gordon, Ann D. "The Young Ladies Academy of Philadelphia." In *Women of America: A History*, edited by Carol Ruth Berkin and Mary Beth Norton, 68–91. Boston: Houghton Mifflin, 1979.

Grasso, Linda M. *The Artistry of Anger: Black and White Women's Literature in America, 1820–1860*. Gender and American Culture Series. Chapel Hill: University of North Carolina Press, 2002.

Green, Nancy. "Female Education and School Competition: 1820–1850." *History of Education Quarterly* 18 (Summer 1978): 129–42.

Greven, Philip. *The Protestant Temperament: Patterns of Child-Rearing, Religious Experience, and the Self in Early America*. New York: Alfred A. Knopf, 1977.

———. "The Self Shaped and Misshaped: *The Protestant Temperament* Reconsidered." In *Through a Glass Darkly: Reflections on Personal Identity in Early America*, edited by Ronald Hoffman, Mechal Sobel, and Fredrika J. Teute, 348–69. Chapel Hill: University of North Carolina Press, 1997.

Gross, Robert A. "Reconstructing Early American Libraries: Concord, Massachusetts, 1795–1850." *Proceedings of the American Antiquarian Society* 97 (1988): 331–451.

Grossberg, Michael. *Governing the Hearth: Law and the Family in Nineteenth-Century America*. Studies in Legal History. Chapel Hill: University of North Carolina Press, 1985.

Guion, J. Marshall IV, compiler, and Violet H. Guion, ed. *Descendants of Louis Guion, Huguenot of La Rochelle, France and New Rochelle Westchester County, Province of New York, A Guion Family Album: 1654–1976*. Olean, N.Y.: [1976?].

Gunther, Candy. "The Spiritual Pilgrimage of Rachel Stearns, 1834–1837: Reinterpreting Women's Religious and Social Experiences in the Methodist Revivals of Nineteenth-Century America." *Church History* 65 (Dec. 1996): 577–95.

Gustafson, Sandra M. *Eloquence Is Power: Oratory and Performance in Early America*. Chapel Hill: University of North Carolina Press, 2000.

Habermas, Jürgen. *The Structural Transformation of the Public Sphere: An Inquiry into a Category of Bourgeois Society*. Translated by Thomas Burger. Cambridge, Mass.: MIT Press, 1989.

Hall, David D. "Books and Reading in Eighteenth-Century America." In *Of Consuming Interests: The Style of Life in the Eighteenth Century*, edited by Cary Carson, Ronald Hoffman, and Peter J. Albert, 354–72. Perspectives on the American Revolution Series. Charlottesville: Published for the United States Capitol Historical Society by the University Press of Virginia, 1994.

———. "The Uses of Literacy in New England, 1600–1850." In *Printing and Society in Early America*, edited by William L. Joyce, et al. 1–47. Worcester: American Antiquarian Society, 1983.

Halttunen, Karen. *Confidence Men and Painted Women: A Study of Middle-Class Culture in America, 1830–1870*. Yale Historical Publications, Miscellany, 129. New Haven: Yale University Press, 1982.

———. "Humanitarianism and the Pornography of Pain in Anglo-American Culture." *American Historical Review* 100 (April 1995): 303–34.

Hansen, Karen V. "Rediscovering the Social: Visiting Practices in Antebellum New England and the Limits of the Public/Private Dichotomy." In *Public and Private in Thought and Practice: Perspectives on a Grand Dichotomy*, edited by Jeff Weintraub and Krishan Kumar, 268–302. Chicago: University of Chicago Press, 1997.

———. *A Very Social Time: Crafting Community in Antebellum New England*. Berkeley: University of California Press, 1994.

Harding, Vincent. *A Certain Magnificence: Lyman Beecher and the Transformation of American Protestantism, 1775–1863*. Chicago Studies in the History of American Religion. Brooklyn: Carlson Publishing, Inc. 1991.

Hayes, Kevin J. *A Colonial Woman's Bookshelf*. Knoxville: University of Tennessee Press, 1996.

Hedrick, Joan D. *Harriet Beecher Stowe: A Life*. New York: Oxford University Press, 1994.

Hemphill, C. Dallett. *Bowing to Necessities: A History of Manners in America, 1620–1860*. New York: Oxford University Press, 1999.

Henderson, Desiree. "The Imperfect Dead: Mourning Women in Eighteenth-Century Oratory and Fiction." *Early American Literature* 39, no. 3 (2004): 487–509.

Hessinger, Rodney. *Seduced, Abandoned, and Reborn: Visions of Youth in Middle-Class America, 1780–1850*. Early American Studies. Philadelphia: University of Pennsylvania Press, 2005.

Hicks, Philip. "Portia and Marcia: Female Political Identity and the Historical Imagination, 1770–1800." *William and Mary Quarterly* 62 (April 2005): 265–94.

Hochschild, Arlie Russell. *The Commercialization of Intimate Life: Notes from Home and Work*. Berkeley: University of California Press, 2003.

———. "Emotion Work, Feeling Rules, and Social Structure." *American Journal of Sociology* 85 (Nov. 1979): 551–75.

———. *The Managed Heart: Commercialization of Human Feeling*. Berkeley: University of California Press, 1983.

———. *The Time Bind: When Work Becomes Home and Home Becomes Work*. New York: Metropolitan Books, 1997.

Hoffer, Peter Charles. *Sensory Worlds in Early America*. Baltimore: Johns Hopkins University Press, 2003.

Hunter, Jane H. *How Young Ladies Became Girls: The Victorian Origins of American Girlhood*. New Haven: Yale University Press, 2002.

Hunter, Phyllis Whitman. *Purchasing Identity in the Atlantic World: Massachusetts Merchants, 1670–1780*. Ithaca: Cornell University Press, 2001.

Illouz, Eva. *Consuming the Romantic Utopia: Love and the Cultural Contradictions of Capitalism*. Berkeley: University of California Press, 1997.

———. *Oprah Winfrey and the Glamour of Misery: An Essay on Popular Culture*. New York: Columbia University Press, 2003.

Jabour, Anya. "Albums of Affection: Female Friendship and Coming of Age in Antebellum Virginia." *Virginia Magazine of History and Biography* 107 (Spring 1999): 125–58.

———. "'Grown Girls, Highly Cultivated': Female Education in an Antebellum Southern Family." *Journal of Southern History* 44 (Feb. 1998): 23–64.

Jagodzinski, Cecile M. *Privacy and Print: Reading and Writing in Seventeenth-Century England*. Ideas Series. Charlottesville: University Press of Virginia, 1999.

Jensen, Joan M. *Loosening the Bonds: Mid-Atlantic Farm Women, 1750–1850*. New Haven: Yale University Press, 1986.

Johnson, Claudia L. *Equivocal Beings: Politics, Gender, and Sentimentality in the 1790s: Wollstonecraft, Radcliffe, Burney, Austen*. Women in Culture and Society Series. Chicago: University of Chicago Press, 1995.

Johnson, David A. *John Pierce IV: His Life as He Lived and Recorded It*. Brookline: The Author, 2002.

Jones, Theodore Francis. *Land Ownership in Brookline from the First Settlement, Illustrated by Six Maps, 1635, 1667, 1693, 1746, 1786, 1822*. Brookline: Riverdale Press, 1923.

Joyce, William L., et al., eds. *Printing and Society in Early America*. Worcester: American Antiquarian Society, 1983.

Juster, Susan. *Disorderly Women: Sexual Politics and Evangelicalism in Revolutionary New England.* Ithaca: Cornell University Press, 1994.

———. "'Neither Male nor Female': Jemima Wilkinson and the Politics of Gender in Post-Revolutionary America." In *Possible Pasts: Becoming Colonial in Early America,* edited by Robert Blair St. George, 357–79. Ithaca: Cornell University Press, 2000.

Kagle, Steven E., and Lorenza Gramegna. "Rewriting Her Life: Fictionalization and the Use of Fictional Models in Early American Women's Diaries." In *Inscribing the Daily: Critical Essays on Women's Diaries,* edited by Suzanne L. Bunkers and Cynthia A. Huff, 38–55. Amherst: University of Massachusetts Press, 1996.

Kaledin, Eugenia. *Mothers and More: American Women in the 1950s.* American Women in the Twentieth Century. Boston: Twayne Publishers, 1984.

Kamensky, Jane. *Governing the Tongue: The Politics of Speech in Early New England.* New York: Oxford University Press, 1997.

Kann, Mark E. *A Republic of Men: The American Founders, Gendered Language, and Patriarchal Politics.* New York: New York University Press, 1998.

Kaplan, Fred. *Sacred Tears: Sentimentality in Victorian Literature.* Princeton: Princeton University Press, 1989.

Kelley, Mary. "Reading Women/Women Reading: The Making of Learned Women in Antebellum America." *Journal of American History* 83 (Sept. 1996): 401–24.

———. "'Vindicating the Equality of the Female Intellect': Women and Authority in the Early Republic." *Prospects* 17 (1992): 1–27.

Kelly, Catherine E. *In the New England Fashion: Reshaping Women's Lives in the Nineteenth Century.* Ithaca: Cornell University Press, 1999.

Kennedy, Gwynne. *Just Anger: Representing Women's Anger in Early Modern England.* Carbondale: Southern Illinois University Press, 2000.

Kerber, Linda K. "Daughters of Columbia: Educating Women for the Republic, 1787–1805." In *The Hofstadter Aegis: A Memorial,* edited by Stanley M. Elkins and Eric L. McKitrick, 36–59. New York: Alfred A. Knopf, 1974.

———. "The Republican Mother: Women and the Enlightenment—an American Perspective." *American Quarterly* 28 (Summer 1976): 187–205.

———. "Separate Spheres, Female Worlds, Woman's Place: The Rhetoric of Women's History." *Journal of American History* 75 (June 1988): 9–39.

Kete, Mary Louise. *Sentimental Collaborations: Mourning and Middle-Class Identity in Nineteenth-Century America.* Durham: Duke University Press, 2000.

Kett, Joseph F., and Patricia A. McClung. "Book Culture in Post-Revolutionary Virginia." *Proceedings of the American Antiquarian Society* 94, pt. 1 (1984): 97–147.

Klein, Lawrence E. "Gender and the Public/Private Distinction in the Eighteenth Century: Some Questions about Evidence and Analytic Procedure." *Eighteenth-Century Studies* 29 (Autumn 1996): 97–109.

Klepp, Susan E. "Revolutionary Bodies: Women and the Fertility Transition in the Mid-Atlantic Region, 1760–1820." *Journal of American History* 85 (Dec. 1998): 910–45.

Kling, David W. *A Field of Divine Wonders: The New Divinity and Village Revivals in Northwestern Connecticut*. University Park: Pennsylvania State University Press, 1993.

Knott, Sarah. "Sensibility and the American War for Independence." *American Historical Review* 109 (Feb. 2004): 19–40.

Kowaleski-Wallace, Elizabeth. *Consuming Subjects: Women, Shopping, and Business in the Eighteenth Century*. New York: Columbia University Press, 1997.

Kring, Ann M. "Gender and Anger." In *Gender and Emotion: Social Psychological Perspectives*, edited by Agneta H. Fischer, 211–32. Studies in Emotion and Social Interaction, Second Series. Cambridge: Cambridge University Press, 2000.

Labaree, Benjamin Woods. *Patriots and Partisans: The Merchants of Newburyport, 1764–1815*. Cambridge, Mass.: Harvard University Press, 1962.

Laqueur, Thomas. *Making Sex: Body and Gender from the Greeks to Freud*. Cambridge, Mass.: Harvard University Press, 1990.

Larkin, Jack. "The Merriams of Brookfield: Printing in the Economy and Culture of Rural Massachusetts in the Early Nineteenth Century." *Proceedings of the American Antiquarian Society* 96, pt. 1 (1986): 39–73.

Lasser, Carol. "'Let Us Be Sisters Forever': The Sororal Model of Nineteenth-Century Female Friendship." *Signs* 14 (Autumn 1988): 158–81.

Lehuu, Isabelle. *Carnival on the Page: Popular Print Media in Antebellum America*. Chapel Hill: University of North Carolina Press, 2000.

Lemay, J. A. Leo, ed. *Robert Bolling Woos Anne Miller: Love and Courtship in Colonial Virginia, 1760*. Charlottesville: University Press of Virginia, 1990.

Lewis, Jan. "Mother's Love: The Construction of an Emotion in Nineteenth-Century America." In *Mothers and Motherhood: Readings in American History*, edited by Rima D. Apple and Janet Lynne Golden, 52–71. Women and Health Series. Columbus: Ohio State University Press, 1997.

———. "Politics and the Ambivalence of the Private Sphere: Women in Early Washington, D.C." In *A Republic for the Ages: The United States Capital and the Political Culture of the Early Republic*, edited by Donald R. Kennon, 122–51. Perspectives on the American Revolution. Charlottesville: Published for the United States Capitol Historical Society by the University Press of Virginia, 1999.

———. *The Pursuit of Happiness: Family and Values in Jefferson's Virginia*. Cambridge: Cambridge University Press, 1983.

———. "The Republican Wife: Virtue and Seduction in the Early Republic." *William and Mary Quarterly* 44 (Oct. 1987): 690–721.

Lewis, Michael, and Jeannette M. Haviland-Jones, eds. *Handbook of Emotions*. 2d ed. New York: Guilford Press, 2000.

List, Karen A. "Magazine Portrayals of Women's Role in the New Republic." *Journalism History* 13 (Summer 1986): 64–70.
Lombard, Anne S. *Making Manhood: Growing Up Male in Colonial New England*. Cambridge, Mass.: Harvard University Press, 2003.
Lutz, Catherine A. "Engendered Emotion: Gender, Power, and the Rhetoric of Emotional Control in American Discourse." In *Language and the Politics of Emotion*, edited by Catherine A. Lutz and Lila Abu-Lughod, 69–91. Studies in Emotion and Social Interaction. Cambridge: Cambridge University Press, 1990.
Lystra, Karen. *Searching the Heart: Women, Men, and Romantic Love in Nineteenth-Century America*. New York: Oxford University Press, 1989.
Macdonald, Cameron Lynne, and Karen V. Hansen. "Sociability and Gendered Spheres: Visiting Patterns in Nineteenth-Century New England." *Social Science History* 25 (2001): 535–61.
Matt, Susan J. "Frocks, Finery, and Feelings: Rural and Urban Women's Envy, 1890–1930." In *An Emotional History of the United States*, edited by Peter N. Stearns and Jan Lewis, 377–95. The History of Emotion Series. New York: New York University Press, 1998.
McCall, Laura, and Donald Yacovone, eds. *A Shared Experience: Men, Women, and the History of Gender*. New York: New York University Press, 1998.
McGiffert, Arthur Cushman, Jr. *Their Stories: Laura Maria Wolcott 1811–1887, Robert Gosman Rankin 1806–1878*. Arthur Cushman McGiffert, Jr. 1991.
McMahon, Lucia. "'We Would Share Equally': Gender, Education, and Romance in the Journal of Rachel Van Dyke." In Lucia McMahon and Deborah Schriver, eds., *To Read My Heart: The Journal of Rachel Van Dyke, 1810–1811*, 309–37. Philadelphia: University of Pennsylvania Press, 2000.
Meckel, Richard A. "Educating a Ministry of Mothers: Evangelical Maternal Associations, 1815–1860." *Journal of the Early Republic* 2 (Winter 1982): 403–23.
Merish, Lori. *Sentimental Materialism: Gender, Commodity Culture, and Nineteenth-Century American Literature*. New Americanists Series. Durham: Duke University Press, 2000.
Michaelson, Patricia Howell. *Speaking Volumes: Women, Reading, and Speech in the Age of Austen*. Stanford: Stanford University Press, 2002.
———. "Women in the Reading Circle." *Eighteenth-Century Life* 13 (November 1989): 59–69.
Miller, Jacquelyn C. "An 'Uncommon Tranquillity of Mind': Emotional Self-Control and the Construction of a Middle-Class Identity in Eighteenth-Century Philadelphia." *Journal of Social History* 29 (Fall 1996): 129–48.
Minkema, Francis. "Hannah and Her Sisters: Sisterhood, Courtship and Marriage in the Edwards Family in the Early Eighteenth Century." *New England Historical and Genealogical Register* 146 (1992): 35–56.
Motz, Marilyn Ferris. "Folk Expression of Time and Place: Nineteenth-Century Midwestern Rural Diaries." *Journal of American Folk-Lore* 100 (April–June 1987): 131–47.

———. "The Private Alibi: Literacy and Community in the Diaries of Two Nineteenth-Century American Women." In *Inscribing the Daily: Critical Essays on Women's Diaries,* edited by Suzanne L. Bunkers and Cynthia A. Huff, 189–206. Amherst: University of Massachusetts Press, 1996.

Mullan, John. "Feelings and Novels." In *Rewriting the Self: Histories from the Renaissance to the Present,* edited by Roy Porter, 119–31. London: Routledge, 1997.

Murray, Gail S. "Rational Thought and Republican Virtues: Children's Literature, 1789–1820." *Journal of the Early Republic* 8 (Summer 1988): 159–77.

Nagel, Paul C. *The Adams Women: Abigail and Louisa Adams, Their Sisters and Daughters.* New York: Oxford University Press, 1987.

Nash, Margaret A. "'Cultivating the Powers of *Human Beings*': Gendered Perspectives on Curricula and Pedagogy in Academies of the New Republic." *History of Education Quarterly* 41 (Summer 2001): 239–50.

———. "Rethinking Republican Motherhood: Benjamin Rush and the Young Ladies' Academy of Philadelphia." *Journal of the Early Republic* 17 (Summer 1997): 171–91.

Neuwirth, Steven. "Her Master's Voice: Gender, Speech, and Gendered Speech in the Narrative of the Captivity of Mary White Rowlandson." In *Sex and Sexuality in Early America,* edited by Merril D. Smith, 55–86. New York: New York University Press, 1998.

Noble, Marianne. *The Masochistic Pleasures of Sentimental Literature.* Princeton: Princeton University Press, 2000.

Nord, David Paul. "A Republican Literature: A Study of Magazine Reading and Readers in Late Eighteenth-Century New York." *American Quarterly* 40 (March 1988): 42–64.

Opal, J. M. "Exciting Emulation: Academies and the Transformation of the Rural North, 1780s–1820s." *Journal of American History* 91 (Sept. 2004): 445–70.

Opie, Iona, and Moira Tatem, eds. *A Dictionary of Superstitions.* Oxford: Oxford University Press, 1989.

Ousterhout, Anne M. *The Most Learned Woman in America: A Life of Elizabeth Graeme Ferguson.* University Park: Pennsylvania State University Press, 2004.

Payne, Rodger M. *The Self and the Sacred: Conversion and Autobiography in Early American Protestantism.* Knoxville: The University of Tennessee Press, 1998.

Pearson, Jacqueline. *Women's Reading in Britain 1750–1835: A Dangerous Recreation.* Cambridge: Cambridge University Press, 1999.

Perlmann, Joel, Silvana R. Siddali, and Keith Whitescarver. "Literacy, Schooling, and Teaching among New England Women, 1730–1820." *History of Education Quarterly* 37 (Summer 1997): 117–39.

Poovey, Mary. "The Liberal Civil Subject and the Social in Eighteenth-Century British Moral Philosophy." In *The Social in Question: New Bearings in History and the Social Sciences,* edited by Patrick Joyce, 44–61. London: Routledge, 2002.

Porterfield, Amanda. *Feminine Spirituality in America: From Sarah Edwards to Martha Graham.* Philadelphia: Temple University Press, 1980.

Rabinowitz, Richard. *The Spiritual Self in Everyday Life: The Transformation of Personal Religious Experience in Nineteenth-Century New England.* New England Studies. Boston: Northeastern University Press, 1989.

Rath, Richard Cullen. *How Early America Sounded.* Ithaca: Cornell University Press, 2003.

Reddy, William M. *The Navigation of Feeling: A Framework for the History of Emotion.* New York: Cambridge University Press, 2001.

Reichardt, Mary R. "'Friend of My Heart': Women as Friends and Rivals in the Short Stories of Mary Wilkins Freeman." *American Literary Realism* 22 (Winter 1990): 54–68.

Rosaldo, Michelle Z. "Toward an Anthropology of Self and Feeling." In *Culture Theory: Essays on Mind, Self, and Emotion,* edited by Richard A. Shweder and Robert A. LeVine, 137–57. Cambridge: Cambridge University Press, 1984.

Rose, Jonathan. *The Intellectual Life of the British Working Classes.* New Haven: Yale University Press, 2001.

Rosenwein, Barbara H. "Worrying about Emotions in History." *American Historical Review* 107 (June 2002): 821–45.

Rosenzweig, Linda W. *Another Self: Middle-Class American Women and Their Friends in the Twentieth Century.* The History of Emotion Series. New York: New York University Press 1999.

Rothman, Ellen K. *Hands and Hearts: A History of Courtship in America.* New York: Basic Books, Inc., 1984.

Rothman, Sheila M. *Living in the Shadow of Death: Tuberculosis and the Social Experience of Illness in American History.* New York: BasicBooks, 1994.

Rotundo, E. Anthony. *American Manhood: Transformations in Masculinity from the Revolution to the Modern Era.* New York: Basic Books, 1993.

Ryan, Mary P. "The Public and the Private Good: Across the Great Divide in Women's History." *Journal of Women's History* 15 (Spring 2003): 10–27.

Scanlon, Jennifer. *Inarticulate Longings: "The Ladies' Home Journal," Gender, and the Promises of Consumer Culture.* New York: Routledge, 1995.

Schmidt, Leigh Eric. *Hearing Things: Religion, Illusion, and the American Enlightenment.* Cambridge, Mass.: Harvard University Press, 2000.

Scott, James C. *Domination and the Arts of Resistance: Hidden Transcripts.* New Haven: Yale University Press, 1990.

Sears, Donald A. "Libraries and Reading Habits in Early Portland (1763–1836)." *Maine Historical Society Newsletter* 12 (1972–73): 151–64.

Sered, Susan Starr. "Mother Love, Child Death and Religious Innovation: A Feminist Perspective." *Journal of Feminist Studies in Religion* 12 (Spring 1996): 5–23.

Shalhope, Robert E. *A Tale of New England: The Diaries of Hiram Harwood, Vermont Farmer, 1810–1837.* Baltimore: Johns Hopkins University Press, 2003.

Shammas, Carole. *A History of Household Government in America*. Charlottesville: University of Virginia Press, 2002.

Shapiro, Stephen. "Sexuality: An Early American Mystery." *William and Mary Quarterly* 60 (Jan. 2003): 189–92.

Shera, Jesse H. "The Beginnings of Systematic Bibliography in America, 1642–1799: An Exploratory Essay." In *Essays Honoring Lawrence C. Wroth*, edited by Frederick Richmond Goff and others, 263–78. Portland, Maine: Anthoensen Press, 1951.

Shields, David S. *Civil Tongues and Polite Letters in British America*. Chapel Hill: University of North Carolina Press, 1997.

Shields, Stephanie A. *Speaking from the Heart: Gender and the Social Meaning of Emotion*. Cambridge: Cambridge University Press, 2002.

Skinner, Gillian. *Sensibility and Economics in the Novel, 1740–1800: The Price of a Tear*. New York: St. Martin's Press, 1999.

Sklar, Kathryn Kish. *Catharine Beecher: A Study in American Domesticity*. New Haven: Yale University Press, 1974.

Small, Nora Pat. *Beauty and Convenience: Architecture and Order in the New Republic*. Knoxville: University of Tennessee Press, 2003.

Smith, Bruce R. *The Acoustic World of Early Modern England: Attending to the O-Factor*. Chicago: University of Chicago Press, 1999.

Smith, Mark W. *Listening to Nineteenth-Century America*. Chapel Hill: University of North Carolina Press, 2001.

———. "Making Sense of Social History." *Journal of Social History* 37 (Fall 2003): 165–86.

Smith-Rosenberg, Carroll. "The Female World of Love and Ritual: Relations between Women in Nineteenth-Century America." *Signs* 1 (Autumn 1975): 1–29.

Sobel, Mechal. *Teach Me Dreams: The Search for Self in the Revolutionary Era*. Princeton: Princeton University Press, 2000.

Spacks, Patricia Meyer. *Gossip*. New York: Alfred A. Knopf, 1985.

———. *Privacy: Concealing the Eighteenth-Century Self*. Chicago: University of Chicago Press, 2003.

Spiro, Melford E. "Some Reflections on Cultural Determinism and Relativism with Specific Reference to Emotion and Reason." In *Culture Theory: Essays on Mind, Self, and Emotion*, edited by Richard A. Shweder and Robert A. LeVine, 323–46. Cambridge: Cambridge University Press, 1984.

Spurlock, John C., and Cynthia A. Magistro. *New and Improved: The Transformation of American Women's Emotional Culture*. The History of Emotions Series. New York: New York University Press, 1998.

Stabile, Susan M. *Memory's Daughters: The Material Culture of Remembrance in Eighteenth-Century America*. Ithaca: Cornell University Press, 2004.

Stansell, Christine. *City of Women: Sex and Class in New York, 1789–1860*. Urbana: University of Illinois Press, 1987.

Stearns, Carol Zisowitz, and Peter N. Stearns. *Anger: The Struggle for Emotional Control in America's History*. Chicago: University of Chicago Press, 1986.

Stearns, Peter N. *American Cool: Constructing a Twentieth-Century Emotional Style.* The History of Emotion Series. New York: New York University Press, 1994.

———. *Anxious Parents: A History of Modern Childrearing in America.* New York: New York University Press, 2003.

———. *Battleground of Desire: The Struggle for Self-Control in Modern America.* New York: New York University Press, 1999.

———. "History of Emotions: Issues of Change and Impact." In *Handbook of Emotions,* 2d ed., edited by Michael Lewis and Jeannette M. Haviland-Jones, 16–29. New York: Guilford Press, 2000.

———. *Jealousy: The Evolution of an Emotion in American History.* The American Social Experience Series. New York: New York University Press, 1989.

Stearns, Peter N., with Carol Z. Stearns. "Emotionology: Clarifying the History of Emotions and Emotional Standards." *American Historical Review* 90 (Oct. 1985): 813–36.

Stedman, Gesa. *Stemming the Torrent: Expression and Control in Victorian Discourses on Emotions, 1830–1872.* Aldershot, U.K.: Ashgate, 2002.

Steinberg, Ronnie J., and Deborah M. Figart. "Emotional Labor since *The Managed Heart.*" *Annals of the American Academy of Political and Social Science* 561 (Jan. 1999): 8–26.

Stowe, Steven M. "The Not-So-Cloistered Academy: Elite Women's Education and Family Feeling in the Old South." In *The Web of Southern Social Relations: Women, Family, and Education,* edited by Walter J. Fraser, Jr., and others, 90–106. Athens: University of Georgia Press, 1985.

Sturkenboom, Dorothee. "Historicizing the Gender of Emotions: Changing Perceptions in Dutch Enlightenment Thought." *Journal of Social History* 34 (Fall 2000): 55–75.

Swidler, Ann. *Talk of Love: How Culture Matters.* Berkeley: University of California Press, 2001.

Tavris, Carol. *Anger: The Misunderstood Emotion.* New York: Simon and Schuster, 1982.

———. "Are Girls Really as Mean as Books Say They Are?" *The Chronicle of Higher Education,* 5 July 2002, B7-B9.

Taylor, Charles. *Modern Social Imaginaries.* Durham: Duke University Press, 2004.

Thoits, Peggy A. "The Sociology of Emotions." *Annual Review of Sociology* 15 (1989): 317–42.

Todd, Janet. *Sensibility: An Introduction.* London: Methuen, 1986.

Tomes, Nancy. "The Quaker Connection: Visiting Patterns among Women in the Philadelphia Society of Friends, 1750–1800." In *Friends and Neighbors: Group Life in America's First Plural Society,* edited by Michael Zuckerman, 174–95. Philadelphia: Temple University Press, 1982.

Ulrich, Laurel Thatcher. *The Age of Homespun: Objects and Stories in the Creation of an American Myth.* New York: Alfred A. Knopf, 2001.

———. *Good Wives: Image and Reality in the Lives of Women in Northern New England 1650–1750.* New York: Alfred A. Knopf, 1987.
———. *The Midwife's Tale: The Life of Martha Ballard, Based on Her Diary, 1785–1812.* New York: Vintage, 1991.
Van Sant, Ann Jessie. *Eighteenth-Century Sensibility and the Novel: The Senses in Social Context.* Cambridge: Cambridge University Press, 1993.
Vickery, Amanda. "Golden Age to Separate Spheres? A Review of the Categories and Chronology of English Women's History." *The Historical Journal* 36 (June 1993): 383–414.
Vincent-Buffault, Anne. *The History of Tears: Sensibility and Sentimentality in France.* Translated by Teresa Bridgeman. New York: St. Martin's Press, 1991.
Waldstreicher, David. *In the Midst of Perpetual Fetes: The Making of American Nationalism, 1776–1820.* Chapel Hill: University of North Carolina Press, 1997.
Welter, Barbara. "The Cult of True Womanhood, 1820–1860." *American Quarterly* 18 (Summer 1966): 151–74.
———. "The Feminization of American Religion, 1800–1860." In *Clio's Consciousness Raised: New Perspectives on the History of Women,* edited by Mary S. Hartman and Lois Banner, 137–57. New York: Harper Torchbooks, 1974.
West, Candace, and Don H. Zimmerman. "Doing Gender," *Gender and Society* 1 (June 1987): 125–51.
Whipple Website. History and Genealogy. Maria or Mary B. Howell. http://genweb.whipple.org/d0158/I70103.html
Winans, Robert B. "Bibliography and the Cultural Historian: Notes on the Eighteenth-Century Novel." In *Printing and Society in Early America,* edited by William L. Joyce, et al., 174–85. Worcester: American Antiquarian Society, 1983.
———. "The Growth of a Novel-Reading Public in Late-Eighteenth-Century America." *Early American Literature* 9 (Winter 1975): 267–75.
Wittmann, Reinhard. "Was There a Reading Revolution at the End of the Eighteenth Century?" In *A History of Reading in the West,* edited by Guglielmo Cavallo and Roger Chartier, translated by Lydia G. Cochrane, 284–312. Amherst: University of Massachusetts Press, 1999.
Woloch, Nancy. *Women and the American Experience,* 3rd ed. Boston: McGraw Hill, 2000.
"Women's History in the New Millennium: Carroll Smith-Rosenberg's 'The Female World of Love and Ritual' after Twenty-Five Years." *Journal of Women's History* 12 (Autumn 2000).
Wood, Gordon S. "Conspiracy and the Paranoid Style: Causality and Deceit in the Eighteenth Century." *William and Mary Quarterly* 39 (July 1982): 401–41.
———. *The Radicalism of the American Revolution.* New York: Alfred A. Knopf, 1992.
Yacovone, Donald. "Abolitionists and the 'Language of Fraternal Love.'" In *Meanings for Manhood: Constructions of Masculinity in Victorian America,* ed-

ited by Mark C. Carnes and Clyde Griffen, 85–95. Chicago: University of Chicago Press, 1990.

Zagarri, Rosemarie. "Morals, Manners, and the Republican Mother." *American Quarterly* 44 (June, 1992): 192–215.

———. "The Rights of Man and Woman in Post-Revolutionary America." *William and Mary Quarterly* 55 (April 1998): 203–30.

Zboray, Ronald J. "Reading Patterns in Antebellum America: Evidence in the Charge Records of the New York Society Library." *Libraries and Culture* 26 (Spring 1991): 301–33.

Zboray, Ronald J., and Mary Saracino Zboray. "Reading and Everyday Life in Antebellum Boston: The Diary of Daniel F. and Mary D. Child." *Libraries and Culture* 32 (Summer 1997): 285–323.

INDEX

Italicized page numbers refer to illustrations.

Adams, Abigail, 16, 51, 159
Adams, John Quincy, 42, 43, 187
Adams, Louisa, 187
adulthood and maturity: fears about, 148; increasing problems and emotional constraints, 147, 178, 189; married vs. single, 182; as new and serious reality, 148–49; role of education, 80–81; tone of resigned gratitude and acceptance, 163, 164, 165, 181; transition to, 12, 147–48, 175, 180–81, 191. *See also* death and loss; marriage; motherhood; pregnancy
Alcott, Louisa May, *Little Women*, 196
Allgor, Catherine, 187
Anderson, Benedict, 27
anger: acceptance of speaking out, 144; ambivalent attitude toward, 118, 131, 141; class, and expression of, 99, 101, 231n99; culture's discouragement of, 118, 119; definition of, 228n7; expression of, 12, 118, 141–42, 231n99; reasons for and targets of, 12, 119, 120, 140–41; as religious issue, 175, 237n117; suppression, avoidance, control of, 63, 117–18, 122, 142–43; women's lack of concern about, 143–44

—diarists who expressed anger forcefully, 118; and class issues, 231n101; delight in words, 142; clear targets for, 140–41; going against culture, 118–19; linked to strong sense of self, 119, 141; writing for an audience, 123–24, 229n24
—diarists who voiced anger tentatively, 118, 122–23; avoidance of anger, 122; linking emotion to a sentimental ideal, 119, 120; self-criticism about, 119–20
Armstrong, Nancy, and Leonard Tennenhouse, 27
Austen, Jane, *Sense and Sensibility*, 91, 92
Averill, James R., 205n41
Ayer, Samuel, 166–70, 173, 236n86
Ayer, Sarah Connell: diary of, 168, 174–75, 235–36n79; —, maternal, as sad, 173; efforts at self-improvement and cheerfulness, 172–73, 181, 196; as feeling shame, guilt, failure, 172, 173, 175; friendships and women's groups, 173–74; husband's emotional control over, 167, 170, 189; motherhood and family obligations, 168, 170–72, 180. *See also* Connell, Sarah

Bacon, Mary Ann, 58, *59*, 204n33
Bartky, Sandra Lee, 13, 188
Bassett, Mary, 219n82

Beecher, Catharine, 215n25, 216n32
Beecher, Lyman, 149–50, 151, 152, 154
Beekman, Sarah, 58, 204n33; diary of, 64, 219n79
Bevier, Henrietta Cornelia, 55, 56, 73, 204n33
Blair, Robert, 43, 72
Bloomfield, Robert, *The Farmer's Boy*, 30, 31
Boardman, Caroline, 67, 75–76, 204n33, 219n82, 234n33
Bourdieu, Pierre, 195
Bowne, Eliza Southgate, 192. *See also* Southgate, Eliza
Boydston, Jeanne, 22
Brace, Frances Ann, 70
Brace, John: Academy positions, 54, 76; assignment of essays, 56–57; celebration of competition, 61–62, 64, 70, 146; conducting examinations and judging students, 57, 61–62, 192; and discipline, 58, 122; and religion, 149–50, 151, 154, 171; student journals read to and critiqued by, 54, 76–77, 215n22; support of rules, 67; as teacher, 214n10, 215n14
Bradley, Cornelia Abbey, 62
Breen, T. H., 17, 28, 41–42
Brereton, Virginia Lieson, 174–75
Brickley, Lynne Templeton, 56, 217–18n61
British imports: books and literature, 21, 23, 24, 86, 208n44; luxury goods and customs, 16–18, 20, 23; manners, 18
Brooks, Elizabeth, 88, 89, 121
Brown, Gillian, 27–28, 192
Brown, Mary Guion, *164*; changed sense of self, 162, 165, 189; church domination of life, 163. Diary: loss of distinctive voice, 163–64, 165; silence in, and loss of plot, 161. *See also* Guion, Mary
Brown, Richard D., 208n43, 239n12

Brown, Samuel, 170; character and situation, 108–9, 227n108; courtship of, 108–11; as good husband and partner, 161, 170; work and household of, 162, 235n66
Brownstein, Rachel M., 225n58
Brumberg, Joan, 227n100
Buel, Maria, 65
Burney, Frances, 224n50; *Camilla*, 23, 24; *Evelina*, 25, 94, 209n53, 225n56
Burnstein, Andrew, 1, 2
Bushman, Richard, *The Refinement of America*, 18, 206n16

Calvinism: conversion to, 182; and motherhood, 170–72; rules of, 167, 169–70; and sadness, 173; sense of shame, 172; talking about sin, 174–75
Camp, Mary G., 54, 55, 61, 204n33
Campbell, Colin, 6
Carlson, John G., and Elaine Hatfield, *Psychology of Emotion*, 13
Catlin, George, portrait of Sarah Pierce, *53*
Cato, 207n27
Chambers, Thomas A., 207n17, 229n49
Champion, Lucretia (attrib.), "Minerva Leading the Neophyte to the Temple of Learning," 79
cheerfulness and amiability: as prized expression, 40; work to achieve, 63, 172–74, 181, 196, 200
Chester, Caroline, 204n33; academic struggle and feelings of shame, 61, 70, 152; anger of, 122; and friendships, 71–72, 74; praise and criticism for, 58; striving for contentment, 64–65, 70; struggle with religion, 154. Diary: chronicles of Academy's religious practices, 150–52; content, 71–72, 205n1; on

memorizing and reciting, 216n32; writing in school, 54
Chesterfield, Lord, 18
Clark, Betsey, "Mechanical View of the Faculties of the Soul," 65–66, 65
Clark, Candace, 239n20
class: education and, 49, 59–60, 214n51; elite, and sensibility, 16, 19, 41, 86; and expression of anger, 231n99, 231n101; fashion and friendship, 75; fear of deceitful men, 83–84, 95; and gender identity, 7; identity and luxury goods, 17; issue of social status, 4, 121; lower, interest in elite culture, 207n33; prosperity linked to reading, 21–22, 93, 208n43, 208–9n46; upper, associated with corruption, 95, 96. *See also* women, upper- and middle-class republican
Cobb, Mary Elizabeth, 72, 74
cognomens, used in diaries, 31, 35, 85, 223n25
commercial development and society: fear of deceit, 84; and idea of comfort, 17, 206n8; interest in refinement, 16–19, 20–21; linked to sensibility, 16, 20. *See also* consumer culture
competition: Academy's contradictory attitudes about, 59, 63–64, 76, 80; comparisons and failure as painful, 61; in courtship, 106; fashion as, 75–76; historical views of, 60; problems caused by, 63, 76, 220n92; at "public exhibitions," 61–63, 70; as reflected in diaries, 68–69; in schools, colleges, literature, 217–18n61
Condict, Jemima, 8
conduct books, 18, 63, 178, 213n125
Connell, Sarah: anger, and reaction to, 119, 120, 121; background and economic circumstances, 22, 40–41, 45, 92, 166; books and reading, 21, 23–26, 29–30; character, 47, 50, 142; emotion work as invisible, 43, 78, 192; and feeling according to gender, 39–40; and friendship, 45–46, 166, 189; importance of sensibility for, 11, 15, 28–29, 32–33, 43, 72, 92, 112, 166; manipulation and adjustment of feelings, 41, 42, 46, 48, 75; turn from sensibility, 166. Diary, 28–29, 206n2; during courtship, 166; on friendship, 43, 45; importance of self, 29, 42–43, 47, 119; published version, assessment, 235–36n79; style, 31, 43, 72, 92, 112. *See also* Ayer, Sarah Connell
consumer culture: in republic, 16–18, 20, 23, 75; twentieth-century, 113–14
contentment and tranquility: concern for consumption as destroying, 75; as desired, 34, 45, 64, 65, 140, 219n82; as elusive goal for sentimentalists, 35, 36, 128; as feeling to be cultivated and taught, 33, 181, 182; role of religion, 158–59; striving to achieve, 41, 70
courtship: attributes, 81, 82, 83, 223n17; competition in, 106; diaries of, and language of the heart, 83, 87; and emotion work, 11–12, 84, 192; influence of sensibility, 86–88, 91–92, 110, 223n35; men with the initiative and power, 86–87, 106; as part of social gatherings, 101; republican meaning, 96, 109–10; research findings on, 60; role of discernment, 84, 85, 87, 92, 157; and sexuality, 87; as time of greatest agency for women, 81, 185, 189
Coviello, Peter, 212n122
Cowles, Julia, 204n33; diary of, 54, 228n19

Crain, Caleb, 38
Cranch, Elizabeth: development of self, 42, 50, 185; emotion work and its rewards, 29, 35, 36, 42, 48, 78; as engaged woman, 157–60, 189; on men, 39, 83; reading, 24, 209n47; and sensibility, 11, 15, 35–36; social situation, 16, 22, 146. Diary: musings on adulthood, 148; selected parts, 206n2; style and expression, 16, 22, 35, 146. *See also* Norton, Elizabeth Cranch
Cranch, Mary, 158
Crowley, John E., 206n8
Culley, Margo, 228n122
culture, 1780–1830: adaptation to, 178; books and, 177; contradictory expectations, 142, 184; courtship and, 113–14; fear of individual self, 188; as romanticizing, 3. *See also* society, 1780–1830
culture, twentieth-century, love and, 114–15

Damasio, Antonio R., 205n43
Darnton, Robert, 209n46
death and loss: of children, 168, 180; of classmates, 180; dealing with, 155, 156, 157–58, 182–83; of fiancé, 157–58; as frequent, 180; hair memorial, 180; as marker of maturity, 147, 180; part of religious message, 153–54, 180; social importance of mourning, 179, 196, 238n129; as women's task, 179
Demos, John, 172
de Sousa, Ronald, 13
diaries: concept of self, 8, 107, 185, 189–90; of courtship, 83; and emotion work, 7–9, 12; "folk," 185; and housework, 22–23; men's, 82–83; mothers in, 207n30; as private, 28, 187, 189, 210n61; of sensibility, as distinct genre, 15–16, 185; as source material, purpose and value, 7–10, 54. *See also* novels and literature, sentimental; reading
—in adulthood: constraints on, 160, 162, 188–89; loss of privacy and sense of self, 159, 160, 161, 174; and the self, 107, 228n122; tone of resigned gratitude, 163, 181–82
—expression and style of: alternative language for peers, 72; creating emotions, 32–34; idealization of nature, 15, 34; influence of fiction on, 25, 28, 31, 33; physical emoting, 32; punctuation, 31–32; sartorial metaphors in, 30–31; sensibility and distinctive language, 29, 30–31; use of disguised names and cognomens, 31, 35, 86, 223n35. *See also* anger; tears
—of Litchfield Academy students: on academic achievement, 57, 69–70; as assignment, 54, 55; and issue of competition, 68–69; as public, 54–55, 76–77, 215nn22–23, 215–16n25; seeking faculty approbation, 57, 69, 70; tendency to blame or criticize self, 54, 61, 68; writers listed, 204n33
diarists: characterized, 9–10, 13, 25; lists, 204–5n33; selected entries, 206n2; writing for self and writing for others, 54
Diderot, Denis, 210n74
Dillon, Elizabeth Maddock, *The Gender of Freedom*, 96, 240n25
Dumont, Jane, 134–35

education, female: Academy vs. high school, 80–81; assignment of essays, 56–57; and building character, 51–52; competition and public exhibitions, 62–63; as dominated by oral culture, 55–57, 216nn29–30; as expanding, 194; as limited, 141; and print culture, 48–49; school as a stage, 59, 80; and social class, 49,

59–60, 214n151; Southern colleges, 218n61, 218n69, 220n91. *See also* Litchfield Female Academy

Edwards, Jonathan, 172

Edwards, Miss (boardinghouse mother), 58, 151–53

Elliott, Carl, 203n13

Ellison, Julie, 37

emotional communities: idea of, 10–11, 26–28; "imagined," 27, 31; institutional, 52, 151, 170; linking to emotion work, 195–96; multiple, and adapting to adulthood, 146, 147, 149, 154; and sensibility, 26–28, 38; single women, 182–83; village courtship, 84, 89

emotion history: definitions of emotion, 13–14; as distinct field, 1–2; gender issues, 2; role of society and its rules, 2, 193–94; studies of first-person literature, 9–10, 194; study of public/private spheres, 194–95; women's disadvantage in prescriptive literature, 194

"emotionology": defined, 2; distinctions in, 205n41

emotions: anger, studies of, 2, 116–18; considered as labor, 5–6, 192, 193; and emotional judgment, 11–12; and expression by gender, 2, 36–40, 193; issue of rules for, 2, 5; and recognition of the self, 6; specific and correct, instruction for, 30; women's assertion of right to emotions, 186. *See also* emotional communities; emotion history; emotion work; *and under names of specific emotions*

emotion work: for Academy students, 68, 70; adaptation to culture, 144, 178, 184; and anger, 12, 142; balancing self and society, 6–7, 185, 189; becoming public, 190; in courtship and marriage, 112, 185, 193; encouragement of acceptable emotions, 36, 55, 60; as hard work, 5–6, 192, 193; importance of reading and writing, 185; as invisible, unnoticed, 43, 78, 192–93; as key subject, 1; literature as instructive, 29–30, 111–12; manipulating, producing, suppressing feelings, 5–6, 32–36, 41, 42; needed for adult womanhood, 154, 171, 176; as pervasive, 184; and religious expectations, 178–79; rewards for, 186; striving for self-control, 34, 50, 65–66, 142–43; value and importance of, 5, 144–45. *See also* diaries: expression and style of; men; sensibility

—study of: importance and need for new approaches, 195; links to archetypal women's work, 199; parallels between early republic and twentieth century, 196–99. *See also* work, women's

—theatrical metaphors for: deep acting, 5, 29, 32, 35, 41, 84, 112, 147; diaries as offstage, 42, 131, 189; diaries as onstage, 55; expression onstage vs. backstage, 42–43, 213n142; idea of performance, 4–5, 41–43, 75, 80; surface acting, 5, 29, 63, 84, 112, 147

Enlightenment, the, 20, 51, 37; aesthetics and religion, 167; Scottish philosophers, 20, 37, 51; scientific, 65

Eustace, Nicole E., 116–17, 204n23, 211n80, 223n17, 223n35, 225n72, 231n101

fancy or irrational affection, 11; as clouding judgment, 103; linked to sexuality, 97; reason vs., 11, 97, 98, 111; as something to watch out for, 82, 97

Farnham, Christie Anne, 214n151, 218n61, 218n69

fear: about adulthood, 148–49; of deceit, 84; marriage and life changes, 159; of passion, 97; as strong emotion in courtship, 11, 83, 96, 108, 109, 112
feelings, definitions of, 14, 205n43. *See also* emotions
Ferguson, Elizabeth Graeme, 206n1
Ferguson, Robert, 117
Fielding, Henry, *Joseph Andrews*, 25, 30
Fithian, Philip Vickers, 37, 39
Fliegelman, Jay, 55–56, 222n9
friendship(s): albums, *44, 72, 180,* 233n28; between men, 37, 191; for boarding school girls, 60, 71; and class differences, 75; descriptions of, 45, 213n142; female, freedom of expression and restraints, 71, 130, 188–89; importance of, 43, 45, 46, 186; lacking, searching for, 107, 130, 133; linked to religion, 152–53; male and female, 105–6; sensibility and, 43, 45, 74–75

Gedge, Karin E., 169
gender issues and differences: and accepted social distinctions, 52–53; competition and, 68, 191; cultural acceptance of intellectuality, 131, 132, 187–88, 190–91; cultural views toward anger, 116–18, 119, 228n2; in education, 191; and emotion work, 7, 176, 190–91, 193–94; and fears, 187; public vs. private, 190–92; and reading, 190–91; and republican ideology, 20, 187; in selfhood, 178, 188–90; sensibility and emotional expression, 2, 36–40, 193; sexual expression and erotic passion, 40, 87; in society, study of, as needed, 194–95; and understanding of God, 152. *See also* men

gentility: and anger, 118; books and, 21; and class status, 121, 142, 193–94; elements of, 18; fusion of material and emotional, 20–21; and gender, 193; manners as British import, 18; marriage as statement of, 86; sensibility linked to, 18, 41, 63, 67; varying expressions of, 34–35
Gilman, Tabitha, 91, 121
Gilmore, William J., 55, 206n7, 208n44, 208–9n46
Gimbrede, Napoleon (attrib.), "View of the Litchfield Academy," *150*
Godbeer, Richard, 222n9
Goddard, Lucretia, 124, 130
Goffman, Erving, *The Presentation of Self in Everyday Life*, 4, 6, 28, 42–43, 104, 213n142
Goldsmith, Oliver, 224n50; *The Vicar of Wakefield*, 21, 23, 50–51, 207n33; read in class, 214n10
Grasso, Linda, 117, 124, 140, 231n101, 237n117, 239n3
Green, Nancy, 218n61
Greven, Philip, 40, 237n121
Grosvenor, Ebenezer (Mr. G.), 131–33, 155
Guion, James: advice from, 103, 104, 124, 163, 189; marriage to Tabitha Lyon, 98, 113
Guion, Jonathan, 224n49; family social and economic situation, 92–93, 224nn45-46, 227n108, 235n67
Guion, Mary: background and daily life, 1, 11, 20, 85, 92–93, 96–97, 105–6, 113, 224n46; and her community, 99, 101, 104–5, 113, 119, 146; distinctive courtship, 108–11, 161; emotion work for, 112–13; importance of books and reading, 93, 224nn49-50; importance of reason, emotional judgment, discernment, 11, 82, 84, 85, 97, 111, 112; interplay of

fiction and reality for, 93–98, 111, 225n58; and men of feeling, 39, 99; model for marriage, 98; protecting her reputation, 99, 101, 104–5; relations with women, 101, 105, 106; search for a man to trust, 95, 96, 106, 107; sister's experience and its lesson, 93–94, 97, 108, 109, 111, 113, 126–27; social life, and importance of conversation, 93, 100–105, 226n76, 226n78; strong sense of self, 113, 119; suitors, 94–95, 96–97, 99, 102. Diary, *100*; characteristics, 92, 100–101, 163; distinctive voice in, 113, 124; as evidence of oral culture, 99–101; expression of anger, 118–19, 123, 124, 126–27, 141; struggle to develop self-assertion, 125–26; as trustworthy confidante, 107, 108, 110; as valuable social document, 8, 84; value to her, 96, 107–8, 112; written with audience in mind, 124. *See also* Brown, Mary Guion

Gunther, Candy, 237n113
Gustafson, Sandra M., 216n26

Habermas, Jürgen, 27
Haight, Abigail, 101, 103, 106
Halttunen, Karen, 4, 211n91, 211n95
Hansen, Karen V., 226n76, 240n25
Hardy, Thomas, *Tess of the D'Urbervilles*, 225n58
Harwood, Hiram, 37, 39
Hatfield, Elaine. *See* Carlson, John G., and Elaine Hatfield, *Psychology of Emotion*
Heath, Betsey, 17
Heath, Ebenezer: character, 137–38; family situation, 136–37, 230n79
Heath, Hannah, 138–40, 183
Heath, Susan, 12; admiration for Abigail May, 143–44; and anger, 22, 118–19, 123, 124, 136, 139, 140; attacks on father and brother, 137–39, 140–41; family as audience, 138; and growing up, 147–48; as mature woman, 182–83; strong sense of self, 119, 124. Diary: choice of material and words, 142; commentary on reading, 24, 209n53, 214n10; as unchanged through maturity, 182; writing for an audience, 124–25

Hemphill, C. Dallett, 213n125
Hessinger, Rodney, 203n7
Hochschild, Arlie Russell, 4–6, 7, 10, 236n82; on deep acting, 32; definition of emotion, 13–14; on emotion work, 192–93, 200; on modern marriages, 197–98
Howell, Mary B.: anger and its targets, 19–20, 140; emotional work and its rewards, 47–48, 78; leisure time, 22; reading, 26, 210n57; on reason, 50; and sensibility, 11, 15, 16, 112. Diary: characterized, 29; style and language, 31, 32, 34, 86
Hunt, Nancy Thompson, 8
Hunter, Jane H., 2, 21–22, 118, 155, 207n30, 218n61, 237n104

Illouz, Eva, 113–14, 198, 199
improvement: as behavioral goal, 52, 56, 93, 153; intellectual, 56, 131; working toward, 77

Jagodzinski, Cecile M., 6, 107
Jasup, Captain Jonathan, 94–96, 97, 103, 107, 108, 224–25n55
jealousy, 2, 218n61; and competition, 76
Jefferson, Thomas, 37, 212n122
journals. *See* diaries
Juster, Susan, 39–40, 176, 236n92

Kann, Mark, 83
Kelley, Mary, 215n14

Kelly, Catherine E., 2; on female friendship, 220n101, 233n28; on marriage and romantic love, 111, 223n19; on social life, 105, 226n76, 227n96, 234n36
Kennedy, Gwynne, 228n2
Kerber, Linda, 53, 214n8
Kete, Mary Louise, 209n51, 238n129
Klepp, Susan E., 22–23
Kling, David, 232n5, 238n122
Knox, Vicesimus, 55; *Elegant Extracts*, 21, 207n32
Kring, Ann M., 198

Lewis, Jan, 238n133
Litchfield Female Academy: assignments, 54, 56–57; atmosphere of competition, 59–63; as contradictory and complex emotional world, 54, 66, 72, 78–80, 146; credit system, 57; curriculum and goals, 53, 78; diary writing, 54–55, 58; emotional community as public, 11, 55, 59, 71, 79–80; founding and aims, 52–53, 67, 76; public recognition and prizes, 146, 186; rules about behavior and emotional control, 52, 63, 67, 72–73, 76, 122, 146, 151, 220n96; weekly public review of faults and virtues, 58. *See also* competition
—students: diarists, listed, 204n33; as elite, 48–49, 59–60, 75; emotion work for, 68, 78–79, 80, 155–56, 192; expression of anger, 122–23; with literary first names, 31; need for proper emotional performance, 75; regimented life and religious conversion, 150–51, 152–55; transition to maturity and marriage, 147, 149, 155. *See also* anger: diarists who voiced anger tentatively; friendship(s)
literature: and gentility, 21; influence on society, 31; multiple forms, 23;
sentimental and popular, 21, 23, 24, 45. *See also* novels and literature, sentimental; poetry; print culture
love: culture and, 113–14; developing in courtship, 108–9, 111; differing meanings for, 86–87; in marriage, views on, 86, 87, 108, 223n19; romantic, in nineteenth century, 111. *See also* fancy or irrational affection
Lutz, Catherine, 12–13
Lystra, Karen, 2, 109

Mackenzie, Henry, *The Man of Feeling*, 37, 97–98, 99; as popular, 38
male/female dichotomy. *See* gender issues and differences
marriage: as emotional demarcation line, 189; emotional life after, 177, 193, 200; fear of husband's domination, 159; Mary Guion's ideal, 98, 107–8; and ideals of sensibility, 86; importance of successful, 84, 85; love in, views on, 86, 87, 108, 223n19; male control and role in, 82, 83, 86–87; as marker of adulthood and change, 12, 82, 147, 148, 157; and money, 86–87, 99; playful speculation about, 105, 147; political ideals for, 96–97; religion and, 149, 152–53; sense of self-effacement, 159, 160, 177; and status, 82, 84, 186, 223n17; treatise on, 98; unhappy, examples of, 93–94, 97, 99, 109, 111, 126–27, 148
May, Abigail, 26; commentary on behavior of others, 18–19, 20, 129–30; expression of anger, 12, 116, 118–19, 123, 124–25, 127–31, 140, 141, 146; as ill and dying, 127–28, 130, 180, 229n49; and men of feeling, 37–39; and reading, 21, 26; and sensibility, 15, 20, 40, 128. Diary: circulation of, and reactions, 143–44; description of behavior, 19; description of

sartorial extravagances, 17; distinctive and unrestrained voice, 124, 130, 140; language of anger, 141; on marriage, 148; records of visits, 208n37; on tears, 211n86; written with audience in mind, 124, 131
McFarland, Asa, Rev., 167, 169
McMahon, Lucia, 131–32
"Mechanical View of the Faculties of the Soul" (Clark), 65–66, *65*
melancholy and sadness: to be controlled, 41; to be cultivated, 34; depression, 155–56, 157, 173, 175; praise of and pleasure in, 72, 86, 237n104; as problematic for Calvinists, 173
men: considered false and untrustworthy, 83–84, 95, 106, 129, 222n9; diaries of, 38, 82–83; as dominant in marriage and society, 82, 83, 84, 86–87, 159, 190–92; emotion work for, 190–91; of feeling, 38, 86, 97, 169; growing up for, 191; reading for, 190–91; same-sex relationships, 239n13; sense of self, 192. *See also* gender issues and differences
Merish, Lori, 20
Mifflin, John, 37; diary of, 38
Miller, Jacquelyn C., 212n123
"Minerva Leading the Neophyte to the Temple of Learning" (attrib. Champion), *79*
motherhood: Calvinist, 170–72; emotion work of, 171, 176; linked to religion, 154; as marker of maturity, 12, 147; republican, 53, 170; as transforming and wearing, 162, 176, 177
Motz, Marilyn Ferris, 185, 210n61
mourning. *See* death and loss
Mulford, Eliza Ann, 63, 67
Mullan, John, 24–25

Nash, Margaret A., 215n14, 215n16
nature: idealized, in diaries, 15, 34; sensibility's responses to, 38, 169

Neuwirth, Steven, 231n104
Newell, Harriet, 176
Nord, David Paul, 209n46
Norton, Elizabeth Cranch, 235n73; diary after marriage, 159, 160. *See also* Cranch, Elizabeth
Norton, Jacob, 157, 158, 160; as emotional support, 158–59
novels and literature, sentimental: British, 21, 23, 24, 86, 208n44; characters and themes from, as lessons, 92, 94–97, 111, 224n51; circulation of, 21, 208–9n46; described in diaries, 24–25, 135, 138, 209n14; feminine centrality of, 24–25; ideal emotions in, 45; influence on diaries, 8, 23–25, 33, 46, 208n42; instruction on correct emotions, 30, 93; readership, age of, 25–27; reading of, in the Academy, 52, 214n10, 216n30; renunciation of, 161, 168, 176–77. *See also* sensibility

Ogden, Eliza, diary entries: on academic achievement, 69–70; on school experience, 56, 57, 59, 61; on school's religious methods, 234n33
Ong, Walter, 141
Opal, J. M., 59–60
oral culture: as dominating education, 55–57, 216nn29–30; link to memorization and recital, 56; and print culture, 55; in the village, 11–12, 85, 89, 100–105, 108–9
Osgood, Harriot, 45, 174

Pain, Oliver, 19, 38, 129
Payne, Rodger M., 237n115
Payson, Edward, Reverend, 168–69, 236n89
Peck, Mary Wallace, 62; Friendship Album, *44*, *180*
Perkins, Thomas, 157–58
Philammon. *See* Tenney, Samuel (Philammon)

Pierce, Sarah, 53, 218n67; aims and philosophy, 52–53, 64, 72, 78, 146, 194; criteria and rules for diary writing, 54–55, 58; guidance in emotional rules and control, 63–67, 73, 79–80; lessons on character and use of time, 76, 153, 176–77; presentation of plays, 66; public punishments and rewards, 57–58, 149; and religion, 149, 153–54; as stage director, 59; student affection for, 58–59, 215nn22-23; views on competition, 63–64, 76, 218n61; and women's relations, 71, 73, 220n102. *See also* Litchfield Female Academy

poetry: and diary expression, 16, 31, 35, 43, 209n51; in friendship albums, 72, 83, 209n51; on male deceit, 83; for newly religious women, 177

politeness: general rules for, 63; school and parental concern for, 67, 73

Pope, Alexander, 102, 224n50

Portius. *See* Woodbridge, William (Portius)

pregnancy, 22–23, 32, 162–63, 168

print culture: and better education, 48; and better expression of emotion, 142; books from Britain, 21, 23, 208n44; link to oral culture, 55; magazines, 23, 96, 209n46; and rise of literacy, 3, 142; and sensibility, 21, 23, 45; and women's rights and status, 190–91. *See also* novels and literature, sentimental; poetry; reading

public/private dichotomy: in the Academy and education, 49, 54–58; and anger, 117–18; and diaries, 54–55, 189–90; and emotional communities, 27–28; and emotion work for men and women, 190–92; and reading, 27–28, 56; and the self, 6, 42, 191–92; and women's weakness and rights, 190

race, issues of, 19–20, 72, 198

reading: as changing in adulthood, 176–77, 178; and emotion work, 3, 185; importance for diarists, 21, 23–24, 25, 28, 31, 33, 185; importance for learning and social life, 21–22, 50, 93; lessons from, 113, 224n51; for men, 190–91; and public/private dichotomy, 27–28, 56; sentimental, examples of, 21, 23, 24, 25; social class and, 21–22, 93, 208n43, 208–9n46; sources, and reasons for, 208–9n46. *See also* literature; novels and literature, sentimental

reason and rationality: vs. fancy, 11, 97, 98, 111; link to sensibility, 50; and republican ideology, 51–52, 66

Reddy, William M., 8

Reichardt, Mary R., 231n100

religion and evangelism, 1780–1830: at the Academy, 149–55; and emotion work, 178–79, 192; God and Christ as friends, 152, 186; and marriage, 149, 152–53; and mature womanhood, 12, 147, 148, 149; motherhood and, 163, 170–72; as sad renunciation, 149, 168, 176, 232n12; sensibility and, 162, 167–70, 177; and submission of women, 150, 176, 238n122; and women's emotions, 3, 162. *See also* Calvinism

republic, revolutionary: courtship in, 114–15; and race issues, 19–20, 198; social values and influence on women's emotions, 3. *See also* commercial development and society; republican ideology; society, 1780–1830

republican ideology: and consumption, 16–17, 20, 23; and courtship, 96, 109–10; female self-assertion and anger, 118; ideal of material simplicity and common good, 20; and marriage, 86, 96–97; and motherhood, 53, 170; role of rationality, 51, 66, 96; role of sensibility, 20–21, 66; and virtue, 20–21, 51–52, 96; women's sphere and role, 20–21, 51–52, 53, 66–67, 96–97, 190, 215n14

Reynolds, Betsey, 204n33; diary reports of, 58, 61, 75, 214n10, 228n18

Richardson, Samuel, 25, 138, 210n74; *Clarissa*, 168

Roberts, Candace, 209n47

Rogers, Martha (Patty), 11; background and household occupations, 22, 85, 180; as consumer of feelings, 114; as engaged in acting, 84, 112; inability to control emotion, 87, 89–92; reaction to anger, and concern with identity, 121–22, 141; reading, 224n50; as unafraid and lacking in caution, 109, 110; in world of sensibility, 22, 85–86, 115, 147. Diary: as mirror for self-admiration, 89; reflecting her world of sensibility, 85–86; use of cognomens, 86, 223n35; use of exclamation point, 32

Rosaldo, Michelle Z., 3

Rose, Jonathan, 4

Rosenwein, Barbara H., 10, 26

Rothman, Ellen K., 2, 111, 224n51

Rotundo, Anthony, 60

Rowe, Mrs. Elizabeth, letters of, 21, 23, 30

Ryan, Mary P., 240n25

sadness. *See* melancholy and sadness

Sarles, Isaac, 94, 102, 103, 108, 109, 148; Mary Guion's anger against, 126–27, 163, 164

Sarles, Sally Guion, 93–94, 97, 108, 109, 111, 112, 126–27, 148, 163

Scott, James C., 189

Sedgwick, Catharine, 25; *A New-England Tale*, 62–63

self, concept of: diaries and, 8, 107, 185, 189–90, 228n122; influence of novels, 24–25; lessons of sensibility for, 33–34; as part of society, 4, 106–7, 113, 189, 210n61; as plummeting after marriage, 177; public vs. private, 6, 42, 191–92; religion, and issues of identity, 178, 179; strong sense of, diarists with, 47, 113, 119, 124, 130, 141, 144, 156; work on self-control, 34–36, 50, 64, 196

sensibility: contradictory demands of, 11; and courtship, 86–88, 91–92, 110, 223n35; defined and described, 15, 47, 205–6n1; elite class and, 16, 19, 41, 86; and formation of emotional communities, 26–28, 38; and friendship, 43, 45, 74–75; and gentility, 18–19, 63, 67; and "imagined" community, 27, 31; influence on emotional expression and language, 28–36, 118, 186; journal of, 15–16, 185; male/female, 37–40; as a mirror, 48, 89; as paradoxical emotional guide, 11, 29, 30, 41, 79; as pervasive in society, 16, 86, 187; religion and, 162, 167–70, 177; and role of the economy, 16, 20; and self control, 34–36; and virtue, 51–52. *See also* emotion work; novels and literature, sentimental; reading; women's history, and emotions

Sered, Susan Starr, 180

sexuality and eroticism; differing gender responses, 40; economic metaphors for, 87; same-sex, 37, 60, 191; wariness about, 97

shame and embarrassment: in competitive context, 61, 218n69; experiencing of, 63; about failure, 61, 70, 172; frequent expression of, 9, 68

Shammas, Carole, 212n111

Sheldon, Charlotte, diary reports, 54, 57, 75, 216n80
Sheldon, Lucy, diary reports, 58, 75, 83, 147; expression of rivalry, 69, 70, 220n95
Shields, David, 211n90
Shields, Stephanie A., 7
Shippen, Nancy, 18
Smith, Adam, 20
Smith, Benjamin, 99, 108, 111
Smith, Jotham, 95, 97, 102–3, 104, 106, 107, 125
Smith, Maria, 132, 133–34, 136
Smith-Rosenberg, Carroll: studies of emotion, 2; on women's friendships, 60, 71, 186, 233n28
Sobel, Mechal, 6
society, 1780–1830: commercial development and interest in refinement, 16–19, 20–21; concern for and expectations of self-control, 34–35; conventions, influence on expression, 3, 9, 11; fear of deception, 83–84, 95, 188, 194; and the individual, 6–7; influence of Scottish Enlightenment, 20, 37, 51; male control in, 82, 83, 86–87, 190–92; question of status, 4, 7, 82, 84, 179, 186, 223n17; rules for women, 3, 40–41, 190; and sensibility, 16, 86, 187; the village community, 84–85; women as performers, 4–5, 41–42, 80, 142, 194; women's inability to change, 187–88. *See also* class; gender issues and differences; gentility; sensibility
Southgate, Eliza, 83, 207n18, 235n63. *See also* Bowne, Eliza Southgate
Spacks, Patricia Meyer, 6, 100, 211n95
Spiro, Melford, 144
Stabile, Susan M., 8
St. Clair, or The Heiress of Desmond, 29–30
Stearns, Carol Zisowitz, 2, 13, 117, 141
Stearns, Peter N., 2, 13, 117, 141, 218n61

Stedman, Gesa, 205n43, 205n1
Stowe, Harriet Beecher, 56–57, 190
Stowe, Steven M., 225n73
Swidler, Ann, 118; *Talk of Love: How Culture Matters*, 114–15, 177

Tavris, Carol, 231n99
Taylor, Charles, 195, 196–97
tears: as epitome of sensibility, 32, 34, 50; as expression of deep emoting, 32–33, 72, 85–86, 199; male, 38; part of real grief, 155–56; religion and, 162; on TV today, 199. *See also* melancholy and sadness
Tennenhouse, Leonard. *See* Armstrong, Nancy, and Leonard Tennenhouse
Tenney, Samuel (Philammon), 86, 121, 122; relationship with Patty Rogers, 90–91
Thomson, James, 23, 31, 35, 135
Thurston, Sally, 90, 94
Todd, Janet, 33
Trumbull, Harriet, Jonathan, and Maria, 17
Tucker, Mary Orne, 211n89, 232–33n12
Twain, Mark, *Huckleberry Finn*, 177

Ulrich, Laurel Thatcher, 22, 93, 223n19

Van Dyke, Rachel, 12, 189; attacks on women, 133–36, 141; attempt to establish identity as woman intellectual, 131, 132, 133, 135; contempt for affectation and deceit, 134, 140, 230n77; depression and turning to religion, 155–57, 180, 234n36; expression of anger, 118–19, 123, 124; published poem by, 231n99; and sentimental literature, 38, 135; strong sense of self, 124, 144, 156. Diary: judgments on, 189; rhetoric of anger, 141; shared with others, 124, 131, 132, 134, 136

Victorian period: anger, 117–18; association of femininity and piety, 170, 171; competition in schools, 218n61, 220n92; courtship practice, 109, 110; emotional communities in, 196; and housework, 21, 22; novels of, 176; reading, 21, 209n51, 239n3; sensationalist fiction, 211n83

"View of the Litchfield Academy" (attrib. Gimbrede), *150*

Warren, Mercy Otis, 51
Welter, Barbara, 187
West, Candace, and Don H. Zimmerman, 7
Wilbor, Mary L., 57–58, 61, 204n33; ambivalent critical remarks, 73–74, 77, 122; on fashion, 75
Winans, Robert B., 208n42, 208n46
Winfrey, Oprah, 198–99
Winslow, Anna Green, 17, 25
Wolcott, Laura Maria, 204n33; and adulthood and marriage, 148, 192; background, 25, 76, 221n124; expression of anger and emotion, 122–23, 144; and female friendship, 71, 73; sense of competition, 69; understanding emotion work, 77–78. Diary: as a fresh voice, 76–77; summaries of essays in, 64, 77–78

women: in fiction, antagonistic relations among, 231n101; public recognition for, 186–87; Southern, 225n73; as vulnerable in courtship, 83, 104; without equal opportunities, 188. *See also* women, upper- and middle-class republican; women's history, and emotions; work, women's

women, upper- and middle-class republican: and education for, 48–49; leisure time for reading, 21–22, 85, 93; reading novels, 23–24; role in class identification and manners, 17–18; role of inspiring virtue, 51–52; and sensibility, 16, 19, 41, 86. *See also* republican ideology

women's history, and emotions: between 1780 and 1830, important developments, 3; and concept of work, 5–6, 193–94; growth of individual and self, 6–7; homosocial relations, and lesbian sexuality, 60; role of emotions and emotion work, 2, 5; role of sensibility, 26–27; studies of, 2; themes of, 12. *See also* emotion work: study of; gender issues and differences

Wood, Gordon, 83
Woodbridge, William (Portius), 86, 88–89, *88*, 121
work, women's: archetypal characteristics, 199–201; described in diaries, 1, 22–23; as dissimulation, 194; emotions as, 5–6; emotion work as hard and increasing through time, 192, 193; household, 21, 22, 193, 197; scholarly reconsideration of, 5; as unnoticed and unending, 5, 43, 192–93, 200–201. *See also* emotion work

Zimmerman, Don H. *See* West, Candace, and Don H. Zimmerman
Zimmermann, Johann, 224n50; *Solitude Considered*, 98, 225n69